Effective Ecology

Ecology is one of the most challenging of sciences, with unambiguous knowledge much harder to achieve than it might seem. But it is also one of the most important sciences for the future health of our planet. It is vital that our efforts are as effective as possible at achieving our desired outcomes. This book is intended to help individual ecologists to develop a better vision for their ecology – and the way they can best contribute to science.

The central premise is that to advance ecology effectively as a discipline, ecologists need to be able to establish conclusive answers to key questions rather than merely proposing plausible explanations for mundane observations. Ecologists need clear and honest understanding of how we have come to do things the way we do them now, the limitations of our approaches, our goals for the future and how we may need to change our approaches if we are to maintain or enhance our relevance and credibility. Readers are taken through examples to show what a critical appraisal can reveal and how this approach can benefit ecology if it is applied more routinely.

Ecological systems are notable for their complexity and their variability. Ecology is, as indicated by the title of this book, a truly difficult science. Ecologists have achieved a great deal, but they can do better. This book aims to encourage early-career researchers to be realistic about their expectations: to question everything, not to take everything for granted and to make up their own minds.

Effective Ecology
Seeking Success in a Hard Science

Roger D Cousens
with
Mark R T Dale, Alkistis Elliott-Graves, Michael J Keough,
Gerry P Quinn, Joshua I Brian, Jane A Catford,
Jannice Friedman, Alyson C Van Natto, Bruce L Webber,
Daniel Z Atwater, Maria Paniw, Chris M Baker, Thao P Le,
Marc W Cadotte and Françoise Cardou

CRC Press is an imprint of the
Taylor & Francis Group, an **informa** business

First edition published 2024
by CRC Press
6000 Broken Sound Parkway NW, Suite 300, Boca Raton, FL 33487-2742

and by CRC Press
4 Park Square, Milton Park, Abingdon, Oxon, OX14 4RN

©2024 Roger D Cousens, with co-authors Mark R T Dale, Alkistis Elliott-Graves, Michael J Keough, Gerry P Quinn, Joshua I Brian, Jane A Catford, Jannice Friedman, Alyson C Van Natto, Bruce L Webber, Daniel Z Atwater, Maria Paniw, Chris M Baker, Thao P Le, Marc W Cadotte and Françoise Cardou

CRC Press is an imprint of Taylor & Francis Group, LLC

Reasonable efforts have been made to publish reliable data and information, but the author and publisher cannot assume responsibility for the validity of all materials or the consequences of their use. The authors and publishers have attempted to trace the copyright holders of all material reproduced in this publication and apologize to copyright holders if permission to publish in this form has not been obtained. If any copyright material has not been acknowledged please write and let us know so we may rectify in any future reprint.

Except as permitted under U.S. Copyright Law, no part of this book may be reprinted, reproduced, transmitted, or utilized in any form by any electronic, mechanical, or other means, now known or hereafter invented, including photocopying, microfilming, and recording, or in any information storage or retrieval system, without written permission from the publishers.

For permission to photocopy or use material electronically from this work, access www.copyright.com or contact the Copyright Clearance Center, Inc. (CCC), 222 Rosewood Drive, Danvers, MA 01923, 978-750-8400. For works that are not available on CCC please contact mpkbookspermissions@tandf.co.uk

Trademark notice: Product or corporate names may be trademarks or registered trademarks and are used only for identification and explanation without intent to infringe.

ISBN: 9781032322940 (hbk)
ISBN: 9781032322926 (pbk)
ISBN: 9781003314332 (ebk)

DOI: 10.1201/9781003314332

Typeset in Minion Pro
by codeMantra

'The scientist is not a person who gives the right answers, he is one who asks the right questions.'
Claude Lévi-Strauss

'Without questions there are no answers. And without answers no truth, no progress, no future.'
Victor Canning

The elevation of ecology beyond the delivery of plausible answers to mundane matters depends on challenging accepted wisdom, defining crucial questions and delivering inspired solutions. Critique – of ourselves and of others – needs to be central to that process.

Contents

Preface	xi
Acknowledgements	xv
About the authors	xvii

1	**Why a hard science needs strong critique**	**1**
	Roger Cousens	
	Why ecology is difficult	1
	Questions and answers in science	3
	The role of critique in science	4
	Ecological goals	7
	So what?	10
	References	11
2	**The evolution of ecology**	**13**
	Roger Cousens and Mark Dale	
	Can Ecology improve?	13
	A conventional history of Ecology	15
	Natural history	16
	Demography and modelling	17
	Coalescence of natural history with demography and beyond	17
	Selection in science space	19
	The evolution of Ecology as a multilayered network	22
	Evolving space for evolving Ecology	27
	So what?	27
	References	28
3	**What sort of a science is Ecology?**	**33**
	Alkistis Elliott-Graves	
	Ecology as a science	33
	Ecological systems are complex	34
	The challenges of complexity	35
	Generalisations	35
	Explanations, predictions and interventions	36
	Scientific and ethical values	37
	What sort of a science Ecology is *not*	38
	The traditional picture of science	38
	Laws of nature	39
	Ecological 'laws'?	40

vii

viii Contents

	Falsificationism	41
	Falsification and prediction	42
	Objectivity	42
	So what?	43
	Modest expectations	43
	Methodological pluralism	44
	References	45
4	**Rigorous ecology needs rigorous statistics**	**49**
	Mick Keough and Gerry Quinn	
	Using models to distinguish signals from noise	49
	Hard, but critical	49
	Some things do not change	50
	Changing (statistical) landscapes for ecologists	51
	It can be complicated	52
	A chance to make mistakes	52
	There are some 'new' challenges	55
	A field guide to getting it wrong	57
	So what?	60
	References	61
5	**Ecological scale and context dependence**	**63**
	Joshua Brian and Jane Catford	
	Scale as a pervasive form of context dependence	63
	The importance of study scale	64
	What is study scale?	64
	The importance of scale for revealing ecological patterns	67
	Systems used to explore scale dependence	68
	Spatial scale	68
	Spatial grain	68
	Spatial extent	69
	Can we retrospectively correct for spatial grain or extent?	70
	Temporal scale	71
	Temporal grain	71
	Temporal extent	71
	Do temporal and spatial scale dependence have the same consequences?	72
	Scale interacts with other sources of context dependence	73
	Darwin's naturalisation conundrum	73
	The invasion paradox	74
	So what?	75
	References	76
6	**Assembling the ecological puzzle**	**81**
	Jannice Friedman and Aly Van Natto	
	From the picture on the outside to the pieces in the box	81
	Difficulties in drawing evolutionary inferences	82
	What are the traits on which selection has acted?	82
	How do we recognise adaptation?	82
	How do we measure fitness?	83
	What if there are trade-offs and correlations between traits?	83
	What are the timescales?	83
	The methods available	83
	Case studies that exemplify integrative methods	88
	Case study 1: threespine stickleback	88

Case study 2: deer mouse	89
Case study 3: seep monkeyflower	90
So what?	91
References	92

7 Assumptions: respecting the known unknowns — **97**

Bruce Webber, Roger Cousens and Daniel Atwater

The biggest 'elephant in the room'?	97
The species' niche concept	99
The niche concept meets the real world	100
Niche shifts in non-native species	102
The data	102
The analysis	106
Interpretation	109
Uptake of conclusions by others	111
Species distribution models	112
Choice of model	112
Training data	114
Software implementation	117
Peer review	119
So what?	120
References	122

8 Theory, prediction and application — **127**

Maria Paniw, Roger Cousens, Chris Baker and Thao Le

A place for modelling in ecology	127
Types of population model	129
Testing the predictions of theoretical models	130
Case study 1: predator-prey cycles	131
Case study 2: rate of population spread	132
Predictions generated from empirical data	133
Which drivers are important for prediction?	134
Case study 3: meerkat abundance	136
Model parameterisation and validation	137
From forecasts to policy	139
Case study 4: dynamical population modelling for COVID-19 policy	142
Case study 5: adaptive management of malleefowl	143
So what?	144
References	145

9 From pattern to process in the search for generality — **151**

Françoise Cardou and Marc Cadotte

The pattern-first approach to ecology	151
Community ecology: a brief overview	154
What do community ecologists try to predict and understand?	154
Crisis	154
The ascent of a process-first approach for ecology	155
The Holy Grail: understanding and predicting community composition	155
Challenge (or strawman) from Hubbell's neutral theory: do species differences even matter?	157
Predictive community-environment relationships based on processes	157
More than one path: understanding and predicting diversity	158
Diversity patterns depend on species pool	159
Matching diversity measures to hypotheses to capture processes	160

Inferring process from (diversity) pattern: a many-to-one problem	161
A little bit of everything all of the time: ecosystem function	162
The perspective from mathematical ecology	163
The perspective from ecosystem ecology	163
All-or-nothing explanations	164
Pending challenge: when the pattern is the process	164
A final word on communities	165
So what?	165
References	166

10 Effective ecology — **173**

Roger Cousens

How to increase the effectiveness of ecological research	173
What we seek to achieve	174
How we go about ecology	175
Descriptive ecology	175
Black box ecology	176
Collection of supporting evidence	178
How can we improve what we do?	179
And, finally, so what?	180
References	181

Index — **183**

Preface

Scientists are consumers of information, not just producers of it. What others do, write and claim to have demonstrated through their research, influences the way that we think. We use their results, interpretations and conclusions to formulate our own ideas and to place our own results in context.

We probably regard ourselves as highly discerning consumers – after all, we are scientists! But the reality is that like any other consumers, we tend not to read the fine print! How often do we critically dissect every method applied or examine every individual assumption that a study makes, from its formulation to its final conclusions? There is far too much literature to read everything in that sort of detail.

In any case, the brevity of modern publications means that many basic details are left out. We are forced to place considerable trust in our colleagues and on our peer-review systems. We trust some sources of information more than others, based on the reputation of the journal or of the scientist. We assume that the researchers knew what they were doing and that those adjudicating on the work were good enough to identify any problems.

We must have considerable faith that other researchers did not make mistakes.

The evidence, however, is that errors in published papers are common. Many of these are perhaps minor and inconsequential, but some have the potential to completely undermine the authors' conclusions. It is not difficult to appreciate how errors can be made and published. If you are like me, you do not understand every detail of every method that you use in your studies, or every nuance involved in their best application.

Your scientific tool-box contains a wide range of items. You try to become sufficiently knowledgeable about them, because you want to do the best job that you can. But you are not perfect: you cannot expect to be! You may seek advice from someone who appears to know more than you, who perhaps taught you. Because of the vastness of the literature, it is impossible for you to read and appreciate everything that has been written about even one method. Your data might not fit all the criteria that the method technically requires, but you think that they may be 'near enough' (and there may not be a better method). You hope that your conclusions will be reliable and that any inabilities on your part, along with mere bad luck, will not mislead the rest of the ecological scientific community.

If you are asked to review a manuscript – and you consider that it is on a subject with which you are sufficiently familiar – you do the best you can with the information available. If you have concerns, you ask that the authors respond to your criticisms or questions, or you might reject the paper. But often you will know no more about the methods than the paper's authors. You cannot be expected to spot every mistake, because you do not have all the information – or the time – for a forensic analysis.

Most journals seek the views of only two or three reviewers, for the good reason that we are all very busy. Such a small sample size has low powers of discrimination (we would seldom accept such low power in our experiments!) and the variance of opinion is high.

It is not just technical errors that have the potential to mislead scientists. We make inferences, from our results – and from other published papers – that may turn out to be wrong. It is quite common for me to be unconvinced by some aspects of studies that I read. I might have done things differently, I might have drawn different conclusions from the same data, or I might not know what to conclude: to me, the study is far less persuasive than to the authors. I cannot necessarily say that the researchers were wrong, but I can have doubts; and some of these doubts may later turn out to be warranted.

Ecological systems are notable for their complexity and their variability. Ecology is, as indicated by the title of this book, a truly difficult science. We seek the truth of how ecological systems behave and try to generate insight that will save species – and even the planet – from extinction. Yet, philosophically, it is impossible to prove anything: we can merely weigh up evidence, of different kinds, that help us to reach an informed opinion.

Everything we do involves assumptions that may, or may not, turn out to be appropriate. We try to be dispassionate observers, but we never can be. We use human concepts to help us try to interpret what we see. We have biases, opinions and other human foibles. We have a history and a respect for others that inspires us but constrains us. Our current and future methods, and our uses of them, as I have just discussed, are fallible. We have a quality control system that is not only imperfect, but also provides inertia, maintaining a set of norms that resist change and allow weaknesses to persist. And despite all of this, ecologists are notable for their confidence in their conclusions: even though a 'due-diligence' of ecology would tell us be sceptical about everything that we read!

The primary aim of this book is to encourage early-career researchers – those who are still developing their particular type of science and having to 'sink or swim' in their chosen career – to be realistic about their expectations. To question everything, not to take everything for granted, and to make up their own minds. Their predecessors have made significant progress but very slowly and, because ecology is inherently so difficult, we remain uncertain about many (indeed most) things. But the book is not only for young researchers. It is also for any of our colleagues who are prepared to sit back and take a cold, hard look at what we have done and what we have achieved.

It is easy to conduct studies and collect data that are new, but it is hard to truly understand what they mean and to push forward the boundaries of ecological understanding. The literature to which our next generation aspires to add their names and ideas is not all 'state-of-the-art' but a range of qualities, all of it 'work in progress' that needs to be challenged, improved and accepted with caution.

The examples that we discuss in this book are intended to encourage all researchers to develop the habit of engaging in critical analysis of both their own work and that of others. Of course, we would be delighted if the superstars of our profession were also to benefit from our discussion and be inspired to engage in subsequent debate. But our primary target – early-career researchers – seldom have books written for them.

It has long struck me that debate – an open expression of differing ideas and views – is extremely limited in ecology. In particular, there is little debate about what we are trying to *achieve*. One-way communication dominates ecology: in our journals and conferences we tell others of our recent work, perhaps briefly float ideas and review the extent of knowledge. But as a way of critically examining ideas and approaches and initiating further development, these media are highly ineffective. Follow-on discourse, debate, dialogue – call it what you will – is limited, difficult and, in the case of journals, subject to extended time-lags. The much more dynamic medium of 'real time' discourse, the life-blood of the ancient philosophers, has become heavily constrained and inaccessible in modern science (not least because of issues of scale). Email, social media, forums and blogs have helped to fix some – but by no means all – of the timeliness and accessibility issues.

About 12 years ago, my great friends Bruce Maxwell (USA) and Michael Williams (Australia) helped me to start the Andina international workshops. Our aim has been to give emerging and more experienced ecologists the opportunity to participate in events tailor-made to facilitate effective, safe and inclusive discourse on what are often challenging and provocative topics. The presence of others in the same room allows the process of critical analysis to reach new levels of rigour and insight, by drawing on a huge combined intellect and a wide diversity of views and experience.

We therefore build into our meetings ways of overcoming natural reservations, social consciences and dominance hierarchies. Simple things, like going hiking together in the afternoons and relaxing together afterwards. Scale and cost remain as problems, but the feedback, from the early-career researchers in particular, has been overwhelmingly positive. Our sixth meeting is scheduled for February 2024. Our hope with this book is to reach out to a much wider audience than Andina has been able to.

The colleagues that I invited to join me in this project are a mix of youth, experience and backgrounds. Their expertise spans empirical, molecular and theoretical ecology, pure and applied modelling, philosophy and statistics, with extensive experience in journal editing, academic book authorship, program management and academic leadership. Some of them have shared experiences with me in Andina workshops; others I knew only by reputation. I am honoured to have such colleagues prepared to contribute their time and – perhaps – to risk their reputations. Importantly, most chapters involve early-career researchers: it would, I feel, have been hypocritical if they had not been included in a debate designed for such people. Indeed, we hope that journals will encourage reviews of the book by this audience.

Our contributions are subjective, biased, incomplete and almost certainly faulty in some instances. All these things are inevitable in a science in which there are few absolute answers. We will, in many places, state our personal opinions: clearly, we have strong views in some areas, about what ecologists should be trying to achieve, the strengths and weaknesses of the past and current approaches, and some things that should be changed. But we do not claim the primacy of these opinions. We do not believe that we are entitled to tell our colleagues what they should be trying to achieve; nor can we give them recipes for how to conduct their own critiques.

We urge readers to identify faults and improvements in our arguments and to communicate these – and alternative analyses – through appropriate, open communication media. We certainly do *not* argue that the topics of our chapters are those most in need of critique: they provide excellent examples and include the areas that we were most interested to engage with. We encourage readers to focus on our overall message and not on the fine details (many of which will always be a matter of opinion).

Our aim is to kick-start the process of critique in the scientific discipline of Ecology, rather than to pretend to present definitive statements on each topic (note that throughout the book we will capitalise the word Ecology where we refer to the bigger picture of the discipline: its community of researchers, their aims and values, the research that they do and the interactions among them).

Finally, a request for tolerance and respect. We explore topics of research rather than the work of particular individuals. However, the number of people active in a topic, and the number of leaders, can be limited and our comments in this book may be taken personally. This is unfortunate, but it is not our intention. Well-intended modern social mores placing an emphasis on the avoidance of conflict would seem to negate the benefits to be gained from the airing and resolution of differences.

Science must be challengeable, otherwise it will lose its credibility. We all learn through our mistakes and so we, the authors, must be prepared to be challenged in the same way that we challenge others.

Roger Cousens

Acknowledgements

Roger Cousens is indebted to Mark Dale for his valuable mentoring and support throughout the project. The team of authors thank Scott Vandervalk for his outstanding editorial help in pulling all the chapters together; Edmund Iffland for his wonderful cover design (https://edmundiffland.com/) and Hiromi Yagui for drawing figures. We thank Chris Cousens for comments on a very early draft of Chapter 1; and the following for their advice and input into Chapter 2 (J C Cahill and Sonia Graham), Chapter 3 (Yiannis Kokosalakis, Robert Frühstückl and Andrew Robinson), Chapter 5 (Maree-Josée Fortin), Chapter 7 (John Scott), Chapter 8 (Michael Dietze). Josh Brian and Jane Catford were supported by the European Research Council (ERC) under the European Union's Horizon 2020 research and innovation program (grant agreement No. 101002987 to JAC). We would like to note our appreciation to Olalekan Obisesan for his work in the early stages of the book. Finally, this book would never have been written without the love, tolerance and support of Jane Cousens.

About the authors

Daniel Z Atwater is an Assistant Professor at Montana State University, USA, in the Department of Animal and Range Science. He studies how ecology and evolution govern the distribution, abundance and productivity of plants responding to global change. In particular, he focuses on effects of drought and temperature on rangeland productivity and biodiversity. His work involves field experiments, genetic analyses, mathematics, geospatial modelling and individual-based modelling. He hopes to use this work to promote sustainable interactions between humans and our surrounding wildlands and agroecosystems.

Chris M Baker is a Senior Research Fellow in the School of Mathematics and Statistics at the University of Melbourne, Australia, and is affiliated with the Centre of Excellence for Biosecurity Risk Analysis (CEBRA) and the Melbourne Centre for Data Science (MCSD). His main interest is in using mathematical models to help inform the way that we manage complex systems. Projects to date have included the optimisation of management of interacting species and the impacts of species removal, such as feral cats and invasive plants, the removal of diseased Tasmanian devils from isolated regions to create devil facial tumour disease-free areas, and modelling the effect of antibiotics on microbes to develop treatment strategies that prevent the emergence of treatment-resistant infections. Most recently, he has been part of a team of modellers working on the management of COVID-19, providing advice to Australian state and federal governments.

Joshua I Brian is a Research Associate at King's College London, UK, in the Department of Geography, following a PhD with Professor David Aldridge at the University of Cambridge. His research presently focuses on the mechanisms of success of invasive plant species, with a particular emphasis on how plant enemies can facilitate or inhibit invasion. More generally, his research spans community ecology, invasion biology, parasitology and symbiosis, and previous research projects include studies of the coral reefs of Timor-Leste and the parasites of European freshwater mussels. He is particularly interested in how ecological processes vary and interact across spatial and temporal scales.

Marc W. Cadotte is Professor of Urban Forest Conservation and Biology at the University of Toronto, Scarborough, Canada. He has a broad interest in the ecological and evolutionary mechanisms generating patterns of species diversity and in applying this understanding to conservation issues. Past research projects have included the role of evolutionary relationships among species in influencing the health and functioning of ecosystems and the effects of forest fragmentation on forest structure in Madagascar coastal rain forests. He was the Executive Editor of the *Journal of Applied Ecology* for many years and now leads a new initiative with the British Ecological Society to help bridge the research-implementation gap. He is also editor-in-chief of *Ecological Solutions and Evidence*, a new open access journal. He was co-author of the book *Phylogenies in Ecology* (Princeton University Press, 2016 with Jonathan Davies) and co-editor of *Conceptual Ecology and Invasion Biology: Reciprocal Approaches to Nature.*

Françoise Cardou is a Post-doctoral Fellow at the University of Toronto, Scarborough, Canada, following a PhD at l'Université de Sherbrooke with

Bill Shipley and a post-doc with Mark Velend. Her aim is to understand the diversity of ways in which humans shape and are shaped by our environment, focusing on the idea that both biological and social systems can be conceptualised under the same general theory of evolution and adaptation. Thus far, her work has featured plant communities within socio-ecological systems: specifically, does increased movement of species, people and information in the Anthropocene generate similar patterns of diversity across natural and social systems?

Jane A Catford is a Reader in Ecology at King's College London, UK, and Senior Editor of the *Journal of Ecology*. She is a plant community ecologist with interests in biological invasions, environmental change and biodiversity. She is particularly interested in the causes, consequences and processes of vegetation change, and typically focuses on species invasions to tackle such questions. Past research has spanned topics that include species coexistence, community assembly, vegetation management, ecosystem restoration, ecosystem services, functional traits, novel ecosystems, climate change, disturbance and river regulation. Fascinated by mechanisms, she maintains long-term field experiments in Australia, the USA and the UK. She currently leads a five-year project *Predicting impacts of alien plant invasions on community diversity*.

Roger D Cousens is an Emeritus Professor at the University of Melbourne, Australia, with over 40 years specialising in agricultural weeds and invasive species. His approaches have featured components of field research, population modelling and statistical analysis, while he has initiated collaborative projects with quantitative geneticists, molecular ecologists, geomorphologists and social scientists. For the last decade, his passion has been unravelling the dynamics of two invasive sea rockets, their hybridisation and the role of their pollinators. Throughout his career, he has been an outspoken communicator on research practices. This book is a direct outcome of his 12 years as the convenor of the Andina international workshops, developing approaches to effective debate and in which the role of early-career researchers has been central. He has been lead author on two previous academic books: *Population Dynamics of Weeds* (Cambridge University Press, 1995 with

Martin Mortimer); and *Dispersal in Plants: A Population Perspective* (Oxford University Press, 2008 with Calvin Dytham and Richard Law). He is an Honorary Fellow of the Weed Science Society of America.

Mark R T Dale is Professor at The University of Northern British Columbia, Canada. His research interests include the spatial structure of plant communities and the development and evaluation of numerical methods to answer ecological questions, including graph theory and network complexity. His graduate students have worked in a diverse set of systems from prairie to alpine and at a range of spatial scales from plant neighbour competition to landscape disturbance patterns. He wrote *Spatial Pattern Analysis in Plant Ecology* (Cambridge University Press, 1999) and *Applying Graph Theory in Ecological Research* (Cambridge University Press, 2017) and was co-author, with Marie-Josée Fortin, of *Spatial Analysis: A Guide for Ecologists* (Cambridge University Press, 2005, 2nd ed. 2014) and *Quantitative Analysis of Ecological Networks* (Cambridge University Press, 2021).

Alkistis Elliott-Graves focuses her research at Bielefeld University, Germany, on the general philosophy of science and philosophy of applied sciences (especially ecology and climate science). She is particularly interested in complex systems: what makes them interesting but also difficult to investigate? Recent publications have addressed the difficulty of making precise and accurate predictions in ecology and climate science, and what this means for the scientific status of these disciplines. She is currently working on the broader implications of this research for the relationship between traditional philosophy of science and applied scientific practice.

Jannice Friedman is an Associate Professor at Queen's University in Kingston, Canada, in the Biology Department. Her research examines the evolution of plant reproductive strategies in response to ecological conditions and the consequences for pollination and mating. It aims to develop a mechanistic understanding of life history decisions. Recent publications look at: the evolution of annual and perennial reproductive strategies; the consequences of variation in allocation for pollination, fitness and mating; and the effects of seasonality on plant life histories.

Michael J Keough is now an Honorary Professor at the University of Melbourne, Australia. He has a particular interest in how populations and communities respond to change, human induced and natural, and the role of recruitment in this process. He has worked on a range of systems, but deep down, he finds field experiments with invertebrates the most satisfying. He has worked hard to improve experimental design and data analysis for all biologists and, with Gerry Quinn, published the book *Experimental Design & Data Analysis for Biologists* with a supporting website (Cambridge University Press, 2002, 2023). He is also a co-author of *Monitoring Ecological Impacts* (Cambridge University Press, 2002). He is a recipient of the Gold Medal of the Ecological Society of Australia.

Thao P Le is a Research Fellow in the School of Mathematics and Statistics at the University of Melbourne, Australia, and is affiliated with the CEBRA and the MCSD. They are interested in mathematical modelling of ecological and epidemiological phenomena and the effects of management. Past and current research includes the benefit of citizen involvement in invasive species management and the relationship between population immunity and future COVID-19 waves.

Maria Paniw is a Research Fellow at the Estación Biológica de Doñana, Spain, and a Research Associate at the University of Zurich. Her research focuses on how intrinsic and extrinsic factors, biotic interactions and individual traits interact to determine population structure and dynamics. She is particularly interested in how population projections under global change can be improved by accounting for trait dynamics, environmental and spatial patterning, and trade-offs between survival and reproduction. She works with long-term data on plants and animals, including carnivorous plants, Mediterranean shrubs, meerkats, yellow-bellied marmots, African ungulates and the Iberian lynx. She also works on the potential evolutionary consequences of environmental change

and the integration of multi-species seasonal population dynamics into viability analyses.

Gerry P Quinn is now an Honorary Professor at Deakin University, Australia, and was previously Chair in Marine Biology and Head of Deakin's Warrnambool campus. He has extensive research experience in the ecology of coastal marine, freshwater and estuarine ecosystems and their environmental management. He has co-authored two books: *Experimental Design & Data Analysis for Biologists* (2002, 2023) with Michael Keough and *Monitoring Ecological Impacts* with various authors (2002), both with Cambridge University Press.

Alyson C Van Natto is a PhD Candidate in the Biology Department of Queen's University, Kingston, Canada, with a keen interest in plant evolutionary ecology. She is particularly interested in the ecology and evolution of plant reproduction and life history strategies in human-altered environments. She has a passion for conservation, having worked with species-at-risk during her undergraduate and master's degrees and invasive species for her current PhD research. Most recently, she has been a part of a team of conservation biologists working to fill knowledge gaps with respect to rare plant conservation in Canada.

Bruce L Webber is Principal Research Scientist with the Commonwealth Scientific and Industrial Research Organisation (CSIRO) and an Adjunct Associate Professor at the University of Western Australia. His work focuses on the impacts of global environmental change on community ecology and the role of plant–ecosystem interactions in shaping community composition. His research spans a variety of ecosystems, with a particular focus on the management of biological invasions and the tropical regions of northern Australia and SE Asia. He has a special interest in methods for modelling species distributions and has been a key contributor to the Andina international debate workshops.

1

Why a hard science needs strong critique

ROGER COUSENS

WHY ECOLOGY IS DIFFICULT

Ecology is one of the most difficult of sciences (though beware that there is a second definition of the term: Box 1.1). Many of the natural phenomena that ecologists study are of great diversity and complexity, and are inherently variable. There are so many different organisms, each with their idiosyncrasies in the ways that they live, occupying so many different environments. Every location on earth provides a unique set of living conditions, determined by their position on the globe and modified by regional and local geology and geomorphological processes. Every location differs in the groups of organisms that have found themselves there at any given point in time and that have then undergone further evolution.

How do we begin to understand it all?

Science and philosophy have provided us with an array of logical, procedural and analytical tools that we can use. There are so many questions that we might ask, any number of ways to proceed, so many things to observe or measure. But, alas, no perfect recipe as to how to proceed.

We can do a great variety of things that we recognise as components of science, each contributing fragments of evidence, like the pieces in a jigsaw puzzle. But unlike a jigsaw, the picture will never be complete and even the pieces themselves may be blurred and indistinct. The same evidence may be explained by multiple alternatives, some of which may not even have occurred to us yet. We may well have cause to wonder whether we will recognise the true explanation when we have it! Can we ever be certain of anything?

An additional layer to this complexity is that ecologists are human observers, with all the constraints that it carries. We see nature through the eyes of humans, who have been taught to view things in particular ways. We are all individuals, who vary in our interests and opinions, and in our technical and cognitive abilities. We will see the same issue in somewhat different ways, do things differently from one another, interpret the results differently and potentially gain different insights. We differ in the levels of evidence that we regard as sufficient to support our views. Different ecologists have different levels of expectation: they will vary in the vehemence of their claims and in the headlines that accompany their publications. It is quite possible that they may well reach different conclusions from the same evidence. Like professionals in any discipline, we also make mistakes, which may be inconsequential but may be more serious, undermining our efforts to make progress. Scientific convention attempts to define standards of rigour, so that this variation can be minimised, but it can never be eliminated.

Ecologists have risen to such challenges over many decades. Judging by the titles and summaries

DOI: 10.1201/9781003314332-1

BOX 1.1: The other ecology

This book is about the science that we call ecology, first coined by Haeckel (1866) and derived from the Greek 'oikos' meaning dwelling place and 'logia' meaning study. Although there have been many modifications of the definition over the years (Andrewartha 1961; Odum 1959, 1975; Margalef 1968), the consensus is that ecology is 'the study of the interactions between organisms and their environments'. As we will show, there are many ways in which ecology can be done and various forms of output. Ecology is not an easy thing to tie down.

Over time, the many people engaged in this activity of ecology have diversified (and subdivided) their objectives and their approaches, established standards, conventions, reputations and traditions, created a machinery for the vetting and publication of its research, concepts and ideas, fashioned an underlying social structure (societies with their conferences, outreach and other services) and developed educational programs. The resulting scientific 'discipline' of Ecology is, in its entirety, so much more than the mere collection and assembly of pieces of knowledge that it deserves its own special recognition. In this book, when we want to draw attention to this overall scientific edifice that ecologists have created, we capitalise the word: Ecology.

It is important, however, to recognise that there is another definition of ecology that has nothing directly to do with science or study. The 'logia' part of the word has become redundant: ecology has entered the vernacular as simply 'the relationship between living things and their environment'.

The 'ecology' of a penguin, for example, relates to its breeding cycle, the food it eats, its predators, how it is affected by weather, climate and so on. The 'ecology' of a lake relates to the community of organisms that it supports, and to its chemistry, hydrology and seasonal weather cycles, since these all interact with the organisms. We refer to the latter as an 'ecological system' or 'ecosystem'.

To put it another way, an entity *has* an ecology. Ecology is used in this sense by scientists and the public alike and it is the definition we most often see used in the media. Scientists are as comfortable using the same word for their own research activities as for the object of their actions. Does this ever result in confusion? This second definition of ecology does *not* specify that our knowledge – the narrative that we would tell – has been achieved through the methods of science. A penguin has an ecology whether we have studied it or not (just like a tree falling in a forest will create pressure waves in the air, even if there is no one there to perceive them!). It is worth noting that the same dichotomy of meaning applies to 'natural history': natural history is both the activity of observers and the attributes that they are observing. Such is the nature of language! It is not always logical, but common usage ultimately dictates the evolution of language and we learn to live with it (Newberry et al. 2017).

Another linguistic consequence of this other ecology is that people may validly label themselves as ecologists simply by having cultivated an interest and a knowledge of the topic, or being employed within the environmental management industry, or active in a policy setting. Membership of ecology's professional societies and institutes may also not require the individual ever to have been involved in quality-controlled research. All may be regarded by the media as experts. This is perhaps why some researchers now refer to themselves as 'ecological scientists' to make the distinction clear.

of our scientific papers, we seem to be remarkably optimistic and positive, uplifted by doing science and thrilled by our discoveries. There is good reason to congratulate ourselves and our predecessors on the ecological knowledge that we have assembled thus far. We make extensive use of surveys, experiments and models. It has been fortunate that technological advances have allowed us to extend and fine-tune a wide range of techniques, in data collection and data analysis. A vast amount of evidence from a wide variety of contexts has been accumulated, so that we can determine whether our ideas have generality. But because we cannot measure many things directly, we have come to rely on surrogate measurements – things that we think, and trust, will reflect the true underlying processes. We are also forced to make a great many assumptions in order to simplify problems and to bring solutions within our reach; and we create a great many concepts, human constructs that help us as observers to better comprehend the systems with which we work.

The paradox is that such tools, which we use to make science easier for us, actually add further levels of uncertainty. It is surely not surprising, then, that progress towards greater understanding in ecology can be frustratingly slow, inconsistent and uncertain. Success can be temporary or, in hindsight, illusory. There is always the possibility of false leads and mistakes along the way. Moreover, progress will seldom come from a single piece of research, but from the accumulation of many decades of effort.

Ecologists are playing ever greater roles in society. We are now routinely involved in preparing advisory reports and are consulted in the development of government policy, in addition to our more traditional roles in communication, education and conservation. With the increasing impacts of global environmental change to the planet, ecologists are going to be critical contributors to the very survival of humanity over the coming decades. Our opinions and our insights are, and will continue to be, valued. However, our reputations ultimately depend on the rigour of our contributions to science, not just the politics of our opinions.

In order to maintain high levels of quality control, we need to apply the highest standards that we can. Here we propose that a strong element of critique applied to our work can help to guide us in this quest.

QUESTIONS AND ANSWERS IN SCIENCE

A great deal has been said in the past about the way that we *should* do science, often by those who do not do science themselves: some of these philosophical issues will be discussed in Chapter 3. These discussions can easily become bogged down in semantics and ideas that can be easy to state but difficult to apply in practice. At a pragmatic level, however, science is about posing questions and using evidence from relevant sources, in ways that are logical and therefore defendable, in order to reach answers. These conclusions can be synthesised and built into frameworks of connected ideas which, in turn, lead to new questions – perhaps through hypotheses based on previous results and syntheses – and a search for new answers.

Through science, we can achieve and share fundamental understanding about how the natural world works and formulate ways in which we might take actions to achieve particular outcomes. Our success in the science of ecology should therefore be judged in terms of our ability to pose and to answer questions about the ways in which organisms and their environment interact.

It is not easy to come up with a set of questions upon which to base a scientific study. There is, undoubtedly, a great deal of art involved in being a scientist and a great deal of variation among scientists. Clearly experience plays a major role in the questions we pose, as does observation. There is also likely to be a role for imagination. Ideas seldom simply strike us like a magic bolt of lightning (the so-called 'Eureka moment'): most thoughts are inspired by something.

The best scientists tend to be the ones with a knack for posing the most illuminating questions and identifying the most effective pathways, sets of procedures, towards the solution. They are also likely to be the ones that are most critical, of both themselves and of others.

The quest for answers can be illustrated with a simple cartoon. It is no easy matter to come up with the right question: a poorly phrased question may make the path to an answer opaque (Figure 1.1a). We might, for example, ask something very mundane about spatial variation in an index of diversity when in fact we want to know something fundamental about interactions within communities, believing naively that the former will somehow lead

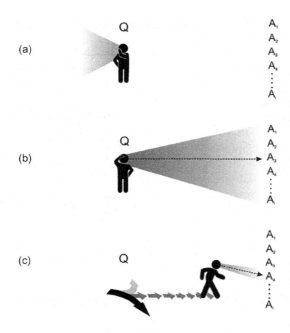

Figure 1.1 The quest for answers (A1, A2, A3 etc.) to a question (Q). See text for details.

to the latter. The first consideration of a researcher needs to be the determination of the ultimate objective of the research, rather than merely coming up with something that we can easily do or calculate, or something that someone has done before. It may not have given them the answer before and it will probably not give you the answer now. Does the question lead us towards the objective?

We often have a favoured answer when we first pose the question (Figure 1.1b); this is especially true as we become more experienced. We may well be right, but it is easy to let our confidence cloud what we do. Indeed, it is common in ecology to set out to 'test' a particular idea or hypothesis and in doing so accumulate evidence that supports what we think. This can lead to 'confirmation bias', since we may subconsciously ignore evidence that is contrary or that is inconclusive. There may be several possible answers to our question, some of which we have not even considered. Support for one answer does not exclude the possibility that another may be correct: we may need to demonstrate lack of support for alternatives rather than just support for our cherished idea (the principle of refutation is discussed in Chapter 3).

Part of the art of science is to design a pathway that will effectively lead towards the true answer (Figure 1.1c). A single step is unlikely to take us all the way there. It may or may not draw upon hypotheses and it may be informed by evidence from a wide variety of sources and methodologies. There may be many alternative steps, each of which contributes something to the answer: the best pathway may need to include steps that go in a variety of directions, and draw on a wide variety of skills other than our own, before coming together as we get closer to the answer. Synthesis plays an important part in science and it is not uncommon that information from scientists asking very different questions becomes relevant to us. Some steps may not take us any closer to the answer and may even be distracting: in itself scientific activity, 'busy work', does not necessarily lead towards an answer. We might spend many decades going nowhere because we are not using the appropriate procedures, or because we have failed to specify an appropriate – or even a tractable – question.

Even if we are going in the right direction, the size of our steps will vary and may diminish over time: the law of diminishing returns. We then have a difficult decision: how close (intellectually) do we need to get before we are willing to claim that we *know* the answer, 'beyond reasonable doubt'? We all differ in our levels of confidence of when we are right, or when we are prepared to accept that we are wrong.

In science, we are part of a community and it is not a simple matter of convincing ourselves, but of convincing others. Like minds may be convinced by the same (incomplete) information. But, to ensure the highest of standards, we must be able to convince the most rigorous of our peers. Even then, there is no guarantee that we will be correct: there will always remain a degree of uncertainty. The need to convince others, as well as ourselves, leads naturally to the discussion of the role of critique (and its cousin, debate) in science.

THE ROLE OF CRITIQUE IN SCIENCE

Critique and criticism have the same root, the Greek *kritikos* meaning 'able to make judgements'. In the Socratic tradition, criticism was a necessary, healthy aspect of enquiry: an evaluation of our logic and our progress to reassure ourselves that our quest for knowledge proceeds in the right direction. History shows that science is not an inexorable accumulation of correct knowledge; we make mistakes (Bronowski 1979). Science feeds upon such errors, testing and often rejecting them, in the realisation that we have made, and rectified, previous errors (though see Banobi et al. 2011). Scientists all have strengths that we can recognise and exploit. And they all have weaknesses. A good scientist – within a healthy scientific discipline – needs to know their limitations (to paraphrase Milius and Cimino 1973).

Regrettably, modern English uses 'criticism' asymmetrically, meaning an expression of disapproval. The result is that criticism, even 'constructive criticism', can offend and cause people to become defensive, so that the benefits of criticism are lost. Failure and weakness are frowned upon in society. If we are seen to have failed, or if we admit the weakness of our understanding, then our reputations will be impaired. We may be seen as having wasted time and money and may raise concerns about the soundness of our policy advice. Governments do not want highly resourced scientists to say *we don't know* or *we've made a mistake and need to go back to the drawing board*. Modern ecologists, perhaps more than any other scientists, pride themselves on their inclusive attitudes and their respect for the views of others. Thus, open criticism may be seen by some as undesirable and unwelcome to the general spirit of collegiality, or even as bullying (Vazire 2017, as is debate: Box 1.2). Language can, of course, be toned down to avoid overt confrontation. But there are perhaps times when unambiguous or emphatic statements are needed to halt the proliferation of poor science and, as a result, ensure the prevalence of strong science.

Sadly, most forms of interaction among ecologists are passive and unidirectional, informing colleagues through our publication media and short, polite questions at conferences, rather than an active multidirectional exchange of thoughts and ideas. Even when we identify serious problems within an area of research or across the entire discipline (Steel et al. 2013; Morales et al. 2017), our responses tend to be informative and advisory, rarely leading to a concerted effort to overcome the problem. To gain the full benefits of criticism we must welcome it into ecology by providing greater opportunities for open and non-threatening discourse.

We use the term 'critique' throughout this book as 'detailed analysis and assessment', a necessary

and ongoing process of evaluation. Critique, if embedded in science, can help us to maintain quality control in what we do because it does more than simply find fault: it identifies our weaknesses so that we can work to overcome them. Ideally, critique should be as dispassionate as possible and, wherever possible, appraise evidence against stated criteria. No critique, however, can ever be completely objective, since it inevitably involves some form of interpretation.

Given the high level of uncertainties involved in ecology, a realist might argue that we should review and question everything that we, and our colleagues, do and claim: to make up our minds on the basis of a rigorous examination of evidence. Such scepticism is a philosophically rational response to difficulty rather than lack of trust or a submission to negativity or doubt. Only intense scrutiny will identify deficiencies that, if it is possible, we can address. The criterion that we should use to evaluate the effectiveness of research should be its purpose or goal. What was a particular study meant to achieve? How was the investigation done? What are the potential problems with it? What was not achieved? How could it be done better?

Statements of what we think we know, as in traditional review papers, are little help in setting directions unless accompanied by an evaluation of precisely what it is that we are trying to achieve. The application of some new method, no matter how 'advanced' it is, does not in itself guarantee a major advance in understanding. We should also be careful not to equate effectiveness with the number of papers that result, even though that criterion may often be used in the judgement of our case for promotion or for our suitability to be allocated a research grant.

Critical assessment need not wait for decades until someone decides that it is about time to write a book or publish an article! It makes sense for critique to be ongoing and forward-looking, rather than merely retrospective; and to be proactive, through the research designer, rather than reactive by reliance on the haphazard and protracted process of peer review. It makes sense, when designing every aspect of every project, to bear in mind specifically what we are trying to achieve, in both the short term and the long term. Is what we are about to do capable of success (or of substantially contributing towards success)? Just because other ecologists are doing the same thing, or because a particular method has not previously been applied to our study system, it does not mean that it is the best thing to do. Could we do something else, or do it in a different way, perhaps with skills that are not currently included?

In hindsight, what did we actually achieve? How could we have achieved more if we were to step back in time? Every ecological researcher goes through such self-examination to some extent: it would be insulting to suggest otherwise. But it is a skill that needs to be appreciated, acquired and honed; some of us are better at it than others. There are also times when our own skills are insufficient, such as when we are 'too close' to something: the best critique may then come from others.

If we are to evaluate ecological research in terms of its effectiveness in answering a given question, then we need to incorporate into this critique an assessment of the question. One is irrevocably dependent upon the other. A great many research questions are short term in focus and context specific. This makes their evaluation relatively easy. For example: what do we need to do in order to increase the abundance of lynx in a particular national park? What is a specific technique capable of telling us about the effect of climate change on a particular coral reef community? The individual researchers, and their colleagues in those fields of research, are in the best position to evaluate their approaches. However, there are also 'higher-order' questions that relate to those working across many – if not all – contexts. These might be considered to represent the ultimate goals of ecology as a discipline, since these indicate where we have developed knowledge and understanding that transcend all the variability inherent in our systems. We will consider them in more detail in the next section.

BOX 1.2: Debate in ecology

A 'debate' is a discussion of opposing views, a process that helps us to assess the veracity of conflicting evidence and opinion and, hopefully, to reach a conclusion. The very words 'debate' and 'argument' are considered by some people to be too focused on winning and losing: they argue that science needs 'discourse', not debate. This may have semantic merit. In many walks of life 'debate' has become all about taking sides, winning and losing, right and wrong. There may be palpable (not just egotistical) rewards for winning and penalties for losing. Examples of intense debates in ecology include those concerning plant communities and life history traits (Grime vs. Tilman: Grace 1991), species co-occurrences (Diamond vs. Simberloff: Diamond and Gilpin 1982) or niche-based and neutral theories of community structure (Clark 2012; Wennekes et al. 2012). Clearly structured debates such as these are rare and often remain unresolved; perhaps the debates are intense and extended because they *are* unresolvable (Peters 1991).

In one extraordinary case, Snaydon (1994) was allowed by editors to liken Sackville-Hamilton (and by implication similar ecologists) to an outdated supporter of the phlogiston theory, for continuing to support the popular 'replacement series' experimental design. This escalated to the point of journal editors forbidding the use of the design for any purpose ('*The tendency to misuse the method is so pervasive that its continued use should be discouraged*': Gibson et al. 1999) and referring to it as '*discredited*' (an editor's comment, pers. comm.).

A few ecologists railed against these opinions on the basis that the imposition of such dogma could infringe intellectual freedom (Jolliffe 2001) and even threaten ecology's status as a science (Cousens 1996). The Snaydon camp argued that because the use of the replacement series was highly questionable for *some* inferences, it should be banned for *all* uses. A similar personal debate was Lawton's (1991) attack on Peters (1991) in a book review, but Peters' right to have his views carefully evaluated was defended by Keddy (1992; see Keddy and Weiher 1999).

'Debate' of this sort, with people having to defend their reputations, is unhealthy, but so is a *lack* of insightful discourse. Discourse should involve the broad ecology community and not be hidden behind the secrecy of peer review or diminished by deference to the individuals with the strongest reputations.

ECOLOGICAL GOALS

Progress is a nebulous thing: we all aspire to achieve it, in all walks of life. It is common to hear the claim that *we are making significant progress*, whether this refers to landing on Mars, defeating a disease, fighting drugs and cybercrime, achieving targets on renewable energy or becoming good enough to win the football World Cup. But how do we measure progress? More specifically, how would we measure the progress in, and therefore the effectiveness of, ecological research? How would we respond to a question from a funding provider who asks us to demonstrate that what we have done with their money has been worthwhile?

The very term 'progress' begs the question 'progress towards what'? Dictionary definitions of progress are typically 'movement towards a destination' (the achievement of a specified goal), or 'towards an improved or more advanced condition' (better than before). To be able to measure progress, we either need a clear goal – so that we can measure our distance from it – or we need to be able to define the current situation, so that we can, in turn, define 'better'. With goals, we can objectively consider what we might do to improve progress. Without a goal, the doing of things *likely* to lead to progress all too readily becomes the goal. Attempts to justify claims that progress is being made, in any field of endeavour, thus often involve lists of the things we have done, rather than objective measurement of how much closer to the goal or how better we now are.

Peters (1991) was particularly critical of ecology's lack of goals in 'fundamental' ecological research: *'It is an elemental proposition that, if we want to get someplace, then we must know where we are and where we want to go'*. Keddy and Weiher (1999) provocatively used the analogy of landing on the moon:

> There appears to be a naïve belief [in ecology] that the way to build a spaceship and land a human on the moon is to trust that, if everyone indulges themselves in an idiosyncratic and self-indulgent pastime at the taxpayer's expense, the outcome will be positive. Like Voltaire's Professor Pangloss, there is the insistence that this must be the best of all possible worlds, however

inefficient or painful it may appear on the surface. If progress is forgotten about entirely... there is no particular need to be concerned about goals, progress and social contribution.

But the counter-argument is that, in ecology's case, we do not know where the moon is, how many moons there are or whether moons even exist! So, how can we set ourselves goals?

There are two common justifications given for ecological research. One, most often identified as pure or fundamental research, is the generation of knowledge for its own sake. Civilisation's quest to understand the world around us (Garfield 1973) would be deficient – for many academically minded people – without an appreciation of the roles played by organisms in that world. This is the type of ecology that fills our ecological textbooks: general principles, concepts and theories, along with case studies that we consider as support for them. With this information, that we might term 'ecological theory', we can help others in society to appreciate the insights from our science, especially how the living component of their world functions, their impacts on it and thus their ethical responsibilities (see Box 1.3).

The other justification, labelled as applied ecology, is to help solve or to mitigate environmental problems, such as conservation, reclamation and environmental risk minimisation. This is probably the most socially compelling reason in the modern era – at least when it comes to the case for financial support. Applied ecology can, but does not necessarily, make use of theory: the mere application of the procedures of science, such as surveys, experiments and data analysis, may be sufficient to draw conclusions.

What ecologists do in our research does not necessarily map directly on to this binary classification of fundamental and applied. There has long been an argument in all sciences that (applied) benefits to society from fundamental research *will* occur, but they are rare and inherently unpredictable: we must invest adequately in fundamental science so that we will not miss out on these opportunities.

This reasoning is similar to that used by people who buy tickets in lotteries: unless you play, you will never stand a chance of winning. But in the case of science, you do not even know if there is

BOX 1.3: A brief note on ecological scientists in society

Ecologists are highly motivated, often passionate, because they see great significance and value in what they can contribute to science, to society and to the planet. It is important at the outset to distinguish among these different contributions, because the subject of this book is research. That is not to discount the other contributions of ecologists: it is merely a statement of boundary. The social and political contributions of ecological researchers, in communication and education, in the development of policy and advice, even the administration of our societies and the management of our journals, are extensive and important but must be explored elsewhere.

Many professional ecologists see themselves as champions of the environment, not just as dispassionate scientists. Our roles in society can be complex and often it is our *opinions* that are sought rather than our provision of factual information: in such a setting, the dividing line between scientifically derived knowledge, expert judgement and guesswork is often unclear. As human beings, we are not immune to other influences such as politics and religion, and we can be biased.

---

a prize! It is purely a matter of faith, rather than fact, that there will be (more) prizes. This serendipity argument is not just applied to the issue of high-level funding allocations to different types of science. It is often used to justify case studies of particular organisms, communities or ecosystems: a 'silver bullet' might be discovered, a way of saving a species from extinction, of managing a pest or a way of making a system more sustainable. Such claims are often made, but rarely justified, in many introductions to scientific papers and research grant applications: '*improved understanding of the ecology of X is* necessary *to improve our ability to manage it*'. A more persuasive argument for fundamental research might be that, when we are inevitably called upon to use our expertise (rather than facts) to make speculations for managers, a fundamental understanding of the ways that ecological systems behave will make it more likely that our informed guesses will be reasonable.

It is difficult to discern clear goals for much of ecology (Peters 1991), other than to achieve *more* or *better* on a case-by-case basis: more knowledge and understanding, more accurate predictions and better management advice. Take, for example, the websites of researchers or their labs. We are told very little about what they are trying to *achieve* through the research, whether it be fundamental or applied. What are the difficult questions that they are trying so hard to answer, the challenges, the things that would constitute breakthroughs? The information we read often refers to the interests of

the researcher – a taxonomic group, an ecosystem or an academic theme – and the techniques they use. We may or may not be told why those topics are considered important. In almost every case we are told that it is anticipated that the research will lead, somehow, to better management. If management is truly a priority, then there are strategies for making research more effective (see *From forecasts to policy*, Chapter 6).

This extract from a website is perhaps typical:

> I am interested in the processes that determine the success or failure of invasive plant species in coastal dune systems. Through experimentation, survey, sampling, laboratory analysis and modelling, I try to predict how abundance and distribution change under different conditions and hence what action we might take to manage populations.
>
> *(The University of Melbourne, undated)*

We assume that more research, guided by peer review of what we do, inevitably leads to better individual project outcomes and therefore progress for the discipline as a whole. But would fundamental ecology be better served if we set ourselves clear goals: specific things that we should strive to achieve? It is often argued that the sense of purpose provided by a goal can motivate and focus, while assisting in planning of a series of actions (Locke and Latham 2006). They can also be used to set milestones along the way and 'key performance indicators'. When goals are shared by multiple researchers, they can – in theory – result in greater collegiality, greater combined capability, but also greater competition and challenge. The negative side of having goals is that they set us up to be criticised if they, or defined milestones towards them, are not achieved. Although ecologists are not in the habit of setting goals, the reformulation of fundamental research projects in terms of goals would appear to be relatively straightforward. If a funding agency demanded it, we would do it (Gannon 2003)!

At the level of individual projects, short-term goals are common in applied research. The funding often comes from a client who wants to achieve something in particular: for example, to develop a decision-making aid to guide efforts to save the Sumatran rhinoceros (*Dicerorhinus sumatrensis*) from extinction, to reduce the impact of facial tumour disease on the Tasmanian Devil (*Sarcophilus harrisii*) or to develop an effective biological control agent for kudzu (*Pueraria lobata*).

This does not mean that every research project is expected to achieve that aim by itself. Saving the Sumatran rhino requires tactical, political and social solutions rather than merely ecological knowledge. But it should be made clear how the scientific project will contribute to the goal. It is largely a matter of extending the short-term objective, to explain – as specifically as possible – the longer-term goal of the body of work into which the project fits.

Consider, for a moment, research on climate change. This has generated a large volume of information over the past two to three decades, the result of considerable government investment. In the great majority of instances, the specific research projects were the creations of individual researchers or small teams. The outcomes have been what we already suspected: that, in various case studies, climate change is already having impacts and – hardly a major surprise – we have predicted that these impacts will increase as climate changes further. Those impacts are also relatively predictable on the basis of our current understanding of ecology – although surprises may arise.

In an analysis of the summary sections of every project application funded by the Australian Research Council from 2003 to 2021 (using the search terms 'climate' and 'ecology'), the dominant objective was to develop a better understanding of what has happened in nature so far. About one-third of projects claimed that the research would lead to a better ability to predict future changes. About one-fifth expected their research to result in unspecified benefits for the management of the impacts of climate change, but only 3% had management of the impacts of climate change specified as the target of the research.

Do we need more of the same types of climate change studies, examining further nuances to these established impacts, or serendipitously uncovering instances of interesting new impacts? Or are there bigger questions that require concerted efforts by researchers around the globe? Can we rely on the decisions of individual researchers to determine where, as a society, to go from here? The process of setting and agreeing on goals for fundamental research, however, is far from clear. Do we need some sort of high-level think-tanks? Who would be invited? Would they be effective: the process of reaching consensus often results in wording of outcomes that is general, encapsulating multiple views, rather than being specific and achievable? Would they gain popular support and be widely adopted?

There have been occasional attempts to find consensus on the most important ecological questions and future issues for research. In the case of a survey by the British Ecological Society (Sutherland et al. 2013), many of the questions would have been considered by Peters (1991) as unanswerable and therefore inappropriate as goals. How, for example, would we ever achieve a definitive answer to the question '*What is the relative importance of trophic and non-trophic interactions in determining the composition of communities*?' Although many of us would agree that it is, indeed, an interesting ecological question, many decades of research are likely to still be inconclusive: it is unclear in most cases what specifiable observations – rather than just data that are somehow relevant – would constitute an answer. A decade and 400+ citations after the survey was published, it is difficult to see what effect its lists have had (or will have) on the direction of research activities in ecology. Instead of ecologists debating and refining the lists, formulating appropriate tests and initiating new collaborative or competitive research projects, the lists seem mostly to have been used to justify projects that were going to be done anyway.

How, then, should ecologists proceed? Does our discipline need to change? And how would change occur?

SO WHAT?

In his book *Critique for Ecology*, Peters (1991) commented upon the whole discipline, arguing that the way we do much of our work is fundamentally flawed and requires a new approach based on prediction. If Peters is correct, we will never achieve answers because they are the wrong questions. His views received little support, eliciting denial and defensiveness rather than useful, formative discussion of his criticisms.

It is pointless expecting that, somehow, ecology will undergo a major paradigm shift, with us all accepting that there is a better way of doing ecology, just because one person – or even several people – says so. Fundamental change does not happen that way. Our aim in this book is quite different from Peters'.

Instead of proposing how our colleagues should change what they do, we encourage them to embrace and to facilitate the process of critique themselves, so that it plays a more central role in their science. We will draw on examples from across the discipline in order to demonstrate what this might look like. In our book, we are not starting from a premise that ecology needs to be completely re-designed; it has achieved much in its current form. But it does require vigilance to maintain quality and, since it can never be perfect, it is capable of being improved.

Many of ecology's core fundamental questions are long-standing and we are yet to achieve satisfactory answers. If we carry on as we are now, we will achieve more and our tools will become better. That is not in doubt. But progress is likely to continue to be slow, even though the researchers are being productive (in terms of outputs), because ecology is inherently a very difficult science.

There is little doubt in our minds – and supported by discussions with journal editors – that some things that we are currently doing are ineffective, sometimes erroneous, and should be changed or discontinued. Critique is a powerful tool for helping us all to identify those things that are most inhibiting progress and to stimulate us to identify what we might change in order to achieve

better progress. Achieving satisfactory implementation of those changes is another matter – one that we cannot expect to resolve here.

We will begin the book with a short exploration of some of the ways in which the discipline of ecology has evolved thus far and the factors – the selection pressures – that influence what we do and how we do it (Chapter 2). We then discuss some of the reasons why it is hard to answer questions in ecology, the conceptual tools that we have at our disposal and some of the outdated thoughts about how scientific progress occurs (Chapter 3). This will be followed by a discussion of why it is difficult to draw conclusions from noisy data even with the best approaches that statistics has on offer (Chapter 4); there are no flawless recipes, and all conclusions need to be treated with care. We also explore the problem – indeed, the intriguing phenomenon – that research results are often qualitatively inconsistent, varying among studies ('context specificity'), some of the reasons for this and how it might affect our approaches (Chapter 5).

We then use case studies to explore four issues that affect our ability to draw conclusions: how stronger inferences can be made from using multiple approaches to a given question (Chapter 6, using evolutionary ecology as an example); our reliance on assumptions (Chapter 7, using the example of studies of niche shifts in invasive species and species distribution models); how we test theories, make predictions and inform decisions (Chapter 8, using population forecasting as an example); and our struggles to achieve generality (Chapter 9, using community ecology as an example). These topics will be dealt with in greater depth than the previous chapters and will be more technical in some parts. Although case study areas may be daunting for the non-specialist, we hope that the generalist reader will take time to follow the critiques on each topic, to learn from the approaches that we take. Finally, Chapter 10 brings together a few loose ends and offers some ways forward in our approaches to what we are trying to achieve, the ways that we go about our quests and the need for better quality control systems.

Each chapter ends with a So what? section that raises both specific and general issues that, in our opinions, warrant greater thought and more extensive debate. The authors draw some conclusions of their own, highlight issues that ecologists everywhere need to consider and set challenges for their peers. What we do not do is to present an instruction manual for how to do better ecological research: that must always depend on the goals that are set and the objectives and questions that each researcher chooses to address. Indeed, that is perhaps the overall message of the book: that we need a critical approach purpose-built for every problem, instead of the replication of prescribed recipes that often seems to dominate ecology.

REFERENCES

Andrewartha, H. G. 1961. *Introduction to the study of animal populations*. Chicago: University of Chicago Press.

Banobi, J. A., T. A. Branch, and R. Hilborn. 2011. Do rebuttals affect future science? *Ecosphere* 2:1–11. doi:10.1890/ES10-00142.1

Bronowski, J. 1979. *The origins of knowledge and imagination*. Yale: Yale University Press.

Clark, J. S. 2012. The coherence problem with the unified neutral theory of biodiversity. *Trends in Ecology and Evolution* 27:198–202. doi:10.1016/j.tree.2012.02.001

Cousens, R. 1996. Design and interpretation of interference studies: Are some methods totally unacceptable. *New Zealand Journal of Forestry Science* 26:5–18.

Diamond, J. M., and M. E. Gilpin. 1982. Examination of the 'null' model of Connor and Simberloff for species co-occurrences on islands. *Oecologia* 52:64–74. doi:10.1007/BF00349013

Gannon, F. 2003. Goal-oriented research. *EMBO Reports* 4:1103. doi:10.1038/sj.embor. embor7400039

Garfield, E. 1977. Science for the sake of science is not without its justification. *Essays of an information scientist*, 1:467–468. Philadelphia, PA: ISI Press.

Gibson, D. J., J. Connolly, D. C. Hartnett, and J. D. Weidenhamer. 1999. Designs for greenhouse studies of interactions between plants. *Journal of Ecology* 87:1–16. doi:10.1046/j.1365-2745.1999.00321.x

Grace, J. 1991. A clarification of the debate between Grime and Tilman. *Functional Ecology* 5:583–587. doi:10.2307/2389475

Haeckel, E. 1866. *Generelle morphologie der organismen*. Berlin: G. Reimer.

Jolliffe, P. A. 2001. The replacement series. *Journal of Ecology* 88:371–385. doi:10.1046/j.1365-2745.2000.00470.x

Keddy, P. 1992. Thoughts on a review of a critique for ecology. *Bulletin of the Ecological Society of America* 73:234–236.

Keddy, P., and E. Weiher. 1999. The scope and goals of research on assembly rules. In *Ecological assembly rules: Perspectives, advances, retreats*, eds E. Weiher, and P. Keddy, 1–20. Cambridge: Cambridge University Press.

Lawton, J. 1991. Predictable plots. *Nature* 354:444. doi:10.1038/354444a0

Locke, E. A., and G. P. Latham. 2006. New directions in goal-setting theory. *Current Directions in Psychological Science* 15:265–268. doi:10.1111/j.1467-8721.2006.00449.x

Margalef, R. 1968. *Perspectives in ecological theory*. Chicago: University of Chicago Press. doi:10.4319/lo.1969.14.2.0313

Milius, J., and M. Cimino. 1973. *Magnum force*. Los Angeles: Warner Brothers.

Morales, N. S., I. C. Fernández, and V. Baca-González. 2017. MaxEnt's parameter configuration and small samples are we paying attention to recommendations? *PeerJournal* 5:e3093. doi:10.7717/peerj.3093

Newberry, M., C. Ahern, R. Clark, and J. B. Plotkin. 2017. Detecting evolutionary forces in language change. *Nature* 551:223–226. doi:10.1038/nature24455

Odum, E. P. 1959. *Fundamentals of ecology*, 2nd edition. Philadelphia, PA: W. B. Saunders.

Odum, E. P. 1975. *Ecology: The link between the natural and the social sciences*, 2nd edition. New York: Holt, Rinehart and Winston.

Peters, R. F. 1991. *A critique for ecology*. Cambridge: Cambridge University Press.

Snaydon, R. W. 1994. Replacement and additive designs revisited: Comments on the review paper by N. R. Sackville Hamilton. *Journal of Ecology* 31:784–786.

Steel, E. A., M. C. Kennedy, P. G. Cunningham, and J. S. Stanovick. 2013. Applied statistics in ecology: Common pitfalls and simple solutions. *Ecosphere* 4:115. doi:10.1890/ES13-00160.1

Sutherland, W. J., E. Fleishman, M. Clout, et al. 2019. Ten years on: A review of the first global conservation horizon scan. *Trends in Ecology and Evolution* 34:139–153. doi:10.1016/j.tree.2018.12.003

Sutherland, W. J., R. P. Freckleton, H. C. J. Godfray, et al. 2013. Identification of 100 fundamental ecological questions. *Journal of Ecology* 101:58–67. doi:10.1111/1365-2745.12025

The University of Melbourne. Undated. Prof Roger Cousens. https://findanexpert.unimelb.edu.au/profile/3991-roger-cousens (accessed 9 September 2022)

Vazire, S. 2017. Criticizing a scientist's work isn't bullying. It's science. https://slate.com/technology/2017/10/criticizing-a-scientists-work-isnt-bullying.html, (accessed 2 September 2021).

Wennekes, P. L., J. Sosindell, and R. S. Etienne. 2012. The neutral-niche cebate: A philosophical perspective. *Acta Biotheoretica* 60:257–271. doi:10.1007/s10441-012-9144-6

2

The evolution of ecology

ROGER COUSENS AND MARK DALE

CAN ECOLOGY IMPROVE?

Ecology – and by this we mean the scientific discipline of Ecology (see Box 1.1) – has achieved much since it was recognised in the mid-19th century. We understand a great deal about the interactions between organisms and their environment and the world about us.

The literature describing what we have learned is vast and ever-expanding. We are solving many practical problems and answering many fundamental questions, to a degree that satisfies the majority of ecologists (though see Chapter 10). Our contributions are increasingly appreciated by decision-makers and, although our advice is not always taken, we have succeeded in having ecological principles considered seriously by society. That seems like success, but...

Ecology remains a hard science, in which significant advances seem difficult to achieve. It is reasonable to ask whether ecology is as good as it can be and whether, or how, it can be improved.

Over the decades, there have been many criticisms of ecology (Box 2.1) and encouragement for ecology to change. Most of these criticisms have some justifiable basis, even if their importance has been hotly debated; solutions have been difficult to identify and ultimately their proposals have been either ignored or summarily dismissed.

Should we trust the existing feedback mechanisms within Ecology to optimise the discipline, maximising its effectiveness and minimising the effects of problems?

In other words: can we rely on the natural evolution of our system of doing science? If one approach to ecology, or one idea, is less effective than another, then it should decline in relative frequency over time, and the stronger the selection (the greater the difference in superiority), the more rapid the change should be. Selection of the fittest. This is how the peer review system should work: our colleagues give their views on our approaches and the consensus drives the direction of research, albeit inefficiently.

Ecologists who identify what they believe are serious flaws can do no more than to publish their concerns and arguments, then wait. No matter how strong an appeal for a paradigm shift is (Choi 2007; Rist 2013), there is no guarantee that it will be accepted (as Peters 1991 discovered: see Lawton 1991; Keddy and Weiher 1999). Scientific communities have strong inertia even in the face of overwhelming evidence – think of plate tectonics in geology, which took several decades to become widely accepted.

Can we give this evolution a helping hand, to move Ecology towards a better direction or more quickly? Having identified something new with clear benefits, can we intervene to encourage its adoption? Or something entrenched in the discipline which we would like to discourage? What would those actions be, in a system based on mutual exchange of ideas and largely without governance? Editorial boards, for example, have been unable to eliminate common statistical errors over several decades in which statisticians have drawn attention to our frequent and consistent errors.

DOI: 10.1201/9781003314332-2

14 Effective Ecology

BOX 2.1: Some criticisms made of ecology

Concerns about the way ecology is done have included:

- dominance of descriptive studies (e.g. Whittaker 1962);
- over-reliance on correlations as demonstrations of cause and effect (Carr et al. 2019);
- paucity of hypotheses (Betts et al. 2021);
- predilection for claims of confirmation (potentially resulting in 'confirmation bias': Brittan and Bandyopadhyay 2019);
- failure to investigate alternative explanations (Betini et al. 2017);
- lack of fundamental laws and testable theories (Marquet et al. 2014);
- popularity of concepts that are inherently incapable of refutation (Scheiner 2013);
- tendency to take up fads (Belovsky et al. 2004);
- poor links between theoretical and empirical research (Simberloff 1981) and between pure and applied studies; and
- divisiveness of subdisciplines (Dayton 1979).

(Note that one example reference has been given for each issue, even though there may be many.)

Another concern is ineffective quality control, which results in a high incidence of statistical errors (Fraser et al. 2018) and poor applications of various analytical methods (Hoekstra et al. 2012). We also see many implied criticisms, in the form of papers extolling a specific new approach and its virtues (at the expense of something else), such as calling for more interdisciplinary research (e.g. Kelly et al. 2019) or more transdisciplinary research (e.g. Marshall et al. 2018).

It is easy to list these criticisms, but it is hard to assess the extent to which they have actually detracted from the work or reduced its impact. Some of the concerns result from a mere philosophical belief that there are better ways of doing things – but without proof that progress could actually have been better (as in so-called 'physics envy': Nelson 2015). We can, perhaps, forgive ourselves a modicum of procedural errors in ecology, since no field of human endeavour, and no quality control system (Smith 2006), is perfect. Not every ecological study can break new ground: studies that might be dismissed as 'busy work' (Dayton 1979) may contribute by consolidating ideas, providing the data for meta-analyses, exploring context-specific conclusions or exploring exceptions that may cause a re-think of ideas. Indeed, any science needs a balance between advance and consolidation, and there is clearly no criterion for what that balance should be.

Any discussion of change needs to be based on a thorough appreciation of how ecological research evolves. In this chapter, we will examine the evolution of ecology in three distinct ways. First, we follow a brief traditional, historical narrative of the changes that have occurred in the practice of ecological science, as ecologists have 'gone with the flow'. With the value of hindsight, we can see how ecology has evolved to be this way – and has become this vast – because…

Next, we consider the place of individual researchers within the great, apparently unplanned effort that constitutes the entirety of the discipline. We use the analogy of an agent-based system, in

which each individual makes decisions and takes directions according to the environment they are in and their own decision criteria. The result is a set of unique trajectories of individual ecologists, each pursuing their research as their ideas develop and proliferate. While the evolution of ecology may appear to be haphazard, the individuals, their efforts and their trajectories are under a form of selection pressure which must surely, over time, shape our discipline.

Finally, we consider the roles of ecologists within the much wider, and multilayered, network of which they are just one part, drawing on the same network theory that is applied in research on ecological systems. We invite readers to apply the same principles to themselves, to better understand what they do and the way they do it.

A CONVENTIONAL HISTORY OF ECOLOGY

Sciences unfold upon a framework of history. In the case of most sciences, including ecology, we can trace their roots back by more than two millennia. One or two people start to ask questions about the world about them and come up with – often – naïve answers. Others come along over time, adding their new styles and ideas; the tools and procedures (such as experimentation, mathematical analysis and logic) that we use become ever more sophisticated and the answers that we reach become more persuasive. The science steadily gains in maturity and in ability. The scientific landscape upon which we can chart our activities starts to become occupied, patchily at first, but then the gaps begin to fill. Most sciences, at least in their early days, have no goals other than to gain greater understanding, so we have little idea in advance when different areas of the scientific landscape will become occupied. The scientists of the time 'go with the flow', following the questions and trends of the time and responding to occasional new directions. Expansion and proliferation seem to go on unabated. Inevitably, a cornucopia of information is produced, some of which allows us to make confident statements and reach generalisations while much of it – at the time – cannot be rationalised and we struggle to achieve insights. But we persist.

The pace of scientific activity also undergoes periods of increased interest and heightened recruitment of scientists, causing an inexorable increase in the cornucopial flow of information and the subsequent desire for explanations. One key aspect of what we call civilisation is that some of the people have the time to *think* and *communicate*, in the past often males in privileged positions who had the resources to do more than just survive. Some could afford travel, during which they made observations of plants, animals, geology or astronomy, which they interpreted and communicated to others. Communication led to the sharing of ideas with a common theme: to describe, classify and explain the natural world. From the ancient Greek philosophers, through the Enlightenment in Europe to the early establishment of universities, the number of people involved in science was relatively small and their capabilities were restricted.

The second half of the 20th century was a time of extraordinary growth for all sciences. Expansion of the tertiary education system produced more students, while increased government investment in research and conservation provided jobs related to ecology. Ecology became a profession rather than a pastime. There were widespread concerns about food supply (resulting in the 'green revolution'), over-population, acid rain, eutrophication, species extinctions and land clearances for agriculture. Governments began to have policies and strategies that required ecological input – whether or not they truly embraced the need for effective action. There was a proliferation of books on ecology and new journals publishing ecological research. The ecologist's toolbox grew to include mathematical and computer modelling, more powerful data collection and handling methods, technological advances in measurement, analytical chemistry, the use of molecular methods and so on. This growth in activity and output on many streams of enquiry, in turn, led to the development of subdisciplines in ecology, each with its own skill set, specialist knowledge, conferences, journals, jargon (and acronyms!). This diversification also brought a degree of compartmentalisation and a reduction in dialogue among some subdisciplines. To some extent, that has been countered by the emergence of new subdisciplines that have bridged former divides: examples would be areas of plant-animal interactions, and the ecology of global change.

And so, to the present. Our textbooks tell their readers what ecology is – or the authors' impressions of what it was at the time when it was written (ecology textbooks have great longevity and, as a result, views persist). But ecology will not remain that way.

Ecology not only *will* continue to change, but it *needs* to change: to keep up with modern scientific techniques and advances in understanding, to fulfil the needs and expectations of society and to strive constantly to improve in quality. The modern world needs ecology as an essential science that will help us to cope with the problems that we face and create. The question we raised in the introduction to this chapter was whether ecologists as a body of scientists continue to just go with the flow. Will the ecology that our discipline evolves into in, say, 40 years' time be the best fit-for-purpose? Or should we attempt to manage the change? Let us reflect on the evolution of ecology in a little more detail.

Elton (1927) stated that *'Ecology is a new name for a very old subject'*. Humans have long appreciated aspects of the interactions between organisms and the environment, but without the basis provided by formal study. Early people living within and relying directly on nature developed their own understanding of the natural world. This understanding was not the structured knowledge of reductionist science, with ideas rigorously expressed and tested. There are different types of knowledge and different ways of knowing (Wildman and Inayatullah 1996). Annual changes in the environment and the landscape determined the resources available to our ancestors, when and where they could be found and, as a result, how best to move around in that world. Over time, people worked out how to alter the environment and to control preferred plants and animals, making food more abundant and more accessible. They observed and they tried new techniques; those that were successful were adopted and agriculture evolved, along with the rest of the paraphernalia that goes with *Homo sapiens*, such as trade, technology, arts, politics, weapons, pollution and environmental change.

Ecology, the science that it is now, derives from two distinct pathways which have, to some extent, coalesced: natural history and demographic modelling.

Natural history

The first pathway to modern ecology can be traced back at least as far as the Greek philosophers Aristotle and Theophrastus and relates to what we might call natural science: a desire to understand the way the world is, the laws of nature.

Early philosophers certainly understood that different species inhabited different environments (later to be reflected in our concept of the niche) and responded to both climate and soil. They also saw that this knowledge could be applied for the benefit of food production. They were also aware of the diversity of organisms and the fact that some organisms were similar to others. Their attempts to understand the natural world, however, were based on simple observations, their version of logic and their attempts to draw inferences.

After a period of relative quiescence, the description of the natural world and the search for explanations were revived in the Middle Ages as travellers began to describe what they saw in different regions and to search for commonalities and for explanations for what lives where: notable among these were von Humboldt, Darwin and Wallace. Others received information and specimens from these travellers, catalogued and classified them, such as Ray and Linnaeus, building a body of knowledge capable of a more methodical (systematic) analysis. Ultimately, their activities led to the establishment of research areas familiar to ecologists today, such as biogeography, evolution, systematics, phytosociology, biodiversity and macroecology.

A great deal of what we see practised in ecology today is clearly a development of early natural history – the observation of particular organisms in their environments – but now using the methods of science to record, analyse and explain. The diversity of the natural world means that we will never be lacking for case studies that have never been investigated previously. Natural history has always fuelled ecology (Anderson 2017), providing the basic information on which ideas could be formed. It became a common amateur pastime among the middle and upper classes of Europe, reaching its height in the Victorian era. Observational natural history is still a popular pursuit, existing alongside increased public concerns about the environment and conservation. Indeed, the National Audubon Society in the USA and the Royal Society for the Protection of Birds in the UK each have over one million members. This resource has been tapped increasingly, with large numbers of observers collecting useful data combined with the spatio-temporal locations, thus acting as 'citizen scientists'.

When Elton referred to ecology in 1927 as 'scientific natural history' he was referring to the fact that scientists were, by then, collecting natural history data in a quantitative and systematic way and searching for explanations and generalisations. As Simberloff (2013) observes, Elton was not using other scientific approaches in his own work, such as hypotheses and experiments, but by that time the use of experiments was firmly established (as in the work of Darwin and others: see Hector and Hooper 2002) and the formal methods of statistics were starting to become popular.

Demography and modelling

The second pathway to modern ecology was fuelled by an interest in animal life histories, reproductive rates, ages at death and population growth curves – things today that we might group under the term 'demography' (see Hutchinson 1978). This arose primarily from the study of humans: lifespans affected calculations for insurance purposes and informed economic policies – as explored by Malthus (1798) in relation to policies regarding aid to the poor. Calculations could be made using census and church records. (There were also religious discussions regarding the age of the earth (by Ussher and others) based on the Bible as a source of evidence.) It was natural to extend demographic calculations to include other animals (see Egerton's 1968 account of van Leeuwenhoek). It became clear that there were natural checks on population growth rates that, in time, themselves became the targets of investigation.

It was but a small step from there to the use of the data to model population dynamics. The classic work on mixtures of species by Lotka and Volterra in the 1920s and Gause in the 1930s and spatial populations by Fisher in the 1930s led to modelling of ever greater complexity. Coincident with this was the development of population genetics and evolutionary theory, championed by Wright, Haldane and Fisher. Alongside these theoretical studies, there were repeated attempts to test the model predictions on experimental systems (see Chapter 8). Like other areas of research, this theoretical work expanded, became ever more complicated, bringing in new approaches and enabled by dramatic advances in computing technology. Two modern examples are the exploration of population genetics at invasion population margins and the conditions needed for persistence of competing species. There is now a vast literature on what became referred to as theoretical ecology.

The empirical side of this work expanded to include the task of measuring and comparing demographic rates (life history parameters, life table analysis) among species and trying to understand the evolutionary causes of those differences. However, it took until the 1960s and 1970s for plant ecology to adopt demographic approaches – which it did in a major way, championed by J L Harper. It was realised that these demographic data could be incorporated into models that would predict the likely dynamics of species under different circumstances and, through various types of sensitivity analysis, could be used to derive advice for the conservation of rare species and the management of pests.

Coalescence of natural history with demography and beyond

By the time that Haeckel (1866) gave ecology its name, 'ecological' research had already achieved momentum, following the conclusions of Darwin and Wallace. Many natural philosophers were beginning to see the powerful ramifications of natural selection for biology, philosophy, society and religion. The key concepts at the time were the 'struggle for life', 'natural selection' and 'evolution' (Allee et al. 1949; Egerton 2013). Haeckel's publication was an attempt to reorganise zoology according to the ideas of Darwin, which effectively brought together the two fields of natural history and demography, expanding ecology's capacity for investigating phenomena. And, over the next 150 years or so, the size of the cornucopia of ecological data accelerated – along with an increase in our frustration to find definitive explanations for so many different things. Ecologists came up with a plethora of concepts, through which they could assemble data, but very few laws and generalisations emerged (Lawton 1999).

Not only did the total quantity of ecological research expand, but it rapidly expanded into new areas of enquiry, fed at first by advances in chemistry, physics and biology – and by physiology in particular. In addition to populations and communities, ecologists had begun to study ecosystems – both empirically and using models. Interest in the environment had grown into a discipline in its own right and, over time, would lead to concepts such as ecosystem services and bioremediation, along with increasing interest in urban ecology and the impacts of unrelenting global change in atmospheric gases, temperatures, sea levels, land use and deforestation. Economics began to be seen as a natural partner for ecology, allowing us to explore some of the social implications of ecosystem management and providing us with a way to converse more effectively with policy-makers and managers. New techniques emerged, such as molecular ecology, offering us the possibility of answering questions that had previously been beyond our reach. Although ecologists had been working on pest and conservation issues for many years, pressure increased for ecologists to focus on useful outcomes. And we began to realise that we were missing entire pieces of the ecological jigsaw puzzle, such as the social components of systems and the social implications for our actions. So, we welcomed these into our discipline. Had ecology grown too broad?

Ecology does not just expand. During its lifetime, some of ecology's most favoured topics for debate and research have waxed, but then waned. There are too many topics to list, but examples are (1) the individualistic continuum concept of communities, (2) the regulation of population abundance, (3) keystone species in communities and (4) species coexistence. New topics may arise due to a new concept or approach, a novel result for which interesting explanations can be explored or simply a new technique that can be applied to a variety of study systems. Each topic can stimulate a number of activities that may last for a decade or two. Thereafter, interest declines as attention moves on to other, newer topics. A topic may reappear because advanced techniques develop, allowing us to answer previously unresolvable questions (e.g. the resurgence of interest in population genetics with gene sequencing) or because a new context arises (e.g. phenology in the context of climate change). But, overall, the picture of ecology is one of expansion. A rapid increase in knowledge calls for synthesis, particularly to assist new generations entering the discipline.

In a review of Krebs' (1972) textbook on ecology, which was a basic text for ecology worldwide for decades, Futuyma (1973) expressed an opinion that ecology was a 'nebulous science' that lacked a focus and meant different things to different ecologists. That multiplicity does not, however, mean that ecology is weak.

A science that has expanded so quickly and in so many directions can be viewed from many perspectives. Just because some ecologists chose to focus on ecosystem processes, and others focus on theory, population dynamics or conservation, it did not mean that these views were in conflict. They are just different, as we might expect to find a variety of viewpoints or areas of emphasis within the sciences of physics or biology. The diversity does, however, require that ecologists make special effort to communicate across specialisations rather than only within their own silo.

One modern trend is an increase in the proportion of ecological studies designed to investigate management issues. At the same time, there has been an acceptance that topics such as wildlife management and agriculture are *bona fide* fields of research for the ecologist (though barriers still exist). Although ecologists have a long history of involvement in conservation, pest management and reclamation, many prestigious journals chose to focus on 'fundamental' ecology. Some of the fundamental ecological work on population dynamics of interacting species, for example, was inspired and funded because of pest management, although the papers' language did not reflect it. In contrast, there is now often a pressure from editors to comment specifically on the applied significance of research (with the risk of the applied relevance being over-stated). However, this has not necessarily resulted in an overwhelming change in what we do. Carmel et al. (2013) considered less than 20% of ecological studies as 'problem-solving', suggesting that despite a greater interest in applied ecology, it was far from dominant.

Another trend is the number of calls for more interdisciplinarity in ecological research (Reyers et al. 2010): for example, the human component of ecosystems and the necessary decisions requires us to consider the social systems in which scientific issues are embedded. There are some barriers to this, including the structures of our funding systems (Bromham et al. 2016) and the rewards for researchers (Goring et al. 2014). Nevertheless, Anderson et al. (2021) concluded that '*Within eight decades, the field* (ecology) *has evolved from focusing on natural history and observational field studies to a multidisciplinary field more applied and quantitative in scope*' (see also Nobis and Wohlgemuth 2004).

In apparent conflict with that conclusion, Carmel et al. (2013) found that two-thirds of ecological activities were still of individual species studied using a single discipline. Descriptive studies using data exploration methods still represented over half of published papers, with only one-third experimental studies. Although that study was almost a decade before Anderson's (but contemporary with Nobis and Wohlgemuth's), there is little to support a conclusion that ecology has, indeed, undergone a radical change. The Anderson et al. study was a culturomic analysis based on the terminology that we use in papers and the things we say, rather than an analysis of what we actually *do*.

While ecology may now be more diverse (a much 'bigger tent'), embracing more spheres of research than it once did (Craven et al. 2019) and we more readily refer in our work to papers from other disciplines (see also Gates et al. 2019), there is little evidence that we are bringing those disciplines together effectively in the performance of the research itself. We have a way to go before we can claim to be an *inter*disciplinary science.

SELECTION IN SCIENCE SPACE

Ecologists are familiar with the concept of the niche as a hypervolume of many dimensions that together describe the set of conditions under which a species can exist.

We can easily extend this idea to consider the underlying conditions present in the entire universe – not just in biology – as a hyperdimensional set of physical rules and relationships that together dictate what can and cannot occur: we might call this 'factspace'. However, the exploration of that universe, in which we attempt to develop knowledge about that factspace, is a human endeavour and therefore involves social dimensions. It is both aided and constrained by the ways in which humans think, feel and behave.

What we will call 'science *social* space' consists of many dimensions determined by all the social factors that can influence its outcomes: people, groups, communication, ecological constructs, investigative methods and so on (Box 2.2) – in addition to the characteristics of the universe.

The evolution of ecology as a discipline results from the actions of individuals, groups and organisations acting in that space, and we can consider the career of a researcher as a unique trajectory through it, though it is linked in both direct and indirect ways to the trajectories of other ecologists.

Influenced by our interests, past experiences, education, training, opportunities and

---

BOX 2.2: Science social space

The multidimensional science social space we explore can be defined by a number of factors. These include:

- People: students, researchers, managers, politicians, citizens, industry directors…
- Collectives: collaborative research teams, schools, faculties, organisations…
- Social constructs: values, identity, attitudes, motivations, intentions, biases, emotions, norms…
- Communications: lectures, publications, conferences, hallway conversations…
- Ecological constructs: concepts, theories, models, diagrams…
- Investigative methods: field observations, measurement, experiment, synthesis, meta-analysis…
- Context: culture, place, date…
- Resources: facilities, grants, contracts, scholarships…
- Environment: the characteristics and underlying laws of the universe which will determine organism behaviour.

Although we can list these things as separate entities, they are nested and interact in a great many ways. We can imagine 'spatial' relationships among people, concepts and activities within that space based on similarity, interactions or causal relationships which provide proximity in that space. For example, the researchers who are closest to us in science space may be competitors, collaborators or working in parallel without any mutual awareness but connected through similar values and influenced by shared norms. We can think of our endeavours in ecology as an exploration or development and expansion of that science space. If we include such a large number of factors to define the space, they cannot all be independent and we might consider reducing its dimensionality, at least in concept. We will have more to say about dimensionality later. We can also think about how that science space must or can change as ecology itself evolves.

relationships with others (including the norms of the discipline), we may move towards that part of science social space that is ecology. Once in that social space, our postgraduate studies continue to depend on many factors within science: marks, an inspiring lecturer, a supervisor with an available place, a scholarship; and beyond: place, attachments, hobbies, personal relationships (Manzi et al. 2019). Thereafter, the work we do, the papers that we publish, the papers we read, the conferences we attend, the places we visit and the people we meet all affect the trajectory we follow within the social subspace that is ecology.

One way to understand the trajectory of an ecologist in science social space involves the overt recognition of ecologists as being part of a social network, similar to the way that ecologists themselves build an agent-based model of a group of interacting animals. However, we need to incorporate individual motivations (other than merely access to resources, mates and avoidance of predation) – for example, values which may influence who people interact with and the nature of their relationships to others.

The direction of each step taken by an ecologist depends on individual motivations, values, interests, the local availability of resources (grants, students, ideas), the opportunities for resources elsewhere and the feasibility of moving from the current 'location' in science social space to another. Access to resources depends on the relationships (in science social space) with other individuals, who compete, stimulate and provide social context. The ability to move from one area of science to another depends on social relationships, technical and cognitive abilities and desires, the current distribution, motivations and expectations of other ecologists, and serendipitous events (such as hearing about a job application from an acquaintance).

The resulting trajectory of a researcher may not resemble a 'simple random walk' (Figure 2.1). Success – perhaps measured in terms of research outputs – in one region of science social space will increase the tendency to remain in the same location or to continue moving in the same direction (i.e. a correlated walk). New advances may come from breaking away from a strong paradigm and looking afresh ('separation and reintegration': Koestler 1959), but moving may carry a greater risk of failure to continue in a strong scientific career. Trajectories are drawn towards spatial attractors in the social landscape, such as calls by funding agencies for specific proposals, which may be influenced by broader social and cultural trends towards or away from particular ideas, such as resilience. As mentioned, popularity is also a powerful attractor. There are also barriers to movement (Börger et al. 2008), such as those imposed by employment. It is easy to appreciate, then, why ecologists become aggregated in particular regions of the scientific landscape.

As with a dispersing organism, an individual research trajectory can exhibit a trend even if it is not goal-orientated. This correlated pathway is still likely to be perturbed by the whims of reviewers, funding agencies and employers, and it may end abruptly or take a sudden turn. In a 'correlated random walk' through research, it may be difficult to distinguish among (1) slow but steady progress towards a major breakthrough, (2) tying up loose ends at a fine scale to complete a story or (3) being in a rut that is hard to escape.

Considering this view of multiple (and connected) individual trajectories in science space, we can appreciate how selection can affect not just which scientists are successful in their careers, but the movement of a population of scientists or their ideas, causing them to congregate in particular regions, through what Richard McElreath in a lecture called the *'population dynamics of how we discover things about the world'*.

It is not just researchers who have trajectories in science space. Consider the evolution of an idea or ecological concept (and using appropriate evolutionary terms as analogies).

We start with a background of *variation* among ecologists and ecological concepts, reflecting a diversity of traits. Novel 'mutations' arise, as when a new concept, theory or technology arrives, often arising out of previous ideas by synthesis rather than novel inspiration. The success of these ideas and approaches can be considered in terms of contributions to ecologists' 'fitness': our survival as scientists depends on how good we are (subject to chance events), and social biases that privilege some over others. Our best ideas proliferate (reproduce) through publication and translation of our findings to broader audiences, adoption by colleagues and civil society and the success of our students. The models that are used to explore the population genetics of organisms under different conditions can be used to investigate the development of knowledge under different sociological

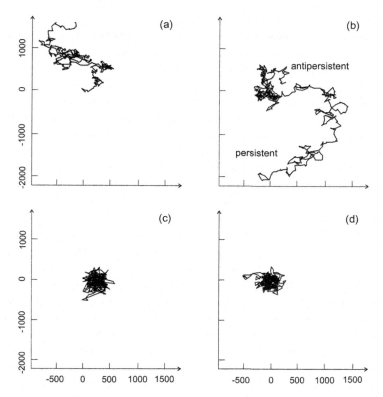

Figure 2.1 Examples of random walks of organisms varying in the constraints to movement that are incorporated. Redrawn from Börger et al. 2008. **(a)** Simple unconstrained random walk; **(b)** correlated random walks of two types; **(c)** simple correlated random walk with simple long-term memory; and **(d)** a biased random walk.

and management regimes and the selection pressures they impose (McElreath and Smaldino 2015; Smaldino and McElreath 2016).

Many changes in scientific methodology can be considered adaptive in that they improve the quality ('fitness') of the knowledge generated, at least in the short term. Examples include the arrival of electronic data-loggers, personal computers or genetic sequencing. Other changes may be more akin to genetic 'drift': someone does something first and the idea catches on, not because it is especially beneficial but because it is appealing and becomes popular (Abrahamson 2009). Other changes may seem merely superficial (equivalent to changes to the phenotype rather than to the genotype), as when we re-package research to appeal to different funding agencies.

Despite the virtues of peer review, some changes may actually be 'mal-adaptive', in that they set the discipline back. Similarly, we may inadvertently accumulate the equivalent of 'deleterious alleles', the bad habits that we have failed to recognise or failed to correct (such as common statistical errors). A final comment on this analogy is that, like the evolution that we see in organisms, the evolution of ideas and knowledge in science occurs at a variable rate, perhaps resembling a series of 'punctuated equilibria'. Periods of slow development based on 'additive variation' (the 'normal science' of Kuhn 1970) may be interspersed by occasional selection for novel 'mutations with major effect'.

All the changes described here, the trajectories of individual researchers or of groups, and the selection and fitness of methods or ideas can be seen as movement through 'science space', almost always with a random component, but with constraints, so that the movement does not completely resemble the random walk as a null model. In fact, it is our contention that the trajectory of ecology as a hard science can be made more direct and more effective if we work together to change the way the science is done. The conceptual model of science space is useful for organising our thoughts, and in the next section, we describe and explore an alternative.

THE EVOLUTION OF ECOLOGY AS A MULTILAYERED NETWORK

Let's start again from a different viewpoint. Many of the systems that ecologists study are best treated as networks; a network is a structure consisting of nodes (shown as points) with edges (shown as lines) joining the nodes in pairs as in Figure 2.2 (see Dale and Fortin 2021). Think of the trophic network of an ecosystem or, for greater simplicity, the mutualistic network of flowering plants and their pollinators: in Figure 2.2, the nodes are species and the edges are the pollination interactions.

Usually a network is more than a simple graph of nodes and edges because the nodes have labels or magnitudes and the edges have categories, quantitative properties of rates or capacities, or even equations describing the dynamics. A network, therefore, has properties related to composition (the identities of the nodes and the categories of interactions between them), structural properties determined by which nodes are joined by what kinds of edges, and functional properties related to the dynamics of the relationships determined by the edges and the interactions that result. A network may have dynamics on it or in it, with the structure of the network unchanged (think of trains running on a railway), but often a network has the dynamics of structural change as it evolves through time (think of a river system changing course through floods and droughts).

Ecologists study many kinds of natural systems that are often portrayed and studied as networks, but the approach we explore here is to consider the science of Ecology itself, including all its components, as a network. In this network of Ecology, there are nodes representing 'things' of different kinds (people, theories, concepts, experiments, publications…) and edges between nodes representing a range of relationships among the nodes (learning, collaboration, creation, modification, synthesis, management…). There are two main features of this representation: it is best structured as a *multilayer* network (see Bianconi 2018), and it is in many ways a *complex* multilayer network.

In many applications of networks, the nodes can be assigned to layers, whether by location or node category, producing a multilayer network which can be seen as a series of subnetworks, one on each layer (as in Figure 2.3). A review of ecological networks will show that almost all are essentially multilayer, with several interaction types, interactions that vary in space or time, or interconnected systems forming networks of networks (Pilosof et al. 2017). The multilayer property can arise in ecological networks in different ways. For example, when the same interaction network (e.g. pollination mutualism) is observed at several different times, each time period in the figure is a layer with (mostly) the same nodes in each, but with differences among the edges within each layer. The same structure may arise from studies of the same ecological interaction network at several locations (Bianconi 2018). In this kind of multilayer structure, edges between layers may indicate the persistent identity of individual nodes or something different such as causal relationships. When the layers are generated by space or time, their order is obviously of significance; in other circumstances, the order of the layers can be arbitrary or merely of convenience.

In the network that is the science of Ecology, the nodes can be classified by their type (people, concepts, theories…) and so an obvious suggestion is to treat it as a multilayer network, with the layers defined by the categories to which the nodes belong and the kinds of interactions that occur (Figure 2.3a). Using this structure allows greater clarity in identifying the most critical nodes and interactions. For example, Figure 2.3b illustrates the layers active in the development and communication of a theory by one researcher through a publication to another researcher and thence to colleagues. A and B are researchers, with three colleagues, C. The blue arrows show the communication of theory T from one person to another. The dashed arrows between layers show different effects. A develops theory T and makes observations O; T and O inform the publication P. Researcher B learns about theory T from A's publication P and presents the ideas in seminar S. Seminar S affects the colleagues C, as they learn about theory T from it.

Figure 2.2 A simple ecological network of pollination interactions. Five pollinator species interact with five plant species, but different pollinators visit different plants. Modified from Dale and Fortin (2021); reprinted with permission.

The idea of a science and its context as a complex network is not really new. Networks of researchers with edges defined by collaboration or co-authorship are frequently used as textbook examples of social networks (e.g. Newman 2010), usually including only the researchers as a kind of society. Halpern et al. (2020) illustrate the inverse of that approach, showing the identifiable clusters in a network of publications based on the authors.

Networks depicting subfields of a science as nodes with weighted edges between them have already appeared in the literature (e.g. Herrera 2010). Similarly, Dale and Fortin (2014, figure 12.9) used a network depiction to show the relationships among methods of spatial analysis (or among quantitative methods for network analysis (Dale and Fortin 2021, figure 5.3). Even the multilayer aspect is not new; for example, Omodei et al. (2016) used a separate layer for publications in each subfield of physics, and Meleu and Melatagia (2021) used three layers for publications, based on authors, laboratories and institutions. With layers representing time slices, Boekhout et al. (2021) studied mobility in co-authorship networks by counting identified categories of multilayer 'temporal motifs', which are small subgraphs of identifiable structure that are frequent structural components of the network.

The 'concept' or 'construct' layer of our multilayer figure could start as the familiar 'concept map' used to organise ideas in a diagram that depicts the relationships among them; it is a common device in both classroom teaching and brainstorming workshops. There is also a close relationship with the semantic networks or 'knowledge graphs' in information science (James 1992), originally maps of words but now used to depict networks of entities and their relationships (Kejriwal et al. 2021), perhaps embedded with their related concepts (Guan et al. 2019). The entities in a knowledge graph can include people, places, products and so on, but they are not organised into layers and the knowledge graph does not actually contain the knowledge that flows in the collection it depicts. On the other hand, in the 'Ecology network' shown in Figure 2.3a, paths of links joining 'MacArthur' and 'island biogeography' would both include and go through the relevant publications and communications and their contents, so that the information is actually included in the structure.

So, what does the Ecology network do? It discovers and creates knowledge through observation, experiment, analysis and synthesis, and it organises and communicates that knowledge, advancing some forms of knowledge over others depending on the social trends, values and norms at the time.

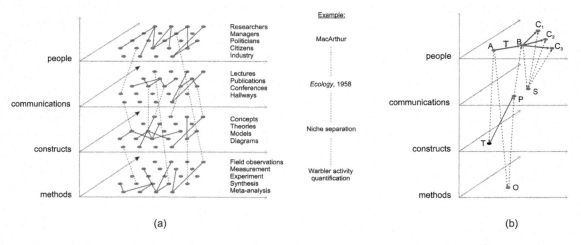

Figure 2.3 **(a)** The science of Ecology is depicted as a multilayer network. Each layer has its own components. Solid edges are interactions within a layer and their nature will vary depending on the layer. The dashed edges are interactions between layers and will also vary. For example, the researcher MacArthur created the publication in Ecology which described the concept of niche separation, and that concept was based on observation and quantification of warbler behaviour. **(b)** The layers active in the development and communication of a theory by one researcher through a publication to another researcher and thence to colleagues. See text for details.

Ecology is a science that studies complex systems and complex networks, such as those just described, *but* it is also true to say that the science of Ecology is itself a complex multilayer network with many of the properties mentioned in Box 2.2. There are layers associated with people: researchers, managers, funders, politicians, citizen scientists... There are layers associated with the development of the science itself: observations, concepts, theories, methods, techniques, models... (Figure 2.3a). There are interactions between these two kinds of layers: publications (Figure 2.3a), presentations, conferences, courses... What about layers of resources? Consider: universities, salaries, research grants, lab facilities, field stations... Each of the layers has nodes representing the appropriate structural units, edges within layers representing intra-layer relationships and then the complex web of interactions between nodes in different layers. There is complexity also in the dynamics of the network: disorder; non-equilibrium; feedback loops; history, memory and adaptive behaviours; and self-organisation and stability to some forms of perturbation. The balance or imbalance of these various dynamic characteristics can lead naturally to the evolution of the system through time.

All this complexity of the science itself, in addition to the complexity of the living systems which we study, is another factor that makes this science hard.

A corollary of the statement that the science of Ecology is a complex network is that it is evolving towards even greater complexity. The units in the layers become more numerous with time, and with more connections between units, whether within or between layers (see Halpern 2020, figure 5, as an example). It is easy to see that we may also acquire more layers.

Complexity is a concept that has different implications depending on the system being studied and whether the focus is on structure or on function (or on both), but there are a number of characteristics that can be associated with it (see Box 2.3).

This general list in Box 2.3 can form a background for the more technical and focused discussion of ecological networks that follows. Of note is the fact that ecologists have pursued their own progression in defining measures of the complexity of networks, without relying on some pre-existing work on the topic such as Bonchev and Buck (2005). Part of the reason has to do with the focus by ecologists on the relationship between network complexity and network stability for ecological systems (but only part). Of the many measures that have been proposed for the complexity of an ecological network, a high proportion are based on or related to random walks on the network (Dale and Fortin 2021). Table 2.1 uses the categories from Box 2.3 to discuss the features of the Ecology network's comlexity:

The challenge of the network model is to make sense of its complexity, the opportunities for synthesis as well as critique and critical thinking. Complexity of our systems is one factor that makes the science hard. We already are familiar with how to understand some of the characteristics of a single layer (e.g. the studies of co-authorship relations and evolution such as Barabási et al. 2001), but we need to extend this to the many layers and the edges between them. There are at least two features of the multilayer networks that will be helpful in dealing

---

BOX 2.3: What is complexity?

Ladyman and Wiesner (2020) consider complex systems generally and provide the following list of ten features – under three headings – that may be either sufficient or necessary for a system to be complex:

- *Structural*: Numerosity (many units: nodes or edges); disorder and diversity; nestedness and modularity.
- *Short-term dynamics*: Feedback loops; non-linear responses; non-equilibrium; stable to some perturbations.
- *Long-term dynamics*: Spontaneous order or self-organisation; adaptive behaviour; memory of past history.

The evolution of ecology 25

Table 2.1 Complexity characteristics of the evolving Ecology network

Structural

Network size ('Numerosity')

Ecology is home to many thousands of ecologists, publications, ideas, projects, approaches, outcomes. Need we say more?

Disorder and diversity

What organisation there is in Ecology is not externally imposed but developed within, in response to changing conditions and its history, local and global. The flexibility of disorder is obvious in every layer as well as in the relationships between layers (see Ohlmann et al. 2019).

A key form of diversity in ecological networks is the existence of indirect interactions (see Figure 2.4). Familiar examples may be the 'trophic cascade' or 'apparent competition'. In essence, a network edge can act as a node in a subsequent level of interactions. This form of diversity in ecological networks is one critical factor in how ecological networks function, but it is also a factor in what makes our science hard. In the network that is Ecology, the same phenomenon is very common: direct interactions between pairs of nodes can be modified by the effects of other nodes in the network or by edges, so that network edges act as nodes for the next level of modification. The network that is Ecology has the potential for hierarchies of indirect interactions of various degrees or levels. Clearly this form of diversity contributes greatly to its complexity and also to the detail of how it can evolve.

Nestedness and modularity

All four layers depicted in Figure 2.3a will be modular with clusters of researchers, and publications and overlapping subnetworks of closely related concepts and closely related methodological approaches. There will also be tight inter-layer clustering of researchers with their favourite methods and concepts and then papers and presentations that result (see Costa et al. 2007).

Short-term dynamics

Feedback loops, positive and negative

As with diversity, feedback loops can be found in every layer as well as among layers. Some of the feedback loops are negative, providing controls to processes and increasing stability, and some are positive, enhancing or reinforcing change. For example, an over-production of PhDs in one subfield may supress employment opportunities and thus its perceived attractiveness to future students. On the positive side, research avenues that succeed can provide increased resources of many kinds that enable further potentially successful research.

Non-linear responses

Equal step incremental changes may produce small effects over a certain range but the same size of change may cause a break-point in behaviour, a flash of insight or a paradigm shift, depending on the layer in question.

Non-equilibrium

Instability and tipping points are found in the structure of Ecology as well as in the natural phenomena it studies. Small changes that made big differences include the understanding of genetics and heredity, and the development of digital computers.

Robustness, stable to some perturbations

New ideas may destabilise old concept maps or may be absorbed into the existing framework depending on the conflicts or extensions they create (see Barrat et al. 2008). The diversity of all elements of the structure may or may not enhance the stability of the network's function and we can speculate whether positive interactions such as collaboration enhance both stability and the function.

(Continued)

Table 2.1 (*Continued*) Complexity characteristics of the evolving Ecology network

Structural

Long-term dynamics

Spontaneous order or self-organisation

> External forces obviously affect the development of the science, but most of the changes as it has evolved through time have been driven by nodes and their interactions both within and between layers. New or refined techniques affect how research is done, the concepts that are generated and the questions that may be asked or answered.

Adaptive behaviour

> Having noted that much of the change we can observe in the evolving network of Ecology is self-generated, we also need to acknowledge that its behaviour can also be adaptive, changing in response to prevailing conditions (see Gross and Blasius 2008). This becomes clear in the changing focus of attention from natural processes in natural systems such as disturbance and succession, to landscape fragmentation and conservation, to climate change and the Anthropocene.

History and memory

> Nodes and the intra-layer edges in the communications layer of the network will be temporal in nature and thus the history aspect of the structure can be explicit. The elements in other layers may be closely tied to a flow of historical development and evolution. Memory can be found in all layers, and it would be interesting, if possible, to contrast the lines of memory in the layer of concepts or constructs with the memory made explicit in the communications layer. The memory shown by citations may sometimes prove to be too short-sighted. Knowledge requires the system's memory, but it is imperfect.

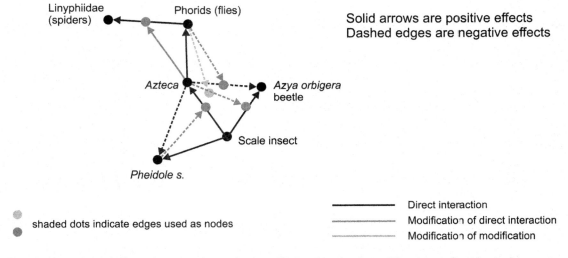

Figure 2.4 Indirect effects in an ecological network: two levels of modifications of ecological interactions. Part of a coffee agro-ecosystem, showing a hierarchy of interaction modifications: edges at one level become nodes for edges at the next. *Azteca* and *Pheidole* are ants. Modified from Dale and Fortin 2021; reprinted with permission.

with the potentially overwhelming complexity. The first is the existence of small structurally defined subgraphs, motifs or graphlets, as an aid to summarising small-scale or local aspects of structure and its consistency. This is complemented by the tendency for many of the individual layers to have structural hierarchies of nestedness or modules (or both). The second is the redundancy of information in separate layers. For almost any network, the density of edges ('connectance') has implications for its function but usually 'connectivity' (how difficult it is to disconnect) is more critical to function and resilience. Connectivity may manifest itself in the form of redundancy of information in different layers. For example, the relationships among concepts in a cluster centred on niche separation will also be reflected in the relationships such as paper citation among publications in the 'communications' layer, and in the clustering of like-minded authors in the 'people' layer. De Domenico et al. (2014) describe a method to aggregate the information in different layers, which was designed for multiplex networks (the same nodes in all layers), but may work for multilayer networks with different node sets in different layers.

EVOLVING SPACE FOR EVOLVING ECOLOGY

If Ecology is treated as a multilayer network, as the science evolves, the network evolves in a non-random way, based on the mutual influence of adjacent nodes, rather like the diffusion of information through the edges.

We might imagine at first that this network is embedded in the same n-dimensional contextual space of time, physical space, conditions and resources, but unlike our individual researcher described in *Selection in Science Space* in this chapter, the Ecology network is not in that same 'science space'; in fact, it is conceptually difficult to see how it could be. The layers constrain the structure although we draw them as parallel planes. Similarly, the indirect interactions among k species won't fit into the k-dimensional species density space. Fortunately, this is not a problem because any graph or network creates its own space (Dale and Fortin 2021). This means that as the network evolves, so does the space within which it is embedded. The coevolution of the embedding space is an important aspect of spontaneous order or self-organisation recognised as a key feature of complex systems. That, in turn, will affect our view of what the evolution of this network is like; it is definitely not like a line of organisms evolving in response to their environment and interactions.

We suggest that this approach resembles using structure as surrogate for a process like diffusion and using a conceptual process like diffusion to understand the structure. As often in the study of graphs, this ties closely with the concept of random walks or constrained random walks (on a graph or in an n-dimensional space), as discussed previously with respect to a researcher exploring science space.

SO WHAT?

Viewing the science of Ecology as a dynamic multilayer network, rather than as an evolving organism, allows more independence to different parts of the endeavour as it develops and helps explain why the science is hard.

However, this view also recognises that indirect influences flow through the network between different and distant projects, whether as directed communication or as a random walk of chance exchanges. The model makes possible the recognition of the different roles of elements in different layers, and of different roles within a single layer (e.g. student versus administrator) while providing scope for the interactions of units within and between layers.

Of course, the network model makes a convenient and helpful metaphor for our science, but someone will undoubtedly ask whether the network might actually be created. The answer is '*yes*', at least for parts of it, and the knowledge graph approach is proposed as a potential summary of the discipline's state (Popping 2007). This can be done by applying and developing methods based on those already in existence to create knowledge graphs from very large data. In parallel with our comment about networks (they are used and studied by ecologists, and the science of Ecology is one itself), knowledge graphs have been fundamental to organising and representing scientific information in a structured manner (Kejriwal et al. 2021) and the science of Ecology can also be portrayed as one. Time will tell…

The network model also enables us to appreciate how the diverse parts of ecology and the system of scientific research interact, but also how change might occur within the discipline. In the early decades of the science, there were few practitioners, large regions of science space had yet to be explored and the discipline network had yet to mature. Not to devalue the contributions of our predecessors, but it was relatively easy for the ideas of a few researchers to be adopted and dominate the discipline. Change seems to have occurred readily. Now, with a more established multilayer structure and a greater volume and diversity of research activity, it is much harder for the ideas of even the most innovative of ecologists to percolate through and to have influence over the whole discipline; influence tends to be localised within subdisciplines. This contributes to the frustration of those who believe that there are fundamental flaws in the way all ecology is done and see the need for wholesale change.

From here onwards, change may be slow and limited in scope. Those calling for paradigm shifts by their colleagues, even within a sub-discipline, cannot expect immediate uptake; complex multilayer networks have their own dynamics.

This is not to suggest that change is impossible, just difficult. Changes to nodes and links within the multilayer network can produce worthwhile benefits: examples frequently discussed include changes to research grant allocation systems (Fang and Casadevall 2016), the adoption of interdisciplinary and transdisciplinary approaches (Kelly et al. 2019; Marshall et al. 2018), and the establishment of mechanisms for synthesis and debate (Halpern et al. 2020; Cousens 2017) workshops and working groups. Improvements at the level of individual ecologists through modified education, training and quality-assurance systems will be beneficial (to address known common errors and weaknesses).

The multilayered network that is Ecology contains little in the way of overall governance or management. No node has individual responsibility for improving the whole network. As scientists, we all share that responsibility but as individuals have little power or authority. So, we must encourage the academy to take up the best suggestions: waving flags, writing papers, introducing local innovations and hoping that they catch on.

In this chapter we have presented two views or two models of what ecology is like and how it evolves – both useful, both interesting. The first model, of selection acting on individual ecologists, emphasises the importance of the traits and context of the researcher and their research projects in multidimensional science space. The second model presents Ecology as a multilayer network that defines its own space. That network is complex

and that complexity is one feature that makes our science hard. The network model emphasises the diversity of nodes and their relationships, accommodating the frequency and importance of indirect interactions, and the potential for hierarchies of indirect interactions of various levels. Basic network analysis would suggest that because its function is knowledge discovery, communication and synthesis, it will do better with more links, more communication and more collaboration.

REFERENCES

Abrahamson, E. 2009. Necessary conditions for the study of fads and fashions in science. *Scandinavian Journal of Management* 25:235–239. doi:10.1016/j.scaman.2009.03.005

Allee, W. C., A. E. Emerson, O. Park, et al. 1949. *Principles of animal ecology*. Philadelphia, PA: W.B. Saunders.

Anderson, J. G. T. 2017. Why ecology needs natural history. *American Scientist* 105:290–297. doi:10.1511/2017.105.5.290

Anderson, S. C., P. R. Elsen, B. B. Hughes, et al. 2021. Trends in ecology and conservation over eight decades. *Frontiers in Ecology and the Environment* 19:274–282. doi:10.1002/fee.2320

Barabási, A. -L., H. Jeong, Z. Néda, et al. 2001. Evolution of the social network of scientific collaborations. doi:10.48550/arXiv.cond-mat/0104162

Barrat, A., Barthélemy, M., and A. Vespignani. 2008. *Dynamical processes on complex networks*. Cambridge: Cambridge University Press. doi:10.1017/CBO9780511791383

Belovsky, G. E., D. B. Botkin, T. A. Crowl, et al. 2004. Ten suggestions to strengthen the science of ecology. *BioScience* 54:345–351. doi:10.1641/0006-3568(2004)054[0345:TSTSTS]2.0.CO;2

Betini, G. S., T. Avgar, and J. M. Fryxell. 2017. Why are we not evaluating multiple competing hypotheses in ecology and evolution? *Royal Society Open Science* 4:160756. doi:10.1098/rsos.160756

Betts M. G., A. S. Hadley, D. W. Frey, et al. 2021. When are hypotheses useful in ecology and evolution? *Ecology and Evolution* 11:5762–5776. doi:10.1002/ece3.7365

Bianconi, G. 2018. *Multilayer networks: Structure and function*. Oxford: Oxford University Press. doi:10.1093/oso/9780198753919.001.0001

Boekhout, H. D., V. A. Traag, and F. W. Takes. 2021. Investigating scientific mobility in co-authorship networks using multilayer temporal motifs. *Network Science* 9:354–386. doi:10.1017/nws.2021.12

Bonchev, D., and G. A. Buck. 2005. Quantitative measures of network complexity. In: *Complexity in chemistry, biology, and ecology*, eds D. Bonchev and D. H. Rouvray, 191–235. Springer: Boston. doi:10.1007/0-387-25871-X_5

Börger, L., B. D. Dalziel, and J. M. Fryxell. 2008. Are there general mechanisms of animal home range behaviour? A review and prospects for future research. *Ecology Letters* 11:637–650. doi:10.1111/j.1461-0248.2008.01182.x

Brittan, G., and P. S. Bandyopadhyay. 2019. Ecology, evidence, and objectivity: In search of a bias-free methodology. *Frontiers in Ecology and Evolution* 7:399. doi:10.3389/fevo.2019.00399

Bromham, L., R. Dinnage, and X. Hua. 2016. Interdisciplinary research has consistently lower funding success. *Nature* 534:684–687. doi:10.1038/nature18315

Carmel, Y., R. Kent, A. Bar-Massada, et al. 2013. Trends in ecological research during the last three decades: A systematic review. *PLoS One* 8:e59813. doi:10.1371/journal.pone.0059813

Carr, A., C. Diener, N. S. Baliga, and S. M. Gibbons. 2019. Use and abuse of correlation analyses in microbial ecology. *ISME Journal* 13:2647–2655. doi:10.1038/s41396-019-0459-z

Choi, Y. D. 2007. Restoration ecology to the future: A call for new paradigm. *Restoration Ecology* 15:351–353. doi:10.1111/j.1526-100X.2007.00224.x

Costa, L. da F., F. A. Rodrigues, G. Travieso, and P. R. Villas Boas. 2007. Characterization of complex networks: A survey of measurements. *Advances in Physics* 56:167–242. doi:10.1080/00018730601170527

Cousens, R. 2017. Do we argue enough in ecology? *Bulletin of the British Ecological Society* 48:58–61.

Craven, D., M. Winter, K. Hotzel, et al. 2019. Evolution of interdisciplinarity in biodiversity science. *Ecology and Evolution* 9:6744–6755. doi:10.1002/ece3.5244

Dale, M. R. T, and M.-J. Fortin. 2014. *Spatial analysis: A guide for ecologists*, 2nd edition. Cambridge: Cambridge University Press. doi:10.1017/CBO9780511978913

Dale, M. R. T., and M.-J. Fortin. 2021. *Quantitative analysis of ecological networks*. Cambridge: Cambridge University Press. doi:10.1017/9781108649018

Dayton, P. K. 1979. Ecology: A science and a religion. In: *Ecological processes in coastal and marine systems*, ed. R. J. Livingstone, 3–18. New York: Plenum Press.

De Domenico, M., V. Nicosia, A. Arenas, and V. Latora. 2014. Structural reducibility of multilayer networks. *Nature Communications* 6:6864. doi:10.1038/ncomms7864

Egerton, F. N. 1968. Leeuwenhoek as a founder of animal demography. *Journal of the History of Biology* 1:1–22.

Egerton, F. N. 2013. History of ecological sciences, Part 47: Ernst Haeckel's ecology. *Bulletin of the Ecological Society of America* 94:222–244. doi:10.1890/0012-9623-94.3.222

Elton, C. 1927. *Animal ecology*. London: Sidgwick and Jackson.

Fang, F. C., and Casadevall, A. 2016. Research funding: The case for a modified lottery. *Mbio* 7:e00422-16. doi:10.1128/mBio. 00422-16

Fraser, H., T. Parker, S. Nakagawa, A. Barnett, and F. Fidler. 2018. Questionable research practices in ecology and evolution. *PLoS One* 13:e0200303. doi:10.1371/journal.pone.0200303

Futuyma, D. 1973. Ecology: The experimental analysis of distribution and abundance. *Quarterly Review of Biology* 48:47–48.

Gates, A. J., Q. Ke, O. Varol, and A.-L. Barabási. 2019. Nature's reach: Narrow work has broad impact. *Nature* 575:32–34. doi:10.1038/d41586-019-03308-7

Goring, S. J., K. C. Weathers, W. K. Dodds, et al. 2014. Improving the culture of interdisciplinary collaboration in ecology by expanding measures of success. *Frontiers in Ecology and the Environment* 12:39–47. doi:10.1890/120370

Gross, T., and B. Blasius. 2008. Adaptive coevolutionary networks: A review. *Journal* of the *Royal Society Interface* 5:259–271. doi:10.1098/rsif.2007.1229

Guan, N., D. Song, and L. Liao. 2019. Knowledge graph embedding with concepts. *Knowledge Based Systems* 64:38–44. doi:10.1016/j.knosys.2018.10.008

Haeckel, E. 1866. *Generelle morphologie der organismen*. Berlin: G. Reimer.

Halpern, B. S., E. Berlow, R. Williams, E. T. Boer, et al. 2020. Ecological synthesis and its role in advancing knowledge. *BioScience* 70:1005–1014. doi:10.1093/biosci/biaa105

Hector, A., and R. Hooper. 2002. Darwin and the first ecological experiment. *Science* 295:639–640. doi:10.1126/science.1064815

Herrera, M., Roberts, D. C., and N. Gulbahce. 2010. Mapping the evolution of scientific fields. *PLoS One* 5:e10355. doi:10.1371/journal.pone.0010355

Hoekstra, R., H. A. L. Kiers, and A. Johnson. 2012. Are assumptions of well-known statistical techniques checked, and why (not)?) *Frontiers in Psychology* 3:137. doi:10.3389/fpsyg.2012.00137

Hutchinson, G. E. 1978. *An introduction to population ecology*. New Haven: Yale University Press.

James, P. 1992. Knowledge graphs. In: *Linguistic instruments in knowledge engineering*, eds R. P. Van de Riet and R. A. Meersman, 97–117. Amsterdam: Elsevier.

Keddy, P., and E. Weiher. 1999. The scope and goals of research on assembly rules. In: *Ecological assembly rules: Perspectives, advances, retreats*, eds E. Weiher and P. Keddy, 1–20. Cambridge: Cambridge University Press.

Kejriwal, M., Knoblock, C. A., and P. Szekely. 2021. *Knowledge graphs: Fundamentals, techniques, and applications*. Cambridge MA: MIT Press.

Kelly, R., M. Mackay, K. L. Nash, et al. 2019. Ten tips for developing interdisciplinary socio-ecological researchers. *Socio-Ecological Practice Research* 1:149–161. doi:10.1007/s42532-019-00018-2

Koestler, A. 1959. *The sleepwalkers: A history of man's changing vision of the universe*. London: Hutchinson.

Krebs, C. J. 1972. *Ecology: The experimental analysis of distribution and abundance*. New York: Harper and Row.

Kuhn, T. S. 1970. Logic of discovery or psychology of research. In: *Criticism and the growth of knowledge*, eds I. Lakatos and A. Musgrave, 1–23. Cambridge: Cambridge University Press.

Ladyman, J., and K. Wiesner. 2020. *What is a complex system?* New Haven: Yale University Press. doi:10.12987/yale/9780300251104.001.0001

Lawton, J. 1991. Predictable plots: A critique for ecology by R. H. Peters. *Nature* 354:444.

Lawton, J. H. 1999. Are there general laws in ecology? *Oikos* 84:177–192.

Malthus, T. R. 1798. *An essay on the principle of population as it affects the future improvement of society, with remarks on the speculations of Mr. Goodwin, M. Condorcet and other writers*. London: J. Johnson.

Manzi M, D. Ojeda, and Hawkins R. 2019. Enough wandering around!: Life trajectories, mobility, and place making in neoliberal academia. *The Professional Geographer* 71:355–363. doi:10.1080/00330124.2018.1531036

Marquet, P. A., A. P. Allen, J. H. Brown, et al. 2014. On theory in ecology. *BioScience* 64:701–710. doi:10.1093/biosci/biu098

Marshall, F., J. Dolley, and R. Priya. 2018. Transdisciplinary research as transformative space making for sustainability: Enhancing propoor transformative agency in periurban contexts. *Ecology and Society* 23:8. doi:10.5751/ES-10249-230308

McElreath, R., and P. E. Smaldino. 2015. Replication, communication, and the population dynamics of scientific discovery. *PLoS One* 10:e0136088. doi:10.1371/journal.pone.0136088

Meleu, G. R., and P. Y. Melatagia. 2021. The structure of co-publications multilayer network. *Computational Social Networks* 8:8. doi:10.1186/s40649-021-00089-w

Nelson, R. R. 2015. Physics envy: Get over it! *Issues in Science and Technology* 31, 71–78.

Newman, M. E. J. 2010. *Networks: An introduction*. Oxford: Oxford University Press. doi:10.1093/acprof:oso/9780199206650.001.0001

Nobis, M., and T. Wohlgemuth. 2004. Trend words in ecological core journals over the last 25 years (1978–2002). *Oikos* 106:411–421. doi:10.1111/j.0030-1299.2004.13496.x

Ohlmann, M., V. Miele, S. Dray, et al. 2019. Diversity indices for ecological networks: A unifying framework using Hill numbers. *Ecological Letters* 22:737–747. doi:10.1111/ele.13221

Omodei, E., M. De Domenico, and A. Arenas. 2016. Evaluating the impact of interdisciplinary research: A multilayer network approach. *Network Science* 5:235–246. doi:10.1017/nws.2016.15

Peters, R. F. 1991. *A critique for ecology.* Cambridge: Cambridge University Press.

Pilosof, S., M. A. Porter, M. Pascual, and S. Kéfi. 2017. The multilayer nature of ecological networks. *Nature Ecology and Evolution* 1:0101. doi:10.1038/s41559-017-0101

Popping, R. 2007. Text analysis for knowledge graphs. *Quantity and Quality* 41:691–709. doi:10.1007/s11135-006-9020-z

Reyers, B., D. Roux, and P. O'Farrell. 2010. Can ecosystem services lead ecology on a transdisciplinary pathway? *Environmental Conservation* 37:501–511. doi:10.1017/S0376892910000846

Rist, L., A. Felton, L. Samuelsson, C. Sandström, and O. Rosvall. 2013. A new paradigm for adaptive management. *Ecology and Society* 18:63. doi:10.5751/ES-06183-180463

Scheiner, S. M. 2013. The ecological literature, an idea-free distribution. *Ecology Letters* 16:1421–1423. doi:10.1111/ele.12196

Simberloff, D. 1981. The sick science of ecology. *Eidema* 1:49–54.

Simberloff, D. 2013. Charles Elton. In: *Oxford bibliographies.* New York: Oxford University Press. doi:10.1093/OBO/9780199830060-0090

Smaldino, P. E., and R. McElreath. 2016. The natural selection of bad science. *Royal Society Open Science* 3:160384. doi:10.1098/rsos.160384

Smith, R. 2006. Peer review: A flawed process at the heart of science and journals. *Journal of the Royal Society of Medicine* 99:178–182. doi:10.1258/jrsm.99.4.178

Whittaker, R. H. 1962. Classification of natural communities. *Botanical Review* 28:1–239.

Wildman, P., and S. Inayatullah. 1996. Ways of knowing, culture, communication and the pedagogies of the future. *Futures* 28:723–740.

3

What sort of a science is Ecology?

ALKISTIS ELLIOTT-GRAVES

ECOLOGY AS A SCIENCE

As the science of the struggle for existence (Cooper 2003) developed and matured into what we now recognise as Ecology, a number of new struggles emerged, this time for its practitioners rather than the organisms they studied. These struggles have plagued the discipline since its beginnings, threatening the value of its concepts and methods (Kingsland 1995). They have even cast doubt on its status as a science (see discussion in Elliott-Graves 2019).

Ecology does not fit neatly into the traditional picture of what a science ought to look like. Laws are hard to find and tend to have too many exceptions to be useful (Elliott-Graves 2019). Predictions often turn out to be inaccurate, even when established explanations of the same phenomena already exist and theoretical results often resist practical application (Shrader-Frechette and McCoy 1994). Yet the aim of this chapter is not to chastise the discipline for its failings to address these problems, rather it is to show that the struggles faced by ecologists are to a large extent due to the special type of complexity of the systems they investigate. This means that we should not expect ecological research to proceed along the lines laid out by 20th-century philosophers of science, who based most of their ideas on certain subdisciplines of physics and chemistry (Mitchell 2000).

Of course, the existence of these problems does not mean that we should cease testing the quality of ecological research or stop striving to increase the value and usefulness of ecological concepts and methods. It simply means that the traditional philosophical framework for evaluating scientific practice will doom Ecology to failure.

This chapter highlights some key aspects of this traditional scientific philosophical framework, explains why they cannot apply to ecological research and suggests some ways to modify this picture so that it applies more fairly – but also more usefully – to ecological research. The chapter begins by outlining the way in which ecological systems are complex and then examines two ways in which complexity affects ecological research: in terms of ecologists' ability to generate generalisations, explanations, predictions and interventions, and in terms of the role of *values* in ecological research. It then shows how the traditional picture of philosophy of science fails to account for the reality in Ecology; and it concludes by suggesting some ways in which these struggles can be overcome, based on existing methods already in use by ecologists.

What sort of a science is Ecology? It is a complex, challenging but ultimately rewarding science. Moreover, the ways in which it diverges from other sciences and challenges our expectations regarding scientific practice ought not to be a source of embarrassment but an opportunity to learn and revise our theoretical frameworks about scientific practice.

DOI: 10.1201/9781003314332-3

ECOLOGICAL SYSTEMS ARE COMPLEX

Discussions of complexity are notoriously thorny in most disciplines (Hooker 2011). The same is true in Ecology. On the one hand, there seems to be general agreement that ecological systems are quintessential examples of *complex systems* (Levin 1998). There seems to be a consensus that complexity is a feature of healthy and mature ecological systems, even though such systems may be susceptible to particular disturbances (Loreau et al. 2001). On the other hand, there is no single, uncontested definition of complexity in ecology (Elliott-Graves, 2023).

One characteristic that is typically associated with complexity – both within and beyond ecology – is having *multiple parts* (Levins 1966), though it is rarely seen as the only relevant characteristic of complexity.

The parts of an ecosystem are not just many, they also *interact* (Pimm 1991). Specifically, complex ecological systems display high levels of *connectance* (the number of interspecific interactions out of those possible) and *interaction strength* (the average value of the interspecific interactions in the community) (Odenbaugh 2011). Other characteristics include *non-linearity* or *feedback*, where a change in one factor can result in a disproportional change – or a complete flip – in the behaviour of the system, and *path dependence*, which occurs when the later states of systems depend on their previous states (Levin 1998). For example, in the colonisation of new areas, such as islands or forest patches, the final composition of the system – which species persist and in what proportion – depends on which species are the original colonisers and how they interacted with each other.

Some characteristics of complexity are important because they lead to methodological and epistemic challenges. That is, they make it difficult for ecologists to conduct scientific investigations and limit the quality or scope of the knowledge ecologists gain from these investigations (see *The challenges of complexity*, this chapter and Figure 3.1). Specifically, in the case of ecological systems, these characteristics are the existence of *multiple, interacting* and *diverse* parts (Elliott-Graves 2020). Ecological systems are made up of a number of

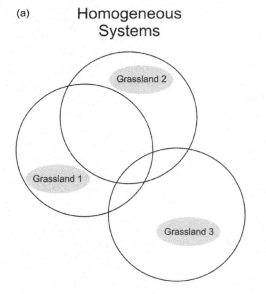
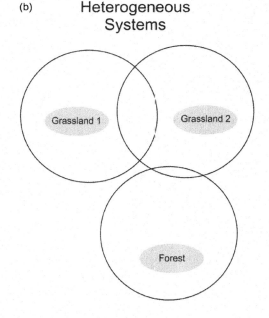

Figure 3.1 How complexity affects generalisations. In homogeneous systems **(a)**, there are factors that are common between systems. In this example, all three grassland systems may share a certain species or dynamic, such as positive plant-soil feedback. Knowledge gained from one system may be transferred to the other systems. In heterogeneous systems **(b)**, there are no factors common across all systems. Generalisations are limited: knowledge gained from one system does not necessarily apply to all the others – though it might apply to some.

heterogeneous individuals of various species in variable environments, which interact with each other and with their environment in diverse and dynamic ways (Levins 1966, 1993). It is important to note that systems, in principle, can have multiple interacting parts but be homogeneous. For example, a chainmail armour suit is made up of many interacting metal rings, yet each of these rings is almost identical to the rest. It is also possible for a system to have multiple diverse parts but be homogeneous across other systems of the same type. For example, a Boeing 747 is made up of many diverse interacting parts, yet each Boeing 747 is very similar to the rest. Thus, despite its complexity, once knowledge from one Boeing 747 is acquired it can be applied to other airplanes of the same type: indeed, air safety relies on this (Elliott-Graves 2018; Matthewson 2011). In contrast, ecological systems score highly on all three characteristics: they have multiple, interacting parts, and there is great variability both within and across ecosystems. For instance, a forest and a marine ecosystem may have similar trophic levels, but they are made up of different types of species. Even two ecosystems of the same 'type' such as two grasslands often have different species and/or display different dynamics and interactions (Figure 3.1).

THE CHALLENGES OF COMPLEXITY

How do these characteristics of complexity affect ecological practice? The short answer is that they make it difficult to acquire and transfer empirical knowledge within and between ecological systems. More specifically, they create difficulties for making *generalisations*, *explanations*, *predictions* and *interventions*.

Generalisations

Being able to generalise beyond the results of a scientific investigation can be extremely useful. At a basic level, generalisations are practically advantageous, since they can help scientists gain insights that go beyond their current investigation. So, we can generalise the results of an experiment (where a particular phenomenon is in a sample of the population) to the larger population or maybe even the whole species. But generalisations are also useful in a deeper sense. Identifying a pattern in nature reveals information about the world. The idea is

that a pattern encompasses what is common across different phenomena or systems. These common factors are thought to be the 'real causal factors' of the system that actually give rise to its behaviour and dynamics. In contrast, the factors that differ across systems – those that are 'idiosyncratic' – are thought to be 'mere details', or noise, in the sense that they do not contribute significantly to the dynamics or behaviour of the system. In other words, successful generalisations provide scientists with knowledge about how the world really is (Strevens 2004). This, in turn, can help scientists explain how a system or phenomenon works, as it allows scientists to 'virtually reduce' the complexity of a system, which makes the system easier to study. Omitting the noisy details from a system means that there are fewer factors that scientists need to take into account, hence they can study the systems as though they have fewer parts and properties. Thus, there are fewer variables and parameters to measure or calculate and fewer dynamics to identify. Moreover, there are fewer possibilities of introducing errors to the models.

Finally, identifying general patterns can help scientists form expectations about how a system or phenomenon will behave in the future. If we understand what is happening now, then we can project this information into the future. In other words, successful generalisations form the basis of explanations, predictions and interventions, three of the main goals of science.

This is all well and good, provided that the generalisations do, in fact, identify real patterns in the world. The problem is that in ecological systems, which are complex and heterogeneous, what seems like a general pattern might be restricted in time or space (Figure 3.1). In fact, patterns can break. If this is the case, then how should ecologists approach generalisations? What sorts of expectations regarding generalisations are appropriate? Should we give up on them completely or should we increase our efforts to find ecological laws, even if they are few and far between?

Prescribing a specific set of rules or actions regarding generalisation is unlikely to be useful, as each set of rules or actions will probably only work well in a small number of cases. Instead, our suggestion is to take a step back and change our overall attitude and expectations of generalisations. What does that mean? It means that we should adjust our expectations of what generalisations mean, what sort of information we can glean from them and what their role is within a scientific investigation. So, for example, we can continue to look for patterns, but not necessarily expect to find them. Even if we do find a pattern, we should expect it to break. In other words, we should expect the level of generality to be constrained to variation within particular types of phenomena, such as disturbance, plant-soil feedback or migration. A parallel suggestion is to pay more attention to testing the scope of a generalisation rather than assuming (or hoping) that a generalisation that seems to hold will continue to do so. This can be achieved in many different ways, including experiment replications, testing for model robustness and using statistical review methods such as meta-analysis.

Explanations, predictions and interventions

Explanation and prediction are two central goals of science (Douglas 2009b). When scientists attempt to explain, they aim to understand *how* and *why* certain phenomena occur in the way that they do, or why certain systems exhibit a type of behaviour. When scientists predict, they make claims based on knowledge of past investigations about the occurrence of an event or phenomenon in the future, or about how a system will behave in the future. In addition, *successful* explanations and predictions are hallmarks of 'good science'. When scientists manage to provide explanations of phenomena and their predictions turn out to be accurate, then we have good reason to have confidence in our theories and methods (Douglas 2009b). In contrast, when explanations and predictions start to fail, then this is usually a sign that something is wrong. A plethora of failed explanations and predictions in a scientific discipline are usually treated as a sign that some fundamental assumptions, theories or methods must be abandoned or at least revised (Douglas and Magnus 2013).

Explanations and predictions are based on generalisations. Providing a scientific explanation used to be synonymous with demonstrating how a particular phenomenon is an instance of a more general pattern, while scientific *theories* were those that subsumed many disparate phenomena under one framework (Douglas 2009b). The simpler the theoretical framework and the greater the number of phenomena it could explain, the more powerful

it was. In causal accounts of explanation such as those of Woodward (2003), generalisations form the basis for explanations, as they describe causal regularities between variables. Here, to explain an event or phenomenon is to show that it is *caused* by another event or phenomenon and that this relationship is invariant or stable within certain parameters. In the case of prediction, the connection to generalisations is even clearer, as a prediction is just the projection of an existing pattern into the future.

But if generalisations fail, and explanations and predictions are based on generalisations, shouldn't we expect explanations and predictions to also fail? We should, or at the very least, we should not be surprised or demoralised when they do. For example, explanations of community structures that were based on the keystone species concept have subsequently been proven to be false, as it turns out that keystone species do not behave in the same way across different systems (Cottee-Jones and Whittaker 2012). Similarly, predictions can fail when underlying patterns change or break. Another example comes from species distribution models (SDMs), which are often used to predict the range of a species colonising a new area, by projecting variables of the species' native region to the new area (Sobek-Swant et al. 2012). However, climate change can render these predictions inaccurate, as unexpected higher temperatures or fewer extreme cold events can increase a species' range to regions that it would normally not be able to colonise (Cuddington et al. 2018).

Ecological research is not exclusively focused on building a body of knowledge for its own sake. Quite often, the reason for investigating a certain phenomenon, system or dynamic is so that ecologists can intervene and induce, change or stop something from occurring. In other words, ecologists often *apply* knowledge from their scientific investigations so as to *intervene* in ecological systems. Yet, as these interventions are based on knowledge of existing systems – knowledge of generalisations, explanations and predictions – when these fail then the subsequent interventions are also likely to fail. If a group of ecologists are planning an intervention to stop the spread of a potential invasive insect, they may base their intervention on the predictions of an SDM. However, if that SDM predicts a significantly smaller range of the insect's spread than it is actually capable of (due to higher temperatures) then the subsequent intervention which focuses on the smaller range is likely to fail.

Scientific and ethical values

Another way in which complexity manifests in ecological research is in the context of values. Philosophers of science distinguish between *epistemic* and *non-epistemic* values. Epistemic values (sometimes called cognitive or even scientific values) are those that directly help with the attainment of knowledge, such as truth, empirical adequacy, explanatory power, simplicity, generality, theoretical unity etc. Non-epistemic values (sometimes called contextual or ethical values) are those that arise from the social and/or ethical context within which a scientific investigation takes place, such as justice, equality, conservation, diversity etc.) (Reiss and Sprenger 2020). For much of the 20th and 21st centuries, there has been an ongoing debate concerning the relationship between the two types of values and the appropriate role for each type of value in scientific practice. More specifically, while there is widespread agreement that epistemic values are important for most aspects of scientific practice, there is much less agreement on the value and role of non-epistemic values in science (Douglas 2009a).

From the Enlightenment until the mid-20th century, the received view was that non-epistemic values had little or no place in science, as they detracted from the *objectivity* that scientists ought to strive for at all costs (McMullin 1982). A slightly less extreme version of this view is that non-epistemic values have a role to play, but only in some aspects of science, for example, when it comes to choosing which topics to study or how to allocate funding to various disciplines or subdisciplines within an academic institution. Still, for each scientific investigation, when it comes to testing, accepting or rejecting hypotheses, this view dictates that only epistemic values ought to play a role (Reiss and Sprenger 2020).

More recent philosophical views show that the prevailing attitude towards non-epistemic values has shifted. Several philosophers have pointed out that it is impossible to keep non-epistemic values out of science completely (Douglas 2009a). More importantly, there are cases where separating epistemic and non-epistemic values and attempting to eliminate the latter from scientific investigations

can actually result in worse outcomes (i.e. inaccurate results and/or an *increase* in bias). For example, there is a large body of research on intellectual and physical differences between men and women that is based on assumptions of female inferiority (Kourany 2003). As long as these assumptions remained unchallenged, they were accepted as part of the scientific body of knowledge, thus perpetuating the illusion that the results of these studies were objective. Only after scientists with an explicit feminist perspective challenged these assumptions were they and the many results based on them questioned. A particularly poignant case is that of archaeological findings, where most tools that indicate advances in human evolution were immediately – and mistakenly – associated with males (Kourany 2003).

The issue of competing epistemic and non-epistemic values is particularly important in ecology, because the behaviour of ecological systems affects and is affected by human societies. This includes exploitation for resources (e.g. forests or marine ecosystems), management of biological invasions, biodiversity conservation measures and so on. Scientific investigations into these systems are inherently and inescapably 'ethically driven' (Justus 2021). Ethical values affect the very concepts and methods used in the investigation, which, in turn, affect how choices for various strategies are made and evaluated. In addition, the results of these investigations inform policy decisions and thus have ethical implications for human societies. For example, research on *biodiversity* is loaded with values. First, the concept itself is not neutral or merely descriptive, but has a positive normative connotation: biodiversity is considered to be a good thing that ought to be preserved. Second, there are different ways to conceptualise biodiversity, which affect how it is measured. Different measurements can result in very different strategies or policies regarding an area or species. Third, policies for biodiversity conservation are made in the context of economic scarcity and in competition with other policies that are often based on very different values. For instance, determining the size of a marine nature reserve will depend on which species are considered important, how many of these are also economically viable, where commercial ferry routes are located, how much funding is allocated to implementing the policy and so on.

WHAT SORT OF A SCIENCE ECOLOGY IS *NOT*

The intent of this chapter so far has been to highlight some ways in which the complexity of ecological systems creates conceptual and practical difficulties for ecologists. But this is only half of the story. The more interesting question is what can and should be done in light of these difficulties. This is where delving deeper into the philosophical foundations of ecology can be illuminating. We will start by sketching out the traditional picture of science, based on philosophical views of the early to mid-20th century, and show how and why it does not work well for Ecology. Luckily, there are philosophical views that can make sense of, and provide a coherent theoretical framework for ecological research.

The traditional picture of science

The traditional picture of science, which appears in many textbooks and scientific lore as *the scientific method* is a mishmash of two philosophical theories: *hypothetico-deductivism* and *falsificationism*. There are quite a few versions of hypothetico-deductivism out there, but at its basis it is a framework for understanding how hypotheses are (or should be) tested: scientists formulate hypotheses (hence the *hypothetico-*) which *entail* certain expectations (E). The *deductivism* comes in because of the 'entail'; that is, the expectations are meant to be *logically deducible* from the hypothesis. This gives us the logical statement: if H then E (if the hypothesis is true, then the expectation must be true). A typical example used in philosophical discussions is the hypothesis 'All ravens are black' which entails the expectation E (the next raven I will see will be black). Apologies to ecologists for perpetuating this example of 'indoor ornithology' (Goodman 1955 in Godfrey-Smith 2009), but it actually works in the ecological context. So, we can go out in the world (or our lab, where we could be waiting for the raven eggs to hatch) and observe whether E occurs. If our observations match our expectations (i.e. the next raven, and the one after that, and so on, is in fact black) then our hypothesis H must also be true. Right?

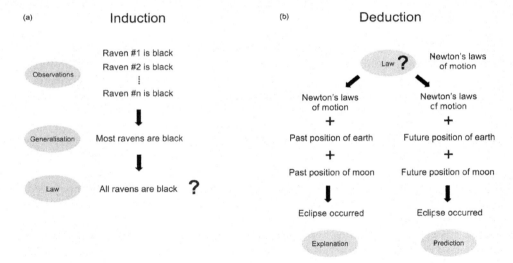

Figure 3.2 Traditional pictures of science. In induction (a), we start by making observations. When we have enough of these, we might be able to make generalisations. But is this generalisation merely accidental or a genuine law? We can never be 100% sure (the problem of induction). In deduction (b), genuine laws of nature can be used to make explanations (by showing that an event is an instance of the more general pattern described by the law) or predictions (by projecting the pattern described by the law to an event in the future). This symmetrical portrayal of explanation and prediction is called the *symmetry thesis* (Hempel and Oppenheim 1948). The problem is that the deductive structure only works if laws are already established. But establishing laws is difficult, due to the problem of induction.

Wrong! *Deducing* particular phenomena or events from generalisations that we know to be true is all well and good *if we already know* that the generalisation is true. The problem with hypothesis testing is that we are in the process of trying to determine *whether* the general hypothesis is true. So, rather than engaging in *de*duction, we are, in fact, engaging in *in*duction – where we are attempting to generalise 'upwards' from a number of particular instances (Figure 3.2). Now, you might think that this is not a problem – scientists do it all the time – but many philosophers, most notably Hume, are *inductive sceptics*. They believe that we can never be 100% sure that a generalisation constructed from many observed instances holds. In other words, just because you have observed 1,000,000,000 black ravens does not mean that every single raven in all of time and space will be black. Here the reason for sticking with the example should become apparent to ecologists – it is quite easy to breed ravens of different colours, while there are also occasional ravens found with leucism (white pigmentation). So, our hypothesis cannot be *confirmed*. This might not be a huge deal in the case of ravens, but the worry is that the same problem (called the *problem of induction*) affects our ability to confirm all hypotheses. If we take the problem of induction seriously, then no experiment or model will ever be sufficient to make us certain about any hypothesis. Every time a test turns out positive (that is, it supports the hypothesis) all we know is that we have no reason to reject it.

In the mid-20th century, there were two main suggestions for how to deal with this problem. The first was to overcome the problem of induction by discovering so-called 'laws of nature' and the second was Popper's falsificationism.

Laws of nature

Laws of nature are generalisations that have three main characteristics: (1) universality (they cover all of space and time), (2) truth (they are exceptionless) and (3) natural necessity (they are not accidental) (Mitchell 2003). The first and second characteristics concern the scope of generalisations. Universal generalisations exist throughout all space and time. They are true if they hold in all instances within their defined scope. Thus, even if a generalisation is not universal, it can still be exceptionless within a specified domain. For example, it is likely that in the first few minutes after the 'Big Bang', only helium, deuterium and lithium were formed. All other elements were formed later, as stars developed (Mitchell 2003). Thus, a law stating that no uranium-235 sphere is larger than 55 kg is only applicable to the time where uranium-235 actually exists. The third characteristic aims to distinguish between generalisations that are necessary and those that are merely accidental. For example, the generalisation *'all the pens in my drawer are blue'*. There is nothing about my drawer or the nature of pens that affects whether or not the statement is, in fact, true. If it turns out to be true, then it is true accidentally (for further explanation on laws versus accidental generalisations see Box 3.1).

The point is that if you discover a law of nature, then you can bypass the problem of induction, by showing (deductively) that a phenomenon or event is a particular instance of the general pattern described by the law. This goes a long way in explaining a lot of scientific and philosophical practice in the subsequent years, especially the obsession with ever increasing the scope of generalisations, and the quest for discovering laws that are specific to particular disciplines such as ecology.

For many philosophers of science, laws became the basis for their scientific 'worldview', as they formed the basis of what counted as 'good' or high-quality science. For example, a popular view of scientific explanation in the mid-20th century was the so-called *deductive-nomological* (DN) model (also called the covering-law model), where a scientific explanation was nothing more than a deduction of a phenomenon or event from an existing law and certain antecedent conditions (Hempel and Oppenheim 1948). Many scientists took these ideas to heart and realised that finding laws of nature that were specific to one's own discipline effectively legitimised the discipline as a true and independent science (Mayr 1996). In other words, if Ecology had its own laws, then it would definitely count as an autonomous science. The problem is that laws of nature – at least of the type that would allow for overcoming the problem of induction – remain elusive in many sciences, ecology included.

BOX 3.1: Laws versus accidental generalisations

Why were scientists and philosophers of the past obsessed with finding laws of nature? A full answer to this question is long and complicated, but here is a short summary: laws of nature can bypass the problem of induction.

If you assume that the natural world is orderly and has patterns, then it is a good idea to identify those patterns. These patterns can then provide the basis for a number of scientific endeavours: you can explain something by showing how it fits into an existing pattern, you can predict something by projecting an existing pattern into the future and you can intervene on a system to enhance or break an existing pattern. The problem is that not all patterns are equally stable, some are contingent on other factors, some are ephemeral, while some are illusory. So, the aim of science (according to some scientists and philosophers) was to identify the most stable of these patterns – which they called laws of nature – and to distinguish them from merely accidental generalisations. In other words, what makes a law a law is that it is not arbitrary or accidental, it has some underlying reason for its existence.

Consider the following three generalisations:

1. All spheres of uranium-235 have a diameter of less than 100 m.
2. All spheres of gold have a diameter of less than 100 m.
3. All the pens in my drawer are blue.

The traditional story is the following: all three of these generalisations are true, yet only the first is *necessarily* true. That is, there is something about uranium-235 that makes it impossible for a sphere of it to exceed 100 m. That 'something' is a chain reaction of nuclear fission, which spontaneously occurs once uranium-235 reaches critical mass. In contrast, there is nothing about pens or my drawer that makes it necessary that all the pens in the drawer are blue. Even if I only buy blue pens, this is still an accidental fact of the world, there is nothing about me or my pens that makes it necessary for me to have made such a decision. What about the gold? It may seem impossible for such a sphere to exist – even if there is enough gold in the world to construct such a sphere, it is extremely unlikely that you could convince everyone to give up their gold for such a project. Still, these constraints are practical, it would be *possible* to construct a gold sphere so large if we managed to collect enough gold.

If you are not entirely convinced that there is a strict dichotomy between laws and accidental generalisations, you are not alone. More recent philosophical views present a much more nuanced picture (Mitchell 2000). On the one hand, established examples of laws, including the uranium spheres, are in some sense contingent – the law only exists in a universe where uranium exists, and only after it has come into existence. On the other hand, many generalisations in biology, such as Mendel's laws, are the products of evolution, and are sufficiently stable to generate explanations and predictions. While generalisations like (3) are unlikely to be useful for science, there are many modest, highly contingent generalisations that are useful. The problem with such generalisations is that they don't neatly bypass the problem of induction. Alas! Uncertainty remains with us.

Ecological 'laws'?

In ecology, various candidates for lawhood have been proposed, including exponential/logistic growth, allometric metabolic/body weight relationships and species/area relationships (Colyvan and Ginzburg 2003). However, none of these potential laws have been proven to be universal or exceptionless (Shrader-Frechette and McCoy 1993). In addition, many of these supposed laws seem like accidental regularities rather than regularities that are necessarily true (Lange 2005). In fact, given the difficulties of generating generalisations, it seems unlikely that ecology will ever be awash with laws of nature.

There are roughly two responses to this state of affairs, both of which have been espoused by philosophers and ecologists.

The first option is to just give up on laws completely, arguing that sciences like biology and ecology just do not have the types of regularities that count as laws (see Lange 2005). Schrader-Frechette and McCoy (1993) argued that Ecology is *'more a science of case studies and statistical regularities than a science of exceptionless, general laws'*. The second option is to revise the notion of laws, so that ecological regularities make the cut. The idea is that the classic dichotomies (necessary/accidental, universal/contingent) are not useful for practicing scientists, as the point of generalisations is that they help scientists achieve various goals, such as explaining and predicting natural phenomena or intervening on the world. In this context, the most important characteristic of ecological laws is that they are invariant (or stable, or resilient – different accounts use different terms, which are not identical, but close enough for the purposes of this discussion) (Mitchell 2000).

Linquist et al. (2016) identify three dimensions of 'resilience'. A generalisation is *'taxonomically resilient'* if it is stable across a different number of species or higher-level taxa. *'Habitat* resilience' occurs when a generalisation is invariant across a broad set of regions or biological contexts. *'Spatial* resilience' occurs when a generalisation remains invariant at the scale of whole organisms, molecular systems and genomic communities. They use meta-analyses to investigate the extent to which various generalisations are resilient across these three dimensions. For example, they found that the generalisation *'Habitat fragmentation negatively impacts pollination and reproduction in plants'* is resilient across *'five distinct habitats and across 89 species from 49 families'*. They believe that these types of generalisations qualify as laws.

It is worth noting that the only agreement, in philosophical circles, is that sciences such as biology or ecology do not have laws *in the traditional sense*. The jury is still out when it comes to whether we should revise our notion of laws or give up on laws in these sciences. The important point is that in the absence of traditional laws, we must find other ways in which to test the quality of ecological research.

Falsificationism

A different suggestion for dealing with the problem of induction is to 'bite the bullet' and accept that it cannot be overcome. A famous proponent of such a view was Popper. Contrary to how his views are often portrayed in scientific textbooks, Popper believed that scientists can never *confirm* hypotheses with 100% certainty, they can only *refute* hypotheses (Popper 1965; see also Godfrey-Smith 2009).

Going back to our raven example, if you observe a white raven, then you have conclusively rejected the hypothesis that all ravens are black. This notion of *refutation* was so important that it formed the foundation of Popper's philosophy of science, including his view of scientific progress and his method for distinguishing science from pseudoscience. For Popper, science progressed through a continual process of conjecture (formulating hypotheses) and refutation (rejecting hypotheses). As soon as a hypothesis is rejected, a new hypothesis is constructed to take its place, which is then tested until it also is rejected, and so on. There are some important implications of this view: while we can be sure that hypotheses accepted by past scientists are false, we have no reason to believe that the hypotheses we currently hold are true. It is inevitable that they too will eventually be refuted. This means that scientific knowledge is nowhere near to being foolproof. It is just as likely to be false than non-scientific knowledge.

But then, how can we distinguish between science and non-science? According to Popper, *true* science is the one that is most likely to turn out false. When put like that it sounds very counterintuitive, but a short explanation might help. The key difference between science and pseudoscience lies in accepting the possibility of your hypothesis being refuted. True scientists, therefore, make *bold* hypotheses that are *falsifiable*. Scientists make hypotheses that can be tested by available methods and observations that are actually possible. These hypotheses are *novel* (not of events that have already been observed) and *precise* (not vague) so that it is possible to determine when they are refuted. In contrast, pseudo-scientists construct hypotheses that are difficult to test and thus not easily refuted.

Falsification and prediction

Unfortunately, refutation has its own set of problems. The main issue is the so-called *Duhem-Quine problem*, or *holism about testing* (Godfrey-Smith 2009) that no hypothesis is tested in isolation but is embedded in a network of additional assumptions (often called auxiliary assumptions). These are assumptions about our instruments of measurement or observation, the circumstances in which the observation is made, the reliability of existing data or records and so on (Godfrey-Smith 2009). This means that the test of the hypothesis is actually a test of the *conjunction* of the hypothesis *and* all the auxiliary assumptions (some of which we might not even be aware of). So, if the expectation (*E*) turns out to be false, we can be sure that something in the whole conjunction is false, but we cannot be sure whether it is the hypothesis or one or more of the auxiliary assumptions.

Imagine that you are conducting a field experiment in some alpine meadows, examining why a particular butterfly population has dramatic fluctuations in population size. You want to test the hypothesis that abnormally warm temperatures in November cause the population to drop. So, you go out, set up your thermometers in July and regularly check them to see that they are working. As it turns out, the November temperatures were abnormally warm, but the butterfly population did not drop (in fact, it grew to higher levels than previous years, which had normal temperatures in November). Now, it could be that abnormally warm November temperatures actually do not have an effect on the butterfly populations. However, a number of other factors could be at play. Maybe mistakes were made in counting the butterfly population (this year, or in previous years) so that this year's population was estimated to be larger than it actually was, or that populations in previous years were estimated to be smaller than they actually were. Alternatively, the thermometers could be faulty, calibrated wrongly or overheating because of the (atypical) lack of snow cover. Another issue could be that warm temperatures do cause population decline, but only in the presence (or absence) of other factors that you have not yet identified. The list of plausible alternative explanations can go on and on. The point is that at least without additional tests, we cannot be sure whether we should consider the hypothesis refuted.

Most scientists and philosophers nowadays do not believe that this problem is insurmountable, provided that predictions turn out to be true *enough*, often *enough*. What exactly counts as true enough and often enough tends to incur some level of debate, but usually certain norms emerge within a particular discipline about when scientists ought to be worried about the quality of predictions. The problem is that in sciences that study complex systems, the success rate of predictions is much lower than it is in other sciences (for the reasons explained in the section on *The Challenges of Complexity*). In Ecology, this has been an ongoing thorn in the side of many prominent ecologists, who with some regularity write papers lamenting the generalisability of ecological theories and the success rate of predictions (two of the most famous of these are Peters 1991, Lawton 1999). Moreover, given the outlook of laws and generalisations in ecology, it seems unlikely that the success rate of predictions is going to increase any time soon. So, does this mean that Ecology is at best an immature science and at worst just a lower quality science?

The answer is no! Ecology is a science that deals with systems that are complex – this complexity was not taken into account by the 20th-century philosophers who constructed the received views about science. In fact, the traditional picture of science has been extensively questioned and criticised. We will examine this critique in the next section and see whether this alternative view better captures ecological reality.

Objectivity

In the section *Scientific and Ethical Values* we outlined the difference between epistemic and non-epistemic values and showed how these values are intertwined in ecological research. We also highlighted the relationship between debates about values and objectivity. In this section, we will delve deeper into this discussion and show that two traditional views on objectivity do not work for ecological research.

To recap, the received view of values in science from the Enlightenment until the mid-20th century was that only epistemic values have a place in scientific investigations, while allowing non-epistemic values into science would result in a failure of objectivity, which would necessarily undermine scientific results. However, this view was successfully challenged by many scientists, historians and philosophers, starting with Kuhn in *The Structure of Scientific Revolutions* (1962). Kuhn was a physicist, historian and philosopher of science, who (correctly) pointed out that the picture of science painted by his predecessors was implausible and inaccurate (Okasha 2002). Scientists were not hyper-rational creatures who acquired knowledge and resolved any disputes by dispassionately observing 'neutral' (unbiased) facts. Despite scientists' best intentions, facts, data and phenomena are 'theory laden', that is, identifying, observing and interpreting these facts, data and phenomena are affected by each scientist's background beliefs.

So far, none of this is hugely controversial. As discussed earlier, in many sciences, especially those like ecology which deal with complex systems and whose results have implications beyond academia, epistemic and non-epistemic values are inextricably intertwined. Moreover, assuming that the status quo is free from non-epistemic values can decrease the overall objectivity of an investigation by obscuring or completely masking underlying biases.

However, Kuhn's (1962) argument can be interpreted in a much stronger way, namely as an argument that science is an entirely *irrational* activity, where any notion of truth is relative to a particular 'paradigm', where a paradigm is a set of theoretical and methodological assumptions that a group of scientists accept at a given time (Okasha 2002). This sparked a movement in some academic circles (such as the strong program in sociology and cultural relativism in anthropology) which denied any role for objectivity, truth and rationality in science (Okasha 2002). The tone in which the book is written is admittedly quite radical, but Kuhn himself disagreed with this interpretation of his work (Godfrey-Smith 2009). He subsequently tried to clarify his views and rein in the most extreme interpretations, but it was too late.

So, we are now left with two extreme views. The first, where science is fully objective and scientists hyper-rational, is unattainable, while the second, where science is fully subjective and scientists irrational, is undesirable. Yet there is a middle ground.

Accepting that scientists are not maximally objective does not mean that they are entirely irrational. Accepting that established theories can be problematic does not mean that we cannot distinguish between higher and lower quality research.

A similar point can be made with respect to values. Non-epistemic values *can* be important does not mean that they *always are* important, nor that they should be prioritised over epistemic values (Justus 2021). The point is rather to recognise that they may have an effect and that this effect is not necessarily problematic. Adopting a more open attitude to the existence and potential of non-epistemic values can sometimes help our scientific endeavours, by highlighting a potential source of bias, or by helping to counteract another hidden source of bias.

SO WHAT?

In this chapter we have painted a few pictures of science that do not accurately capture Ecology. Ecology is not a hyper-rational, fully objective science based on exceptionless laws of nature, whose hypotheses are constantly tested through precise predictions. Still, this does not mean that ecology is wholly unobjective, irrational and untestable. Not all ecological research is of equally high quality, and it is important to have standards to distinguish between high- and low-quality research – yet these standards are not to be found in (outdated) 20th-century philosophical writings. So, what can ecologists do in light of these issues? We end the chapter with some suggestions. These are not intended as specific methodological prescriptions, but more abstract recommendations for our attitudes and expectations regarding concepts and methods in ecological research.

Modest expectations

The first suggestion is to change our attitude and expectations regarding generalisations. In other words, rather than assuming that an observed pattern holds widely, we should focus time and resources for probing, exploring and testing whether a generalisation is possible and what its scope and limitations are. This may seem like a small point, but it is actually very important.

Changing our attitude and expectations towards generalisations is a key step in recognising the potential of generalisations in ecology. We should not be dismissive or embarrassed when generalisations turn out to be limited in scope or break down completely. We should not even expect many generalisations to actually exist in complex, heterogeneous systems. This does not mean that we should stop trying to identify them. It means that we should value them for what they are when we do find them. Examples of successful and useful generalisations where the scope is limited to variation *within* particular types of phenomena include disturbance (Peters et al. 2006), plant-soil feedback (Casper and Castelli 2007) and migration (Kelly and Horton 2016).

Methodological pluralism

The second suggestion is to make wider use of the methodological toolkit that ecologists have at their disposal.

There are numerous ongoing debates in Ecology concerning the best method to use for a set of issues or phenomena. One example is the debate concerning optimal model complexity, where one camp argues for using simple models with few parameters and the other argues for using more complex models that incorporate a larger number of parameters and dynamics (Evans et al. 2013; Levins 1966). However, rather than assuming that a single model or method will be superior, ecologists could adopt a more pluralistic strategy.

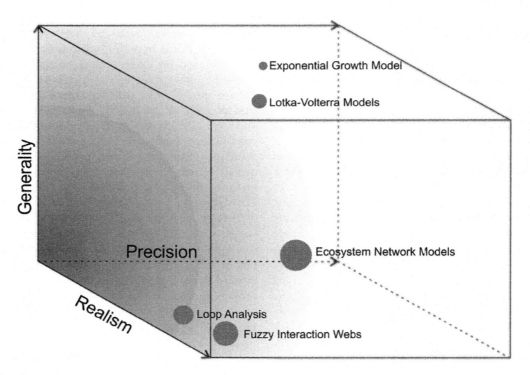

Figure 3.3 Methodological pluralism. Ecologists do not need to limit themselves to one type of approach, even in a single investigation. Models can differ in terms of generality (how many systems they apply to), realism (how many real-world parameters they contain) and precision (how finely specified their predictions are). The size of each circle represents how far along the realism axis a model is (larger circles are more realistic models). Using different models allows us to explore more of the space of possibility. Moreover, if these different models are independent, i.e. not based on the same assumptions, then if their outputs converge we can be more confident that the results are accurate (inferential robustness). Based on Levins (1966).

This pluralism can be achieved at two levels. At the basic level, it is important to recognise that each investigation occurs in a different context with different goals (Figure 3.3). Thus, in some cases generalisation will be more important, while in others predictive accuracy will be more important – each of these goals might render a different method optimal, such as models that aim at identifying a pattern versus models that aim at predicting within a particular system (Justus 2021; Levins 1966). Here are three examples:

- *The exponential growth model* (general and precise but not realistic) applies to many systems but is not very realistic. All populations *would* grow exponentially if there were no other factors limiting them, but many such factors are present in the real world.
- *Ecosystem network models* (realistic and precise but not general) incorporate many factors present in the real world, such as many of the ecosystem's populations and the interactions between them, but they are built each time for a particular system.
- *Loop analysis* (realistic and general but not precise) can incorporate many factors present in the real world and apply to many systems in the world, but their results (predictions) are not finely specified.

At a deeper level, ecologists can adopt a pluralistic strategy within a particular investigation. Here, the idea is that scientists should use multiple models to investigate a particular phenomenon (Reiners and Lockwood 2010). As long as the models are independent from each other, then they can cancel out, or at least mitigate, each other's errors and biases. If we are lucky, the model outputs will converge, yielding *inferential robustness*, which can increase our confidence in the models (Weisberg 2006). In Levins's words, '*truth is at the intersection of independent lies*' (Levins 1966).

In short, ecology is not an immature science; it is a difficult science. Ecological systems are surprising, irregular and mercurial. The scientists who manage to get information about them should be commended in their endeavours, even if they suffer setbacks and complications. Luckily, ecologists already possess the concepts and methods necessary to achieve high-quality research, though they may not always recognise it.

REFERENCES

Casper, B. B., and J. P. Castelli. 2007. Evaluating plant-soil feedback together with competition in a serpentine grassland. *Ecology Letters* 10:394–400. doi:10.1111/j.1461-0248.2007.01030.x

Colyvan, M., and L. R. Ginzburg. 2003. Laws of nature and laws of ecology. *Oikos* 101:649–653. doi:10.1034/j.1600-0706.2003.12349.x

Cooper, G. J. (ed.). 2003. *The science of the struggle for existence: On the foundations of ecology*. Cambridge: Cambridge University Press. doi:10.1017/CBO9780511720154.002

Cottee-Jones, H. E. W., and R. J. Whittaker. 2012. Perspective: The keystone species concept: A critical appraisal. *Frontiers of Biogeography* 4:117–127. doi:10.21425/F5FBG12533

Cuddington, K., S. Sobek-Swant, J. C. Crosthwaite, et al. 2018. Probability of emerald ash borer impact for Canadian cities and North America: A mechanistic model. *Biological Invasions* 20:2661–2677. doi:10.1007/s10530-018-1725-0

Douglas, H. 2009a. *Science, policy, and the value-free ideal*. Pittsburgh: University of Pittsburgh Press. doi:10.2307/j.ctt6wrc78

Douglas, H. 2009b. Reintroducing prediction to explanation. *Philosophy of Science* 76:444–463. doi:10.1086/648111

Douglas, H., and P. D. Magnus. 2013. State of the field: Why novel prediction matters. *Studies in History and Philosophy of Science* 44:580–589. doi:10.1016/j.shpsa.2013.04.001

Elliott-Graves, A. 2018. Generality and causal interdependence in ecology. *Philosophy of Science* 85:1102–1114. doi:10.1086/699698

Elliott-Graves, A. 2019. The future of predictive ecology. *Philosophical Topics* 47:65–82. doi:10.5840/philtopics20194714

Elliott-Graves, A. (2023). *Ecological complexity*. Cambridge: Cambridge University Press

Evans, M. R., V. Grimm, K. Johst, et al. 2013. Do simple models lead to generality in ecology? *Trends in Ecology and Evolution* 28:578–583. doi:10.1016/j.tree.2013.05.022

Godfrey-Smith, P. 2009. *Theory and reality*. Chicago: University of Chicago Press.

Goodman, N. 1955. *Fact, fiction and forecast*. Cambridge, MA: Harvard University Press.

Hempel, C. G., and P. Oppenheim. 1948. Studies in the logic of explanation. *Philosophy of Science* 15:135–175. doi:10.1086/286983

Hooker, C. (ed.). 2011. *Philosophy of complex systems*. Amsterdam: North Holland. doi:10.1016/C2009-0-06625-2

Justus, J. 2021. *The philosophy of ecology: An introduction*. Cambridge: Cambridge University Press. doi:10.1017/9781139626941

Kelly, J. F., and K. G. Horton. 2016. Toward a predictive macrosystems framework for migration ecology. *Global Ecology and Biogeography* 25:1159–1165. doi:10.1111/geb.12473

Kingsland, S. 1995. *Modeling nature*. Chicago: University of Chicago Press.

Kourany, J. 2003. A philosophy of science for the twenty-first century. *Philosophy of Science* 70:1–14. doi:10.1086/367864

Kuhn, T. S. 1962. *The structure of scientific revolutions*. Chicago: University of Chicago Press.

Lange, M. 2005. Ecological laws: What would they be and why would they matter? *Oikos* 110:394–403. doi:10.1111/j.0030-1299.2005.14110.x

Lawton, J. H. 1999. Are there general laws in ecology? *Oikos* 84:177–192.

Levin, S. A. 1998. Ecosystems and the biosphere as complex adaptive systems. *Ecosystems* 1:431–436. doi:10.1007/s100219900037

Levins, R. 1966. The strategy of model building in population biology. *American Scientist* 54:421–431. doi:10.2307/27836590

Levins, R. 1993. A response to Orzack and Sober: Formal analysis and the fluidity of science. *The Quarterly Review of Biology* 68:547–555. doi:10.1086/418302

Linquist, S., T. R. Gregory, T. A. Elliott, et al. 2016. Yes! There are resilient generalizations (or 'laws') in ecology. *The Quarterly Review of Biology* 91:119–131. doi:10.1086/686809

Loreau, M., S. Naeem, P. Inchausti, et al. 2001. Biodiversity and ecosystem functioning: Current knowledge and future challenges. *Science* 294:804–808. doi:10.1126/science.1064088

Matthewson, J. 2011. Trade-offs in model-building: A more target-oriented approach. *Studies in History and Philosophy of Science Part A* 42:324–333. doi:10.1016/j.shpsa.2010.11.040

Mayr, E. 1996. The autonomy of biology: The position of biology among the sciences. *The Quarterly Review of Biology* 71:97–106.

McMullin, E. 1982. Values in science. *PSA: Proceedings of the Biennial Meeting of the Philosophy of Science Association* 1982 2:2–28. doi:10.1086/psaprocbienmeetp.1982.2.192409

Mitchell, S. D. 2000. Dimensions of scientific law. *Philosophy of Science* 67:242–265. doi:10.1086/392774

Mitchell, S. D. 2003. *Biological complexity and integrative pluralism*. Cambridge: Cambridge University Press. doi:10.1017/CBO9780511802683

Odenbaugh, J. 2011. Complex ecological systems. In *Philosophy of complex systems*, ed. C. Hooker, 421–431. New York: Elsevier. doi:10.1016/B978-0-444-52076-0.50015-8

Okasha, S. 2002. *Philosophy of science: A very short introduction*. Oxford: Oxford University Press.

Peters, D. P. C., B. T. Bestelmeyer, and J. E. Herrick. 2006. Disentangling complex landscapes: New insights into arid and semiarid system dynamics. *BioScience* 56:491–501. doi:10.1641/0006-3568(2006)56[491:DCLNII]2.0.CO;2

Peters, R. H. 1991. *A critique for ecology*. Cambridge: Cambridge University Press.

Pimm, S. L. 1991. *The balance of nature?* Chicago: University of Chicago Press.

Popper, K. R. 1959. *The logic of scientific discovery*. New York: Basic Books.

Reiners, W. A., and J. A. Lockwood. 2020. *Philosophical foundations for the practices of ecology*. Cambridge: Cambridge University Press.

Reiss, J., and J. Sprenger. 2020. Scientific objectivity. In *The Stanford encyclopedia of philosophy*, ed. E. N. Zalta (Winter 2020 edition). https://plato.stanford.edu/archives/win2020/entries/scientific-objectivity/ (accessed 26 September 2022).

Shrader-Frechette, K., and E. D. McCoy. 1994. Applied ecology and the logic of case studies. *Philosophy of Science* 61:228–249.

Shrader-Frechette, K. S., and E. D. McCoy. 1993. *Method in ecology: Strategies for conservation*. Cambridge: Cambridge University Press.

Sobek-Swant, S., D. A. Kluza, K. Cuddington, and D. B. Lyons. 2012. Potential distribution of emerald ash borer: What can we learn from ecological niche models using Maxent and GARP? *Forest Ecology and Management* 281:23–31. doi:10.1016/j.foreco.2012.06.017

Strevens, M. 2004. The causal and unification approaches to explanation unified: Causally. *Noûs* 38:154–176. doi:10.1111/j.1468-0068.2004.00466.x

Weisberg, M. 2006. Robustness analysis. *Philosophy of Science* 73:730–742. doi:10.1086/518628

Woodward, J. 2003. *Making things happen: A theory of causal explanation.* Oxford: Oxford University Press. doi:10.1093/0195155270.001.0001

4

Rigorous ecology needs rigorous statistics

MICK KEOUGH AND GERRY QUINN

USING MODELS TO DISTINGUISH SIGNALS FROM NOISE

Most ecologists use data to answer questions or to develop new ones. When answering questions, we take a model or hypothesis about how the world works and compare it to data, to see whether the model is consistent with the data (Chapter 1).

In developing new questions, we typically take a broad verbal model with lots of possible explanations and use the data to refine those explanations into a smaller number with the most support. These explanations are often themselves questions that need to be challenged with further data, particularly when we are interested in inferring causal relationships.

The process of matching ecological models and data uses statistical analysis to help us distinguish between 'signals' (the ecological processes of interest) and background 'noise'. This step involves translating an ecological model into a formal statistical one. Analysis gives us confidence that we're not being fooled by noise (Gelman and Loken 2014) or by our preconceptions.

Our conclusions, decisions about next research steps and advice we might offer to end-users all rely on our ability to separate signal from noise and to characterise that signal accurately and precisely.

This task, common to most biological disciplines, is particularly difficult for ecologists because our background noise is complex and often large. Working on whole organisms integrates the noise at subcellular levels up, and community and ecosystem work adds further emergent properties. Sources of noise also broaden as we move from controlled laboratory situations to the field. As we try to establish study systems at meaningful spatial and temporal scales, pragmatic decisions mean that we often finish with small sample sizes (and low power) that hinder the separation of signal from noise.

Good study design enables us to reduce noise and increase the likelihood of discovering ecological effects, while the statistical analysis appropriate to that design allows us to draw valid conclusions about those effects from the data.

HARD, BUT CRITICAL

While we acknowledge the difficulty of the task of separating signal from noise, we need to respond to what our statistical analysis tells us and we need two aspects of analysis: the evidence that we are not being fooled – that is, there's a signal from the ecological effect of the process(es) under examination – and a description of the nature of that signal. When we know the signal, we can think about its ecological importance.

An ecological study does not exist in isolation. For many of us, it will be one step in a process towards deeper understanding of a topic, and we would like to know the steps that follow from the result. We also want peers to see how our work changes their understanding of the topic and how

DOI: 10.1201/9781003314332-4

it might influence their next steps. For example, if the work is at the behest of a natural resource management agency, we want to know what the results mean for the management problem that prompted the research – should some management options be moved aside and others raised in priority?

At a personal level, the conclusions we draw from a statistical analysis guide our future research path. Errors are easy to make, and common. If we get fooled, we are also likely to fool others who read our work. We then need to rely on the self-correcting nature of scientific discovery, which recent reviews show not to work especially well, because repeating studies is rare (e.g. Fidler et al. 2017). At best we move briefly down an incorrect path, until our understanding is corrected. At worst, we and our peers are sent down an incorrect path for an extended period. The conclusions from an analysis also influence where we disseminate the work. In academia, exciting results are submitted to higher profile journals and more mundane results to lower ranked journals. Inconclusive results may lead to non-publication, entailing considerable 'research waste' (Purgar et al. 2022). Where we publish still matters, particularly for those early in their careers, as long as selection panels, funding agencies and promotion criteria keep using relatively uninformative journal-based metrics rather than consideration of the impact of individual research outputs.

Robust ecology relies on rigorous statistical analysis. For this link to be strong, we need to be very clear about the logical and statistical issues involved and aware of the pitfalls that can weaken it. Statistics is something that requires deep thought and care: it is not something that should be done by accepting defaults in software packages or thoughtless selection of drop-down menu options. Some methodological issues are relatively recent, while others are recidivists. We'll outline a few of these issues and suggest ways of avoiding pitfalls. We will do this using examples from ecological experiments, while recognising that many of the issues are also applicable to other kinds of data collection.

The past decade has seen an increase in the diversity of approaches ecologists use for data analysis, particularly the use of mixed effect models and more sophisticated methods for model selection. Much of this diversity is summarised in the book edited by Fox et al. (2015), *Ecological*

Statistics: Contemporary Theory and Application, and reflected in dedicated journals such as the *British Ecological Society*'s now open-source *Methods in Ecology and Evolution*.

SOME THINGS DO NOT CHANGE

As the range of methods expands, some issues around statistical analysis still bubble away. We still argue about the 'right' way to draw statistical inferences, most notably in the case of the debate between frequentist versus Bayesian approaches (the 'statistics wars'; Mayo 2018). These arguments are like low-level disturbances, recurring without obvious impact. In broad biological and, within that, ecological circles, the discussion can be relatively superficial, but there are some important issues of statistical philosophy involved (Spanos 2019). Each approach has its strengths and weaknesses, and a logically coherent framework can be developed for each (e.g. Mayo 2018; Gelman and Shalizi 2013). It is critical that we understand exactly how the different statistical approaches are used to answer ecological questions. Robust conclusions depend far more on how well data are collected and getting the design and statistical models right than on the inferential approach used, a point also made by McCarthy (2015). The right way to analyse data is to fit a statistical model appropriate to the data that is also linked directly to the ecological model or question.

Dubious statistical practices are highlighted periodically. The unethical sifting through data to find a response variable that is 'statistically significant' – fishing or P-hacking – is still a concern and can be hard to detect. As we use more complex mixed models, there is more scope for this behaviour by manipulating the classification of predictors as fixed or random (Box 4.1). Preregistration of questions, sampling designs and statistical models can help prevent this problem (Gelman and Loken 2014), although its implementation can be difficult or flawed (Claesen et al. 2021).

Within these broad statistical discussions, there has been some positive change. The most notable one is the shift away from using the term 'statistically significant' (Wasserstein et al. 2019), which includes several issues, including the meaning of significant, the use of P-values and thresholds for separating signal from noise. These issues are not new, and have been discussed by ecologists (e.g. the papers curated by Ellison et al. (2014)). For ecologists, there are four important points:

- 'Statistically significant' indicates that a signal has been detected in the data, but does not reflect the biological importance of that signal. A disappointingly high proportion of results sections of ecological papers and theses start with *we found a significant effect of…*', usually referring to a threshold like $P < 0.05$. This description does not convey the strength of the effect, which is likely the thing of most interest to readers.
- Conversely, a statistically non-significant result is not automatically evidence of a weak or non-existent effect. It means only that no signal has been detected; whether that result is because the signal is weak or we have limited detection capacity requires further work.
- P-values, while frequently misused, can be an important part of an analytical toolbox if interpreted correctly and used in conjunction with measures such as effect size (Wasserstein et al. 2019).
- Thresholds, including those based on P-values, can be part of deciding whether we are being fooled by noise or see a signal, again if they are used carefully (Mayo and Hand 2022). Regardless of how we do it, we need to make decisions about signal and noise in deciding how we use the results of an ecological study.

Describing results in biological (rather than statistical) terms, which are linked to the original questions, has the added benefit of making us think more about effects that matter for the ecological question. Ideally, that thinking happens during study planning, rather than when crafting discussions after data analysis.

CHANGING (STATISTICAL) LANDSCAPES FOR ECOLOGISTS

Irrespective of whether they use frequentist or Bayesian inference, modern ecologists have access to a much wider range of statistical tools than the traditional normal-based linear regression and 'ANOVA' models, and their generalised extensions to include binomial and Poisson distributions, that dominated previously. These include the widespread use of mixed effects models, along with species distribution models, generalised additive models that relax the requirement for models to be linear, boosted regression trees, etc. Of these, we will focus here on mixed effects models, since they are a widespread example of where new methods provide new pitfalls for the unwary. This broadening of approaches has been accompanied by a shift in statistical software, from a range of commercial packages to widespread use of R, which has benefits and challenges.

Mixed effects models have become popular among ecologists in part because they can be applied to some common experimental and sampling designs that rely on techniques like blocking, partial nesting and repeated measurements to reduce noise and make more effective use of scarce resources. These designs have been used widely in field experiments, but in the past they have been commonly analysed by shoehorning data into statistical models that assume normality, homogeneity of variance and independence of errors (e.g. ANOVA). The complication is that these designs have observations 'clustered' into experimental units such as subjects, plots, etc., and observations within clusters are more likely to be correlated than those in different clusters. Mixed effects models allow errors to be correlated, rather than be random and independent (Gelman et al. 2020).

When we try to generalise ecological results by extending our own studies to other places and times, perform coordinated large-scale experimental replication and conduct meta-analyses, we are asking whether ecological interactions vary. Mixed effects models are appropriate for these tasks.

The shift to mixed effects models can be liberating, as they can, depending on the software package used, accommodate a range of correlation patterns within the data, so they can allow us to model the data more precisely (Ives 2022). They rely on the classification of predictor variables as fixed or random (see Box 4.1). In a single experimental design, a random effect typically involves plots, times or subject organisms, while in coordinated studies, it is the individual site-specific data collection, and in a meta-analysis, the individual studies are seen as coming from a larger population of potential ecological studies, from each of which an ecological process is measured. Misclassification of effects can be an important source of error, usually treating random effects as fixed, treating them

BOX 4.1: Fixed versus random effects

When we build a statistical model for ecological data, one important decision is whether each predictor in the model is fixed or random. It is important because it influences the structure of the model and how effects are assessed. It also decides how we interpret the analysis results. Fixed versus random has been a subject for discussion in the statistical literature for some time, with no clear resolution. For ecologists, Bolker (2015) provided a good summary table of criteria, illustrated here for a categorical predictor.

An effect is fixed where:

- The groups we use are all those of interest.
- We are interested in comparing the effects of some of these specific groups.
- If we did the study again, we would choose the same groups.
- Some authors calculate the ratio of groups used (p) to groups available (P) and use it to determine the form of the statistical model, with $p/P \Rightarrow 1$ for fixed, 0 for random.

A random effect is where:

- The groups have been chosen from some larger population of potential levels.
- The individual groups are not of much interest, but their variance might be.
- We have some interest in generalising from the groups used to the larger population.
- If we did the study again, it is unlikely that the same groups would be selected.

The idea of random effects allowing extrapolation, but inference from fixed effects being restricted, matters when trying to generate more general or more complex ecological understanding. If we document a particular set of processes in one study, our next step might be to see if those processes act similarly in other contexts. This might take the form of asking if the processes vary in different specific contexts or wanting to estimate the variance in ecological processes across space or time.

Statistically, any interaction that includes a random predictor is also a random effect.

---

inconsistently within single studies or when random effects are inappropriately omitted from statistical models.

It can be complicated

A specific predictor might be considered fixed or random depending on the aims of the study and the hypotheses of interest (e.g. Gelman and Hill 2006; West et al. 2015), and Quinn and Keough (2023) provide a more extended discussion (their Chapter 10). For the example in Box 4.2, we could view sites as fixed or random, depending on how we wanted to use the results. This can be the cause of much confusion.

If we include time (e.g. months or years) as a factor, we might wish to generalise to other times than the ones we use. However, it is hard to define a statistical population of times from which we could randomly draw specific values for our study. It might be possible for organisms with very short life spans, but hard to see choosing years randomly for long-lived organisms and still being funded or awarded a degree. The other problem with time is that even if we estimate temporal variances at the end of our study, the statistical population of times can only include past times. Generalising to the future requires many more assumptions than just in our statistical analysis.

A chance to make mistakes

The classification of an effect as fixed or random can alter how we fit and interpret statistical models, and random effects counterintuitively alter how we assess fixed ones. Redesignating a random effect as fixed typically results in some other fixed effects being assessed with more degrees of freedom. Only when we are clear how particular effects of interest will be evaluated can we make sensible decisions about where to allocate resources in our design.

Rigorous ecology needs rigorous statistics 53

BOX 4.2: A complex ecological design, its rationale and implications for analysis

We'll use the example of a field experiment on rocky shores to show the practical decisions that need to be made when designing a study and some sources of error in analysis and interpretation.

The research question was how an ecological 'engineer', the habitat-forming alga *Hormosira banksii*, recovers from physical disturbances varying in intensity and spatial pattern (Wootton and Keough 2016). Intensity was three levels of biomass removal, removed in a uniform, tightly clumped or random fashion, giving nine treatment combinations as a 3×3 factorial design. Two additional treatments were 'benchmarks' (or 'controls'), no additional disturbance and complete canopy removal. Recovery was measured at five times.

DESIGN ISSUES

1. Resources
   So far, we have a design with 11 treatments and five times, applied to $60\times40\,cm$ experimental units. For a completely randomised design, we would need $55n$ units on the shore, each of which would need to be marked (by drilling into the rock). In this study, we chose $n=4$. This would take lots of space, time and resources. An alternative design would be to measure recovery through time in the same experimental units, so each unit is recorded five times, and we only need $11n$ units.

2. Noise reduction
   Rocky shores are heterogeneous and spreading experimental units randomly across a wide area could result in lots of variation. To account for this noise, the experimental units were placed into four blocks of 11 units, with the blocks spread across the shore, but units within each block much closer together. This decision does not save resources but is intended to improve our ability to detect disturbance signals.

3. Generalising our results
   We, and coastal managers, would like to know if we can generalise results from this kind of experiment, so this design was repeated at another shore 10km away.

STATISTICAL ANALYSIS ISSUES

1. Correlated observations
   There are two ways in which observations of canopy cover may be correlated with each other. We have time series of five values, and an experimental unit in one of our treatments is physically closer to units from different treatments in the same block than to other units of the same treatment.

2. Fixed and random effects
   Some effects are clearly fixed – we established the treatments and chose when to sample recovery. Other effects are clearly random – the blocks were spread haphazardly across the shore, and the experimental units within each block were assigned randomly to treatments. We used two sites – shores separated by sandy stretches and a few kilometres apart, to assess generality. They could be considered fixed or random effects – they were chosen from a 'population' of geologically similar rocky shores, so they could be random, but with only two, it is not clear what that larger population might be, so they might better be considered fixed (Bolker 2015).

(Continued)

WHERE COULD WE GO WRONG?

1. Forget about the repeated measurements and fit a model for a completely randomised design. There are problems here:
   - Our overall tests of the disturbance treatments have roughly five times more degrees of freedom than there are independent replicate units (i.e. we have one of the forms of pseudoreplication).
   - The assumption of independence of errors will be violated, and the consequences are hard to assess.

2. Omit blocks from our model
   - Degrees of freedom assigned to blocks are now pooled into the residual.
   - We should still be wary about assumption of independence.
   - If the spatial heterogeneity at the scale of blocks matters, we now have more background noise and less sensitivity.

3. Analyse shores as a fixed effect but discuss it as a random effect.

There are two temptations to resist during analysis and interpretation; both involve flipping predictors between fixed and random. The first is to complete the study using fixed effects models but then generalise the results as if we had random effects. Our sense from the literature is that interpreting fixed effects as if they were random is common, but the reverse is rare.

A second situation is where a designed random effect is analysed as fixed. There are rare circumstances when this may be appropriate, largely when unexpected events disrupted data collection (Quinn and Keough 2023). Our impression is that changes at the analysis stage happen when there were design errors, and it is realised that tests for specific effects are weak or, most worryingly, as a form of *P*-hacking, producing a 'statistically significant' effect that was absent when a model with the right combination of fixed and random effects was used. So, getting it right matters, because it can affect the inferences that we draw from our results.

Such reclassification of predictors is inappropriate because the interpretation is not consistent with the model fitting. It is sometimes done deliberately, we suspect, as a way of 'selling' the results to a broader audience or higher impact journal, on the basis that the results are broadly applicable to other situations. The first temptation should be resisted, but it should be dealt with by vigilant referees and readers. The second is more worrying. Preregistration of experimental designs and statistical models is the best way to prevent this behaviour.

As an example of some of the issues around using linear mixed models, consider a standard repeated measures design, such as we might use to follow recovery from disturbance (Box 4.2), with areas sampled over time through their recovery. The observations in these data are not independent, because there are 'sets' derived from physical plots. We might expect that observations from the same plot would be more similar than those from plots further away and that observations closer in time would be more similar than those further apart. A 'traditional' approach to analysing this design requires quite restrictive assumptions about the patterns of covariance in the data, the compound symmetry or sphericity assumption familiar to many (see Quinn and Keough 2023).

Mixed effects models based on maximum likelihood estimation require us to be explicit about fixed and random effects, are more robust for complex or unbalanced designs, and allow more flexibility in data analysis, but in their simplest form they rely on response variables that are normal or can be transformed to approximate normality.

Like linear fixed effects models, they can be expanded to consider biological responses that do not follow normal distributions as generalised linear mixed models (GLMMs) and relationships that are not linear as generalised additive mixed models (GAMMs). While these approaches broaden our horizons, they are not a panacea.

Somewhat cynically, a bigger toolbox allows the unthinking user more chances to use an inappropriate tool and perhaps get the wrong answer.

GLMMs and GAMMs are inherently more complex and approaches to analysis and reporting practices are less standardised than in the more familiar 'make normal and fit an ordinary least squares model' approach. There is also the perception that the ability to deal with correlated data can solve the problem of some forms of pseudoreplication, but this is not the case – the same logical problems exist (Arnqvist 2020).

Along with the broadening of statistical methods, there has been a striking shift to R as the software package of choice. The R user community provides a bewildering diversity of packages, and it is not uncommon to come across multiple packages or ways to fit the same statistical model. The amount of modelling guidance varies with packages, but we suspect many users simply google their design to find appropriate R code. This approach should be a major positive step – anything that encourages us as ecologists to think more about how we fit statistical models to our data is an improvement over 'cookie-cutter' approaches. However, just using someone else's code could also be seen as using a cookie-cutter approach, albeit a more unusually shaped one. In the absence of the validation and well-documented examples associated with standard analyses, it is critical that we examine code carefully and check that it is specifying the model we believe it to be.

THERE ARE SOME 'NEW' CHALLENGES

There are some emerging aspects of statistical analysis that challenge ecologists. We see the increased attention on the nature of ecological signals – effects – rather than merely significance as a positive step. These effects can be complex in many cases because we know that most ecological processes do not act independently of each other (i.e. interactions are important, and many are modulated by external environmental factors). If we cater to this complexity, the result can be designs with multiple predictors and combinations of fixed and random predictors, as in the example of Box 4.2. With this complexity, predicting and measuring effects become difficult.

Predicting effects should be an important part of study planning. We try to make sure we collect enough data to answer questions or distinguish between competing models. The framework used most for doing this is statistical power analysis. It will be familiar to most ecologists as a technique linked to hypothesis testing approaches, particularly specification of decision-error rates, but there are also Bayesian approaches. In principle, it is a very useful concept, but in practice it is difficult to apply except to the most simple of cases. Using power analysis to determine an appropriate sample size requires several things – specifying the exact statistical model that we will fit (good practice), understanding the background noise in the data (desirable) and identifying the kind of effect it is important to detect (crucial). When we have interactions, especially involving categorical predictors with many categories, identifying this effect gets difficult. As discussed earlier (in Chapters 1 and 3), our understanding of many ecosystems is not at a stage that allows precise predictions, and complex interactions can take many forms. These different forms can vary widely in their detectability, so the amount of sampling required depends on the form of that interaction. It is telling that most guides to power analysis focus on simple effects, rather than interactions! Specifying a meaningful effect size is a task that most biologists, not just ecologists, find very difficult. However, it is necessary for meaningful study planning. It could be argued that doing a study without this step is still a planning decision, albeit to detect any effect larger than our sample size and noise allow! We should also be thinking about whether effects are ecologically meaningful as part of interpreting analyses and crafting discussions, anyway, and we argue strongly for moving that thinking to the planning stage.

There are multiple, often software-specific, methods for obtaining ML/REML estimates of random effects, and providing a measure of uncertainty around them, and they can produce different answers (Box 4.3; Bolker 2015). Estimating random interaction effects is challenging, even though they might be effects of most interest (e.g. random slopes in multi-level regression models) and there is no simple recommendation for best practice in interpreting the effects. For example, our starting point in the case study of Box 4.2 could be the interaction between disturbance pattern and intensity (a fixed interaction), and whether that interaction varies between sites (a fixed or random effect, depending on how we frame the question). Technically, it is the interaction between these factors and time that assesses the recovery pathway

BOX 4.3: Estimating random effects – some nuts and bolts

Linear models are fitted in various ways, most commonly ordinary least squares (OLS) and maximum likelihood (ML), plus its variant restricted maximum likelihood (REML).

Random effects are usually defined in terms of the amount of variation that can be attributed statistically to them. OLS has been used in the past, but it does not produce reliable estimates or confidence intervals for random effects when sample sizes vary across the design, as is often the case with ecological data. ML and REML are preferred. Within a mixed model, ML is best for estimating fixed effects, but REML is more reliable for random effects. This can make the analysis stage messy when fixed and random effects are both of interest.

Added complications for ecologists include:

- The terminology for mixed models can be confusing, including the formal model equations.
- Different software, and even different packages within R, use different methods for fitting mixed effects models and obtaining ML/REML estimates of their fixed and random effects (e.g. penalised quasi-likelihood, Laplace approximation, etc.: see West et al. 2015; Bolker 2015). These methods can result in different parameter estimates and confidence intervals, especially for complex models with interactions involving random effects.
- The ability to incorporate different covariance structures varies across packages, as does the interpretability of what are often confusing warning messages

---

from disturbance. After assessing these effects, we might move to site×intensity and type×pattern interactions.

The other issue to emerge recently with implications for ecologists is the replication crisis, originating in psychology, but spreading through scientific disciplines, and possibly to ecology (Fraser et al. 2020). At its core has been the inability to replicate influential results when studies are repeated, which incorporates several aspects already touched on here, including selective data analysis to produce 'statistically significant' results and failure to design studies to resolve questions unambiguously. Sadly, it is also linked to apparent fraud (see https://retractionwatch.com/). For ecologists, the idea of replication is more complex and scale-dependent (Shavit and Ellison 2017). It can mean creating multiple instances of the same conditions within a study (e.g. experimental treatments), so we can be confident about identifying effects and excluding noise as an explanation. It can also mean repeating studies to compare conclusions.

Replicating a study, in the sense of repeating it exactly, is not possible in ecology, because another study, even if done in the same laboratory or field site, will be under different background environmental conditions, at a different time and with

organisms that were likely different genetically from those used in the earlier study. We suspect that most ecologists would not expect to get the same result, and in many ways, it may be more interesting if a strong ecological effect in one study disappears or reverses in another, because that suggests that the ecological effect is context dependent, and this topic is explored in greater depth in Chapter 5 (see Catford et al. 2022).

A more informative way to view the repeating of a study, using the same methods, is that it helps us generalise ecological ideas by determining how consistent they are across space and time – either testing context dependence or estimating the variation in ecological effects, as in the example of Box 4.2. We need to be conscious of two design aspects – replicating a study done at one place and time sufficiently to characterise the ecological effects in question, and then repeating the study enough times and places to be able to measure the variance of these effects or doing the study under different fixed conditions to measure the dependence of the ecological processes on other factors. Filazzola and Cahill (2021) explore some of these issues in more detail, and there are emerging protocols for large-scale coordinated repetition of experiments to measure context dependence (Borer et al. 2014).

A FIELD GUIDE TO GETTING IT WRONG

We have so far outlined several ways that we might go astray.

How common are errors and poor statistical practice in ecology? It is hard to estimate the rates reliably. In the best example, the issues of pseudoreplication, confounding and inappropriate replication, introduced by Hurlbert (1984), one follow-up study a decade later (Heffner et al. 1996) found little had changed and Arnqvist (2020) cites several examples elsewhere in biology that suggest the issue is still common.

Our impression is that other problems raised earlier, such as confusing fixed and random effects and the persistence of 'statistical significance' rather than focusing on ecological effects, are common. The extent of these problems is hard to assess, because the worst examples we encounter tend to be at the review stage, and papers with substantial flaws may vanish. Whether or not we can quantify the flaws, each inconclusive study is a waste of resources, and when the flaws preclude publication, there is a cost to individual ecologists as well. Our goal is to identify the risks and avoid them.

A way to structure this risk avoidance is to think of the examination of an ecological idea as formulating a series of increasingly specific models. An ecological explanation or hypothesis is a simplified explanation of an ecological phenomenon. This initial model is often a qualitative description (e.g. growth of estuarine cordgrass is affected by salinity (S) and insect herbivory (H)). We'd like to know if this model is plausible, so the best way is to confront that model with data (Hilborn and Mangel 1997). There are various ways to do it (Chapter 3), but the most convincing is to do an experiment – create a scenario in which salinity and herbivory vary. A mismatch between expectations and data would expose our ecological model's shortcomings.

The comparison of our ecological model to data cannot be done directly, and we need to translate the ecological model into a statistical one, which we can fit to the data. In this example, one model is $G = \mu + S + H + HS + \varepsilon$.

This model will be familiar to many. It is a linear model, relating cordgrass growth to an overall population average growth (μ), plus independent effects of salinity and herbivory, plus a combined effect of salinity and herbivory, plus background 'noise' represented by the error terms (ε). For our statistical analysis, we want to know how well this model fits the experimental data and whether it fits better than models lacking HS, HS and H, HS and S, or HS, H and S.

Our goal is to use the result of this model fitting to make confident conclusions about our ecological model, and we need several conditions to be satisfied. These conditions include, with potential errors in italics:

- In our data, we should not be able to identify competing explanations that could produce the same pattern. In the cordgrass example, creating our experimental treatments should have only involved changing salinity and herbivory, and not introducing artefacts associated with how we made these changes (i.e. we have appropriate controls). *If there are multiple explanations, your ecological model is actually a group of models that cannot be separated.*
- The statistical model must match the biological one. *Your analysis might give you a clear answer, but to a different question and not relevant to your ecological idea.*
- The statistical model must match the structure of your data. In most cases, problems happen when additional, often random, predictors should have been in the model. In the cordgrass example, we might model the growth of individual leaves without explicitly including the plant from which they arose and the experimental plot in which they grew. *Your analysis probably appears more sensitive than it really is.*
- All statistical models have assumptions, often about the background noise. For example, the linear model above assumes that the ε values (error terms for individual observations) are independent, follow a specified distribution (normal, Poisson, etc.) and have a specific pattern of variation (e.g. equal variances among groups). *If these assumptions are not met, estimates of effects may be unreliable, along with conclusions about how well different models fit the data.*
- We should be confident about the conclusions (i.e. we have collected enough data to distinguish between different models and/or estimate the effects confidently). *If we have not, rather than confident conclusions about (e.g.*

BOX 4.4: Ways of looking at pseudoreplication, the problem that won't go away

We will stay with the cordgrass example. Let us suppose, in the worst case, that insect herbivory could only be manipulated in large plots, and we set up our experiment with eight large plots, each with one combination of two herbivory and four salinity levels. Within each plot, we measure the growth of 20 plants. Everything is normal, so we fit a linear model and generate a familiar analysis of variance table. We will illustrate the issues using F-ratios to test hypotheses. Let us pretend for now that the experimental unit is the plant rather than the plot.

Source of variation	Degrees of freedom	Denominator for test
Herbivory	1	Residual
Salinity	3	Residual
Herbivory×salinity	3	Residual
Residual (error)	152	

This might fill us with joy, as, for example, an F-test with 3, 152 degrees of freedom is powerful. This joy is unwarranted, and may even turn to despair with appropriate analysis.

Here is why the above analysis is wrong:

1. Clear thinking about replication means that the 'treatment' was to exclude herbivores (and vary salinity) at a *plot* scale, and we have only done this once for each combination. This experiment is unreplicated. Stop, do not pass Go, and regret all those plants tagged and measured unnecessarily. If desperate, we could make crude tests about the simple (independent) effects of herbivory and salinity using mean values for each plot.
2. Our 'replicate' observations share two features, the same combination of herbivory and salinity, and whatever other things associated with that specific plot – the things we did to alter herbivory and salinity, the ecological history of that plot, its sediment characteristics, tidal elevation, etc. We might perform the analysis, but we cannot separate the effects of herbivory and salinity from these other things. Our explanations are confounded, and several ecological models could explain the data.
3. If we want to include all of the observations in the analysis, we need a more complex model that includes plots: $G=\mu+H+S+HS+P(HS)+\varepsilon$. We could fit that model to the data:

Source of variation	Degrees of freedom	Denominator for test
Herbivory	1	Plots
Salinity	3	Plots
Herbivory×salinity	3	Plots
Plots within HS combinations	0	Residual
Residual (error) – variation within plots	152	

Looking at this model makes the problem stark. With $n=1$ plot per treatment combination, the degrees of freedom, $4*2*(n-1)$, is 0. We have no test for the effects of herbivory and salinity, unless we are willing to assume that the small-scale variation within plots is a good proxy for larger scale variation (see Chapter 5). Our original statistical model does not match the data structure, and when we use the right model, it breaks down. Harking back to original discussions, plots are a random effect that must be included in the statistical model.

the effect of herbivory), we have a third outcome – we cannot tell. This third outcome might be expressed as very wide intervals around estimates of effects or low power around tests of specific effects. Both represent wasted resources.

- Missteps at any of these points mean that we cannot link the statistical model back to the original ecological model or idea – we have not challenged that idea strongly, or severely, in Mayo's (2018) approach.

There are two areas of high risk in this process. We have already touched on them, and they are related – misunderstanding replication and mismatch of statistical models to data structure (and ecological models).

Replication within studies is fundamental to statistical analysis – observing ecological responses under repeated instances of the same set of predictor variables is how we estimate the amount of noise that is unrelated to the predictors and estimate ecological effects confidently. Knowing this noise allows us to interpret patterns in the data when values of the predictors change (e.g. in an experiment). Estimates of background noise need to be representative of the noise in the overall (statistical) population and estimated confidently enough to allow good separation of signal and noise. The repeated instances should be independent occurrences of the same situation – multiple experimental or sampling units.

Multiple observations within the same experimental or sampling unit are not independent. In an experiment, they can tell us about the noise within that experimental unit (plot, cage, pot, etc.), but they tell us nothing about the variation between different units. Observations that are drawn from within individual sampling or experimental units (i.e. subsamples) are the source of one of the best known and persistent design and analysis flaws, pseudoreplication (Hurlbert 1984). At its most egregious, inappropriately using subsamples as true experimental or sampling units in an analysis can dramatically shrink confidence intervals around effects and greatly and erroneously increase the chance of gaining 'statistically significant' results from hypothesis tests. We can look at this issue in three ways using the framework we've outlined in Box 4.4, but the message is clear – the link between statistical model and ecological model is badly broken.

The example of Box 4.4 introduces the other main area for making mistakes – mixing up fixed and random effects and what we do with random effects included to reduce noise. Including random effects into a fixed effects model changes how we estimate and test the fixed effects, e.g. in a two-factor design, the effect of the fixed factor is tested against the residual if the other factor is fixed but tested against the interaction with fewer df if the other factor is random. Getting the effects classified correctly is an essential part of fitting the statistical model and being sure it gives the answers of interest, rather than answers to different questions. Our impression is that random effects are more often misclassified as fixed than vice versa, and the net effect is usually to increase the likelihood of a 'statistically significant' effect when testing hypotheses or inappropriately narrow confidence intervals around effects.

Ecologists generally include random effects in data collection, as a tool to reduce noise or as part of assessing the generality of ideas, and when subsampling has been used. Subsampling is used when whole treatment units are too large or expensive to measure, and several subsamples can provide a reliable estimate of a treatment unit's state. When used for noise reduction, there has been discussion whether a random effect that accounts for very little variation should be omitted from the model and a simpler model fitted to the data. This simpler model could be seen as setting the random effect to zero or pooling it with the residual variation. Opinions differ on this approach (West et al. 2015; Janky 2000). In the example of Box 4.2, if we focus on the treatments that represent the nine combinations of disturbance intensity and pattern and the four blocks, we have three fixed effects (intensity, pattern and intensity×pattern) and three random effects (blocks, blocks×intensity and blocks×pattern), so we are 'sacrificing' degrees of freedom to remove medium-grained (Chapter 5) environmental noise. Would we be better off excluding some of the random effects? The answer depends in part on our aims – are we trying to assess which predictors are important or do we want to find the most parsimonious model?

We have three pieces of advice:

- If the random predictors were part of the design structure (e.g. the blocks in Box 4.2), we would be reluctant to drop them. If they were measured as an additional variable and not part of the design structure, we could consider dropping them from the model. We would only do that when we are confident that those random effects explain very little variation.

- If the random effects are associated with experimental or sampling units from which subsamples were taken, they should never be dropped, because that would effectively treat the subsamples as true units, creating the issues associated with inappropriate replication (Colegrave and Ruxton 2017; Arnqvist 2020).
- One valuable step at the analysis stage is to look at the true replication in the data, and if there are subsamples of the replicate units, aggregate them into summary statistics for each replicate unit when preparing data files for formal analysis. This step has the dual benefits of reducing the likelihood of artificially inflating degrees of freedom and making the response variable more likely to match the assumptions of the statistical model (e.g. through the 'central limit theorem').

SO WHAT?

We know how to avoid pitfalls in study design and data analysis.

It does not require new approaches, but application of what is often touted as criteria for strong inference. Somewhat pithily: think clearly, think in advance and think before you analyse.

The first part of thinking clearly is not statistical, but about the logic of enquiry. The ecological question the phenomenon and its possible explanation(s) – must be described clearly; and we need to think clearly and critically about the kind of data we need to distinguish between different models or explanations.

As we move to data collection and statistical analysis, there is a sequence of decisions to be made, and they should be made before data are collected.

That sequence could be framed as a series of questions:

- What (ecological) question do you hope to answer with your data?
- Describe the structure of your sampling:

  - What kind of data would answer the question?
  - What are the experimental or sampling units?
  - Should other predictors be included to reduce noise?
- What kinds of ecological responses will you record?
- What randomisation procedures will you use?
- What statistical model will you fit to your data? If you'll be using a linear model of some kind, write it out.
  - Are there interactions between predictors?
  - Which predictors are fixed effects, and which are random?
- What are the assumptions of this model? Are some assumptions more important than others?
- How many samples are required to confidently distinguish an ecologically important effect from noise?

These steps should all occur before you start. It can help to treat them as a formal checklist, even if we have not moved to formalised protocols such as the PRISMA scheme for meta-analysis (O'Dea et al. 2021).

Doing this 'pre-analysis' makes us well placed for when we have data, and it should speed things up. In the field, however, things will often go wrong, and some of our initial expectations (e.g. about data distributions and variances) may prove to be inaccurate. We may need to adjust our statistical analysis to account for additional messiness, and check data for outliers, assumptions, etc.

We must resist the temptation to change the model we use to improve our chances of getting a 'desirable' result. Transparency about our analysis is essential and is an argument for preregistration. Preregistration does not preclude changing the analysis, but it pushes us to explain any changes. The recent trend towards availability of raw data and, where relevant, R code, also improves confidence in the statistical analysis.

The last check we should do is when interpreting the results – and we need to remain vigilant here – particularly remembering earlier decisions about fixed and random effects. We need to be sure that ecological and statistical models are interpreted consistently.

Collecting data to answer ecological questions, particularly in the field, is messy, and there are pitfalls. Those pitfalls can be avoided. We can avoid some of the mess through careful design. Statistical analysis needs to be flexible, rather than recipe based, while making sure that ecological and statistical models are tightly linked. We should be our own harshest critics.

REFERENCES

Arnqvist, G. 2020. Mixed models offer no freedom from degrees of freedom. *Trends in Ecology and Evolution* 35:329–335. doi:10.1016/j.tree.2019.12.004

Bolker, B. M. 2015. Linear and generalized linear mixed models. In *Ecological statistics: Contemporary theory and application*, eds G. A. Fox, S. Negrete-Yankelevich and V. J. Sosa, 309–334. Oxford: Oxford University Press.

Borer, E. T., W. S. Harpole, P. B. Adler, et al. 2014. Finding generality in ecology: A model for globally distributed experiments. *Methods in Ecology and Evolution* 5:65–73. doi:10.1111/2041-210x.12125

Catford, J. A., J. R. U. Wilson, P. Pysek, et al. 2022. Addressing context dependence in ecology. *Trends in Ecology and Evolution* 37:158–170. doi:10.1016/j.tree.2021.09.007

Claesen, A., S. Gomes, F. Tuerlinckx, and W. Vanpaemel. 2021. Comparing dream to reality: An assessment of adherence of the first generation of preregistered studies. *Royal Society Open Science* 8:211037. doi:10.1098/rsos.211037

Colegrave, N., and G. D. Ruxton. 2017. Statistical model specification and power: Recommendations on the use of test-qualified pooling in analysis of experimental data. *Proceedings of the Royal Society B-Biological Sciences* 284:20161850. doi:10.1098/rspb.2016.1850

Fidler, F., Y. E. Chee, B. C. Wintle, et al. 2017. Metaresearch for evaluating reproducibility in ecology and evolution. *BioScience* 67:282–289. doi:10.1093/biosci/biw159

Filazzola, A., and J. F. Cahill. 2021. Replication in field ecology: Identifying challenges and proposing solutions. *Methods in Ecology and Evolution* 12:1780–1792. doi:10.1111/2041-210x.13657

Fox, G. A., S. NegreteYankelevich, and V. J. Sosa, eds. 2015. *Ecological statistics: Contemporary theory and application*. Oxford: Oxford University Press.

Fraser, H., A. Barnett, T. H. Parker, and F. Fidler. 2020. The role of replication studies in ecology. *Ecology and Evolution* 10:5197–5207. doi:10.1002/ece3.6330

Gelman, A., J. Hill, and A. Vehtari. 2020. *Regression and other stories*. Cambridge: Cambridge University Press. doi: 10.1017/9781139161879

Gelman, A., and E. Loken. 2014. The statistical crisis in science. *American Scientist* 102:460–465. doi:10.1511/2014.111.460

Gelman, A., and C. R. Shalizi. 2013. Philosophy and the practice of Bayesian statistics. *British Journal of Mathematical and Statistical Psychology* 66:8–38. doi:10.1111/j.2044-8317.2011.02037.x

Gotelli, N. J., and A. M. Ellison. 2012. *A primer of ecological statistics*. 2nd edn. Sunderland: Sinauer.

Heffner, R. A., M. J. Butler, and C. K. Reilly. 1996. Pseudoreplication revisited. *Ecology* 77:2558–2562. doi:10.2307/2265754

Hilborn, R., and M. Mangel. 1997. *The ecological detective: Confronting models with data*. Princeton: Princeton University Press.

Hurlbert, S. H. 1984. Pseudoreplication and the design of ecological field experiments. *Ecological Monographs* 54:187–211. doi:10.2307/1942661

Ives, A. R. 2022. Random errors are neither: On the interpretation of correlated data. *Methods in Ecology and Evolution* 13:2092–2105. doi:10.1111/2041-210X.13971

Janky, D. G. 2000. Sometimes pooling for analysis of variance hypothesis tests: A review and study of a split-plot model. *American Statistician* 54:269–279. doi:10.2307/2685778

Mayo, D. G. 2018. *Statistical inference as severe testing: How to get beyond the statistics wars*. Cambridge: Cambridge University Press. doi:10.1017/9781107286184

Mayo, D. G., and D. Hand. 2022. Statistical significance and its critics: Practicing damaging science, or damaging scientific practice? *Synthese* 200:220. doi:10.1007/s11229-022-03692-0

McCarthy, M. A. 2015. Approaches to statistical inference. In *Ecological statistics: Contemporary theory and application*, eds G. A. Fox, S. Negrete-Yankelevich and V. J. Sosa, 15–43. Oxford: Oxford University Press.

O'Dea, R. E., M. Lagisz, M. D. Jennions, et al. 2021. Preferred reporting items for systematic reviews and meta-analyses in ecology and evolutionary biology: A PRISMA extension. *Biological Reviews* 96:1695–1722. doi:10.1111/brv.12721

Purgar, M., T. Klanjscek, and A. Culina. 2022. Quantifying research waste in ecology. *Nature Ecology and Evolution* 6:1390–1397. doi:10.1038/s41559-022-01820-0

Quinn, G. P., and M. J. Keough. 2023. *Experimental design and data analysis for biologists*. 2nd edn. Cambridge: Cambridge University Press. doi:10.1017/9781139568173

Shavit, A., and A. M. Ellison. 2017. Toward a taxonomy of scientific replication. In *Stepping in the same river twice*, eds A. Shavit and A. M. Ellison, 3–22. New Haven: Yale University Press.

Spanos, A. 2019. *Probability theory and statistical inference: Empirical modeling with observational data*. 2nd edn. Cambridge: Cambridge University Press. doi:10.1017/9781316882825

Wasserstein, R. L., A. L. Schirm, and N. A. Lazar. 2019. Moving to a world beyond '$p < 0.05$'. *The American Statistician* 73:1–19. doi:10.1080/00031305.2019.1583913

West, B. T., K. B. Welch, and A. T. Galecki. 2015. *Linear mixed models: A practical guide using statistical software*. 2nd edn. Boca Raton: CRC Press.

Wootton, H. F., and M. J. Keough. 2016. Disturbance type and intensity combine to affect resilience of an intertidal community. *Marine Ecology Progress Series* 560:121–133. doi:10.3354/meps11861

5

Ecological scale and context dependence

JOSHUA BRIAN AND JANE CATFORD

SCALE AS A PERVASIVE FORM OF CONTEXT DEPENDENCE

To understand nature and develop ecological theory, we rely on synthesis: combining the results of multiple studies to reach general conclusions as no single study can adequately capture the complexity of the natural world. To make advancements in ecology we typically need to compare studies that have been carried out in different times and places, in different ecological conditions, on different taxa and by different people. However, there is a high degree of variability in the findings of seemingly comparable studies, a phenomenon that is often described as 'context dependence' (Catford et al. 2022).

Context dependence refers to situations where the magnitude or sign of an ecological relationship – say between diversity and productivity – varies (or appears to vary) due to the abiotic, biotic, spatio-temporal and methodological conditions under which that relationship is observed (Catford et al. 2022). Widespread observation of context dependence can make it appear that ecological patterns are species- or site-specific and that results from a given study are not useful outside of the specific circumstances in which it was carried out. We do not believe this is true, but generic claims of context dependence provide little practical information about why studies may have reached different conclusions (Miller et al. 2007; Catford et al. 2022). Therefore, an important part of developing ecological theory or management strategies is the identification of sources of context dependence.

Catford et al. (2022) summarised a range of reasons why the results of two studies may appear context dependent (Box 5.1). In this chapter, we focus specifically on scale dependence, though we note that consideration of all possible sources of context dependence is important, especially when comparing the results of two or more studies (see *Scale interacts with other sources of context dependence*, this chapter).

A common reason that conclusions may differ across studies stems from scale dependence (Levin 1992). Different ecological processes can be observed at different scales, and so the answer to a particular ecological question can depend on the scale at which it was asked and the scale at which measurements are made (Crawley and Harral 2001). For example, movement of migratory birds is affected by surface winds and food resources at an oceanic scale, but roost choice for those same birds is affected by the risk of mammalian predation at the scale of individual islands (Carlile et al. 2003; Frankish et al. 2020). As an example of how scale can affect theory, studies at small spatial scales are more likely to find that neutral-based dynamics govern community assembly, while studies at larger scales typically find that niche-based

DOI: 10.1201/9781003314332-5

processes dominate (Connolly et al. 2014; Mitchell et al. 2019). If studies are compared without considering the spatial and temporal scales at which they were carried out, it becomes even harder to quantify the relative contributions of niche and neutral processes in community assembly.

Ecological methods and study systems are diverse. Unless different studies are specifically designed to be carried out at identical spatial and temporal scales, it is likely that cross-study comparisons will involve some change in scale. The potential confounding effect of scale therefore underlies much of observational and experimental ecology (Sandel and Smith 2009). Despite this ubiquity, many studies do not consider scale dependence in their results (Chase et al. 2018), and increasingly refer to any differences with previous research as 'context dependence' (Catford et al. 2022). We therefore need to properly understand the diversity of ways in which scale can affect our conclusions and lead to apparent contradictions between studies.

In this chapter, we explore the effect of scale across both space and time, using examples from non-native plants and host-parasite relationships. This will show how scale dependence can lead to uncertainty within studies, and context dependence between studies. We then discuss two extended examples (Darwin's naturalisation conundrum and the invasion paradox), which we use to show how spatial and temporal scale interact with each other, as well as with other sources of context dependence. Our goal in this chapter is to highlight the importance of taking study scale into consideration when planning research and when taking lessons from one study and applying them to another. We also show that scale dependence, when used appropriately, can enhance our understanding of ecological processes driving the distribution and abundance of organisms.

THE IMPORTANCE OF STUDY SCALE

To begin, we explore the basic ways in which we can conceptualise study scale. We first define the issue of study scale and the forms it can take. This helps to explain how scale dependence presents an opportunity to better understand ecological processes. We also briefly introduce two case studies

that we will use in further discussions of spatial and temporal study scale.

What is study scale?

There are two main forms of scale that we need to consider in relation to the design of a study: extent and grain (Turner et al. 1989; Wiens 1989). These forms apply both spatially and temporally. Extent refers to the total area or time encompassed by a study (Figure 5.1, solid squares and arrows). If a study analyses the presence of a non-native species across a 100 m × 100 m field, the spatial extent of the study is 10,000 m², and would probably be considered a small extent depending on the type of organism. In contrast, studying the spread of a non-native species across North America would be a large extent. The system might be sampled over the course of a year, or over a 200-year period, representing very different temporal extents (Ryo et al. 2019).

Grain, or resolution, is the size of the sampling unit (Figure 5.1, dashed squares and arrows). The grain represents the finest possible resolution in a dataset (Turner et al. 1989). In the example above, the presence of a non-native species could be scored (present or absent) in 1 m × 1 m plots, a relatively small (fine) spatial grain that would have been selected based on the target organism and study. However, if the species was scored as present or absent in counties or states of the United States of America, the grain would be larger (coarser). Depending on the study system, sampling once a year might be a coarser temporal grain, in contrast to sampling once a day which would be more fine-grained. The choice of study scale is a vital part of research design, ensuring that the grain and extent of an individual study are appropriate for the target study taxa and research question. We do not deal with within-study scale selection in this chapter, but rather focus on between-study comparisons when scales have already been set. For a detailed overview of the importance of choosing appropriate grain and extent for a research study, and how to do it, excellent primers include Addicott et al. (1987) and Münkemüller et al. (2020).

Temporal grain also has additional complexity associated with it, since it can include both

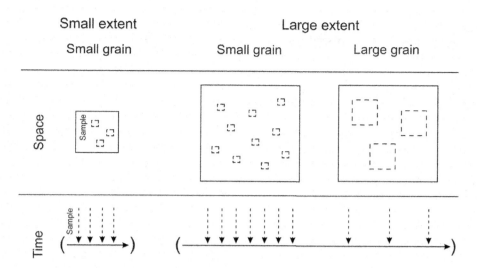

Figure 5.1 Grain and extent. Solid lines represent the total extent of a study in space (squares) or time (arrowed lines in brackets), while dashed lines represent sampling events.

frequency and duration (see Ryo et al. 2019 for comprehensive discussion). Over the course of a fortnight-long experiment (extent), temperature might be measured every day (grain). However, these daily temperature readings could be recorded as a spot measurement (i.e. an instantaneous reading), or taken as the average temperature over an hour of recording. The latter incorporates duration, which can also vary, e.g. the duration measured could have been 15 minutes or 2 hours instead. In this chapter, we treat temporal grain in terms of frequency (recurrence interval of spot sampling events, e.g. daily measurements), as this is the more common usage, though we note that duration may also be important. We will return to a discussion of the added complexity of temporal scale relative to spatial scale in a later section. We note that spatial grain may also incorporate density, in terms of the number of sampling units in a given area, which could change geostatistical analysis for example (see Hui et al. 2010). However, we do not consider this further in this chapter.

Because there are two sources of scaling variation (extent and grain), both need to be considered when comparing studies (e.g. in meta-analysis and meta-synthesis). Two studies might be carried out at identical spatial extents and appear to be directly comparable. However, if one was carried out at a smaller grain, it may capture fine-scale environmental heterogeneity or biotic interactions that are not observed in the study with larger grain, even if those factors are equally important in both studies.

We also note that scale is relative for different organisms (Fortin et al. 2021). A study that examines competition at a kilometre scale may appear incomparable to one that examines competition at a metre scale. However, if the studies examine organisms that differ in size (such as lions and ants), the studies may be comparable as those organisms experience competition at their respective study scales (Miguet et al. 2016). The scale at which an organism competes, disperses and so on will vary considerably, and so the appropriate study scale to detect a specific ecological process will also vary (Addicott et al. 1987; Fortin et al. 2012). By the same token, what may appear comparable (e.g. two studies with matching scales) may not be, if the studied taxa differ widely in their spatial and temporal neighbourhoods and ranges.

We will later show how variation in both extent and grain can alter how we interpret patterns, with consequences for synthesising the results of studies executed at different scales.

BOX 5.1: Four sources of context dependence

Context dependence occurs when the relationship between two variables varies (or appears to vary) under different conditions. Catford et al. (2022) recently proposed a typology of context dependence, which arises from four sources (Figure 5.2).

The figure shows the relationship between independent variable X and dependent variable Y, with illustrative examples and actions that can reduce unexplained variation and the likelihood of apparent context dependence. 'Mechanistic context dependence' (Figure 5.2i) is caused by interaction effects and reflects an underlying ecological process that drives differences between observed relationships. In contrast, 'apparent context dependence' (Figure 5.2ii–iv) occurs when the relationship between two variables appears to differ, but in reality does not. A very common type of apparent context dependence is 'methodological context dependence' (Figure 5.2iv), where varying methods used by different studies cause observed patterns to differ between them. Scale dependence is a form of apparent context dependence, caused by methodological differences when studies use different grains or extents. Other sources of apparent context dependence include confounding factors and statistical inference.

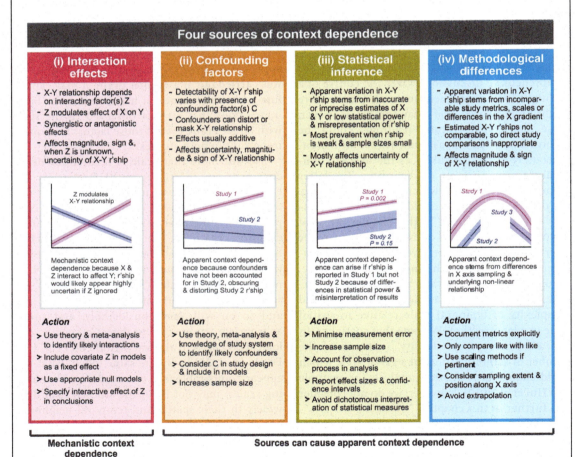

Figure 5.2 Illustration of four sources of context dependence, reprinted from Catford et al. (2022). See text for discussion. 'Relationship' is sometimes abbreviated to 'r'ship'. https://creativecommons.org/licenses/by/4.0/

(Continued)

Confounding factors (Figure 5.2ii) are arguably the hardest to address, because it is likely that multiple factors will affect ecological outcomes, not all of which can be accounted for. Methodological differences are generally easier to address if properly identified, though scale dependence may be an exception (see *Can we retrospectively correct for spatial grain or extent?* in this chapter). Once interacting factors are identified, variation from interaction effects (Figure 5.2i) should be predictable. The sources of variation are not mutually exclusive and are often interrelated and can manifest in various ways (see *Scale interacts with other sources of context dependence*, this chapter). White boxes show examples only; many other scenarios could occur (for example, different metrics for source in Figure 5.2iv).

The importance of scale for revealing ecological patterns

The general importance of scale is well understood, and many empirical and theoretical papers have been published on its influence on the observation and interpretation of ecological patterns (e.g. Swenson et al. 2006; Chase et al. 2018; Spake et al. 2021). Scale affects how we view ecological patterns, altering how we see everything from drivers of biodiversity, to the predictors and effects of biological invasions, to the assembly of host-parasite communities (Chase and Knight 2013; Bolnick et al. 2020a). We focus on how this manifests as context dependence (Box 5.1), by impeding the comparison of two or more studies.

Scale is not a property of a system – it is a property of how we observe that system (Fritsch et al. 2020). Indeed, much like 'populations' and 'communities', it represents a human construct invented to better conceptualise and measure what we observe. An individual plant doesn't know if we are studying only it, all of the plants of that species in a given field or its global distribution. Scale itself cannot produce or affect ecological processes: it just affects our ability to detect them. In this way, it is important to distinguish spatial and temporal scale from 'space' and 'time'.

Some ecological processes are inherently spatial or temporal: the properties of an ecological system may change through time or in space. This is known as non-stationarity (Rollinson et al. 2021). For example, the relationship between two variables (such as soil nitrogen and plant growth) may vary depending on mean temperature, which varies in space. This is therefore *mechanistic* context dependence (Box 5.1). The result of non-stationarity is that the mean or variance of ecosystem traits varies through space and time. However, only a certain spatial scale may allow us to detect this

(Levin 1992): a study with a small extent might only sample a small temperature range, and the role of soil nitrogen may appear to differ from that of another study with a small extent that sampled a different region of the temperature range. A larger extent would allow for more of the temperature range to be seen (Figure 5.2iv). We therefore identify 'scale' as a source of *apparent* context dependence (Box 5.1), as it represents a methodological window of observation, rather than an ecological mechanism. While the interaction between spatially or temporally variable ecological processes (non-stationarity) and observational scale poses a problem, it also represents an opportunity.

A careful consideration of scale, particularly if patterns at multiple scales from the same system are compared, can reveal emergent ecological processes (Kopp and Allen 2021). For example, a medium grain may identify the role of the local environmental conditions in determining what species will be present, while a small grain may detect local-scale interspecific competition between those species. When testing a hypothesis, identifying the appropriate spatial and temporal scales of analysis is recommended as the first step in producing suitable models (Miller et al. 2007; Getz et al. 2018). Considering possible scales of analysis encourages us to explicitly consider the link between our observations and the ecological processes driving them. Alternatively, if we want to measure specific mechanisms, thinking about the scale at which we expect to see them will aid in this goal.

We argue that a greater focus on scale dependence therefore provides a dual benefit. First, acknowledging differences in scale between studies will explain some of the apparent context dependence in ecology. Second, scale provides a useful lens to study ecology, as it integrates many processes that determine the distribution and abundance of organisms. Considering multiple scales can inform our understanding and detection of the variation in ecological mechanisms through time and space. While we focus on the former point in this chapter, we highlight the latter where appropriate.

Systems used to explore scale dependence

Through the rest of the chapter, we will use two broad case studies to explore scale dependence. Non-native plants are widely distributed, often representing a large financial cost as well as an ecological threat (Novoa et al. 2021). Their distribution and spread are driven by factors at multiple scales, from global-scale human transport to fine-scale interactions with local native taxa (Smith et al. 2020). Non-native plants provide a useful and highly important system to understand the influence of scale dependence in ecology.

The second case study is host-parasite interactions. Parasites play important roles in ecosystems, from stabilising food webs to influencing the behaviour of individual hosts and the way that whole ecosystems function (Morton et al. 2021; Brian et al. 2022). Parasite community assembly is also strongly hierarchical. A single host can encompass a parasite community: each parasite interacts with the host environment (the environment within the host) as well as other parasites in that environment, including individuals of both the same species and different species (Rynkiewicz et al. 2015). Other factors at larger scales, such as host identity and dispersal limitation, determine the possible pool of parasites that could recruit to a given within-host community (Dallas et al. 2019). Parasite communities, therefore, also provide a convenient system to explore scale dependency in ecology.

SPATIAL SCALE

Both spatial grain and spatial extent could lead to apparent context dependence between studies. In this section, we discuss why this should be so. This leads us to touch upon the importance of considering the traits and life history of organisms when thinking about the appropriate spatial scale of study. We end by showing how it is difficult to correct for spatial scale, and that increased attention

needs to be paid to the fact that different ecological processes will be observable at only certain spatial scales.

Spatial grain

The grain of a study can strongly influence its conclusions. This can be seen most clearly in studies that carry out identical analyses at multiple grains.

A recent example comes from Kotowska et al. (2022). The authors explored the relationship between the presence of a plant genus (goldenrods, *Solidago* spp.) that is non-native in Europe and landscape heterogeneity, which was measured in terms of both diversity (number of different landscape types) and fragmentation. They looked for the presence or absence of goldenrods along replicate transects, and related goldenrod presence to landscape diversity and fragmentation. To investigate the effect of scale, they quantified landscape diversity and fragmentation at different-sized radii around the transect, from 250 to 5000 m (i.e. going from small grain to large grain, Figure 5.1). They found that goldenrod presence was positively associated with both measures of landscape heterogeneity (Kotowska et al. 2022). However, the effect of landscape diversity strengthened with increasing spatial scale, while the effect of fragmentation declined with increasing spatial scale. They surmised that this is likely because landscape diversity generally increases with scale (i.e. a larger grain typically encompasses a greater range of environments), which effectively increases the number and diversity of niches, increasing the likelihood of goldenrods being observed somewhere in that area. In contrast, high fragmentation produces finer-scale disturbance through edge effects, and so strongly facilitates non-native introduction at small scales but less so at larger scales where environmental filtering is more influential than disturbance from edge effects (Kotowska et al. 2022).

The goldenrod example highlights two important points. First, the observed strength of an ecological relationship (between landscape heterogeneity and non-native plant presence) varied depending on the grain examined. Grain is a clear potential source of variation between studies, which could lead to apparent context dependence. If two studies used different grain sizes, they would reach different conclusions about the strength of landscape heterogeneity. Second, this example shows that exploring multiple grain sizes allows assessments to be made about the ecological processes driving non-native plant success. Here, it appears that environmental filtering is an initial, larger-scale driver determining whether goldenrods are present in the general area. Then, their fine-scale position in that area is linked to higher disturbance, which creates spaces for successful establishment.

Spatial grain can also be related to how the organisms in a study are assessed. For example, it may be important to understand how water usage differs between native and non-native plants. One of the most well-known hydrological impacts of plant introductions is the increased water use by non-native plants (Catford 2017). A meta-analysis of over 160 native-introduced species pairs on a range of continents explored the generality of this effect (Cavaleri and Sack 2010). At the leaf scale, evidence suggests that non-native species tend to have greater stomatal conductance than native species, indicating higher water usage (grain size: leaf). However, native and non-native plants were roughly equal in their sap flow rates (grain size: plant), indicating that native and non-native plants had similar water uptake. This difference between the two grain sizes is likely due to a complex combination of leaf properties, canopy cover, and plant age and height. Therefore, the relationship between two variables (plant origin and water use) differs depending on the grain size examined. The example that different patterns are observed between different characteristics of the same organisms also demonstrates that it is difficult to retrospectively correct for scale, as processes can change between scales. It would be incorrect to assume that the effect size seen at the leaf scale could be applied to whole plants.

Spatial extent

The spatial extent of a study may determine how well the study can detect ecological patterns and processes. Two studies conducted at different extents could therefore conclude that different factors are most strongly related to a given response variable, when in reality no such difference exists.

As an example, Bolnick et al. (2020a) explored the factors explaining parasite richness inside freshwater fish (three-spined sticklebacks, *Gasterosteus aculeatus*) in different lake populations. They included characteristics of the individual fish (e.g. sex, size, gape width) and characteristics of the different lakes (e.g. lake area, elevation, distance from the ocean). Their grain size was the individual fish. However, they carried out their analysis at two different extents: at the within-lake scale (extent: single lake) and the between-lake scale (extent: multiple lakes). They found that some factors, such as host sex, were only important at the single lake extent. Other factors, such as lake area and elevation, were only important at the multiple lake extent. Some factors were also important across both scales, such as host size and gape width. In general, when the extent was a lake, host factors were more important. When the extent was multiple lakes, environmental characteristics become more important (Bolnick et al. 2020a).

These patterns can be interpreted in terms of ecological 'assembly'. Upon arriving in a new area, organisms need to first be able to survive in the environment and then negotiate biotic interactions in areas of suitable habitat (Götzenberger et al. 2012).

Spatial extent alters our ability to detect these ecological assembly processes. At the extent of single lakes, effects of the broader environmental filters cannot be observed; we are unable to detect that some lakes are more suitable for parasites than others. Instead, parasite patterns appear dominated by biotic factors that occur within a lake, such as host size and how much that host consumes. Only when we make observations at a larger extent can we detect the role of environmental variation in determining why some lakes (and therefore the fish within those lakes) have more parasites than others. Because these processes (environmental filtering, biotic interactions) take place over different spatial scales, our interpretation of what process drives an observed pattern is unavoidably linked with the scale at which we study. Unless two studies take place over identical extents, there is always likely to be some degree of apparent context dependence due to their differential ability to detect the same process.

Host-parasite examples nicely illustrate scale dependence as they help highlight that the *same* spatial extent can mean different things to different organisms. While the immediate environment for the fish is the lake, the immediate environment for the parasite is the fish, and parasite-parasite competition occurs at the within-fish level. In a paper on the same stickleback-parasite system, within-host parasite-parasite competition was shown to influence parasite abundances (Bolnick et al. 2020b). However, for the fish, interspecific competition occurs within the lake. Therefore, extreme caution is required when comparing studies on organisms that may vary by orders of magnitude in size. An identical spatial extent (e.g. a lake) may give a meaningful signal of competition for a fish, but not for a parasite within that fish. Studies may appear to be context dependent not because a different spatial extent is used, but because the same extent is used to inappropriately compare two organisms whose life history occurs at different scales. These scaling differences between organisms are often underappreciated and can lead to arguments (for example, about the appropriate management of vulnerable populations) (Wiens 1989).

Can we retrospectively correct for spatial grain or extent?

There are techniques for correcting for differences in sampling spatial scales, but it can still be difficult or impossible to eliminate sampling artefacts. We give an example of why this is the case using the relationship between spatial extent and species richness. If two studies are carried out at different extents, researchers may use rarefaction to calculate a standard species richness for a given level of sampling (Chase and Knight 2013). Essentially, this involves moving up or down a species accumulation curve, where the x-axis is spatial extent, and the y-axis is the number of species observed. By estimating the shape of the curve mathematically based on available data it is possible to extrapolate up or down to get an estimate of species richness for a given spatial extent, and standardise that extent across multiple samples or studies.

There are two problems with the rarefaction approach. The first is that two studies will have different species accumulation curves, that are highly unlikely to be parallel (Figure 5.3a). An attempt to standardise for spatial extent will still be scale dependent because the difference between species accumulation curves varies with what spatial extent is considered (Chase and Knight 2013). The difference between curves 1 and 2 at extent x in Figure 5.3a is only half that at extent y, and the comparison between study 1 and study 2 remains scale dependent.

The second problem is relevant when comparing studies that examine the effect of habitat loss or modification on species responses. Through a disruption of ecological processes (e.g. mutualisms) at smaller scales, species reductions in small and isolated spatial extents are greater than expected (Chase et al. 2020). Therefore, we cannot simply 'move up and down' a single species accumulation curve: the entire curve (not just our position on it) will change with the total spatial extent. In Figure 5.3b, the actual species richness when scaling down to extent x will be lower than predicted by the original curve (solid line). To compare between different spatial scales, more sophisticated tools such as Hurlbert's probability of interspecific encounter are required (see Chase and Knight 2013). Unfortunately, tools such as this are designed specifically for biodiversity comparisons and do not cover all cases of spatial scale dependence.

Another related issue is that of the modifiable areal unit problem (MAUP) (Hui et al. 2010). This problem describes the phenomenon that observed patterns of species distributions will vary with scale, due to spatially explicit processes such as dispersal and social organisation (Peres-Neto and Legendre 2010). Therefore, conclusions about species distributions – for example, the degree of aggregation – remain scale dependent, even if multiple studies are standardised to the same scale. Possible solutions include explicitly including spatial dependence in modelling procedures, though once again this is only suitable for certain types of data (see Dray et al. 2012).

Different spatial grains or extents between studies can cause apparent context dependence. However, the results of any corrections for spatial scale may still not clarify exactly how (and therefore why) two studies differ, because the differences between two studies will vary depending on the scale that is chosen as the 'standard' scale for comparison. Because of the tight link between spatial scale and our ability to observe different ecological processes, the best way to deal with spatial context dependence is to carefully consider what processes you are likely to be capturing at your studied extent and the scales over which those processes are likely to occur (Fortin et al. 2012). This will involve considering the scale at which your studied organism lives its life (e.g. how far it can disperse). Comparisons between studies should

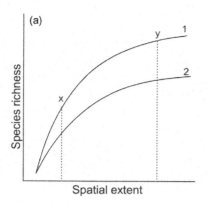 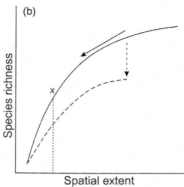

Figure 5.3 Issues when trying to correct for differences in spatial scale. **(a)** Species accumulation curves from different situations (1 and 2) are unlikely to be parallel, so conclusions still depend on the scale you choose to standardise upon. Adapted from Chase et al. (2018). **(b)** Ecological processes may change or be lost when spatial extents become smaller (e.g. fragmentation of a previously intact forest), which changes the shape of the species accumulation curve (dashed arrow and line).

focus on these qualitative assessments of ecological processes, rather than trying to directly compare between studies at incompatible scales.

TEMPORAL SCALE

The temporal context of a study, in terms of both grain and extent, also affects its conclusions. However, there are additional complexities associated with temporal scale relative to spatial scale.

Temporal grain

The frequency at which systems are sampled can affect our conclusions. For example, it is common to model the abiotic niche of species, to predict how species distributions may change with climate change, or to estimate climatically suitable areas that may be vulnerable to non-native introductions. Species distribution models frequently treat environmental variables in terms of their annual average (Karger et al. 2017). However, incorporating environmental variation at smaller grain size, such as quarterly temperature and precipitation extremes, can significantly improve model predictions (Pérez-Navarro et al. 2020).

The chosen temporal grain could alter ecological projections. One species might experience an annual average temperature of 25°C, with an annual range of 20°C–30°C, while another might have an identical average but experience a range of 10°C–40°C. The latter species will likely survive in a much greater range of conditions, and therefore have much stronger potential to spread to other regions. Using a large temporal grain would under-predict this potential (Pérez-Navarro et al. 2020). While incorporating too many variables can lead to poor model performance (see Chapter 7), and gaining good spatial predictions depends on more than choosing a fine temporal scale, considering the variability present in an organism's life cycle (and our ability to capture it) can improve ecological understanding.

Grain has the capacity to change the resolution at which conclusions can be drawn, and should be considered as a possible explanation for differences between studies that incorporate variables that can vary through time. In this example, refining the grain would provide a better estimate of the true ecological conditions experienced by the organism and facilitate a more accurate assessment of its potential to spread to regions outside its native range. In general, choosing an appropriate grain size is vital to detecting important ecological interactions, such as priority effects which play a major role in early assembly of communities (Fukami 2015).

Temporal extent

The total length or duration of a study can also make the relationship between two variables appear to differ between studies. This is because ecological processes act through time to change observable patterns. For example, there is continued interest in the enemy release hypothesis (ERH) as an explanation for the success of non-native species. The ERH states that non-native species lose their native enemies (parasites, pathogens and predators) when arriving in their new range, and thus experience a competitive advantage over native species (Keane and Crawley 2002). However, enemy loss and gain is a dynamic process. While they may lose their specialist enemies quickly, they can also be targeted by generalists in their new range (Wan et al. 2019). Therefore, non-natives may experience rapid initial release, but then accumulate enemies slowly through time (Hawkes 2007).

If patterns change through time, then studies at different temporal extents have different capacities to detect this (Ryo et al. 2019). In this example, a long-term study would be better placed to detect the fact that enemy pressure is *changing* – non-native species may begin with much lower enemy richness than natives, but then slowly experience equivalent enemy pressure over time. In contrast, a short-term study would document a 'snapshot' of the pattern. The conclusions that the study drew (whether a species was experiencing enemy release or not) would then depend on how soon after initial introduction the study was carried out. If studies are to be fairly compared, there needs to be an acknowledgement that ecological processes change over time and that different temporal extents have different abilities to reflect this.

We recommend, for both temporal extent and grain, that an important first step in dealing with scale dependency comes before a study takes place. The temporal scale of sampling or experimentation should be linked with the process of interest (invasion, enemy release, etc.) and designed to match it. If this is not practical, it should be acknowledged that the study likely captures only a certain part of the process (e.g. likelihood of successful introduction in summer months only; the strength of enemy release ten years after introduction). This will facilitate more informed comparisons between studies.

Do temporal and spatial scale dependence have the same consequences?

So far, we have presented spatial and temporal scale dependence as behaving in a similar fashion. Both are a product of extent and grain, with variation in this extent and grain altering the detection and interpretation of ecological processes. Nonetheless, spatial and temporal scale dependence are not completely analogous. We provide a hypothetical example of this in Figure 5.4 that considers the

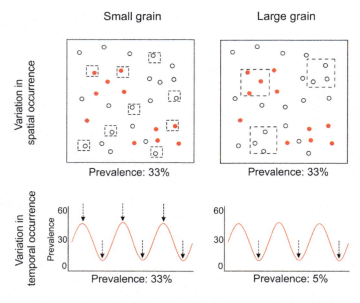

Figure 5.4 Comparing small versus large grains, using a hypothetical example where parasite prevalence is variable in both space and time. Red dots indicate an infected host, while white dots are uninfected hosts.

consequences of changing grain when parasite prevalence varies in both space and time.

In space, changing grain may affect our ability to detect the cause of fine-scale parasite distributions (the clusters of red points in Figure 5.4). Small grains would allow parasite distributions to be compared with fine-scale environmental correlates, while larger grains capture broader environmental drivers (Falke and Preston 2022). However, assuming a random distribution of plots in space, small and large spatial grains will recover similar estimated prevalence for a single sampling event (Figure 5.4). This is because larger spatial grains merely average out the variation among smaller spatial grains (Wiens et al. 1989). This is fundamentally different from temporal grain, where larger grains do not average out the pattern observed at smaller grains if parasite prevalence varies throughout the year. Instead, the opposite occurs: they are far more vulnerable to bias due to stochasticity or periodicity (Figure 5.4). Small temporal grains are better able to reliably capture trends. More frequent sampling identifies the periodicity and allows an accurate recording of mean prevalence, while intermittent sampling only ever observes low prevalence.

Both temporal and spatial scale dependence can influence the perceived importance of ecological processes between studies by altering our ability to observe them. Temporal scale dependence is also potentially more likely to produce explicit errors within studies, providing another source of apparent context dependence between studies. This may be because the two aspects of scale (grain and extent) do not apply as neatly to time as they do to space. Spatial grain and extent both cover an area of space: they functionally examine the same metric and can be expressed in the same units. In contrast, while temporal extent covers a period of time, temporal grain technically refers to the frequency of sampling within that period and does not represent a period of time in itself.

Despite this vulnerability, theory concerning temporal scale dependence is less well-developed than that of spatial scale dependence (Ryo et al. 2019). We recommend further attention needs to be paid to the role of temporal grain and extent in producing contradictions between studies. Such work is vital for the assessment of space-for-time substitutions, which have been criticised due to the frequent mismatch between variability in temporal and spatial scales (Damgaard 2019).

SCALE INTERACTS WITH OTHER SOURCES OF CONTEXT DEPENDENCE

When comparing between ecological studies, it is unlikely that there will only be one source of variation that could cause context dependence. Instead, both mechanistic context dependence and apparent context dependence could occur simultaneously, and they themselves have diverse sources (Box 5.1).

We now give two extended examples from non-native plant introductions about how spatial and temporal scale interact with each other, and with other sources of context dependence, which can further complicate comparisons between studies.

Darwin's naturalisation conundrum

Darwin's 'naturalisation conundrum' stems from two opposing predictions made by Darwin (1859). First, he predicted that non-native plants with close phylogenetic relatives in their new range should experience lower growth and fecundity because they will likely have higher trait overlap and therefore compete for similar resources ('Darwin's naturalisation hypothesis', or 'limiting similarity'). Second, he also predicted that non-native plants with close relatives should be more successful because they will be well-adapted to the environmental conditions there (pre-adaptation hypothesis). Previous work has shown support for both these contrasting hypotheses (e.g. Schaefer et al. 2011; Park and Potter 2013), and the relationship between native and non-native phylogenetic relatedness and non-native success is unclear.

Recent work has suggested that spatial extent (as a source of apparent context dependence) may be responsible for these contradictions. At large extents (regional scale), successful non-native species appear more closely related to native communities than would be expected by chance, because we can detect the role of environmental filtering (Cadotte et al. 2018; Park et al. 2020). Closely related non-natives are more likely to be able to survive the broad environmental conditions in their new range, supporting the pre-adaptation hypotheses. At small extents (local scale), successful non-natives appear less closely related to native communities than would be expected, because they can use different resources to the native species. This minimises competitive exclusion, supporting Darwin's naturalisation hypothesis. Therefore, non-native species follow a broad pattern of tending to occur in the same region as closely related natives (to match the environment), while spatially segregating over small scales (to avoid competition).

Despite this reasonably intuitive explanation, relying only on spatial extent to reconcile Darwin's naturalisation conundrum is an over-simplification. Mechanistic context dependence may also have a role to play in determining the relatedness between native and non-native species. For example, at small scales, non-native species tend to be less phylogenetically related to natives in warmer and wetter climates (Park et al. 2020). This pattern may arise because these environments are relatively favourable and homogeneous, and so competition plays a larger role in coexistence. Thus, the context of local environmental conditions also plays a role in the naturalisation conundrum (mechanistic context dependence), but this can only be observed at smaller scales (apparent context dependence).

As another example, phylogenetic relatedness between native and non-native species was strongly dependent on the fire frequency in an oak savanna system, suggesting that both environmental filtering and biotic interactions determine the success of non-native species (Pinto-Ledezma et al. 2020). This pattern also depended on temporal extent. The non-native grass *Poa pratensis* was generally closely related to species it co-occurred with, supporting the pre-adaptation hypothesis. However, in plots with no fire, this pattern shifted over time until *P. pratensis* was distantly related to co-occurring species, supporting Darwin's naturalisation hypothesis (Pinto-Ledezma et al. 2020). Different conclusions would be drawn depending on when the system was studied, or how long it was sampled for. This example shows how the factor of fire frequency (mechanistic context dependence) interacts with temporal extent (which could lead to apparent context dependence) to produce complex ecological patterns, all within a single spatial extent (local scale). These patterns may also present differently across larger spatial scales.

Finally, time since introduction may interact with the ecological effect of non-native species. This could also produce patterns that cause apparent context dependent between studies. In an analysis of plant communities in Auckland,

New Zealand, the number of non-native species (i.e. richness) was positively related to the number of native species in the same genus, supporting the pre-adaptation hypothesis. However, the *abundance* of each of those non-native species was negatively related to native congeners, supporting Darwin's naturalisation hypothesis and opposing the pre-adaptation hypothesis (Diez et al. 2008). One possible explanation is that non-natives are competitively displacing native species (Cadotte et al. 2018). At early stages of introduction, they appear phylogenetically similar to native species because of environmental filtering. A longer time after introduction, they have competitively displaced closely related native species due to high niche overlap, and so are phylogenetically distant from the remaining native species (Cadotte et al. 2018). Methodological context dependence, in terms of how we choose to measure processes, can influence subsequent interpretation, and requires critical thought.

Various studies show that the observed temporal scale and spatial scale can alter interpretations of interacting factors to produce complex ecological patterns. Considering multiple sources of context dependence simultaneously may be necessary to fairly compare studies that are carried out at different scales and under different ecological conditions. Doing so can help to bring clarity to supposedly contradictory hypotheses, and aid predictions about the circumstances under which certain patterns may be observed.

The invasion paradox

The invasion paradox relates to the relationship between native and exotic species richness. Some studies find that there is a positive relationship between native and non-native species richness, while others find a negative relationship (reviewed in Fridley et al. 2007).

Once again, spatial scale has been implicated as a key cause of this contradiction. Large spatial grains show a positive relationship between native and non-native richness, while small spatial grains show a negative relationship (Peng et al. 2019). This was thought to be for the same reasons as outlined throughout this chapter: at large scales, environmental heterogeneity increases and so more species can be supported, both native and non-native (Fridley et al. 2007). At small scales, competitive interactions are influential and so diverse native communities may resist invasion by using all available resources.

However, multiple additional sources of methodological context dependence may confound the conclusion that spatial grain is responsible for the invasion paradox. Studies with small grains tend to be experiments, which are controlled and explicitly designed to test the effect of native richness on non-native species. In contrast, studies at larger grains and extents are typically observational, which include all the abiotic and biotic variability at a given extent. Therefore, the invasion paradox may be caused by the differences between observational and experimental studies, which are confounded by spatial scale (Peng et al. 2019; Smith and Cote 2019).

Another methodological source of apparent context dependence is the way in which non-native species are assessed. Experiments often use non-native performance (e.g. growth) as a metric of invasive success, while observational studies often use non-native richness (Smith and Cote 2019). These are quite different pieces of information. For example, non-native performance might correlate with non-native abundance and affect native species a lot more than non-native richness. When comparing between studies that use the same metric, the contrast between experimental and observational studies disappears (Smith and Cote 2019).

The invasion paradox shows that there are other methodological sources of apparent context dependence that can covary with spatial scale. Disentangling them, and thus detecting a generalisable ecological signal, requires careful consideration of which ecological processes each method can detect.

SO WHAT?

Different studies will inevitably be carried out at different scales. Two researchers may analyse the same system (or different systems) at different grains, different extents or both, leading to apparent contradictions in their results.

Different sources of scale dependence may interact with each other, or with other forms of context dependence, leading to a complex array of reasons why the conclusions of two studies appear to differ. In order to disentangle true ecological interactions from methodological artefacts, we need to

account for the influence of scale, and understand how it influences our interpretation of ecological processes (Spake et al. 2021). Doing so will allow for comparisons between studies that are accurate and informative, and lead to reliable developments in theory and management of ecological systems. Comprehensive guidelines now exist for addressing mechanistic and apparent context dependence as a whole (Box 5.1, Catford et al. 2022). Below, we emphasise the key points that have arisen through this chapter that are specific to scale dependence, which contributes to methodological differences between studies and thus apparent context dependence.

It is becoming increasingly common for a single study to analytically explore different spatial or temporal grains. For a given extent, studies can repeat analyses at different grain sizes (e.g. Dansereau et al. 2022; Kotowska et al. 2022). This can effectively demonstrate how our ability to detect ecological processes changes with scale (Kopp and Allen 2021). We also argue that this approach could make results more comparable between studies, by allowing studies to 'match' appropriate grains for comparison. Given that a large majority of studies are restricted to short-term investigations over a small area (Stricker et al. 2015), any approach which expands our knowledge of scale dependence will be of benefit to the wider ecological community.

When studying organisms or environmental factors with known periodicity (e.g. parasite life cycles or climate), we need to acknowledge that one or two samples are unlikely to capture the full story, and try to decrease temporal grain and increase temporal extent where possible (Poulin 2019).

We also need to be aware of how scale relates to statistical inference, another source of context dependence. This is particularly relevant for meta-analyses. Studies with small extents can generally achieve higher replication, and thus receive higher weighting in meta-analyses (Spake et al. 2021). However, they may miss patterns that could be detected at larger scales and bias the meta-analysis conclusions. We have demonstrated that interpretation of ecological processes is heavily scale dependent. Extreme caution is required when synthesising results of multiple studies that may have been carried out over variable scales.

There needs to be an increased emphasis on considering spatial and temporal scale dependence together. Having a fine grain in space does not necessarily mean that all relevant fine-scale processes will be captured if time grain is very coarse.

In general, spatial scale has been considered far more than temporal scale (but see e.g. White et al. 2010). Sophisticated measures exist for accounting for some kinds of spatial scale dependency (Chase and Knight 2013). Methods of accounting for temporal spatial dependence have gained less attention, though work is progressing in this area, particularly in network analysis (e.g. CaraDonna et al. 2021; Fortin et al. 2021) and conservation (e.g. Wauchope et al. 2019). These developments need to be built on to be able to fully account for temporal sampling context.

The scale at which a study is carried out should be informed by the ecological processes expected at that scale. Different questions, such as the role of competition versus the role of temperature in community assembly, can best be answered at different scales, with the former likely requiring a smaller grain than the latter to be effectively observed (Hulme and Bernard-Verdier 2018). This also involves thinking about the traits of the studied organism, such as dispersal. For example, different types of communities (plant, bird, microbial) show different rates of spatial turnover. These differences in turnover are partly explainable by differences in body or propagule size, which covaries with dispersal ability (Graco-Roza et al. 2021). The different scales at which species perceive space and time are vital (Fortin et al. 2021): the same scale may mean different things to different species or functional groups, and cross-study comparisons should take this into account. Because scale affects how we see ecological processes, and processes for different organisms may occur at different scales, we cannot merely standardise for scale (Chase et al. 2019). We need to think critically about the relationship between processes, organisms and scale.

Finally, it may be that studies at different scales cannot be effectively compared. If this is the case, synthesis should be attempted cautiously, with comparisons being very explicit when it comes to scale. Attempting to develop ecological theory by comparing studies that answer different questions – by virtue of being carried out at different scales – may be misleading and will exacerbate rather than ameliorate confusion about ecological patterns and the processes driving them.

As a discipline, Ecology will ideally move from declaring a result as 'context dependent' to exploring and explaining *why* conclusions appear different between studies. Accounting for study scale, and its interaction with other sources of context dependence, is one important way of reconciling apparently contradictory or variable results. Doing so will allow us to better understand how methodological choices and inference strategies can affect ecological interpretations. Ultimately, understanding and accounting for these sources of bias will lead to greater mechanistic understanding of the factors and processes that drive variation in ecology.

REFERENCES

Addicott, J. F., J. M. Aho, M. F. Antolin, et al. 1987. Ecological neighborhoods: Scaling environmental patterns. *Oikos* 49:340–346.

Bolnick, D. I., E. J. Resetarits, K Ballare, Y. E. Stuart, and W. E. Stutz. 2020a. Host patch traits have scale-dependent effects on diversity in a stickleback parasite metacommunity. *Ecography* 43:990–1002. doi:10.1111/ecog.04994

Bolnick, D. I., E. J. Resetarits, K. Ballare, Y. E. Stuart, and W. E. Stutz. 2020b. Scale-dependent effects of host patch traits on species composition in a stickleback parasite metacommunity. *Ecology* 101:e03181. doi:10.1002/ecy.3181

Brian, J. I., S. A. Reynolds, and D. C. Aldridge. 2022. Parasitism dramatically alters the ecosystem services provided by freshwater mussels. *Functional Ecology* 36:2019–2042. doi:10.1111/1365-2435.14092

Cadotte, M. W., S. E. Campbell, S. P. Li, D. S. Sodhi, and N. E. Mandrak. 2018. Preadaptation and naturalization of non-native species: Darwin's two fundamental insights into species invasion. *Annual Review of Plant Biology* 69:661–684. doi:10.1146/annurev-arplant-042817-040339

Carlile, D. P. N., F. Zino, C. Natividad, and D. B. Wingate. 2003. A review of four successful recovery programmes for threatened sub-tropical petrels. *Marine Ornithology* 31:185–192.

Catford, J. A. 2017. Hydrological impacts of biological invasions. In *Impact of biological invasions on ecosystem services,* eds M. Vilà and P. E. Hulme, 63–80. Cham: Springer. doi:10.1007/978-3-319-45121-3_5

Catford, J. A., J. R. Wilson, P. Pyšek, P. E. Hulme, and R. P. Duncan. 2022. Addressing context dependence in ecology. *Trends in Ecology and Evolution* 37:158–170. doi:10.1016/j.tree.2021.09.007

Cavaleri, M. A., L. and Sack. 2010. Comparative water use of native and invasive plants at multiple scales: A global meta-analysis. *Ecology* 91:2705–2715. doi:10.1890/09-0582.1

Chase, J. M., and T. M. Knight. 2013. Scale-dependent effect sizes of ecological drivers on biodiversity: Why standardised sampling is not enough. *Ecology Letters* 16:17–26. doi:10.1111/ele.12112

Chase, J. M., B. J. McGill, D. J. McGlinn, et al. 2018. Embracing scale-dependence to achieve a deeper understanding of biodiversity and its change across communities. *Ecology Letters* 21:1737–1751. doi:10.1111/ele.13151

Chase, J. M., B. J. McGill, P. L. Thompson, et al. 2019. Species richness change across spatial scales. *Oikos* 128:1079–1091. doi:10.1111/ele.13151

Chase, J. M., S. A. Blowes, T. M. Knight, K. Gerstner, and F. May. 2020. Ecosystem decay exacerbates biodiversity loss with habitat loss. *Nature* 584:238–243. doi:10.1038/s41586-020-2531-2532

Connolly, S. R., M. A. MacNeil, M. J. Caley, et al. 2014. Commonness and rarity in the marine biosphere. *Proceedings of the National Academy of Sciences of the United States of America* 111:8524–8529. doi:10.1073/pnas.1406664111

Crawley, M. J., and J. E. Harral. 2001. Scale dependence in plant biodiversity. *Science* 291:864–868. doi:10.1126/science.291.5505.864

Dallas, T. A., A. L. Laine, and O. Ovaskainen. 2019. Detecting parasite associations within multi-species host and parasite communities. *Proceedings of the Royal Society B: Biological Sciences* 286:20191109. doi:10.1098/rspb.2019.1109

Damgaard, C. 2019. A critique of the space-for-time substitution practice in community ecology. *Trends in Ecology and Evolution* 34:416–421. doi:10.1016/j.tree.2019.01.013

Dansereau, G., P. Legendre, and T. Poisot. 2022. Evaluating ecological uniqueness over broad spatial extents using species distribution modelling. *Oikos* 2022:e09063. doi:10.1111/oik.09063

Darwin, C. 1859. *On the origin of species by means of natural selection, or the preservation of favoured races in the struggle for life.* London: John Murray.

Diez, J. M., J. J. Sullivan, P. E. Hulme, G. Edwards, and R. P. Duncan. 2008. Darwin's naturalization conundrum: Dissecting taxonomic patterns of species invasions. *Ecology Letters* 11:674–681. doi:10.1111/j.1461-0248.2008.01178.x

Dray, S., R. Pélissier, P. Couteron, et al. 2012. Community ecology in the age of multivariate multiscale spatial analysis. *Ecological Monographs* 82:257–275. doi:10.1890/11-1183.1

Falke, L. P., and D. L. Preston. 2022. Freshwater disease hotspots: Drivers of fine-scale spatial heterogeneity in trematode parasitism in streams. *Freshwater Biology* 67:487–497. doi:10.1111/fwb.13856

Fortin, M. J., P. M. James, A. MacKenzie, et al. 2012. Spatial statistics, spatial regression, and graph theory in ecology. *Spatial Statistics* 1:100–109. doi:10.1016/j.spasta.2012.02.004

Fortin, M. J., M. R. T. Dale, and C. Brimacombe. 2021. Network ecology in dynamic landscapes. *Proceedings of the Royal Society B* 288:20201889. doi:10.1098/rspb.2020.1889

Frankish, C. K., R. A. Phillips, T. A. Clay, M. Somveille, and A. Manica. 2020. Environmental drivers of movement in a threatened seabird: Insights from a mechanistic model and implications for conservation. *Diversity and Distributions* 26:1315–1329. doi:10.1111/ddi.13130

Fridley, J. D., J. J. Stachowicz, S. Naeem, et al. 2007. The invasion paradox: Reconciling pattern and process in species invasions. *Ecology* 88:3–17. doi:10.1890/0012-9658(2007)88[3:TIPRPA]2.0.CO;2

Fritsch, M., H. Lischke, and K. M. Meyer. 2020. Scaling methods in ecological modelling. *Methods in Ecology and Evolution* 11:1368–1378. doi:10.1111/2041-210X.13466

Fukami, T. 2015. Historical contingency in community assembly: Integrating niches, species pools, and priority effects. *Annual Review of Ecology, Evolution, and Systematics* 46:1–23. doi:10.1146/annurev-ecolsys-110411-160340

Getz, W. M., C. R. Marshall, C. J. Carlson, et al. 2018. Making ecological models adequate. *Ecology Letters* 21:153–166. doi:10.1111/ele.12893

Götzenberger, L., F. de Bello, K. A. Bråthen, et al. 2012. Ecological assembly rules in plant communities: Approaches, patterns and prospects. *Biological Reviews* 87:111–127. doi:10.1111/j.1469-185X.2011.00187.x

Graco-Roza, C., S. Aarnio, N. Abrego, et al. 2022. Distance decay 2.0: A global synthesis of taxonomic and functional turnover in ecological communities. *Global Ecology and Biogeography* 31:1399–1421. doi:10.1111/geb.13513

Hawkes, C. V. 2007. Are invaders moving targets? The generality and persistence of advantages in size, reproduction, and enemy release in invasive plant species with time since introduction. *The American Naturalist* 170:832–843. doi:10.1086/522842

Hui, C., R. Veldtman, and M. A. McGeoch. 2010. Measures, perceptions and scaling patterns of aggregated species distributions. *Ecography* 33:95–102. doi:10.1111/j.1600-0587.2009.05997.x

Hulme, P. E., and M. Bernard-Verdier. 2018. Comparing traits of native and alien plants: Can we do better? *Functional Ecology* 32:117–125. doi:10.1111/1365-2435.12982

Karger, D. N., O. Conrad, J. Böhner, et al. 2017. Climatologies at high resolution for the earth's land surface areas. *Scientific Data* 4:1–20. doi:10.1038/sdata.2017.122

Keane, R. M., and M. J. Crawley. 2002. Exotic plant invasions and the enemy release hypothesis. *Trends in Ecology and Evolution* 17:164–170. doi:10.1016/S0169-5347(02)02499-0

Kopp, D., and D. Allen. 2021. Scaling spatial pattern in river networks: The effects of spatial extent, grain size and thematic resolution. *Landscape Ecology* 36:2781–2794. doi:10.1007/s10980-021-01270-2

Kotowska, D., T. Pärt, P. Skórka, et al. 2022. Scale dependence of landscape heterogeneity effects on plant invasions. *Journal of Applied Ecology* 59:1313–1323. doi:10.1111/1365-2664.14143

Lawton, J. H. 1999. Are there general laws in ecology? *Oikos* 84:177–192.

Levin, S. A. 1992. The problem of pattern and scale in ecology: The Robert H. MacArthur award lecture. *Ecology* 73:1943–1967.

Miguet, P., H. B. Jackson, N. D. Jackson, et al. 2016. What determines the spatial extent of landscape effects on species? *Landscape Ecology* 31:1177–1194. doi:10.1007/s10980-015-0314-1

Miller, J., J. Franklin, and R. Aspinall. 2007. Incorporating spatial dependence in predictive vegetation models. *Ecological Modelling* 202:225–242. doi:10.1016/j.ecolmodel.2006.12.012

Mitchell, E. G., S. Harris, C. G. Kenchington, et al. 2019. The importance of neutral over niche processes in structuring Ediacaran early animal communities. *Ecology Letters* 22:2028–2038. doi:10.1111/ele.13383

Morton, D. N., C. Y. Antonino, F. J. Broughton, et al. 2021. A food web including parasites for kelp forests of the Santa Barbara Channel, California. *Scientific Data* 8:1–14. doi:10.1038/s41597-021-00880-4

Münkemüller, T., L. Gallien, L. J. Pollock, et al. 2020. Dos and don'ts when inferring assembly rules from diversity patterns. *Global Ecology and Biogeography* 29:1212–1229. doi:10.1111/geb.13098

Novoa, A., D. Moodley, J. A. Catford, et al. 2021. Global costs of plant invasions must not be underestimated. *NeoBiota* 69:75–78. doi:10.3897/neobiota.69.74121

Park, D. S., and D. Potter. 2013. A test of Darwin's naturalization hypothesis in the thistle tribe shows that close relatives make bad neighbors. *Proceedings of the National Academy of Sciences of the United States of America* 110:17915–17920. doi:10.1073/pnas.1309948110

Park, D. S., X. Feng, B. S. Maitner, et al. 2020. Darwin's naturalization conundrum can be explained by spatial scale. *Proceedings of the National Academy of Sciences of the United States of America* 117:10904–10910. doi:10.1073/pnas.1918100117

Peres-Neto, P. R., and P. Legendre. 2010. Estimating and controlling for spatial structure in the study of ecological communities. *Global Ecology and Biogeography* 19:174–184. doi:10.1111/j.1466-8238.2009.00506.x

Poulin, R. 2019. Best practice guidelines for studies of parasite community ecology. *Journal of Helminthology* 93:8–11. doi:10.1017/S0022149X18000767

Peng, S., N. L. Kinlock, J. Gurevitch, and S. Peng. 2019. Correlation of native and exotic species richness: A global meta-analysis finds no invasion paradox across scales. *Ecology* 100:e02552. doi:10.1002/ecy.2552

Pérez-Navarro, M. A., O. Broennimann, M. A. Esteve, et al. 2021. Temporal variability is key to modelling the climatic niche. *Diversity and Distributions* 27:473–484. doi:10.1111/ddi.13207

Pinto-Ledezma, J. N., F. Villalobos, P. B. Reich, J. A. Catford, D. J. Larkin, and J. Cavender-Bares. 2020. Testing Darwin's naturalization conundrum based on taxonomic, phylogenetic, and functional dimensions of vascular plants. *Ecological Monographs* 90:e01420. doi:10.1002/ecm.1420

Rollinson, C. R., A. O. Finley, M. R. Alexander, et al. 2021. Working across space and time: Nonstationarity in ecological research and application. *Frontiers in Ecology and the Environment* 19:66–72. doi:10.1002/fee.2298

Rynkiewicz, E. C., A. B. Pedersen, and A. Fenton. 2015. An ecosystem approach to understanding and managing within-host parasite community dynamics. *Trends in Parasitology* 31:212–221. doi:10.1016/j.pt.2015.02.005

Ryo, M., C. A. Aguilar-Trigueros, L. Pinek, et al. 2019. Basic principles of temporal dynamics. *Trends in Ecology and Evolution* 34:723–733. doi:10.1016/j.tree.2019.03.007

Sandel, B., and A. B. Smith. 2009. Scale as a lurking factor: Incorporating scale-dependence in experimental ecology. *Oikos* 118:1284–1291. doi:10.1111/j.1600-0706.2009.17421.x

Schaefer, H., O. J. Hardy, L. Silva, et al. 2011. Testing Darwin's naturalization hypothesis in the Azores. *Ecology Letters* 14:389–396. doi:10.1111/j.1461-0248.2011.01600.x

Smith, N. S., and I. M. Cote. 2019. Multiple drivers of contrasting diversity–invasibility relationships at fine spatial grains. *Ecology* 100:e02573. doi:10.1002/ecy.2573

Spake, R., A. S. Mori, M. Beckmann, et al. 2021. Implications of scale dependence for cross-study syntheses of biodiversity differences. *Ecology Letters* 24:374–390. doi:10.1111/ele.13641

Stricker, K. B., D. Hagan, and S. L. Flory. 2015. Improving methods to evaluate the impacts of plant invasions: Lessons from 40 years of research. *AoB Plants* 7:plv028. doi:10.1093/aobpla/plv028

Swenson, N. G., B. J. Enquist, J. Pither, et al. 2006. The problem and promise of scale dependency in community phylogenetics. *Ecology* 87:2418–2424. doi:10.1890/0012-9658(2006)87[2418:TPAPOS]2.0.CO;2

Turner, M. G., V. H. Dale, and R. H. Gardner. 1989. Predicting across scales: Theory development and testing. *Landscape Ecology* 3:245–252.

Wan, J., B. Huang, H. Yu, and S. Peng. 2019. Reassociation of an invasive plant with its specialist herbivore provides a test of the shifting defence hypothesis. *Journal of Ecology* 107:361–371. doi:10.1111/1365-2745.13019

Wauchope, H. S., T. Amano, W. J. Sutherland, and A. Johnston. 2019. When can we trust population trends? A method for quantifying the effects of sampling interval and duration. *Methods in Ecology and Evolution* 10:2067–2078. doi:10.1111/2041-210X.13302

Wiens, J. A. 1989. Spatial scaling in ecology. *Functional Ecology* 3:385–397.

6

Assembling the ecological puzzle

JANNICE FRIEDMAN AND ALY VAN NATTO

FROM THE PICTURE ON THE OUTSIDE TO THE PIECES IN THE BOX

Ecologists often choose to focus on particular aspects of an organism, community or ecosystem. Despite reducing the scope of their questions, they are still dealing with the outcome of a myriad of components, processes and interactions. Examining any one aspect in isolation may fail to lead to an adequate understanding of the entire (sub)system.

The steps necessary to fully understand any scientific issue ideally involve a series of studies, at appropriate scales, addressing the interactions between the components and their effects on each other. Surveys can generate hypotheses about what is going on; theoretical modelling can suggest what is liable to occur under particular scenarios, while experiments can test hypotheses by showing how the system changes as variables are altered in a controlled manner. Researchers learn from each of these steps, propose further questions that will unravel the system and develop appropriate follow-up studies: an iterative process that leads to ever-greater knowledge. Perhaps they model it or simulate its workings in greater detail; they test whether some explanations are better supported by others; and they modify their ideas accordingly. And, step by step, they get closer to a true comprehension of how the system works (see Figure 1.1).

Ecology is rooted in natural history, and indeed natural exploration and observation form the foundation of almost every discipline in biology. Natural history surprises us, amazes us and often leaves us wanting more explanation. It is intuitive to go directly from an interesting observation to the inference of a process that caused it – whether it be explanations for a giraffe's long neck, why bipedalism evolved in humans or how the leopard got its spots. These 'just-so stories' reflect a desire to explain form and function by imagining and reconstructing the processes that gave rise to them. The phrase 'just-so stories' is often used pejoratively and critically in the scientific academic literature; however, these types of observations can form the basis of hypotheses and be an important part of the scientific process (Smith et al. 2016). The crux of science is that we do not accept claims without evidence and substantiation. Plausible hypotheses need to be challenged and tested until we are as certain as we can be that we have found the probable explanation. The early speculations need to be just that, the beginning step that will lead towards rigorous explorations. Follow-up research that tests hypotheses, modifies explanations, interprets data and builds upon knowledge is essential.

Research in the area of evolutionary ecology provides outstanding examples of how to move through the steps described above. The goal of research in this area is to understand the processes generating and maintaining variation in

DOI: 10.1201/9781003314332-6

nature. Having observed patterns of phenotypic and genetic variation in time and space, we use a wide array of techniques to best determine how, and over what timescales, those patterns arose. We can start by speculating. We can look at survey data for evidence of particular processes, and use theory and modelling to understand what to expect under specific circumstances. We can conduct experiments to show that these explanations are plausible because we can replicate them; we can further elucidate those mechanisms. And we can end up identifying the genes or mutations encoding differences in phenotypes.

In this chapter, we break down the foundational concepts that underlie the integration of some of the main techniques used in evolutionary ecology, and then use three case studies that exemplify the kind of traits and species that have been used to successfully connect the multitude of factors relating to the environment, phenotype and genotype that underlie adaptive variation.

DIFFICULTIES IN DRAWING EVOLUTIONARY INFERENCES

Despite a deep history and rich tradition of research in evolutionary ecology, there remain fundamental issues that we need to grapple with in every study, complications at the core of how we define the concepts that ultimately constrain the inferences that we can make. These complications include things like how we specify the traits on which selections acts, how we decide on the fitness 'currency' through which evolution proceeds, how we cope with correlations among traits and interactions among processes, and how we recognise adaptation when we are confronted with it. Thorny issues such as these are part of the reason why iterative and integrative methods are necessary to link together the pieces of the research puzzle, so that a complete picture of the system can emerge. While the issues we discuss in this section are specific to a particular type of research, we hope they act to exemplify the value of being fully cognisant of our assumptions and obstacles in all ecological research. Each of us makes many assumptions, some small, some large. It is only by critical deliberation of them that we can determine what to measure and what to do with the data that we collect (see also Chapter 7).

What are the traits on which selection has acted?

Identifying a trait of ecological significance often begins with natural history observations of variation within or among populations. The very existence of this variation often hints at its evolutionary potential. While these traits may not be causally related to fitness, they may be related to components of fitness, either mechanistically through genetic, developmental, morphological or physiological connections, or statistically through their correlational impact on survival and reproduction. While identifying the existence of trait variation can be a starting point in a research program, careful experiments and modelling are needed to demonstrate the role of natural selection and adaptation in determining the extent and maintenance of that variation (Stinchcombe et al. 2002). Crucially, the relative fitness of any particular trait depends on the environment the organism experiences. Thus, traits that confer high fitness now may become less fit in the future if the environment changes (and vice versa). On the other hand, currently beneficial traits may have been present long before the current environmental conditions, without having conferred any previous advantage.

How do we recognise adaptation?

Living organisms have some amazing complex adaptations that, it is tempting to assume, are the result of natural selection. But not all characteristics or seemingly adaptive traits are adaptations at all. Evolutionary biologists (and natural history documentaries) are sometimes inclined to invoke 'just-so stories' or speculate that selection could have produced a particular trait for a particular function.

While it is tempting to look for adaptive explanations to describe the extraordinary diversity around us, alternative explanations must be considered. For example, it is possible that a particular trait of interest reflects genetic drift; or that it is constrained through physiological, developmental or genetic mechanisms; or that it emerged as a by-product of selection on other traits; or that it was once adaptive but due to environmental changes it is no longer. Carefully designed experiments or robust comparisons between appropriate groups are necessary to demonstrate adaptation (Olson-Manning et al. 2012).

How do we measure fitness?

The word 'fitness' is meant to capture the total relative performance of individuals that will predict their success and their long-term contribution to population dynamics. But the definition of fitness often depends on the question of interest and the biological system under consideration (Hendry et al. 2018). A useful metric of fitness comprises both survival and reproduction, measured as lifetime reproductive success. For species that persist for multiple years and with multiple bouts of reproduction (i.e. iteroparous species), determining lifetime fitness can be challenging or near impossible. Thus, we usually measure just components of fitness, or make measurements in a single year or season. Additionally, for many organisms it can be difficult to ascertain male reproductive success, and co-sexual organisms can have different fitness through female and male function. Molecular approaches to assigning paternity have facilitated the ability to quantify male fitness empirically, but quantifying male fitness continues to pose technical and logistical challenges.

What if there are trade-offs and correlations between traits?

A trade-off exists when an evolutionary change that increases fitness in one phenotypic trait or context causes a decrease in fitness in another trait or context. Correlations between traits can constrain or facilitate evolutionary responses to selection (e.g. Etterson and Shaw 2001). Various analytical approaches can help to parse out the tangle of correlations between traits (Lande and Arnold 1983). Using multiple regression, it is possible to determine how much of the covariance between a trait and fitness is independent of other correlated traits. This approach has changed the way that selection is studied in the wild, and it ameliorates the problem of confounding trait correlations. Furthermore, the genetic architecture underlying trait correlations can help us understand both their evolutionary causes and consequences. For example, when one gene affects two or more traits – known as pleiotropy – the two traits are unable to evolve independently. A similar outcome can occur when the genes for traits are in close physical proximity on a chromosome and experience 'linkage disequilibrium' (see Slatkin 2008). Alternatively, one trait may be influenced by more than one gene – known as epistasis – and depending on the nature of the interactions between the genes, can mean that the phenotypic outcomes are constrained. Well-designed experiments using genetic mapping populations, or lines where genotypes are known and fixed, can allow researchers to gain an understanding of the independent effects of single traits or genes.

What are the timescales?

One of the challenges of linking ecology and environmental differences to evolutionary processes that generate phenotypic variation is the timescale that underlies these processes. Research in the past few decades has demonstrated that selection and evolution in natural populations is often much faster, more dynamic and on shorter timescales than originally conceived (Hairston et al. 2005). In many recent studies, rapid evolutionary change has been shown to occur on the timescale of 1–100 years (Messer et al. 2016). To understand the processes generating and maintaining trait variation, it is useful to look at the evolution of novel traits when they first arise. This approach often relies on comparisons between populations that differ in their environment, in which natural selection has acted on genetic variation to produce phenotypic differences between the populations. A challenge in studying variation at short timescales is that the differences (genetic or phenotypic) between individuals may not be great. Nonetheless, studying recent evolutionary changes is informative because we know or can reliably infer the ecological context in which selection is acting.

THE METHODS AVAILABLE

How do we go about dealing with the conceptual or methodological issues above and assess the validity of how the different parts of a system work and contribute to the overall outcome? The specific methods employed will depend on the research field and the type of information required. The important aspect that we wish to emphasise here is that relying on any one method, or only one approach, is unlikely to lead to a complete picture. To demonstrate this, we use examples from evolutionary biology highlighted by the complications from the previous section.

In many cases, there is a clear logical flow beginning with natural history observations, to identifying the mechanisms and processes that *could* give rise to the phenotypic and genotypic variation and then demonstrating which *have* (probably) given rise to that variation (Figure 6.1). One of the strengths of evolutionary ecology is that it has a rich tradition of formal theoretical modelling, which often provides the foundation for how we tackle empirical research. Here we outline the key research themes and the types of methods available to first drill down and understand mechanisms and processes, and then to integrate and connect between the various pieces of research.

An understanding of natural selection is at the core of evolutionary ecology, and yet identifying and studying natural selection is notoriously difficult (Endler 1986). Natural selection is generally ubiquitous in nature and a characteristic of populations everywhere. Breaking down the process of evolution by natural selection reveals the nature of its parts.

Whenever trait values are associated with differential reproductive success (fitness) within a generation, phenotypic selection is at play. The effect of phenotypic selection is then mediated through the heritability of the trait, and its underlying genetic architecture, to determine evolutionary change. The first step then for understanding evolution by natural selection is to quantify the nature and strength of selection and the patterns of phenotypic selection observed in nature.

To determine whether selection is likely to be acting on a particular trait in a population, we first estimate the fitness associated with the various trait values (Box 1; Figure 6.2a). This allows us to establish that there exists an average, non-random variation in fitness, and that the difference in fitness between individuals is caused by, or correlated with, their phenotypes (trait values). Typically, this is done by measuring trait values for a sample of individuals within a population that are of similar age (e.g. juvenile animals or annual plants). Individuals are marked and then followed over a period of time to determine their survival and/or reproductive success. In an ideal scenario,

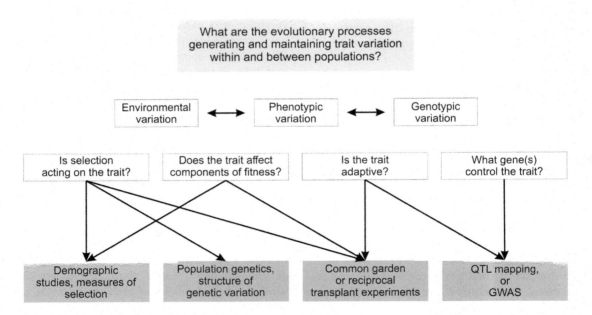

Figure 6.1 A schematic of the ideas discussed in this chapter. Beginning with the broad question aimed at understanding the evolutionary processes generating and maintaining trait variation in nature, we illustrate the component questions that can be tackled with specific methods, and then integrated to return to the larger question.

Assembling the ecological puzzle 85

BOX 6.1: Integrating diverse methods

We provide a brief description of some of the methods used as part of an iterative process to understand the factors generating and maintaining trait variation within a species. Although these methods can be used to answer a myriad of questions, this example focuses on the process of natural selection and how it affects phenotypes in different environments.

Many studies of adaptation by natural selection begin with an observation of variation in a trait of interest within or among populations. The trait of interest may range from the molecular level (e.g. expression of an immunity-related gene) to easily identifiable traits (e.g. flower colour), and usually precedes a prediction of adaptive significance. In Figure 6.2a we illustrate a trait that is under both directional and stabilising selection, and the pattern suggests that the trait influences fitness directly in that environment. However, the fitness function may not be consistent between populations, years or environments.

One approach to testing for adaptive significance of a trait is to determine if populations are locally adapted to their home environment. To compare populations, common garden and reciprocal transplant experiments are useful methods. These traditional approaches have stood the test of time because of their effectiveness. Figure 6.2b (left) shows differences between traits in two populations. Figure 6.2b (right) shows hypothetical results from a reciprocal transplant study where individuals from 'Population 1' are transplanted into the environment of 'Population 2' and *vice versa*. The change of phenotypes expressed by a genotype in different environments indicates local adaptation resulting from divergent selection because fitness is higher in the home environment (see Anderson et al. 2011 for further details). Researchers may conclude that the trait has diverged due to selection in opposing directions in these populations.

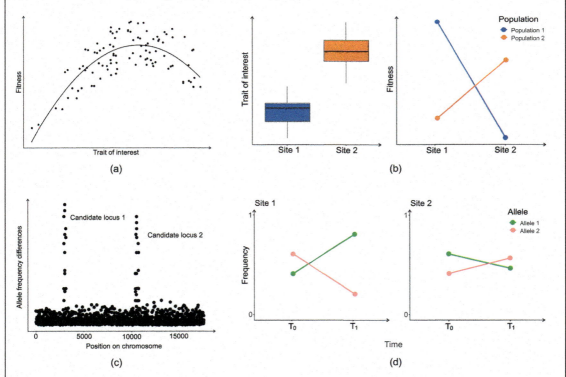

Figure 6.2 Some of the methods used as part of an iterative process to understand the factors generating and maintaining trait variation within a species. See text for details.

(Continued)

The next question may be to understand the evolutionary history of the causal genes underlying the trait differences. One approach to this is to use population genomic sequencing to compare allele frequency differences across the genome between populations (Figure 6.2c). Regions of the genome that have higher differences than expected by neutral processes (e.g. Candidate loci 1 and 2 in Figure 6.2c) can identify putative candidate genes that have evolved under spatially divergent selection and indicate adaptive loci. Further investigations may assess possible function of candidate genes by comparing them to an annotated genome. Genome-wide studies can tell us about the evolutionary history of adaptive loci (Barrett and Schluter 2008). For example, if selection favours a beneficial allele from the moment it enters the population as a single copy mutation (hard selective sweep) there is a different pattern of genetic variation around the locus compared to when multiple mutations at the same gene or existing variation becomes beneficial (soft selective sweep).

Once researchers have identified the genes controlling adaptive traits, they can connect the genotypic differences back to the ecological mechanisms causing selection. One way to do this is to combine a common garden experiment with genetic sequencing. For example, in Figure 6.2d, individuals were genotyped at 'candidate gene 1' and then put into a reciprocal transplant experiment and the frequency of the allele is then sampled through time. In this example, 'Allele 1' originates from 'Population 1', and 'Allele 2' originates from 'Population 2'. If allele frequencies change more drastically at one site, then it suggests that selection is stronger in that environment: linking evolution back to ecology (see Savolainen et al. 2013).

we would attain total lifetime fitness. In reality, this is seldom achieved, and most researchers measure just some components of fitness: survival, mating success or fecundity. Statistical approaches are then used to relate the trait values to fitness: a regression analysis allows us to determine the strength and mode of selection acting on the trait of interest.

The process of adaptation occurs as populations of organisms evolve to become better suited to their environments, through natural selection increasing the prevalence of advantageous traits. A curious feature about the concept of natural selection leading to adaptation is that the chief action of natural selection is to eliminate or reduce the frequency of low-fitness traits. In fact, most forms of natural selection will deplete genetic variation within populations. Nonetheless, adaptation has given rise to extraordinarily elaborate and complex characters. The key generative process occurs as new genetic variation is introduced by mutation and recombination (in sexually reproducing organisms), or through gene flow via migration or hybridisation with other species. Beneficial traits increase through time, and the direction of adaptive change depends on the environment. Implicit in this (and sometimes underappreciated) is that adaptations are always to the conditions experienced by past generations.

Ecologists and evolutionary biologists often focus on differences between populations, and these differences are frequently interpreted in the context of selection and adaptation. But not all differences among populations or species are adaptive, an idea eloquently described by Gould and Lewontin (1979). Differences between populations or species could be caused by genetic drift and reflect neutral processes (e.g. Husband and Barrett 1992). It is also possible that the traits of interest that differ between populations did not evolve for those purposes at all or evolved as a by-product of selection on other traits (e.g. Bourdeau 2010). Particularly when considering differences between species, it is possible that trait differences are due to historical contingency and that they are simply the features that happened to be inherited from ancestors (Blount et al. 2018). For all these reasons, defining and studying adaptation can be challenging.

Experiments are among the most powerful tools to isolate the effect of a single, well-defined factor. A powerful and long-established experimental approach for identifying adaptation, and particularly local adaptation, involves the use of common garden experiments and reciprocal transplant experiments (Blanquart et al. 2013). Because local adaptation occurs when organisms have higher average fitness in their local environment compared to individuals from elsewhere, by using an approach that explicitly measures fitness of individuals from different environments, researchers can compare their performance and aim to identify the traits that contribute to those fitness differences (Box 1; Figure 6.2b). The history of transplant experiments goes back to studies of spatial phenotypic variation in plants (von Marilaun and Oliver 1895). Turesson (1922) first used transplant experiments to reveal that spatial variation across a species range is genetically based and could be associated with performance differences and adaptive traits between populations.

The mid-20th century reciprocal transplant experiments of Clausen et al. (1940), demonstrating adaptation by plants along an altitudinal climatic gradient, are arguably the most famous, and following these classic experiments, a large number of studies have since estimated local adaptation in a wide variety of species (Hereford 2009; Briscoe Runquist et al. 2020). These studies indicate that habitat-mediated natural selection plays a pervasive role in the maintenance of genetic variation among locations with contrasting environments.

Natural variation within populations has long been the fodder of ecologists and evolutionary biologists alike. The largely phenotypic approaches discussed above allow us to predict and interpret changes in traits over time or space. However, not all approaches require an understanding of the traits under selection – researchers can use DNA sequence variation to examine population genetic processes, like the effects of gene flow, population structure and inbreeding. Further, many longstanding questions about the genetic basis of phenotypic evolution and adaptation can be addressed by combining an understanding of trait variation with the genetic mechanisms. Identifying the genetic changes underlying adaptation allows researchers to address whether phenotypic convergence involves repeatable genetic changes (Stern 2013), whether adaptive mutations are more likely to occur in coding or regulatory regions (Wittkopp and Kalay 2012), whether adaptive alleles are more often of large or small effect (Yeaman 2015), and assess the relative contributions of adaptive evolution, balancing selection, deleterious variation and genetic drift in maintaining variation (Mitchell-Olds et al. 2007).

Before modern molecular biology, studying genetic variation in natural populations was limited to visible phenotypes with a known genetic basis, and early theoretical population geneticists used this type of variation to study evolutionary processes (e.g. Fisher 1930; Wright 1931; Haldane 1932). Many of the studies on major gene polymorphisms come from highly visible trait variation, with examples including male horn type in sheep (Johnston et al. 2013), wing spot variation in butterflies (Reed et al. 2011) and flower colour variation (Brown and Clegg 1984). However, organisms vary in complex ways in their anatomy, physiology and behaviour. For most traits, this variation reflects the combination of multiple environmental and genetic factors. Later we will discuss three case studies of selection – coat colour in deer mouse, freshwater adaptation in stickleback and copper tolerance in monkeyflowers – all of which identify the cause of natural selection, connect this with changes in allele frequencies, and use genomic and bioinformatic approaches to identify the loci responsible for phenotypic variation.

Advances in technology enabled experimental approaches to identify the genetic architecture of more complex characters, using a combination of genomics and bioinformatics. First, quantitative trait locus (QTL) mapping was used to identify the genomic location, number and effect sizes of genetic changes that underlie phenotypic differences among natural populations of plants and animals. Approaches that use whole genome sequencing, such as genome-wide association studies (GWAS), can allow researchers to address whether the genetic changes that underlie phenotypic evolution and adaptation are found together in particular regions of the genome or whether the genes are distributed across the genome (Box 1; Figure 6.2c, d). These questions are important if we wish to understand the process of an organism adapting to a new environment, because adaptation usually requires multiple phenotypic changes. For example, consider an ant species that is adapting to a warmer, urban environment from a cooler, rural environment (Martin et al. 2021). Adaptation to the new environment will require multiple phenotypic differences, including morphology, life history and physiology. The process of adaptation may be facilitated if the same genetic changes give rise to multiple phenotypic differences (pleiotropy), or if multiple phenotypes are inherited together due to linkage of genes. Filling in these details allows us to broadly understand the evolutionary process without making simplifying assumptions.

CASE STUDIES THAT EXEMPLIFY INTEGRATIVE METHODS

Here we use three case studies to highlight study systems where researchers have combined some of the methods outlined above to make significant progress in assembling the pieces of the evolutionary ecological puzzle. The foundation for this research was natural history observations on populations that varied in key traits or experienced different ecological conditions. From these observations, researchers proceeded to design successive careful experiments to test the evolutionary and genetic mechanisms responsible for the variation, through an iterative process where discoveries feed back to refine and reformulate future research.

Case study 1: threespine stickleback

An understanding of the genetics of adaptive evolution has emerged from extensive studies on the evolution of threespine stickleback fish as they adapted from living in the ocean to living exclusively in freshwater environments. Threespine sticklebacks (*Gasterosteus aculeatus*) are fish that inhabit saltwater and freshwater habitats in the Northern Hemisphere.

Most populations of sticklebacks are either exclusively marine or live in coastal waters and enter streams and lakes to spawn and then move back out to sea, but some populations have adapted to live their entire lives in lakes. We know that ancestors of the species were trapped in lakes that formed at the end of the glacial maximum approximately 12,000 years ago (McPhail 1993). Fish in freshwater populations have fewer spines and drastically reduced lateral plating compared to their marine relatives, and this phenotypic variation suggested the differences were adaptive. The research on freshwater stickleback populations highlights the benefit of combining rigorous studies of natural selection, with research on developmental and genetic mechanisms underlying phenotypic differences, to develop a holistic picture of the adaptation to freshwater environments.

One of the earliest studies aimed at identifying whether lateral armour in threespine stickleback was associated with environmental variation demonstrated a phenotypic correlation, where fish from saline environments had more plates and fish from freshwater had fewer plates (Bertin 1925). To investigate whether the morphological differences were due to genetic or environmental variation, Heuts (1947) used a reciprocal transplant experiment to compare the development of eggs parented by fish of varying armour in aquaria that differed in temperatures and salinities. The results indicated that survival and hatching success existed in narrow ranges of temperature and salinity for each plate morph and were thus the result of natural selection. Later studies have investigated other possible mechanisms influencing body armour in threespine stickleback including predation (Reimchen 2000; Vamosi and Schluter 2004; Marchinko 2009), buoyancy (Myhre and Klepaker 2009), swimming performance (Bergstrom 2002; Blake 2004; Hendry et al. 2011), growth rate (Marchinko and Schluter 2007; Barrett et al. 2009) and ionic concentrations (Giles 1983; Bell et al. 1993). Contemporary studies are still aiming to determine the key ecological factors driving the evolution of body armour in threespine stickleback.

The next question in the research program was to connect the phenotypic variation to causal genetic variants, and to ask whether there were consistent differences between oceanic and freshwater populations. First, phylogenetic relations among populations of fish were examined with mitochondrial and microsatellite markers to show independent introductions to freshwater environments (Taylor and McPhail 1999). Next, genetic crosses between freshwater and marine fish revealed the genetic loci controlling the phenotypic differences in body armour, initially using a linkage map with about 200 microsatellite markers (Peichel et al. 2001). The introduction of population genomics expanded threespine stickleback research dramatically. Shortly after, researchers used QTL mapping to identify the genetic loci related to differences in plate morph number (Colosimo et al. 2005), and genome-wide patterns of differentiation to identify novel regions of the genome responsible for adaptation (Hohenlohe et al. 2010). One of the genes involved is known as *Eda*, which codes for a signalling protein involved in the growth of lateral armour plates in fish. By comparing the genetic differences in the low-*Eda* allele in different freshwater populations, researchers found that it likely arose at least two million years ago in the marine ancestors of freshwater sticklebacks. Because the allele is recessive, it would have lingered at very low frequencies in ancestral marine populations, and this standing genetic variation provided a selective advantage when populations colonised freshwaters. These new environments lacked predators and contained different ionic compounds, so that elaborate defences no longer resulted in higher fitness. The low-*Eda* allele now increased fitness and rapidly increased in frequency across replicate freshwater populations.

The genetic patterns of variation in the *Eda* gene strongly suggested that these alleles were associated with adaptation, but formal experiments are necessary to confirm the connection between genotypic variation and phenotypic performance in natural populations. Experiments using living populations of fish directly tested how natural selection caused the increase in the low-*Eda* allele in freshwater populations. Researchers used a common garden experiment, where they populated ponds with marine and freshwater fish, tracked individual survival and growth, and genotyped fish at the *Eda* locus. The results revealed that individuals with less body armour, and low-*Eda* alleles, had an advantage in predator-free lakes (Barrett et al. 2008). For example, the reduction in armour gives insect predators less area to grab onto juvenile fish in freshwater environments. The energy investment to grow armour is also costly, and in freshwater environments this is compounded with low concentrations of the ions necessary for bone growth. Juvenile fish with low armour can grow faster and increase lipid storage, which result in higher overwinter survival and earlier reproduction the following season, both key components of fitness.

Case study 2: deer mouse

Variation in coat colour pigmentation in deer mice (genus *Peromyscus*) has provided a rich backdrop for understanding natural selection and the genetic basis of colour adaptation. Deer mice are ubiquitous in North America with '*not one square mile not inhabited by* Peromyscus' (Osgoode 1909). Early research documented variation in coat colour across populations in different environments. Based on measurements of thousands of deer mice in field observations and experiments in laboratory conditions, Sumner (1929) showed a strong relation between coat colour and soil colour among field populations and demonstrated that

coat colour was genetically inherited. A plausible inference was that coat colour evolved for camouflage against visual predators. These extensive natural history observations form the basis of more recent research on *Peromyscus*, which has become one of the best model systems for connecting ecology with genetics to understand evolutionary processes.

One of the species of *Peromyscus* that varies dramatically in coat colour and associated soil colour is *P. maniculatus*. Populations of this species live on the Sand Hills of Nebraska, a dune field with light quartz grain soil that is lighter in colour than the surrounding soils. Mice living on these soils have evolved a dorsal coat that matches the soil, plausibly due to selection imposed by visual avian predators against dark coats that would be conspicuous on light soils. Because the Sand Hills are geologically young, dating back to the receding of the Wisconsin glacial period 8000 to 15,000 years ago (Loope and Swinehart 2000), the light-coloured mice are evidence of recent adaptation. Research for the past 75 years has aimed to answer what ecological factors drive this evolution and what genes cause the divergent phenotypes.

While it seems intuitive that light mice should have a survival advantage on light soils, empirical evidence is necessary to demonstrate that colour differences matter and to what extent they matter. Using experiments to show that coat colour influences predation risk, Dice (1947) employed a common garden approach in which mice with varying dorsal coat colours were released in two indoor enclosures with either dark and light soil colours and subjected to predation by two owls. They found that mice that matched the soil colour were 70% less likely to be captured by a predator, providing direct support for the hypothesis that coat colour does indeed aid in predation avoidance.

In a more recent experiment, this time in the natural Sand Hills environment, Linnen et al. (2013) measured attack rates on light and dark clay models and similarly found that conspicuous dark models were attacked significantly more than light models. These experiments demonstrate that natural selection is almost certainly occurring, due to survival differences in mice with different coat colours.

The next question was to understand how colour varies. To begin, researchers drew on knowledge from the extensively studied mouse, *Mus musculus*, where knockouts of the *Agouti* gene resulted in dark-coloured mice, while overexpression of *Agouti* resulted in light-coloured mice. Using a crossing experiment between light and dark mice, and mRNA expression levels, Linnen et al. (2009) found that *Agouti* is responsible for the light-coloured phenotype in *P. maniculatus*. Now that the phenotypic effect of *Agouti* was understood, the ecological consequences of changes in *Agouti* could be investigated.

To test whether selection favours locally adapted colour phenotypes, Barrett et al. (2019) conducted a reciprocal transplant experiment similar to experiments done by Dice (1947) and Linnen et al. (2013) but with live mice in natural habitats. They collected dark- and light-coloured mice and released them in enclosures that either had dark- or light-coloured soil. All enclosures were open to predators. They tracked the survival of all mice regularly using a mark-recapture method until mortality reached almost 100%. They found that mice introduced to enclosures that matched their original habitat type had greater survival than mice from a different habitat, demonstrating local adaptation in each environment. Additionally, they demonstrated selection on pigmentation: in light enclosures, mice were 1.44 times lighter than mice from the founding populations; and in dark enclosures, mice were 1.98 times darker. Finally, they fully connected the research on natural selection with the genetics of adaptation by determining how allele frequencies at the *Agouti* locus changed over the course of the experiment. They found significant allele frequency changes consistent with selection in the dark enclosures, and similarly in the light enclosures, although low survival reduced their statistical power.

Case study 3: seep monkeyflower

Much like the research on stickleback and deer mice, natural history observations of extensive variation in nature underpin current research on plants in the genus *Mimulus* (*sensu lato*; monkeyflowers). Several species in this genus have become model systems in evolutionary ecology and evolutionary genetics because of their variation in reproduction, life history and physiology. *Mimulus guttatus* (syn. *Erythranthe guttata*) is a widespread species with a native range from Mexico to Alaska and from the Pacific coast to the Rocky Mountains. It is part of a species complex with about a dozen other species that have evolved in response to a wide range of abiotic and biotic conditions. Populations can be found in grasslands, forests, desert streams, peat bogs, alpine meadows and seeps, coastal cliffs and sand dunes and even in toxic soils of serpentine barrens and copper mine tailings (Wu et al. 2008).

Here we use the research on copper tolerance in *M. guttatus* to demonstrate an integrative research program. Common garden greenhouse experiments were first used by Allen and Sheppard in the early 1970s to confirm genetic differences among plants from copper-contaminated soils compared to nearby plants on unpolluted land. They demonstrated that populations from non-contaminated soil had less root growth (a proxy for tolerance) than populations from contaminated soils when grown in contaminated aqueous solutions or soil, suggesting that plants from contaminated populations had adapted to high metal concentrations. Further, they used progeny from tolerant and intolerant parents to demonstrate that the trait was heritable. This study (Allen and Sheppard 1971) set the stage for future efforts to determine the exact genetic mechanism underlying copper tolerance.

Early experiments to identify genetic mechanisms underpinning copper tolerance used classic Mendelian crossing experiments. MacNair (1977) crossed putative tolerant individuals with non-tolerant individuals, backcrossing them and measuring root growth in copper-contaminated solution. The ratio of back-crossed plants that were copper tolerant was consistent with a hypothesis that copper tolerance is controlled by two major genes. However, upon continued breeding experiments with selfed and back-crossed F1 hybrids, research found ratios more aligned with a single gene controlling copper tolerance (MacNair 1983). These crosses also indicated that the locus controlling copper tolerance may also cause hybrid lethality in crosses with non-tolerant populations, perhaps due to pleiotropic effects or a tightly linked locus that has hitchhiked with the copper tolerance locus.

Thirty years later, Wright et al. (2013) took advantage of advances in molecular technologies by using QTL genetic mapping and bioinformatic approaches to identify the loci controlling copper tolerance. They discovered the gene *Tol1* was responsible for copper tolerance. Using additional crosses between tolerant and non-tolerant plants, they found that copper tolerance and hybrid inviability between tolerant and intolerant plants are controlled by two distinct but tightly linked genes rather than a pleiotropic by-product of copper tolerance. The allele for hybrid inviability causes necrosis (and consequently named *Nec1*), and exists in surprisingly high frequencies in copper-tolerant populations.

Hypotheses as to why *Nec1* exists at high frequency include: (1) genetic drift caused the allele to increase in frequency, (2) the hybrid lethality allele confers a fitness advantage in the mine habitat and has been directly selected and (3) the allele may have hitchhiked to high frequency due to tight linkage with *Tol1* which is under positive selection.

To distinguish between these hypotheses, researchers used population genomics and bioinformatics to compare genetic variation and divergence between copper mine and non-mine populations at the genomic region of *Tol1* and *Nec1*. They found mine populations have low genetic variation and high genetic differentiation compared to non-mine populations, indicating that the alleles increased in frequency due to selection. The results could not distinguish whether there was direct selection on both loci independently. However, the *Tol1* allele has been discovered at multiple mine sites, while the *Nec1* allele has only been found at one recently derived population, suggesting that direct selection is much more likely on the *Tol1* allele (Wright et al. 2013).

The presence of *Tol1* alleles in multiple mine populations provides an opportunity to investigate the potential for repeated evolution and local adaptation. A reciprocal transplant study coupled with genomic sequencing and coalescent analyses provided a powerful approach to identify the evolutionary processes generating and maintaining trait variation. First, to determine if mine and off-mine populations were locally adapted, researchers reciprocally planted individuals from mine habitats and non-mine habitats into both environments (Wright et al. 2015). They found that populations from mine populations performed better in mine habitats and *vice versa*, demonstrating strong local adaptation to mine conditions. Interestingly, they did not find a cost (or trade-off) to copper tolerance in off-mine environments. Next, they tested whether the fitness advantage in mine environments is directly related to *Tol1* alleles, by creating introgression lines with individuals from mine and non-mine sites, with or without the tolerance

allele. They found that individuals with tolerant alleles perform equivalently in non-mine sites and have increased survival in mine sites. Finally, to understand how copper tolerance arose at multiple mine sites, they used population genomics and bioinformatics to compare genetic variation around the candidate gene across populations to determine whether the allele arose from standing variation or new mutations. They found low genetic differentiation among mine populations, indicating that tolerance alleles at *Tol1* likely arose from standing genetic variation rather than independent mutations. This hypothesis is plausible because mine sites where *M. guttatus* exist are only about 150 years old and thus time for multiple mutations to arise is unlikely.

SO WHAT?

In this chapter we have explored the process of combining and integrating research methods to understand the generation and maintenance of trait variation in wild populations. Although we have focused on a specific area of study – evolutionary ecology – the approach is generalisable to all of ecology. We usually begin with speculation based on experience and common sense, but to understand the process and how the system works, we need to use an iterative and integrative approach that employs a variety of methods. Research that aims to mechanistically link the ecological and environmental differences among populations to the evolutionary processes that generate diversity is no easy task.

One of the strengths of evolutionary biology is that it is deeply rooted in a robust theoretical framework. This provides the foundation for making predictions about population genetic changes and the way selection operates. Although we may begin with highly plausible speculations about the selection pressures that are involved, or the traits that are responding to these selection agents, those factors may not necessarily be the most important influences. Even a carefully designed experiment may fail to control or account for the environmental variation that really matters to fitness. We may identify genetic differences among populations, or identify the genetic architecture of traits, but these may not be general across populations even within a single species. These challenges are often what make evolutionary ecology dynamic and stimulating, and why there remain many fundamental questions to address and hypotheses to test.

Regardless of the specific research question or field of study, there will always be merits to applying a diversity of methods (see Chapter 3). Ecology is, by nature, a field with complex, interacting pieces. By focusing solely on only one piece of the puzzle, or employing only one type of method, we are prone to making simplified (wrong) assumptions. We advocate for using a diversity of interlocking techniques and approaches, and encourage researchers to borrow across fields. Applying evolutionary perspectives to traditional ecological questions has proved fruitful and provided novel insight, and *vice versa* (e.g. Urban et al. 2020). The case studies discussed here exemplify this strategy.

Nonetheless, not all research requires this level of detail, and indeed intensive research on a large number of 'model systems' may be overkill. There will always be a place for a spectrum of research that ranges from broad-based observations to projects that go into incredible detail using the most advanced methodologies. It is an issue of balance, as well as a matter of scientific credibility and using suitable methods for the question. Natural history observations and straightforward experiments can tell us what is plausible. The field of Ecology can be developed further with studies that go deeper to demonstrate that the initial ideas are valid (Figure 1.1c).

A common concern among new researchers is that all the interesting studies have already been conducted, or that there are few new research avenues. As highlighted in the case studies discussed in this chapter, insightful new research is conducted by using different approaches, borrowing techniques from other fields, and testing old, fundamental ideas with new methods. New molecular technologies and analytical tools are facilitating new research directions, enabling us to answer questions that seemed impossible to achieve only a few decades ago.

Few researchers will have the expertise or time to independently apply a diversity of methods. Actively seeking out collaborators with varied skills can be rewarding, productive or fun – and perhaps essential for progress. But it is not always easy to identify appropriate collaborators. How does an early-career researcher attract collaborators with the skills, knowledge and experience

that they need to further their research or apply different methods? Collaborators need not be leaders in the field; peers at the same career stage working on different research questions can make excellent collaborators for integrative work. Regardless of who you are approaching, being well-informed and well-read on the person's work is respectful and necessary. Most researchers are excited to hear about other people's ideas and to share their own. It's okay if you find it intimidating at first – it becomes easier with experience. It's also okay to admit that you don't know everything and that there are gaps in your research expertise – that is the very point of seeking out collaborations! When you identify researchers with specific expertise, offer them a seminar on your intriguing fledgling research questions, this can help communicate the excitement of your investigations and the need for your work. Such offers are seldom rejected and can sow the seeds for collaboration. Small, intimate workshops (see Chapter 10) may provide better rewards for your attendance, even at the cost of missing out on big international conferences. With hope, your persistence will eventually be rewarded.

REFERENCES

Allen, W. R., and P. M. Sheppard. 1971. Copper tolerance in some Californian populations of the monkey flower, *Mimulus guttatus. Proceedings of the Royal Society B: Biological Sciences* 177:177–196. doi:10.1098/rspb.1971.0022

Anderson J. T., J. H. Willis, and T. Mitchell-Olds. 2011. Evolutionary genetics of plant adaptation. *Trends in Genetics* 27:258–266. doi:10.1016/j.tig.2011.04.001

Barrett, R. D. H., S. Laurent, R. Mallarino, et al. 2019. Linking a mutation to survival in wild mice. *Science* 363:499–504. doi:10.1126/science.aav3824

Barrett, R. D. H., S. M. Rogers, and D. Schluter. 2008. Natural selection on a major armor gene in threespine stickleback. *Science* 322:255–257. doi:10.1126/science.1159978

Barrett, R. D. H., S. M. Rogers, and D. Schluter. 2009. Environment specific pleiotropy facilitates divergence at the Ectodysplasin locus in threespine stickleback. *Evolution* 63:2831–2837. doi:10.1111/j.1558-5646.2009.00762.x

Barrett, R. D. H., and D. Schluter. 2008. Adaptation from standing genetic variation. *Trends in Ecology and Evolution* 23:38–44. doi:10.1016/j.tree.2007.09.008

Bell, M. A., G. Ortí, J. A. Walker, and J. P. Koenings. 1993. Evolution of pelvic reduction in threespine stickleback fish: a test of competing hypotheses. *Evolution* 47:906–914. doi:10.1111/j.1558-5646.1993.tb01243.x

Bergstrom, C. A. 2002. Fast-start swimming performance and reduction in lateral plate number in threespine stickleback. *Canadian Journal of Zoology* 80:207–213. doi:10.1139/z01-226

Bertin, L. 1925. *Recherches bionomiques, biométriques et systématiques sur les épinoches (Gastérostéidés).* Paris: Éd. Blondel La Rougery.

Blake, R. W. 2004. Fish functional design and swimming performance. *Journal of Fish Biology* 65:1193–1222. doi:10.1111/j.0022-1112.2004.00568.x

Blanquart, F., O. Kaltz, S. L. Nuismer, and S. Gandon. 2013. A practical guide to measuring local adaptation. *Ecology Letters* 16:1195–1205. doi:10.1111/ele.12150

Blount, Z. D., R. E. Lenski, and J. B. Losos. 2018. Contingency and determinism in evolution: Replaying life's tape. *Science* 362:eaam5979. doi:10.1126/science.aam5979

Bourdeau, P. E. 2010. An inducible morphological defence is a passive by-product of behaviour in a marine snail. *Proceedings of the Royal Society B: Biological Sciences* 277:455–462. doi:10.1098/rspb.2009.1295

Briscoe Runquist, R. D., A. J. Gorton, J. B. Yoder, et al. 2020. Context dependence of local adaptation to abiotic and biotic environments: a quantitative and qualitative synthesis. *American Naturalist* 195:412–431. doi:10.1086/707322

Brown, B. A., and M. T. Clegg. 1984. Influence of flower color polymorphism on genetic transmission in a natural population of the common morning glory, *Ipomoea purpurea. Evolution* 38:796–803. doi:10.2307/2408391

Clausen J., D. D. Keck, and W. M. Hiesey. 1940. *Experimental studies on the nature of species. I. Effect of varied environment on Western North American plants.* Washington, DC: Carnegie Institution of Washington. Publications No. 520.

Colosimo, P. F., K. E. Hosemann, S. Balabhadra, et al. 2005. Widespread parallel evolution in sticklebacks by repeated fixation of Ectodysplasin alleles. *Science* 307:1928–1933. doi:10.1126/science.1107239

Darwin, C. 1859. *On the origin of species by means of natural selection, or the preservation of favoured races in the struggle for life.* London: John Murray. doi:10.4324/9780203509104

Dice, L. R. 1947. Effectiveness of selection by owls of deer-mice (*Peromyscus maniculatus*) which contrast in color with their background. *Contributions of the Laboratory of Vertebrate Biology, University of Michigan* 34:1–20

Etterson, J. R., and R. G. Shaw. 2001. Constraint to adaptive evolution in response to global warming. *Science* 294:151–154. doi:10.1126/science.1063656

Endler, J. A. 1986. *Natural selection in the wild.* Princeton: Princeton University Press. doi:10.2307/j.ctvx5w9v9

Fisher, R. A. 1930. *The genetical theory of natural selection.* Oxford: Clarendon.

Giles, N. 1983. The possible role of environmental calcium levels during the evolution of phenotypic diversity in Outer Hebridean populations of the three-spined stickleback, *Gasterosteus aculeatus. Journal of Zoology* 199:535–544. doi:10.1111/j.1469-7998.1983.tb05104.x

Gould, S. J., and R. C. Lewontin. 1979. The spandrels of San Marco and the Panglossian paradigm: a critique of the adaptationist programme. *Proceedings of the Royal Society B: Biological Sciences* 205:581–598. doi:10.1098/rspb.1979.0086

Haldane, J. B. S. 1932. *The causes of evolution.* Princeton: Princeton University Press.

Hairston, N. G., S. P. Ellner, M. A. Geber, et al. 2005. Rapid evolution and the convergence of ecological and evolutionary time. *Ecology Letters* 8:1114–1127. doi:10.1111/j.1461-0248.2005.00812.x

Hendry, A. P., K. Hudson, J. A. Walker, et al. 2011. Genetic divergence in morphology-performance mapping between Misty Lake and inlet stickleback. *Journal of Evolutionary Biology* 24:23–35. doi:10.1111/j.1420-9101.2010.02155.x

Hendry, A. P., D. J. Schoen, M. E. Wolak, and J. M. Reid. 2018. The contemporary evolution of fitness. *Annual Review of Ecology Evolution and Systematics* 49:457–476. doi:10.1146/annurev-ecolsys-110617-062358

Hereford, J. 2009. A quantitative survey of local adaptation and fitness trade-offs. *American Naturalist* 173:579–588. doi:10.1086/597611

Heuts, M. J. 1947. Experimental studies on adaptive evolution in *Gasterosteus aculeatus* L. *Evolution* 1:89–102. doi:10.2307/2405407

Hohenlohe, P. A., S. Bassham, P. D. Etter, et al.. 2010. Population genomics of parallel adaptation in threespine stickleback using sequenced RAD tags. *PLoS Genetics* 6:e1000862. doi:10.1371/journal.pgen.1000862

Husband, B. C., and S. C. H. Barrett. 1992. Genetic drift and the maintenance of the style length polymorphism in tristylous populations of *Eichhornia paniculata* (Pontederiaceae). *Heredity* 69:440–449. doi:10.1038/hdy.1992.148

Johnston, S. E., J. Gratten, C. Berenos, et al. 2013. Life history trade-offs at a single locus maintain sexually selected genetic variation. *Nature* 502:93–95. doi:10.1038/nature12489

Lande, R., and S. J. Arnold. 1983. The measurement of selection on correlated characters. *Evolution* 37:1210–1226. doi:10.2307/2408842

Linnen, C. R., E. P. Kingsley, J. D. Jensen, and H. E. Hoekstra. 2009. On the origin and spread of an adaptive allele in deer mice. *Science* 325:1095–1098. doi:10.1126/science.1175826

Linnen, C. R., Y.-P. Poh, B. K. Peterson, et al. 2013. Adaptive evolution of multiple traits through multiple mutations at a single gene. *Science* 339:1312–1316. doi:10.1126/science.1233213

Loope, D. B., and J. B. Swinehart. 2000. Thinking like a dune field. *Great Plains Research* 10:5–35.

Macnair, M. R. 1977. Major genes for copper tolerance in *Mimulus guttatus*. *Nature* 268:428–430. doi:10.1038/268428a0

MacNair, M. R. 1983. The genetic control of copper tolerance in the yellow monkey flower, *Mimulus guttatus*. *Heredity* 50:283–293. doi:10.1038/hdy.1983.30

Marchinko, K. B. 2009. Predation's role in repeated phenotypic and genetic divergence of armor in threespine stickleback. *Evolution* 63:127–138. doi:10.1111/j.1558–5646.2008.00529.x

Marchinko, K. B., and Schluter, D. 2007. Parallel evolution by correlated response: lateral plate reduction in threespine stickleback. *Evolution* 61:1084–1090. doi:10.1111/j.1558–5646.2007.00103.x

Martin, R. A., L. D. Chick, M. L. Garvin, and S. E. Diamond. 2021. In a nutshell, a reciprocal transplant experiment reveals local adaptation and fitness trade-offs in response to urban evolution in an acorn-dwelling ant. *Evolution* 75:876–887. doi:10.1111/evo.14191

McPhail, J. D. 1993. Speciation and the evolution of reproductive isolation in the sticklebacks (*Gasterosteus*) of southwestern British Columbia. In: *The Evolutionary Biology of the Threespine Stickleback*, eds M. A. Bell, and S. A. Foster, 399–437. Oxford: Oxford Science Publications.

Messer P. W., S. P. Ellner, and N. G. Hairston. 2016. Can population genetics adapt to rapid evolution? *Trends in Genetics* 32:408–418. doi:10.1016/j.tig.2016.04.005

Myhre, F., and T. Klepaker. 2009. Body armour and lateral-plate reduction in freshwater three-spined stickleback *Gasterosteus aculeatus*: adaptations to a different buoyancy regime? *Journal of Fish Biology* 75:2062–2074. doi:10.1111/j.1095–8649.2009.02404.x

Mitchell-Olds, T., J. H. Willis, and D. B. Goldstein. 2007. Which evolutionary processes influence natural genetic variation for phenotypic traits? *Nature Reviews Genetics* 8:845–856. doi:10.1038/nrg2207

Moran, E. V., F. Hartig, and D. M. Bell. 2016. Intraspecific trait variation across scales: implications for understanding global change responses. *Global Change Biology* 22:137–150. doi:10.1111/gcb.13000

Olson-Manning, C. F., M. R. Wagner, and T. Mitchell-Olds. 2012. Adaptive evolution: evaluating empirical support for theoretical predictions. *Nature Reviews Genetics* 13:867–877. doi:10.1038/nrg3322

Osgood, W. H. 1909. Revision of the mice of the American genus *Peromyscus*. *North American Fauna* 28:1–285

Peichel, C. L., K. S. Nereng, K. A. Ohgi, et al. 2001. The genetic architecture of divergence between threespine stickleback species. *Nature* 414:901–905. doi:10.1038/414901a

Reed, R. D., R. Papa, A. Martin, et al. 2011. Optix drives the repeated convergent evolution of butterfly wing pattern mimicry. *Science* 333:1137–1141. doi:10.1126/science.1208227

Reimchen, T. E. 2000. Predator handling failures of lateral plate morphs in *Gasterosteus aculeatus*: functional implications for the ancestral plate condition. *Behaviour* 137:1081–1096. doi:10.1163/156853900502448

Savolainen, O., M. Lascoux, and J. Merilä. 2013. Ecological genomics of local adaptation. *Nature Reviews Genetics* 14:807–820. doi:10.1038/nrg3522

Slatkin, M. 2008. Linkage disequilibrium: Understanding the evolutionary past and mapping the medical future. *Nature Reviews Genetics* 9:477–485. doi: 10.1038/nrg2361

Smith, R. J. 2016, Explanations for adaptations, just-so stories, and limitations on evidence in evolutionary biology. *Evolutionary Anthropology* 25:276–287. doi:10.1002/evan.21495

Stern, D. L. 2013. The genetic causes of convergent evolution. *Nature Reviews Genetics* 14:751–764. doi:10.1038/nrg3483

Stinchcombe, J. R, M. T. Rutter, D. S. Burdick, et al. 2002. Testing for environmentally induced bias in phenotypic estimates of natural selection: Theory and practice. *American Naturalist* 160:511–523. doi:10.1086/342069

Sumner, F. B. 1929. The analysis of a concrete case of intergradation between two subspecies. *Proceedings of the National Academy of Science of the United States of America* 15:110–120. doi:10.1073/pnas.15.6.481

Taylor, E. B., and J. D. McPhail. 1999. Evolutionary history of an adaptive radiation in species pairs of threespine sticklebacks (*Gasterosteus*): insights from mitochondrial DNA. *Biological Journal of the Linnean Society* 66:271–291. doi:10.1111/j.1095-8312.1999.tb01891.x

Turesson, G. 1922. The species and the variety as ecological units. *Hereditas* 3:110–113. doi:10.1111/j.1601-5223.1922.tb02727.x

Urban, M. C., S. Y. Strauss, F. Pelletier, et al. 2020. Evolutionary origins for ecological patterns in space. *Proceedings of the National Academy of Sciences of the United States of America* 117:17482–17490. doi:10.1073/pnas.1918960117

Vamosi, S. M., and D. Schluter. 2004. Character shifts in the defensive armor of sympatric sticklebacks. *Evolution* 58:376–385. doi:10.1111/j.0014-3820.2004.tb01653.x

von Marilaun, A. K., and F. W. Oliver. 1895. *The natural history of plants, their forms, growth, reproduction, and distribution.* New York: Henry Holt. doi:10.5962/bhl.title.54631

Wittkopp, P. J., and G. Kalay. 2012. Cis-regulatory elements: Molecular mechanisms and evolutionary processes underlying divergence. *Nature Reviews Genetics* 13:59–69. doi:10.1038/nrg3095

Wright, S. 1931. Evolution in Mendelian populations. *Genetics* 16:97–159. doi:10.1093/genetics/16.2.97

Wright, K. M., U. Hellsten, C. Xu, et al. 2015. Adaptation to heavy-metal contaminated environments proceeds via selection on pre-existing genetic variation. *bioRxiv* 029900. doi:10.1101/029900

Wright, K. M., D. Lloyd, D. B. Lowry, M. R. Macnair, and J. H. Willis. 2013. Indirect evolution of hybrid lethality due to linkage with selected locus in *Mimulus guttatus*. *PLoS Biology* 11:e1001497. doi:10.1371/journal.pbio.1001497

Wu, C. A., D. B. Lowry, A. M. Cooley, et al. 2008. *Mimulus* is an emerging model system for the integration of ecological and genomic studies. *Heredity* 100:220–230. doi:10.1038/sj.hdy.6801018

Yeaman, S. 2015. Local adaptation by alleles of small effect. *American Naturalist* 186:S74–S89. doi:10.1086/682405

Young A., T. Boyle, and T. Brown. 1996. The population genetic consequences of habitat fragmentation for plants. *Trends in Ecology and Evolution* 11:413–418. doi:10.1016/0169-5347(96)10045-8

7

Assumptions: respecting the known unknowns

BRUCE WEBBER, ROGER COUSENS AND DANIEL ATWATER

THE BIGGEST 'ELEPHANT IN THE ROOM'?

Ecology is built on and enabled by assumptions.

Just about everything we do, from measuring the length of a leaf or the pH of a liquid to the most complex of bioinformatic analyses or mathematical models, requires assumptions. An assumption is something that is believed to be true, or considered to be true for the sake of argument, but is not *known* to be true.

By making assumptions, we can simplify nature so that we can deal with it intellectually and effectively. For example, we can assume that there are things that we call populations, communities and ecosystems, even though these are human constructs. We assume that these entities have traits with which we decide to imbue them, such as size, diversity, resilience and energy flow. We assume that we can devise qualities and quantities that adequately represent those traits. We assume that the data that we then collect are appropriate, accurate and unbiased. We assume that our models are adequate representations of reality (Wiens et al. 2009) and that the assumptions of the statistical methods that we use are robust. And we make assumptions every time we draw inferences from our results, such as whether, how and why the results are statistically, biologically, economically or socially of any relevance. Indeed, the entire

research process, from its conception to its final conclusions, consists of layers and combinations of assumptions (Schröter et al. 2021). Our science, therefore, is no better than the assumptions that we make.

Every time we make an assumption, we run the risk of making a mistake: every assumption has the potential to be false. This reality may not matter in many instances, as long as the assumption is *close enough* to the truth. Some methods that we use may be relatively insensitive to a particular assumption, especially if the error is the same across all of the entities that we are comparing. If we overlook the assumption that a ruler – and where we choose to place it – gives accurate measurement of length, the consequences may be minor, especially if the same person always makes the measurements. Likewise, the assumption that we can accurately measure vegetation cover with a visual assessment of a quadrat is often a known source of bias. Yet again, as long as we do not make comparisons of cover across studies by different people, or if the effect size we detect is large, then the bias may be inconsequential.

But some things we do can be highly sensitive to erroneous assumptions. For example, failure to correct for departure from homogeneity of variance can be sufficient to convert an interpretation of a statistically 'significant' result to one of 'non-significant' (Cousens 1988). If we fail

DOI: 10.1201/9781003314332-7

to recognise an important assumption, check its validity or consider the consequences if it is wrong, then potentially we can mislead ourselves as well as those engaging with our work. If assumptions are our windows on the world, then we need to make sure we scrub them off every once in a while to ensure that the light still comes in (Alda 1980 in Ratcliffe 2017).

Many assumptions in ecology are implicit and we do not bother to explore them every time we make them. When we say that we are studying 'population dynamics' we seldom define 'population' unambiguously. We may not specify how we attribute individuals to a particular population, where the boundaries of the population are or even whether we are assuming random mating and homogeneity within the population. We either take it for granted that the reader will fully appreciate the assumptions that we are making, or that any failure to appreciate them is of little consequence.

Other times, we state our assumptions explicitly because we, and our peers, know that they matter, or because there is a culture of defining certain assumptions. Sometimes we comment on specific analyses that we have conducted in order to show that we have checked that the assumptions are at least approximately correct.

There is a great deal of variation among researchers in their familiarity with the importance of particular assumptions – and in whether or not the scientist explores the validity of these assumptions. A failure to address critical assumptions is likely to occur when someone picks up an unfamiliar machine or a piece of common user-friendly software and applies it without being adequately trained. It takes time and experience to acquire skills in applying the methods, to become aware of the existence of key assumptions and to appreciate the need (and find time) to adequately address them. Casual users of ecological methods may never develop a high level of skill in their application. Until assumptions are given greater consideration in the design of research, their limitations better acknowledged during data interpretation and suitable caveats stated explicitly in discussions of results, scientific progress can be compromised.

As we will show, published ecological research contains a high frequency of errors, even in situations where it would be quite straightforward to avoid them. Moreover, the reasons for this threat to best practice ecological standards are often complex and frequently not attributable to ignorance alone.

If our research is only as good as the assumptions that we make, then the onus is on every scientist to make themselves aware of their assumptions – preferably before they carry out the research (so that they can minimise the effect on the data) and definitely after they have collected the data (so that they can take *post hoc* action and select appropriate language to minimise the probability of a false inference). Equally, end-users of our research need to be aware of the assumptions commonly made by scientists, and the pitfalls that can be encountered when applying that research to particular problems.

While readers of our publications should be able to expect that we have considered all relevant assumptions, the research publication and peer review system is an imperfect quality control system. For reasons of tradition or concern for space, it is not standard practice for every publication to list every assumption that is made. Indeed, we should be able to expect adherence to many basic procedures that ought to be known (so-called 'best practice'). Some scientists would even consider it demeaning to be asked to demonstrate that basic procedures have been followed (such as where we place a ruler against the stem to measure seedling height). But the fact of the matter is that not every author of an article and not every reader actually knows what all the assumptions made in the research are, which ones are important or how they ought to have been checked. A collective effort is required to ensure that ecological assumptions are 'safe' for a given context.

In this chapter, we present the detection of niche shifts for introduced plants as a case study for exploring ecology's reliance on assumptions. We have chosen this example because it is timely, because it illustrates the powers and pitfalls of assumptions in ecological research and because we as authors have long nurtured our own frustrations with the standards tolerated of research in this area and the role of assumptions both spoken and unspoken.

This chapter is very long, but necessarily so, because we seek to illustrate just how many assumptions can be hidden within a few lines of text in a concise scientific article. Unlike the other chapters that consider the breadth of ecology or superficially cover entire fields of research, this chapter is a detailed critique of a single research topic in its entirety. The reader is challenged to stay with us through the lengthy discourse, even if niche shifts are not their area of interest. They will hopefully learn how to undertake such a detailed forensic analysis of their own research projects: it can be both eye-opening and jaw-dropping!

To make any scientific headway on species' niches requires two basic assumptions and a number of subsequent ones. Firstly, we must assume that the thing we choose to call the 'niche' serves a useful scientific purpose. Secondly, that we can measure it. Both of these assumptions are widely taken for granted, but they deserve closer scrutiny. We can only measure the niche by making a series of further assumptions in relation to the data that we use and the analyses that we perform. To make the next step, to draw conclusions from the results, requires yet further assumptions. These assumptions conspire to create a morass of cascading uncertainty that if ignored threatens to derail any hope of progress. But if fully appreciated and carefully managed, assumptions are the great enablers of progress in ecology.

THE SPECIES' NICHE CONCEPT

Ecology is awash in words and concepts that instantly mean something to most people, but not necessarily the same thing to all people. Many of them – the niche is a good example – were adopted from other non-scientific uses and at a time in ecology's early history when we were still grappling with basic concepts.

Early definitions of the niche were vague, because ecological paradigms were still being defined. Each *species* was regarded as having a way that it fitted within the communities and ecosystems in which it was found. This was termed the 'niche' of a species, referring both to the role that species played in an ecosystem and to the species' general ecological needs.

This early conceptualisation of the niche was a species-level attribute, assuming that any infraspecific variation was of little consequence. For non-specialists, it is sufficient to define the niche as the role a species plays in an ecosystem. Yet, as specialists searched for ever-greater levels of ecological understanding, it was inevitable that they found a need for language that was semantically more precise and less conceptually ambiguous, allowing

us to communicate subtleties of meaning and to become more quantitative.

There are two distinct ways in which ecologists have come to view the niche of a species. To those involved in the development of theory relating to community structure, the niche concerns the way in which a species accesses the resources it needs to survive and reproduce. It is about how different species impact on one another within a given location, how local processes may have caused these patterns of resource use to evolve, what governs species' coexistence, and thus community diversity. This functional role of a species is often referred to as the Eltonian niche, after Charles Elton who pioneered such thinking. Elton developed this concept in turn after Grinnell's (1917) first definition of the niche, as a layer in a hierarchy of forces that controlled the distribution and abundance of species. In the same seminal paper, Grinnell advanced the competitive exclusion principle. This role-centred view of the niche has, since its inception, been entangled with species' coexistence.

The other commonly considered concept of the niche, which will concern us from here onwards, is usually referred to as the Hutchinsonian niche, after G. Evelyn Hutchinson. This niche concept relates to the tolerance limits of an individual species to the various biotic and abiotic components of its environment. Hutchinson (1978) distinguished between 'scenopoetic' environmental variables, the extrinsic and immutable conditions an organism experiences in the course of its life (Begon et al. 1996), such as temperature, humidity, concentrations of gases and pH, and 'bionomic' variables, the labile resources that organisms must access, such as light, nutrients and water. Hutchinson defined the 'fundamental species niche' as the n-dimensional environmental hypervolume, based on these variables, containing all possible environments within which the species could persist indefinitely. If we are able to validly measure responses to these variables, we can make interesting comparisons between the environmental preferences of the species (as Hutchinson and many others have since done).

Hutchinson pointed out that the niches of species are not independent of one another. If a part of the scenopoetic environment is occupied by a competitor, fewer resources will be available because of competition. In other words, the bionomic variables will be reduced, potentially resulting in a net reproductive rate $\lambda < 1$ and excluding the species from those environments. Predation and herbivory will have similar effects, reducing (or precluding) the species' ability to capture bionomic resources. We might also extend this thinking to mutualist species such as a pollinator, which might constitute bionomic resources in their own right. Hutchinson therefore introduced the term 'realised niche' for the region of the fundamental niche that the species can occupy in the presence of other species.

The assumption of a *species* having a fixed environmental tolerance range – a niche – is, of course, naïve. We should not forget either that the very concept of a species is an assumption in and of itself, which often does not stand up to more detailed interrogation. The principle of natural selection is based on the assumption that *individuals* vary in their environmental tolerances. The match between the individual's tolerance curve and its environment determines how many of their progeny will be available for the next generation. As a result, *populations* in different environments could evolve different tolerance limits. Indeed, if we were to ignore convention, we might refer to all levels of this hierarchical series of tolerance ranges, of individuals, populations, subspecies and species as niches.

From an evolutionary point of view, then, we can develop a population genetics definition of the Hutchinsonian fundamental species niche – though still an abstract and naïve one.

If sufficient numbers and genotypes of the species were to arrive (i.e. enough for establishment) into every possible environment from every suitable occupied environment, and they reproduce, mutate and adapt indefinitely with limited subsequent dispersal, then the fundamental niche of the species would be all those environments in which populations would have a finite population growth rate $\lambda \geq 1$. However, the more we think about the detail of this model of the fundamental niche, the more we expose creakiness in the concept. Even the optimal distribution of a species depends upon its particular ecology. The population dynamics of such a system will depend upon emigration and immigration among subpopulations, and not all subpopulations will be perfectly adapted to the regions they inhabit, particularly at range edges. Further, evolution to biological aspects of the niche, such as competition and predation, may trade-off against abiotic conditions, such as temperature and soil conditions.

THE NICHE CONCEPT MEETS THE REAL WORLD

If we believe that the fundamental niche of a species is something that is worth knowing, can we measure it? Quite simply, the answer is 'no'. It is impossible to quantify experimentally the n-dimensional hypervolume that constitutes a niche: there are simply too many possible combinations for us to recreate effectively. Even if we know *a priori* which subset of environmental variables is the most important, it is difficult to design experimental protocols in which to measure their tolerances, particularly for interactions between variables. Many complexities are difficult to resolve, such as the creation of sufficiently natural conditions, keeping long-lived species healthy and behaving naturally, the calculation of λ (and not a component of it or some surrogate measure) and which genotypes to work with (as we discussed earlier, not all genotypes will have the same tolerances). The fundamental niche is an entirely theoretical concept.

We can measure *something* about a species' niche, and this has become popular among ecologists, but it is definitely not the fundamental niche. Most commonly, we do this by resorting to the incomplete and biased information provided by the geographic distribution of species. The fundamental niche of the species determines the set of locations on the globe where the species *could* potentially persist. So, the distribution of a species must tell us something about the niche. If we comprehensively map a species and then measure all the relevant environmental variables at every location, we could – in some way – depict the suite of environments actually occupied. The jargon in this area of work is that we collect data in geographic space (G-space) and convert it to data in environmental space (E-space).

The problem is that species' geographic distributions past and present represent only a (biased) subset of potentially suitable environments. There are three main reasons for this. Firstly, the vagaries of our planet – the positions of our oceans and land masses, the types and locations of climates and soils, and so on – mean that only a subset of environments within the fundamental niche actually exist for the species ever to experience (referred to as the *potential niche* by Jackson and Overpeck 2000). Secondly, other organisms will be present and their interactions may prevent the species from persisting in scenopoetic environments that would otherwise be suitable. The region in which the species does persist, despite these biotic interactions, is Hutchinson's realised niche *sensu lato*. Thirdly, the species may be absent from regions of suitable E-space because it has never been able to reach them or, if it has, it has been unable to establish for some reason. We will refer to the occupied E-space that results from all three circumstances as the realised niche *sensu stricto*.

We present a two-dimensional representation of this in Figure 7.1. The ranges of two scenopoetic variables within which a population can potentially persist ($\lambda \geq 1$) is the fundamental niche (blue ellipse). Reductions in availability of resources, interactions with further scenopoetic variables and with other species combine to reduce the extents of the variables for which $\lambda \geq 1$ (red ellipse). In addition, only some combinations of suitable variables (green shaded areas) actually exist within the region of study. The species will therefore only occur (black dots) in the environments for which the green areas and the red ellipse overlap – provided that it has been able to reach and establish there (the hatched area is unoccupied due to dispersal limitation). We refer to this as the realised niche *sensu stricto*.

Here, then, is the major problem inherent in the use of geographical presence data to characterise a species' niche: we are inevitably only observing the realised (i.e. occupied) niche in that region, with its particular range of available environments and its particular suite of interacting species. There is no way of telling how much this realised niche and the fundamental niche differ. And although we can speculate on some of the factors that might influence the extent of the realised niche, and perhaps demonstrate scientifically which factor is likely to be having some effect, there are no easy ways of quantifying their individual, interactive or synergistic contributions. Moreover, we cannot be sure that the realisation of the niche found in one geographic region will be the same if the species is introduced into another region of the globe, with its particular set of environments and its different suite of interacting species. If we make a quantitative comparison between realised niches (for example, in relation only to scenopoetic variables) in different parts of the globe, we must make a leap of faith in considering that they represent similar things and are quantified in equivalent ways. If we conclude that there are different realised niches in different areas (as in a comparison of native and introduced regions), what does this actually mean and is it ecologically of any significance?

If the fundamental niche is what we really care about – because it is the immutable, ideal ecological truth at the heart of what makes a species individual and unique – then how do we contend with the fact that the fundamental niche is ultimately unmeasurable and therefore unfalsifiable? Is the fundamental niche even appropriate material for scientific discourse? To answer these questions, we must not ask whether the niche is a *true* concept, but whether it is a *useful* one, and if so, how it can best be utilised. We must also clearly communicate how we conceptualise the niche and for what purpose. Otherwise, readers will get confused if they operate with different assumptions and different goals. Thus, if we are using the concept of a niche pragmatically, merely to better understand the spread of an introduced species, it does not matter that we are assuming a realised niche and cannot possibly interpret the results in terms of a fundamental niche: as long as we are clear and honest about what we have done and the many assumptions that we have made along the way.

For now, we will leave this discussion of niche theory and focus on what ecologists actually do.

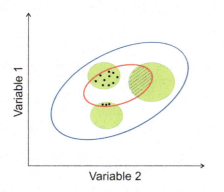

Figure 7.1 Hypothetical species tolerance ranges to two environmental variables. See text for details.

NICHE SHIFTS IN NON-NATIVE SPECIES

Human-mediated introductions of species to new geographic regions have received a great deal of attention in recent years because of the significant threat they represent to economic, environmental and social values. The pragmatic concerns of invasive pest and weed management dominate many studies. But many ecologists regard introductions as invaluable 'natural experiments', from which we can learn a great deal about basic ecological processes (though experimental design issues of replication, randomisation and power tend to be overlooked). These 'experiments' are represented by vast databases of geographic occurrences and dates, which are now readily available online and are commonly analysed in attempts to reveal broad empirical principles. Natural introductions, particularly on islands, featured strongly in the early development of ideas on evolutionary theory and population genetics (Baker and Stebbins 1965). From a conceptual point of view, it makes little difference whether the introductions occurred naturally or through the actions of humans. We know a great deal, in terms of ecological and evolutionary processes, about what happens as a species spreads into new regions. But what can we learn from a comparison of the environments that a species evolved in and the environments that it now comes to occupy in far-off regions? Can we predict the latter from the former? And if not, why not? If so, can we use that knowledge to protect biodiversity and natural resources? It is against this background that an interest in niche conservatism, and its alternative of niche shifts, has developed.

Niche theory was originally driven by an interest in community diversity and largely arose from an Eltonian perspective of the niche. The idea that a species had a niche naturally led to a consideration of the consequences of overlap with the niches of other species. If niches overlap, there will be intense competition between the species for certain resources, perhaps leading to competitive exclusion of one by the other. There might, in response to this, be associated coevolution that reduces niche overlap. 'Niche complementarity', i.e. niche differences among species, should lead to more efficient acquisition of limiting resources and therefore perhaps higher overall productivity by the community.

Theoretical modelling explored factors likely to drive the evolution of niche differentiation at a local scale (e.g. Roughgarden 1974). On the other hand, species tend to retain ancestral ecological characteristics, and evolution often appears to be highly phylogenetically constrained (Pyron et al. 2015). There has been a great deal of debate, for example, over why species are unable to adapt to conditions just beyond the edge of their native range (Hargreaves et al. 2014), why so few species ('extremophiles') have been able to evolve tolerance to very extreme conditions (Xu et al. 2020) and under what conditions we might expect fundamental niches to evolve (Holt 2009). It is, then, logical to ask whether or not, in general, niches tend to be conserved when a species invades a new region. New opportunities are often available to the species and existing constraints are frequently relaxed. Perhaps under such conditions niches will be able to shift more readily than they do in their native ranges.

Before we consider the methods that researchers use to draw their conclusions on these questions, it is worth considering what it means when we say 'niche shift' in regard to an invasion and some of the jargon that is being used (Box 7.1).

The data

If we want to estimate realised niches empirically, we require data on environmental conditions at locations where the species occurs in the native and introduced regions. This requires a number of assumptions. Here, we discuss those assumptions regarding the qualities of the data in databases, addressing sampling issues, conversion of spatial coordinates to environmental variables and the selection of the environmental variables for consideration.

Occurrence records. We usually begin by accessing information on species presence in G-space and then determining environmental variables for those locations. The first assumption is that our 'presence' data are reliable and representative of the species niche we are trying to characterise. The vast majority of available presence records come from global databases compiled from information provided by a variety of collectors, such as the Global Biodiversity Information Facility (GBIF: https://www.gbif.org/). Extreme caution is needed when using these sources (Newbold 2010) as little

BOX 7.1: The new language of invasion ecology

Consider the available environments in a region where a species originally evolved and expanded (yellow region in Figure 7.2a). Part of this overlaps with the fundamental niche (dark blue ellipse) and can potentially be occupied by the species. However, because of limited bionomic variables and the impacts of other species, only a subset is actually occupied (the realised niche, green shaded area). Regions I are too inhospitable for the species to be able to evolve; regions II would be suitable but do not exist. If we were to plot all known occurrences of the species in this graph (often referred to as a map in 'E-space', rather than a map in geographic or 'G-space'), they should all fall within region III.

Now consider that propagules from a population (its tolerance range shown by the small ellipse) at point X in the home region are transported to a new region, whose available environments are shown in pink in Figure 7.2b. The initially suitable scenopoetic range in the new region (small ellipse) may be smaller than that of the source population because only a subset of genotypes will arrive. If the point of arrival is a location with suitable scenopoetic variables, sufficient bionomic resources and tolerable biotic interactions, it can successfully colonise – even though the conditions may be outside the realised niche from the home region. It can then spread and evolve, ultimately being present throughout a new realised niche.

A new set of terminology (Figure 7.2c) has been coined to distinguish between regions of E-space with respect to niche shifts (Guisan et al. 2014):

- *Non-analogue* environments: environments in the new region that were not present in the native region (that part of pink region of Figure 7.2c which does not overlap with the yellow region).
- *Abandonment*: occupied environments in the native region that are unavailable in the new region (A).
- *Unfilling*: environments that were suitable in the native region but not occupied in the new region for some reason (U).
- *Pioneering* of non-analogue environments: environments occupied in the introduced region that were unavailable in the native range (P).
- *Expansion* of the realised niche: environments occupied in the introduced region that for some reason were not occupied in the native region (E).
- *Overlap* (or stability) in the new and old realised niches (O).

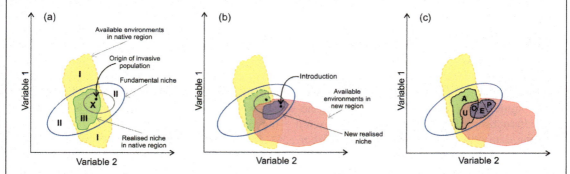

Figure 7.2 Representation of environments in native and introduced regions, along with fundamental niche and realised niches. Also shown are the points of origin and introduction of the invading phenotypes with their tolerance ranges. See text for details. (c is modified from Guisan et al. 2014.)

quality control has been performed on the data. Such databases are not primary information and have often been transposed from other sources, and for older records, the exact locations might have been guessed and the taxonomic determination may be outdated or based on features inadequate to determine identity with confidence. Three factors threaten to derail niche estimation at the first step: spatial accuracy, taxonomic accuracy and microclimates not captured by the variables used to define the niche.

First, spatial errors are particularly common in some widely used databases. Older records collected before handheld GPS units were common often had little information on their spatial location. Digitisation of information on the labels of herbarium specimens can also introduce errors, as it is often conducted rapidly, by non-experts and without the funds necessary for high levels of quality control. Sometimes an occurrence may be deliberately allocated to the latitude and longitude of the capital of the country or the country (or regional) centroid, rather than the actual place of collection (Kriticos et al. 2014).

Second, it is common to find errors in identification of the species, even for accredited sources such as herbaria, again with the potential to cause bias (Webber et al. 2011a). Some taxa are inherently difficult to identify, especially if key traits (such as flowers or fruits) are missing and herbaria are seldom able to keep up with all taxonomic revisions; in one study (of sea rockets, *Cakile* spp.: Cousens et al. 2013) the error in invaded regions was around one-third of samples. Databases such as iNaturalist are now often including samples from unverifiable surveys or from amateurs ('citizen scientists'). If our aim is to make definitive ecological statements, it is surely essential to have all records verified by an expert in that species. This is rarely done in published studies of niche shifts, simply because of the volume of data. It is, however, becoming easier to conduct some level of quality control, even if accessing data online: many (but not all) herbarium specimens are now available at good resolution online, and citizen scientist records are often accompanied by photos.

Third, and of particular relevance for introduced populations, is the role of microclimate in enabling the presence of a species in a given area. That is, if a microclimate facilitating local persistence is not adequately represented in the environmental variables (generally gridded rasters) used to define the niche, then the resulting niche will be misrepresentative. For organisms that can modify their experienced climatic niche by moving through space or time (animals, dormancy), microclimates (forest understorey communities) or mutualisms (assisted seed dispersal), or for species where interannual variation in climate is significant, broadscale climate averages are largely irrelevant to defining the realised niche.

For example, the issue of resolution and scale is frequently encountered for records that are spatially restricted to riparian environments in arid landscapes, or for introduced populations that rely on localised human landscape modifications (e.g. the watering of seedlings during dry summers) to establish and/or persist (Webber et al. 2011b). Ensuring that the spatial accuracy of presence records accords with the resolution of the environmental variables is therefore critical. Moreover, as we discuss in the section on environmental variables below, this is not an issue that is fixed by simply down-scaling the environmental layer to create a false perception of finer resolution.

All three factors can result in frequent errors in G-space for presence records and thus considerable error in E-space. Data are, therefore, sometimes 'cleaned' prior to analysis. The most common cleaning performed is to remove spatial outliers, and procedures are available for automating this process. However, outliers in either G- or E-space may not necessarily be mistakes and in fact can hold useful information about the species (e.g. coastal species spreading through the use of salt on interior road networks). It is straightforward to search for and remove individual records that suggest the species occurs in a highly unlikely place, such as a terrestrial species in the middle of the ocean. Validating taxonomic determinations and correctly identifying microclimate-restricted records is, on the other hand, especially challenging, particularly for older records.

Even if these three factors have been adequately addressed, other cleaning, called 'occurrence thinning', may be done to remove multiple records at the same geographic location or in the same grid square. This approach can reduce bias from over-sampling of some regions or environments. Occurrence thinning is often recommended in the literature, and in some cases it does improve outputs, but it exposes a serious issue: as we fiddle with our data (and our models) we obscure our assumptions, in turn obfuscating our ability to make inferences.

In the case of occurrence thinning, the chief assumption is that in grid cells where records exist, differences in the number of records are due to sampling bias and not to ecological differences in abundance, detection probability or habitat suitability. Conversely, it is assumed that ecology – and not sampling bias – is the only thing determining whether a grid cell has any points to begin with. If the downstream goal is to characterise all possible environments a species can inhabit (e.g. with an envelope model), this assumption might be appropriate. If the goal is to estimate occurrence probability or to quantify habitat suitability, it is not at all clear what an occurrence-thinned distribution represents, especially if it is applied to a real-world system where these two assumptions certainly do not hold.

Which environmental variables to consider. Once we resolve the data cleaning issues to our satisfaction and select occurrence data to use, the next step in data processing is to identify the environmental variables we want to use to measure the niche. Numerous environmental datasets, varying in temporal and spatial scales, are now available for different regions and include marine environments (Fréjaville and Garzón 2018; Tyberghein et al. 2011). Continent-wide data, for example, are primarily climatic or related to physical variables, whereas edaphic data (soil type, pH, salinity) tend to be more restricted. Some programs will generate environmental variables based on various future climate change scenarios (incorporating all manner of assumptions; e.g. Noce et al. 2020).

Assumptions are required by the algorithms used in software to generate values of environmental variables at a given set of spatial coordinates. For example, primary environmental observations recorded at point locations – meteorological recording stations – need to be converted to gridded data rasters through some sort of smoothing procedure. This also requires us to assume an appropriate grid size, but different grid sizes will result in different levels of error. While there seems to be a race to produce ever-finer climate data layers (e.g. the WorldClim database now comes in 1 km grids: Fick and Hijmans 2017), there is a real danger in equating greater resolution with improved realism (Daly 2006). For example, given

the often sparse density of station point data that underpin climate layers, the excessive precision of finely gridded data layers can lead to spurious conclusions. In turn, inappropriately large grids in areas where environmental gradients are steep can also cause problems. Consider, for example, a large grid size in a steeply mountainous area, for which an 'average' environmental value may be highly misleading. We therefore need to match the resolution of the environmental variables chosen to the precision of the occurrence records and the nature of the research question being addressed.

In studies of niche shifts, we are required to assume that the variables used are the most appropriate ones for the species and regions under consideration. That is, either through theoretical framing or experimentally informed decisions we have concluded a mechanistic relationship of some kind between the particular variable and the range-defining factors for the species. But how do we make that decision?

The Hutchinsonian concept of the niche considers environmental variables that directly impact on the life of an organism, such as temperature and humidity. There are programs – again incorporating various assumptions – that will generate physiologically relevant variables anywhere on earth and even the metabolic rates for the species (Kearney and Porter 2020). However, most niche shift studies rely on a set of variables, referred to as ecoclimatic, bioclimatic, climatic or more prosaically 'Bioclim' variables (after the program that made these widely accessible; Booth et al. 2014). Indeed, the term 'climatic niche' is now used in many studies: the availability of data is driving our concept of what the niche is!

Instead of being the environmental factors experienced by the organisms at a given point in time, these bioclimatic variables are often assumed (implicitly or explicitly) to be environmental surrogates that are correlated with proximate drivers of the distribution, such as annual mean temperature, annual precipitation and seasonal patterns such as the mean temperature of the wettest quarter. In some cases, ecological theory or experimental evidence is used to support this choice of variables, which has driven an increasing focus on variables that capture extreme conditions rather than average conditions. There is also a need to make assumptions about the most appropriate time window over which to generate bioclimatic variables. As a result of climate change, it is possible that the data no longer apply to a given location and an element of bias may be present, particularly if there is a mismatch between the temporal windows over which bioclimatic and presence record data have been gathered. For this reason, some researchers now restrict their data sets to averages over only recent decades and avoid using historical presence records.

The use of simplified surrogate variables assumes that the surrogate has a stable causal connection to the actual variable driving species distribution for the time and region under consideration. If this assumption is invalid, inference is dangerous. For example, in one region a short-lived species may find the appropriate conditions at one time of year (e.g. autumn), while in another region it may find those same conditions at a different time (e.g. spring). Two regions may share a similar climate, but the species may only occur in one of them because they require a particular range of soil pH or drainage (the importance of the edaphic environment has long been appreciated by phytosociologists; e.g. Ellenberg 1974).

Which of the many climatic variables should we then use? The WorldClim database, for example, provides 19 variables (Fick and Hijmans 2017), while the CliMond database provides 35 variables (Kriticos et al. 2012). In the early days of the analysis of species distributions, researchers chose as many variables that appeared to align well with geographic limits, such as some temperature at a particular time of year. Many researchers chose to throw all variables at the model in the hope that something would stick. If we have many covariates readily available, it is tempting to use them all (we will return to this issue later in regard to species distribution models). Some of them may be effectively redundant for the species/region under consideration and there may be high levels of correlation between variables, both issues leading to statistical issues in any subsequent calculations.

Many niche shift researchers allow the data to tell them what is correlated, by using principal component analysis (PCA) to reduce the dimensionality of the data from n variables to just a few composite 'climate' axes (sometimes only two). This also allows the results to be presented visually (see Figure 7.3) and facilitates comparison of native and non-native range data. While in some ways it is useful to distil data down in this way, any

simplification discards a considerable amount of information on environmental differences among locations. This is a problem if the proximate ecological drivers are not correlated with the composite variables that are retained, and an even greater problem if the proximate drivers have correlations with the causal variables but these correlations differ between the native and non-native range. Ecological interpretation of composite variables is challenging at best – yet another assumption that we choose to make – and composite variables do not transfer well into other regions or across studies. Finally, PCA involves correlations among the predictor variables, but we are often more concerned with covariation between predictors and species occurrences. When we do PCA and cluster the most tightly correlated predictors, we should not assume that these are also the most *effective* predictors.

Once we have chosen the environmental variables we will be working with, the next step is to convert the spatial coordinates (in G-space) to environmental coordinates in the E-space we have just defined. This process is called ordination and it is as simple as plotting the environmental values for each occurrence in E-space. We now have a cloud of points in E-space representing occupied environments in the native and non-native ranges.

The analysis

At this stage, our goal is to measure whether a niche shift has occurred, by comparing the native- and non-native-range data sets we have gone through so much trouble to create. We need to assume that each of these clouds of points gives an adequate description of the n-dimensional space potentially occupied by the species in each region (see Box 7.2).

There are many difficulties with this assumption. Firstly, unless we set out to evaluate the dynamics of invasions, such as the lengths of lag phases, we must be prepared to accept that each species has managed to access all suitable environments. While this might be reasonable for the native region, where dispersal has been able to take place over millennia, species in introduced ranges may have only had opportunities for a matter of decades or a few centuries at most. Can we be sure that the species has stopped spreading (Forcella 1985), when we know that lag phases can be common and potential environments may extend over

BOX 7.2: The use of composite axes to determine niche overlap

A word of warning is necessary regarding the common practice of collapsing clouds of multivariate points on to just two composite axes, prior to comparison of native and non-native niches.

While environments are multidimensional, it is much easier to think of data if we can depict them in a simple, two-dimensional graph. There are multivariate statistical methods which do this very effectively, such as principal component analysis: they allow us to reduce the number of axes, but at the same time retain as much of the original information as possible. Thus, 20+ independent environmental axes might be reduced to just two or three composite axes and retain, perhaps, 60–70% of the variation in the data.

An example is given in Figure 7.3. Occurrences of Cakile edentula in native (green) and two non-native (blue) ranges are plotted against the first two axes from a principal component analysis of 19 'bioclimatic' variables. The large empty region within the native polygon shows climates that simply do not exist in eastern North America. In the non-native ranges, there has been both a shift in the centroid and an expansion of the E-space occupied. According to standard methods of analysis of climate niches this would constitute a shift in the 'realised niche' of the species. A plausible explanation for the shift is that it is the result of a very broad innate climatic tolerance of the species and highly restricted available combinations of climate in each region. This is supported by the ability of native range genotypes to establish in non-analogue climates (two of the three white symbols). Although other research has shown that adaptation by C. edentula in new locations has occurred, that may well not be the reason for a shift in the realised niche.

The use of two-dimensional ordinations, however, can cause serious misinterpretations of niche overlap. It is highly likely that clouds of points that have no overlap whatsoever in multiple dimensions will appear to overlap in two dimensions. Just imagine being in a three-dimensional world and taking two-dimensional photographs of two balloons, flying separately. From some directions, a 2D image would look as if the balloons overlap, but they do not in the real 3D world. How many of the cases of apparent niche overlap in the literature, based on analysis of PCA data, are actually false?

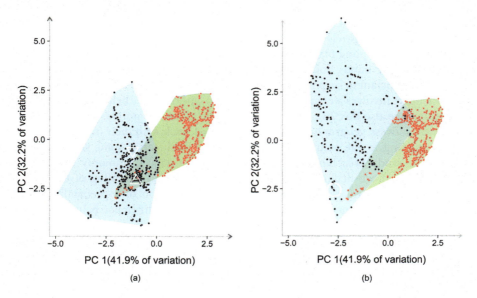

Figure 7.3 PCA ordinations of Cakile edentula in native (red dots, eastern North America) and two of their non-native ranges (black dots): (a) Australasia, (b) western North America (courtesy Philipp Robeck). Data were sourced from GBIF (https://doi.org/10.15468/dl.yc5cxc). Records from non-native regions were checked visually to confirm the species and incorrect records discarded. White symbols indicate first non-native records: △ Australia; ▽ New Zealand; ○ western North America.

thousands of kilometres, or where sharp geographical barriers exist (e.g. steep mountain ranges)?

Secondly, we know that the distribution of data from databases within E-space can be very uneven, which potentially biases subsequent analyses (Meyer et al. 2016). Sampling bias in E-space comes from two sources. Environmental sampling bias occurs when certain environments are more common than others, creating hotspots in E-space. Geographic sampling bias occurs when certain locations are more sampled than others. Sampling bias can easily result in a change in the location of the centroid of the data (a common measure used for niche shift), without there necessarily being any change in the niche at all.

While there are ways of trying to remove such bias and for smoothing data (Atwater et al. 2018), these methods have their own assumptions and are unlikely ever to perfectly overcome the issue. Nonetheless, removal of sampling bias is absolutely vital. If there is bias in either of our clouds of points, then there may be bias in our conclusions about niche shifts.

Finally, there are a range of other sampling problems subsumed within the data. For example, is the sample size sufficient for a good representation of the entire environment space in all of its dimensions? The extremes of distributions may be poorly recorded due to the rarity of the species, leading to an underestimation of niche overlap or niche shift. Because we rarely have accurate estimates of geographic sampling bias, we may be tempted to throw up our hands and ignore the issue. However, it is important to keep in mind that every decision we make involves a commitment to certain assumptions (see also Box 7.3).

If we decline to address geographic sampling bias, we are committing to the assumption that every region of our study area has exactly the same sampling effort. If we decline to address climatic sampling bias, we are assuming that no environments are more common than others. Because these assumptions are likely to be far removed from the truth, we must challenge ourselves to do better.

Calculating the niche and niche overlap. The cloud of occurrence records in E-space may expand, contract or remain unchanged from the home region to the introduced region and it may or may not move its location. There are various ways of summarising clouds of data points mathematically so that their properties – and any change in those properties –

can be analysed; each has its own assumptions. We consider three approaches here.

First, we might measure the volume of the cloud of points by establishing a boundary (such as a minimum convex hull or contoured spline) around each data set and then assess the degree of overlap of the hulls in some way. This assumes that the outermost points represent the maximum extent of the species and that the edges of the polygon introduce negligible error. It is essentially the same approach used by Hutchinson (1978; Chapter 5). Second, we might assume that the niche has a given statistical distribution (e.g. elliptical) across E-space and then compare the home and invaded distributions in an appropriate way (e.g. Guisan et al. 2014). Third, we might calculate some sort of index of overlap based on grid cells in E-space that contain occurrences from one or both clouds (e.g. Schoener 1968). Again, we assume that the index is a valid estimator of overlap.

To compare two niches, however defined, some metric of difference is used. There are many possible indices, each likely to have different sensitivities to the distribution of data, and the options are restricted by the method that has been used. For example, with hulls and contours we can compare areas of overlap (Petitpierre et al. 2012). With any approach it is common to calculate the positions of the centroids of the clouds, in order to measure the direction and magnitude of any niche shift rather than just whether or not it occurs. This assumes that the centroid, an arithmetic mean of the data, is an appropriate summary of the data. It is possible for there to be a significant change in the centroid without there being any change in the overlap of the clouds of points, so other metrics are also needed, each with their own set of assumptions.

The final step is some sort of statistical analyses of the data. Commonly this is a permutation test, involving resampling of the data clouds and the construction of a probability distribution for the estimated difference being simply the result of chance. Such tests are, in themselves, highly robust and avoid problems that can be introduced when using parametric statistics. Following these tests, we need to make a binary decision about whether or not the probability is low enough that we can safely conclude that the difference is real (statistically 'significant'). It has become traditional in ecology to use a cut-off probability of 0.05. This is another assumption, that this high and entirely arbitrary level of confidence is an appropriate default threshold.

BOX 7.3: Take care with software

A word of warning is worthwhile in relation to the use of user-friendly or semi-automated software for research on this topic, on SDMs and in research more generally. Most software assumes, implicitly, that the user knows and understands what they are doing when they parameterise their model and produce outputs, that the issues they are exploring are appropriate to address with this method, that they appreciate potential issues with their data, that they have taken appropriate remedial actions and that they are appropriately interpreting the outputs. If remedial actions are included as part of the package, they are usually *options* that the user needs to make a conscious decision to select.

A real possibility is that casual users, who are unaware of the potential pitfalls, will use the package with default settings unchanged, producing results that will look (at least superficially) appealing and may make some sense, but yet are not actually appropriate. Default settings may cause the user to overlook important departures from the assumptions of the methods. It is left to the researcher and the reviewers of their papers to know what to look out for – which will not always be the case. We will return to this issue when we discuss species distribution modelling.

Interpretation

We now reach a point at which we interpret our results. Has there been a shift in the realised niche? We start with a word of warning – one that applies not just to niches, but across any science using statistics. The search for evidence of whether *or not* there are niche shifts may lead some researchers to interpret non-significant results as instances of no difference between the clouds of points. This is unwise. From a logical viewpoint, absence of evidence is not the same as evidence of absence. 'Non-significant' only tells us that, to the high levels of confidence that we have set, we do not know whether there was truly no difference in the calculated metrics or whether the data were simply too noisy to be able to tell (see Chapter 4). As a result, false negatives will strongly bias a conclusion towards an absence of differences.

It is common to conduct niche shift analyses for many species in order to draw conclusions on the generality of a niche shift. If one or other outcome is more common in a meta-analysis, then we accumulate support not just for the fact that niche shifts *can* occur (or seldom occur), but that they are common (or uncommon) enough that there may be a fundamental ecological principle behind the results. A finding that niche shifts for non-native introductions are common (or, alternatively, that they are rare) could be considered to be a robust conclusion: *despite* all of the assumptions and all the uncertainties about the data, the same result is found for a great many species in a wide diversity of environments. So, the evidence seems compelling. However, it could be that bias in the data is extremely common, making it more likely than not that an apparent niche shift would be found – but which would, in fact, be an artefact.

A spanner in the works, however, is the fact that the qualitative outcomes of studies vary. Some studies have announced that niche shifts are rare or often unable to be detected (Guisan et al. 2014), while others have concluded that they are common (Atwater et al. 2018). Can both conclusions be true? Perhaps it is the differences in the methodology between the studies that resulted in the difference in conclusion (Webber et al. 2012), or the selection of species. Such conflicts in conclusions are of concern. How do we resolve them? Do we accept the most up-to-date study using the most advanced methods as being more likely to be true?

But how do we know, for example, that newer methods have not introduced new invalid assumptions that bias our conclusions? The statistically significant positive conclusion of a niche shift (or the conclusion of no evidence of a niche shift) may still be false – because the data do not fulfil the many assumptions that we have made about them, the data cleaning may not have achieved its aims, our assumptions in the choice of variables were wrong or our calculations of overlap may have been inappropriate. Perhaps we might need some sort of independent forensic analysis of the conflicting studies with respect to the validity of the assumptions and the properties of the data. Even then, after consuming countless hours of effort, we suspect that no unequivocal conclusion would be reached.

Comparisons of climatic environmental data in two regions are regularly used to indicate some of the things that may have happened to cause a shift in the 'climatic' niche (see Box 7.1). Some of these are particularly useful for excluding niche shifts that may well be geographic quirks: chance differences in availability of environments in the two regions. Unfilling (Box 7.1) – a failure to have (yet) occupied apparently suitable environments in the new region – was notably frequent in Atwater et al.'s (2018) study at a continental scale (Figure 7.4). This might not indicate a fundamental niche shift in any ecological sense (just a time lag as an invasion proceeds), but unfilling will have a considerable effect on the centroid and range of a set of points in E-space and make it more likely that a niche shift will be calculated. Abandonment – the mere unavailability of suitable climates from the native range – was also strongly represented in the Atwater et al. data: in other words, the apparent shift in the niche is heavily influenced by a change in climate

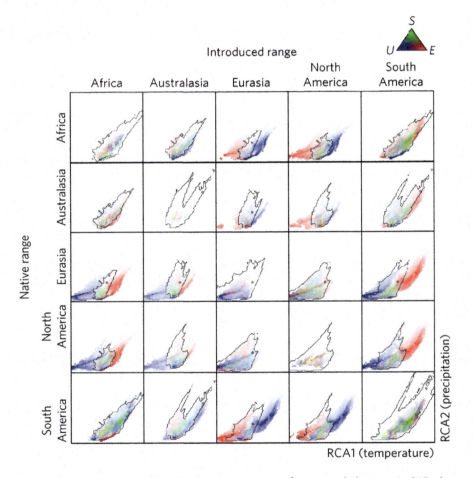

Figure 7.4 Principal component analysis (PCA) comparisons of occupied climates in 815 plant species in their native and non-native range (first published by Atwater et al. 2018). Environmental data were rotated to fall along two axes: an axis indicating increased temperature (RCA1) and precipitation (RCA2). Black line shows climate space in common between native and invaded regions. Blue points inside analogue space represents 'unfilling'; blue points outside analogue space indicate 'abandonment'. Red points inside analogue space represent 'expansion'; red points outside analogue space represent 'pioneering'. See Box 7.1 for definitions of these terms. Green points are 'stability' (similar climates occupied in both regions).

availability, and not necessarily by a change in the fundamental niche of the species.

Whatever the analysis has been, we must make a final judgement that a shift in the realised niche actually means something ecologically. Or that it tells us something that is useful in a practical sense. As we discussed in *The Niche Concept Meets the Real World* (this chapter), there are several reasons why a difference in realised niche might occur.

It may be due to the differential geographic availability (and accessibility) of suitable habitats in the two regions – into which the species can 'shift' because of its inherent tolerance (not to be confused with phenotypic plasticity; Lande 2014) – or because it undergoes local adaptation. It may be because of unspecified differences in the biotic environment, bionomic resources and their interactions in the two regions.

It could be that for some reason the species extends its fundamental niche in the new regions (which begs the question of why it did not do so in the native region, so is this a realistic expectation?). It could be a combination of all these things. How can we tell which? There is no simple answer. For example, there will *always* be differences in the biota in geographically remote regions: this underpins the often-tested enemy release hypothesis explaining the success of biological invasions (Keane and Crawley 2002). How can we tell how much impact these factors have on the realised niches and their overlap? It is common to find evidence that there has been local adaptation in the new region (e.g. van Boheemen et al. 2019), but we expect local adaptation to occur in the native region and within the fundamental niche. Adaptation, of itself, is not necessarily evidence of a niche shift.

Uptake of conclusions by others

As discerning scientists, we should always be aware of the assumptions that a study has made and treat the results with the appropriate caution. If the study is someone else's, we must not ignore the 'fine print' – though experience is needed in order to know what to look for, particularly when the fine print is missing. Weakly supported assumptions can only result in weak inferences and it is poor science to perpetuate these.

In the context of niche shifts for introduced populations, we have reviewed the considerable number of assumptions that need to be made in drawing conclusions from location data. The data that are commonly used for these analyses are known from the outset to have many problems that make them in many ways inadequate. Yet, authors commonly make bold statements about what they have demonstrated, while papers by other authors referring to the results readily accept those bold conclusions at face value.

As an example, consider Atwater et al.'s (2018) paper analysing data on 815 plants which stated boldly in its title that '*climatic niche shifts are common in introduced plants*'. If we read the detail in the paper (the fine print), we find many caveats recognised by the authors. The paper also relies on a number of assumptions not detailed explicitly in the paper. Many of the assumptions relate to the reliability of geographic presence data from a restricted range of environments in order to make statements about the species' tolerance to all possible environments. Unfilling – resulting possibly from a failure to have (yet) occupied apparently suitable environments in the new region – was notable in Atwater et al.'s study at a continental scale. Abandonment – the mere unavailability of suitable climates from the native range – was strongly represented in the data (Figure 7.4). In other words, the apparent shift in the niche may have been heavily influenced by dispersal limitation, and not necessarily by a change in the fundamental niche (or strict-sense realised niche) of the species. Tellingly, Atwater et al. (2018) were pressured to remove a more nuanced discussion of these issues by reviewers who found it uninteresting.

In another example, '*Most invasive species largely conserve their climate niche*' was used as a headline by Liu et al. (2020) – the opposite conclusion to Atwater et al. – even though these authors stated in the text that the work had 'two important caveats' (one of them related to the meaning of the realised niche). Interestingly, these conflicting accounts often rely on the same data. Where they often differ – as between Atwater et al.'s (2018) account and Petitpierre et al.'s (2012) – is in how the data are handled, and in particular what assumptions are made about sampling bias.

The greatest message from this work may be that the conclusions we draw depend heavily on the assumptions we make, but disentangling these issues requires deep, working knowledge of the subject area and particularities of model implementation that is inaccessible to almost everyone, sometimes including the authors themselves. No wonder, then, that readers have so much trouble interpreting the conclusions that have been made!

We examined 67 citations of Atwater et al.'s study. Of these, 63% of papers cited the study as conclusive evidence that niche shifts exist and are common, with a strong implication that this tells us something significant about the biology of the invading species (rather than just about the environments on offer). The reviewers and the editors had accepted these opinions of the citing authors (or the rights of the authors to state them). Most papers (94%), however, made no mention of the fact that the study only tells us about the *realised* niche. The reported niche shifts were sometimes considered by the citing authors to be the result of phenotypic plasticity or tolerance, but also alongside adaptation: 10% of citing papers used the paper as evidence that selection, adaptation or evolution occurs during an invasion, even though there is no logical basis on which to draw such a conclusion. Just one paper questioned what a shift in a realised climate niche actually means, while one other paper used it to draw attention to the importance of unfilling as a component of apparent niche shifts. It is not difficult to see how a process akin to the 'telephone game' (i.e. cumulative errors) can enter ecology and be detrimental to syntheses of results.

SPECIES DISTRIBUTION MODELS

Not all ecological analyses of species distributions have the niche *per se* as their focus. The end goal may, instead, involve some quite mundane statement about the species' geographical range: for example, we may want to know where to search for unknown populations of a rare species (e.g. Maycock et al. 2012) or how widely a species may spread when introduced into a new region. From this, we might be able to draw implications of various forms of management options or to calculate some measure of persistence likelihood or introduction risk. We collect data on species geographic occurrences, use this to make a model of the species' known distribution in E-space and then project it back into G-space (Figure 7.5). This type of model is called a species distribution model (SDM), otherwise known as a habitat distribution model (HDM) or more generally as a type of ecological

niche model (ENM), and it represents a hypothesised species distribution. Since many studies consider only climatic data, SDMs are sometimes referred to as climate matching or bioclimatic models (Sutherst 2003). Terminology remains inconsistent and often confusing. However, by far the most common type of SDM is built by correlating occurrence data with environmental data. Some SDMs also use absence data, where available, or surrogates for absence (pseudo-absence data, backgrounds), which also come with their own set of assumptions and potential pitfalls.

While the study of niche shifts for introduced species does not necessarily involve correlative SDMs, and SDMs can be used for the study of issues other than biotic invasions, the two topics have much in common. As a result, studies of niche shifts and species distributions share many assumptions, but SDMs also introduce new assumptions related to the ways that data are used. Over a few decades, correlative SDMs have become a standard research tool for many ecologists, but not all of them are necessarily familiar with how the methods should be applied (Lowry et al. 2013). Increasingly widespread, user-friendly software also introduce variability in application, output and user expertise (see Box 7.3). Papers describing and comparing the various methods have achieved huge citation rates (Peterson and Soberón 2012), reflecting their popularity. By 2011, SDMs were included in around 1000 scientific papers per year and these volumes do not seem to be declining. It has become common, for example, for an introductory chapter of an ecological PhD or MSc thesis to include the results of an SDM of the study species. Free, menu-driven software (e.g. Phillips et al. 2017) make SDMs available and easy to use, but also an incredibly easy way to make mistakes (Yackulic et al. 2013).

Here, we will deal with three types of issue specific to SDMs: the assumptions and performance of different models, the training data that are used on a case-by-case basis and software implementation issues. We caution that there are many more assumption-related pitfalls that can impact SDMs but these are beyond the scope of this summary.

Choice of model

There are many correlative SDM methods available: Elith et al. (2006) divide these into envelope methods (mirroring Hutchinson's original concept

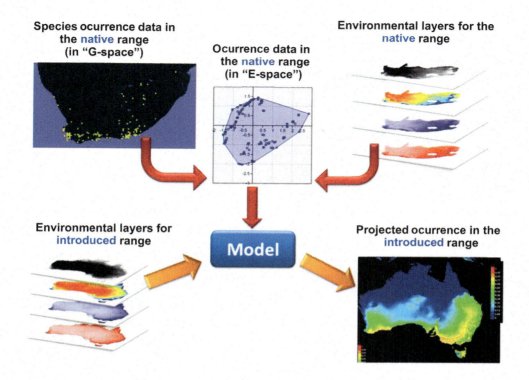

Figure 7.5 Principles behind correlative species distribution models and their use for projecting the eventual ranges of introduced species. The example shown is, a native of southern Africa that has become widespread in Australia. Only native range occurrence data (source GBIF https://doi.org/10.15468/dl.nf2w3y) were used for the projection, using Maxent. (Figure courtesy M. Mesgaran. See text for details.)

of the niche, such as BIOCLIM), regression methods, machine-learning methods (including the most commonly used Maxent) and dissimilarity methods. They all go about their tasks in different ways and make different assumptions. The reason we have so many different SDMs is that there were obvious weaknesses in the early approaches, researchers were starting to ask different questions of the models and improvements were sought. We will not go into a detailed exploration of each approach here; there are excellent guides already published.

Basically, geographic occurrences are converted into points in E-space using appropriate software or environmental layers for that region (Figure 7.5). These are used as input (as 'training' data) for the parameterisation of a model that then makes a projection to the same or another geographic region (in the case of Figure 7.5, Australia). As noted earlier, some methods use known absences (or other surrogates of absence) as well as known occurrences. Note that we often refer to 'projections' rather than 'predictions': see Chapter 8 for a further discussion of the strict difference between the two. When applying a model to novel conditions in space or time relative to those in which it was parameterised (e.g. climate change scenarios, non-native regions), the output relies heavily on assumptions and cannot be tested in the near term with independent data, and therefore is a projection rather than a prediction (the latter of which can be assessed using independent data; Keyfitz 1972).

So, which SDM should we choose? This decision can make a considerable difference to the predicted or projected geographic ranges: outputs from different models can vary considerably. If we assume that model choice is unimportant, then we might be making an important error. While it has been concluded that machine-learning methods and other nonparametric approaches often 'out-perform' older SDMs (Elith et al. 2006), the difference in their outputs depends on the data set and the objective of the research. If they are all used on the same input data to describe the native range of the species (and if the data are well-suited to the task), differences in outputs among SDM methods may be quite subtle and unimportant from a practical viewpoint. If the data depart from the ideal (even after cleaning and screening procedures) then the differences between model outputs can become appreciable.

Logically, we should choose a model that is appropriate for our particular situation, to minimise model choice problems. This requires considerable familiarity with a range of models, which only expert users develop. It can be difficult to master the idiosyncrasies of every method so that we use them all properly and to their maximum effect, so that we make the best choice.

Most SDM users work with only a single SDM package, simply because they are familiar with it, its software may be user-friendly and advice is readily available from colleagues. If a method is widely used, surely this indicates that the method must be widely applicable and reliable? Not necessarily! Popularity does not mean that a method is the best – or even adequate – for every situation. Indeed, this rationale for model choice creates a real danger that the model will be used in situations where it is not (the most) appropriate. And there is a strong likelihood that it will be misused for other lack-of-familiarity reasons, as we will see below. Despite all the published comparisons methods showing that on certain types of data Maxent is one of the better methods, it is probably the most widely used SDM simply because of its accessibility and ease of use. And perhaps for the same reasons, also the most widely misused.

As an alternative to choosing a single method, some ecologists recommend an ensemble/consensus approach, running several SDMs on the same data and then subjectively considering their similarities (Hao et al. 2019). However, it would seem to be inadvisable to include in such a consensus any models whose assumptions are clearly violated or which is known for its consistently extreme outputs (see also Kriticos et al. 2013). The latest version of this approach is to convert the outputs of multiple models to some common currency and render one ensemble prediction or projection, often weighting models based on performance metrics (e.g. Thuiller et al. 2009). We have encountered both

continuous outputs (which produce some continuous metric of habitat suitability) and threshold outputs (which produce a binary occupied/unoccupied map) being created in this way. Interpreting Maxent outputs is already troublesome because it produces frequently misinterpreted estimates of 'habitat suitability' rather than occurrence probability (Royle et al. 2012). Interpreting ensemble outputs is exponentially more difficult because model averaging obfuscates what the data actually mean. Moreover, the average of many bad models is still going to be a bad model. Greater effort put into carefully parameterising and interrogating a single SDM is likely to produce far more robust results.

Training data

In the section on niche shifts, we dealt at length with the many assumptions that we make of the data that we subsequently use for SDMs. Several points are worth repeating or expanding, as they have been explored at some depth in the SDM literature.

All SDMs assume that the data used in their formulation – the training data – are reliable (free from significant errors), appropriate for the purpose and sufficiently numerous for accurate model calibration. SDMs assume that occurrence data are independent, random samples from the species' distribution with respect to the relevant environmental variables (i.e. within E-space) and that the niche has been adequately sampled with respect to the n dimensions under consideration. Such assumptions are explicit, statistical and clearly governed by the SDM being used. We tend to give the most attention to such explicit assumptions, yet for them to run 'well' SDMs also require a number of implicit assumptions about the overall quality of the data. For example, they also assume that the species is in equilibrium with its environment and that it has reached all areas within the region that are suitable for them to persist: more a *potential* distribution than an *actual* distribution (Guisan and Thuiller 2005; Elith 2017). It is possible that a species no longer exists at some former locations: perhaps climates have changed or the species was unable to persist there, even though it was found alive in the past. We tend to assume implicitly that such issues are minor. Another implicit assumption is that selection in the home region has produced all possible phenotypes of which the species is capable and that these are either represented in the sampled data or will be readily selected for in a new region.

If there is a significant departure in any of these assumptions, then model projections could be unreliable. Some assumptions, however, are more important than others. Sampling distribution is one of these assumptions (Phillips et al. 2009; Elith et al. 2011; Elith 2017).

There may be instances where fewer than 15 occurrences give reasonable model outputs (van Proosdij et al. 2016), but such a small number is unlikely to be reliable if they fail to represent the full range of the relevant niche variables, or if there are a large number of predictor variables. Wisz et al. (2008) recommend a sample size of at least 30 for adequate power. Unfortunately, we may not know what is adequate until data have been collected. Some SDM methods are relatively robust to outliers but others are not; methods for removing outliers statistically are included in some software packages. But why should outliers be removed if they are valid records?

Another implicit assumption that is often overlooked is that the niche is not 'truncated', meaning that the environmental niche of a species is constrained by its ecological tolerances – and not dispersal barriers – on all edges of its distribution. If a species is endemic to southern portions of the main island of Japan, we might think we know a lot about the conditions of its northern range limit, but we cannot know if it could survive in climates warmer and wetter than those encountered in the southmost portion of its range. The niche would be said to be truncated at the southern end. Importantly, truncation occurs in *multivariate* space, not just along environmental axes. Our imaginary species may actually tolerate cooler temperatures than it encounters in its northern range edge, provided that there is enough rainfall, or it may tolerate greater aridity if the temperature is right, but those combinations of climates that would allow it to extend its range do not exist in or near its current distribution. Thus, the niche can be truncated even if it appears not to be.

Truncation may not cause major problems if the model outputs have the same spatiotemporal parameters as they were trained in. However, the goal with an SDM is often to project into new places and/or times. If the new region has conditions, or combinations of those conditions, that were not present where the SDM was trained (i.e. non-analogue climates, see Box 7.2), the SDM will extrapolate unpredictably and the modeller will be none the wiser. This is the reason it is often recommended to pool a species' entire global distribution (including the non-native range, if there is one) when training an SDM. However, pooling relies on the assumption that species niches are stable and do not shift realised niches among continents.

Certain SDM techniques are then left to process conflicting information between continents in regard to occupied and unoccupied E-space. If the niche does shift, then the pooled model is specious because it does not represent any niche the species actually occupies! Again, the modeller is trapped in a tangle of assumptions from which there appears to be little hope of escape.

The assumption by far the most discussed in the SDM literature is that of bias in data collection. It is common for some regions of the species' niche in E-space to be less well sampled than others or not at all. Some regions, for example, are more accessible than others (correlated with particular environmental conditions; see also Syfert et al. 2013 in regard to proximity to roads) while there may be sociopolitical constraints to data collection in some regions. Methods have been developed for 'cleaning' the data (Zizka et al. 2019) and, to the extent to which this is possible, to adjust for bias due to clumping of data in some regions of E-space.

One source of bias that is impossible to adjust for is the absence of data from regions of the species' E-space that is within the innate tolerance of the species but from which the species is currently absent. When we extrapolate from our calibrated models, into non-analogue environments, it would not be surprising if errors in projection were to occur for such reasons (Elith et al. 2010; Elith 2017). Islands, and even continents, where the species occurs naturally simply do not contain all of those environments, or the species has been unable to reach there, or perhaps there are un-modelled variables that preclude their occurrence (such as interactions with other species); hence, there are no data to adequately calibrate the model for other regions. Many SDM users, however, appear to be happy to make the assumption that realised niches in the native and non-native ranges will be identical, despite the high frequency of apparent realised niche shifts (Atwater et al. 2018). Is this wise? If not, then we really should not be using SDMs for this purpose!

Ideally, we would have just as much information about where species *are* as where they *are not*. Yet, when recording a species' observation, people rarely note what species they *did not* see. This causes a problem, because if our data suggest that a region lacks occurrences, we cannot tell whether the species does not exist there, or whether it exists there but has never been looked for (or found). To get around this problem, some SDM procedures allow users to specify 'pseudo-absence' or 'background' data, as surrogates for that missing information. To be effective the distribution of the background data must resemble the actual sampling effort: in other words, it should correspond to how hard a species was looked for throughout the area being studied. If not, any biases or errors in the background will automatically – and undetectably – transfer to the final SDM.

The simplest approach is to assume that sampling effort is even, in which case background points are randomly selected with equal probability everywhere. In effect, the uniformly distributed background data tell the model that a species was equally likely to be observed everywhere, and a low density of occurrences can only mean that a species is rare. Unfortunately, where geographic sampling bias exists (and it usually does), an SDM based on such background points will underestimate occurrences in remote places and overestimate occurrences in heavily sampled places. On the other hand, if researchers know that more populated areas are better sampled, they might estimate a sampling bias distribution and randomly sample background occurrences from that same distribution. This approach might produce more accurate models if their assumptions are good, or it might amplify problems if their assumptions are bad. The problems compound if approaches such as occurrence thinning are used: such data processing obscures underlying assumptions about the distribution of the occurrences, making it unclear how those assumptions interact with assumptions made about the distribution of the background points.

If we cannot track our ever-increasing list of assumptions through our chain of modelling decisions, we lose sight of what, precisely, our SDMs represent, and they become functionally uninterpretable despite producing pretty maps.

A final point on the use of occurrence data involves the confidence with which we accept projections that clearly include regions of extrapolation outside the range of the input data. While we can make projections for the changes in species distribution that would result from (hypothetical) changes in the spatial distribution of climate using a space for time substitution, we cannot validate them until enough climate change has occurred so that we can compare before-and-after maps. Nevertheless, we produce such outputs because we consider that we need to. We must, however, be circumspect with regard to the conclusions that we reach.

We have made a best guess of what would happen to a species under conditions that are themselves a best (albeit scientifically based) guess. In the case of species introductions, we may have some evidence from the extrapolated environments: an invasion may be well underway or even completed. When we project SDM predictions parameterised with native occurrence data on to maps of known occurrences in the non-native range, it is common to see regions where the species already occurs outside the projected range: the model is clearly wrong, even though it was calibrated with the best data we had from the native region. So why base management advice on a faulty model? Why not include occurrences from the non-native range as training data when calibrating the SDM? Whether we are prepared to do this depends on our objectives: if we want to give the best guess that we can to biosecurity agencies, then it might be better to include non-native range data than to just use occurrences from the region of origin, even if this approach risks confusing the model (Webber et al. 2011b).

While the non-native range data may include novel environments into which we want to project our models, they will almost certainly invalidate the assumption that the species is in equilibrium. If our aim is to understand the species and its niche, however, we should keep the data sets separate, so that we learn as much as possible from the lack of match between the modelled projection and the current extent in the new region. So much of how we structure, analyse and interpret our SDM outputs depends on the intent of the modelling being done, the assumptions required and the questions being posed.

Software implementation

Even once a particular SDM has been chosen and the data processed, there is still a great need for caution. Although those who work on SDM methodology advise that the user needs to be aware of how each method works, to choose a method appropriate to each task and take appropriate actions to deal with a range of potential problems, that advice is not easy for the non-expert to adopt.

When implementing the software for a particular method, we need to make decisions that relate to assumptions; often the decisions involve parameterising the model by clicking boxes in a menu. The boxes mostly pre-selected when a particular software package is opened are not necessarily 'typical' choices that will generally be sound. They are starting points for the user to begin their investigations and to then make their own informed decisions for their particular data set. Many users probably do not appreciate this. The vast majority of published uses of Maxent appear to use its default values (Merow et al. 2013; Morales et al. 2017) and only 16% examined the effects of varying these (Morales et al. 2017). Importantly, for most models, there can often be an appreciable difference between projections from the defaults and likely optimal combinations of options, especially when the number of occurrence observations is low (Hallgren et al. 2019).

One of the most important implementation issues is which environmental variables to select for inclusion. If we fail to identify the most important variables for the species and thereby exclude them, then the obvious consequence will be an unreliable set of outputs. But it should not be assumed that an SDM needs to use as many environmental variables as possible – the default for most software. As we discussed in relation to niche shifts, it is so tempting with large, accessible databases and the current fad for 'big data', data mining and machine learning (Elith 2017) to include everything, on the assumption that more explanatory variables will lead to better predictions or projections. The inclusion of too many variables into a statistical model is often referred to as 'over-fitting' (e.g. Figure 7.6c).

There is no automated way in most SDM software of reducing the number of variables to retain just those giving the most robust model outputs (in the same way that we commonly do with multivariate regression). A considerable level of judgement (and art; Elith et al. 2010) is required, which inexperienced users or those not informed on the ecophysiology of their target species may find difficult to acquire. One common approach for reducing the number of environmental variables is to use principal component analysis (PCA) to combine a huge number of possible predictors to just a few representative variables. The CliMond database, for example, automatically supplies five PCA variables derived from 35 climatic variables. However, PCA carries with it its own set of complicating assumptions (as described in Box 7.2) and PCA variables are difficult and dangerous to apply beyond the original region being studied (see Figure 7.6).

Most species distribution models by their nature are correlative. When we apply models to the geographic spaces where they were fitted, we are interpolating. Yet, one of the great powers of SDMs is their ability to project into new geographies, and many researchers cannot resist doing so despite the inherent dangers of extrapolation. Extrapolation can occur when projecting models beyond the covariate range of the training domain as well as due to correlation change between covariates (Mesgaran et al. 2014).

Leading proponents and developers of some of the most widely applied SDMs have specifically and repeatedly called for interpreting extrapolated models with extreme caution, if at all (Elith et al. 2010, 2011). This, therefore, makes correlative SDMs poorly suited to most questions of climate change and non-native ranges (Elith and Franklin 2013). Applying SDMs to these questions may well be ecologically and statistically invalid (Davis et al. 1998, Fitzpatrick and Hargrove 2009) and different SDMs often differ wildly from each other in their outputs (e.g. Dormann et al. 2008). Yet, these questions are the most common uses of the methods in recent years!

Extrapolation is particularly risky when environmental variables are correlated, especially if we are extrapolating into regions of E-space with no known occurrences. There are tools that can indicate in both E- and G-space where a model is extrapolating (e.g. Mesgaran et al. 2014, Zurell et al. 2012), allowing modellers to identify where projection results should not be interpreted. However, few published models provide or present

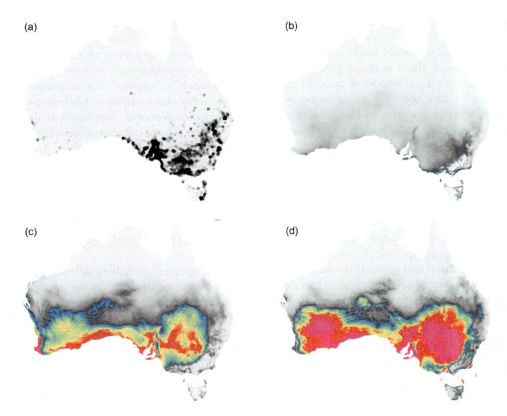

Figure 7.6 Maxent projection of climate suitability in Australia for the southern African species *Lycium ferrocissimum*. (a) Australian distribution according to GBIF. (https://doi.org/10.15468/dl.v68j87); (b) projection using four best PCA variables, (c) using the default 19 bioclimatic variables and (d) using only five bioclimatic variables justified upon examination of climate covariance. Southern African occurrence data for model training were obtained from GBIF (https://doi.org/10.15468/dl.nf2w3y) and subjected to minor cleaning only. Models produced qualitatively similar results when projected into South Africa, but not when extrapolated to Australia.

data to identify where their models are extrapolating, and many publications ignore the issue of extrapolation entirely, obfuscating their assumptions and possible errors.

Having used the model to create a set of outputs, how robust and plausible are the projections? There are several methods available for quantifying model performance. Some are incorporated into SDM software packages and each has its own assumptions, attributes and sensitivities (Meyer and Pebesma 2021).

Elith and Graham (2009) recommend that multiple metrics should be used for assessing the quality of model outputs. Guisan and Zimmermann (2000) and Warren et al. (2020), however, argue that the metric should depend on the objective of the study: metrics for quantifying the fit of the model to data from within its known range (i.e. model sensitivity), for example, rarely measure the model's ability to extrapolate or its ability to describe the niche. Even if the model outputs measure up as statistically robust, are they at all ecologically plausible? A quick scan of the plethora of modelling papers from recent years will reveal biogeographic patterns that would confound the purists. Many of these illogical projections relate to inappropriate application of the model in extrapolation space, emphasising the need to tread carefully (if at all) when going beyond what is known (Mesgaran et al. 2014).

A final issue regarding SDMs relates to the way that the results are presented. This decision is usually left to software developer defaults rather than a choice of the user. Maps of projected 'suitability' (or the range of other spatially displayed metrics that models produce) are an essential component of the interpretation and communication of SDM results. Even if we use mathematical methods to calculate the levels of error, decisions on whether to accept a projection are heavily influenced by the visual cues: does the map look sensible? We assume that the map conveys a reliable interpretation of the SDM's output.

Most attributes of map design are arbitrary, but it would be a mistake to dismiss them as irrelevant (Douglass and Fish 2022). Research on data visualisation shows that the choice of colours, the steepness of the colour gradient and the number of colour categories can influence the perception of information by the reader (Crameri et al. 2020). The output from an SDM is usually an index on a continuous scale and the cut-off value, for a location to be regarded as suitable to the species, can be subjective. The steepness of the colour gradient could influence decisions about the extent of relative suitability, especially where there are no occurrence observations to use for validation (such as projections into changed climates or introductions into new regions). Pixel size is also likely to be influential: a map showing the output from a poorly parameterised SDM using small pixels (i.e. an apparently high spatial precision of the input data) may easily be construed as being more trustworthy (higher quality output) than a more ecologically plausible SDM projection presented with larger pixels, simply because of its grain. Again, the risk of conflating resolution with realism is high. In any case, the SDM itself is only a hypothesised distribution; one of the most common mistakes is to treat this hypothesis as a project endpoint rather as a precursor of future research.

Peer review

Species distribution models continue to be developed, incorporating more biologically based mechanistic approaches (Schouten et al. 2020) and being linked to demographic and dispersal models. They are undoubtedly a useful technique if applied to the right question, parameterised appropriately and interpreted conservatively. It is easy, however, with minimal familiarisation or basic training, to produce visually appealing output from an SDM. Within a short period, anyone can download data from an online records database, run an off-the-shelf SDM using default values and put the results into a paper that is accepted by reviewers and editors with no more training than the author.

Indeed, automated software with next to no warning messages has been created to deliver this exact output. We deliberately do not include examples here to discourage the use of these highly automated packages. When these results are published in a scientific journal, readers almost invariably make the assumption that what they read is trustworthy, since the paper has been through peer review. Yet our quality control systems in science rely on a high degree of trust in the author that they are proficient in the methods they apply and that the review process will filter out sub-standard work.

Yackulic et al. (2013), however, found that 87% of articles using Maxent were based on data that were likely to suffer from sample selection bias, 36% arbitrarily discarded absence data in order to use that model and 54% incorrectly interpreted the output as occurrence probability. Kriticos et al. (2013) also listed several common problems:

- inappropriate model application; incorrect attribution of causality to model extrapolation artefacts;
- oversight of significant, inconvenient methodological caveats;
- extrapolation without identifying the extrapolation space; and
- failing to reconcile models with ecological theory.

The issues had clearly been missed, or regarded as unimportant, by the researchers, the reviewers and the editors!

With so many researchers publishing SDM work, it is increasingly challenging to identify reviewers who are competent enough to detect shortcomings in the deluge of SDM manuscripts that are submitted to journals each week. It may be that, in many cases, these issues had little impact on the model outputs, but most readers are not provided with the material to make this assessment. A related issue is that bad practices can snowball. While reviewing papers, the authors of this chapter have seen severely flawed modelling approaches being defended by virtue of already having been published elsewhere.

As editors and referees, we have seen examples of papers that we have recommended to be rejected (with justification), published at a later stage in other journals with few (if any) additional changes. Given how hard it can be to confidently interpret SDM outputs, there would be a strong case for deciding against publishing at all, even for carefully parameterised models. However, the pressure to publish means that rarely would a researcher get to the end of a modelling activity and decide that the outputs are not of a high enough standard to take on into the publication process.

How, then, are non-specialist readers to judge whether the authors of a given paper have chosen an appropriate model, adequately considered the properties of the data and the assumptions of the methods and taken all these things into account when considering their results? Clearly this judgement is impossible!

We know that all models are wrong (Box 1979), but maybe it is impossible for non-specialist readers to know which are useful. In response to the documented high incidence of problems, only one journal seems to have formally adopted a reporting protocol published by concerned authors (for which an app is also available; Zurell et al. 2020). Why have more editorial boards not taken action when they are alerted to widespread misuse of methods? Even if they did, who would decide on what falls on the right side of the line when it comes to methodological options for a given context? If there's one thing that we all know, ecologists are known to regularly and robustly disagree. Creating further inertia, the incredible citation rates of SDM papers and the relative ease by which they can be generated is a powerful drug to give up in an industry where employment opportunities and career progressions remain heavily influenced by publication metrics.

It can be argued that, ultimately, it is the responsibility of the users of SDMs to make sure that they are adequately trained. Such training is now more widely available than it was perhaps a decade ago, but there is little evidence to suggest that it is being taken up or that the recommendations are being implemented. Crucially, we must also remember that the models we produce are not endpoints of research, but instead are hypotheses to be tested.

To do better, we need to inform users not just about what they need to do, but what they should *not* do. When should a modelling venture be abandoned due to inadequate data or poor model performance? How are SDM practitioners to know when their knowledge is sufficiently adequate? Warnings by expert practitioners and model developers do not appear to reach the attention of occasional users (Yackulic et al. 2013; Morales et al. 2017), especially now that most scientists do not browse journal contents. Likewise, reviewers and editors may not know what to look for. Our peer review system would grind to a halt if we insisted that every piece of work be adjudicated on by an expert in every technique used in a study.

SO WHAT?

Ecology would not be possible without assumptions. Assumptions are indispensable to scientists, because they help us to cope with the complicated world that we are trying to interpret. We must embrace them and respect them, because they are at the heart of what we can and cannot claim to have discovered in our research. If our assumptions are inappropriate or incorrect, then we can make serious errors in our conclusions. It is therefore essential for us to develop a robust knowledge of what they are, the context in which they are relevant, the extent to which they matter and what we can do to make sure that we are not misled. To proceed in research as if the plausibility of our assumptions does not matter would surely be unwise.

Some of the assumptions that we make in ecology may be impossible to test, or at least it would require major additional investigation to do so. This challenge is a common reason why assumptions are required! For example, testing the extent to which individuals within a study area undergo random mating or whether immigration and emigration balance one another would require unjustified effort for most studies. We rely on any departure from the assumption being either unimportant or acting equally across all situations that we are comparing, so that it is relatively unimportant. Without making assumptions, it might be difficult to make progress.

In some situations we may use an assumption without even expecting it to be valid, but we use it as a way to better understand our study system. There are many examples where we use a theoretical model to tell us what we would expect – a null prediction – and then see how far our data depart from that prediction. But there are also a great many situations in which departures from our assumptions can seriously affect the interpretations of our data and, in turn, the entire findings of our research.

A good example of this is analysis of variance. In this chapter, we highlighted the many assumptions that, if they are not fulfilled by our data, have the potential to undermine or invalidate conclusions about invasion niche shifts and species distribution outputs. It would be self-deluding for us to make the bold additional assumption that, in any given study, inappropriate assumptions either do not occur or that they do not matter, if we have not made the effort to test their validity and communicate this effectively in our reporting. There is considerable evidence, particularly from the descriptions of data analysis, that many researchers do not follow good practice for checking assumptions and that unsafe conclusions may, as a result, easily be reached. Readers and end-users of this research could also potentially be misled – especially if they are not themselves experts in the methods that have been used and who accept our conclusions at face value (Box 7.2).

A discussion with an expert in almost any ecological method will often reveal that examples of poor practice are frequent. Faced with this, our advice to any reader of a paper, at least initially, is to be sceptical of every paper that they read unless the author explicitly states what the assumptions were, how they checked them and whether they considered them influential on the findings. We encourage the future leaders of ecological research to hone their skills by probing these papers further: identifying assumptions that remain implicit, probing for those that could undermine the findings and seeking out exemplar papers that lead the way in best practice research methods.

Is it time for the recent progress we have seen in the open data movement (Wessels et al. 2017) to motivate equivalent momentum in open, transparent and accountable research as it applies to assumptions?

In empirical research, such as the analysis of species ranges that we used here as a case study, ecologists frequently try to extract as much as they can – no matter how inadequate the data – and to see how much support there is for an established idea or concept. The research becomes driven by the data that we currently *have*, rather than what

we would *need to have* in order to achieve a particular objective. The more assumptions that we have to make about our data and our methods, and the weaker the support for those assumptions, then the less confident we should be in our assertions. Meta-analyses of many weak studies should not be interpreted as strong support for a particular conclusion, since all the studies may have the same weak underlying assumptions. We should beware of strong assertions of fact in banner headlines of papers.

As we discussed in the case of species distribution models, lack of attention to assumptions in ecological research is often not picked up in the peer review process. In our experience (and in discussions with other editors), it would appear to be rare for the editor-in-charge of a journal to communicate about topical problems – such as the recently and widely reported frequent misuses of SDMs – with their associate editors or to announce a policy for addressing the issue. Some journals publish, and perhaps even seek out, articles for their journal on a topic of particular concern. We assume – falsely – that these papers will be widely read and that their recommendations will be adopted.

Only one journal, to our knowledge, has adopted a code of practice for SDMs. When we asked a senior editor of a major ecological journal why actions have not been taken by that journal to address the widespread publication of misuse of SDMs, they pointed out that SDMs are only one of many methodological problems in the ecological literature and it is impossible to seek to overcome them all. This is almost certainly true, but it is surely also a disturbing report. We are cognisant of the fact that a great deal is expected of our journal editors and reviewers. But while the responsibility for good ecological practice may ultimately be with the researcher, the discipline as a whole would benefit from more comprehensive efforts to clean up particular bad practices.

At what point is the lack of congruence between data and assumptions a problem? Does it matter enough for us to either dismiss our study or to take some form of remedial action? There are objective criteria for some methods, which we can report on in a paper's supplementary information in order to satisfy others. But often the decision is a subjective one, requiring experience and judgement. Many users of ecological methods, however, are yet to develop sufficient expertise. It is not surprising if there is some element of 'hoping for the best'. It is worth noting here that, increasingly, we use readily available, user-friendly software or someone else's code to analyse data. Just because we can process data efficiently does not mean that it provides a quality control mechanism for the user: it simply means that it is easy to produce output. The capacity to check for the acceptability of assumptions is usually available, but often as an option and not as a default.

If the user does not appreciate the need to check particular assumptions, then they cannot be expected to do so. It could be argued that software developers should be responsible for including routine checks into their programs, even at the risk that these will antagonise experienced researchers. Yet native scripting (e.g. in R or Python) is fast coming to dominate ecological analyses and the variability in associated documentation is considerable. Once again, we see the onus on ensuring best practice methods, including giving consideration to any assumptions, falling back to the user (and in turn those who educate new users).

We are in danger of losing our science down a rabbit hole of unfounded assumptions, bewildering methodologies and untested hypotheses.

Facing this precipice, we might feign ignorance, inattentively copying whatever has been done in the past. After all, advancement in academia is increasingly difficult, and researchers worldwide have increasingly less time to devote to contemplative thought and pushing back on convention. Or perhaps we should throw up our hands in disgust and abandon the effort entirely – as the authors of this chapter are often tempted to do with SDMs! Alluring as these options may be, the fact remains that complex ecological methodologies are here to stay with their layers of underpinning assumptions, and are needed to protect biodiversity, natural resources and human health in an era of rapid global change.

As daunting as it may seem, we encourage you (our ecologist superstars of the future) to warmly embrace assumptions for what they are. We must, as a research discipline, get better at keeping track of our assumptions as they accumulate in computational, conceptual or statistical models, and give explicit consideration to how those assumptions influence our inferential power. It should become

de rigueur to weigh the 'assumption cost' of the decisions we make and to share our concerns, caveats and limitations with our readers in an open and accountable way.

We also need brave, clear-headed scientists who can cut through the noise, critically evaluate our assumptions and chart a path forward. This is true not just for the examples we have used in this chapter, but for all of ecology, which is reckoning with the need to anticipate the future in an increasingly confusing and volatile landscape (Maris et al. 2018).

We hope that readers of this chapter will approach their own research and reading with a renewed sense of both scepticism and of the importance and power of assumptions. If we treat an assumption not as a thing to be ignored or evaded but as a tool to be wielded, we may need to limit our scope of inference, but our predictions and projections will be more focused and powerful. Time will tell what role our currently applied ecological methods will play in the future of ecology, but whatever value they have will be maximised only if we treat our assumptions with the respect that they deserve. Our science is, after all, only as good as our assumptions.

REFERENCES

Atwater, D. Z., C. Ervine, and J. N. Barney. 2018. Climatic niche shifts are common in introduced plants. *Nature Ecology and Evolution* 2:34–43. doi:10.1038/s41559-017-0396-z

Baker, H. G., and G. L. Stebbins. (eds). 1965. *The genetics of colonizing species*. New York: Academic Press.

Begon, M., J. L. Harper, and C. R. Townsend. 1996. *Ecology*, 3rd edition. Oxford: Blackwell Science.

Booth, T. H., H. A. Nix, J. R. Busby, and M. F. Hutchinson. 2014. BIOCLIM: The first species distribution modelling package, its early applications and relevance to most current MaxEnt studies. *Diversity and Distributions* 20:1–9. doi:10.1111/ddi.12144

Box, G. E. P. 1979. Robustness in the strategy of scientific model building. In *Robustness in statistics*, eds R. L. Launer and G. N. Wilkinson, 201–236. Cambridge: Academic Press. doi:10.1016/B978-0-12-438150-6.50018-2

Cousens, R. 1988. Misinterpretations of results in weed research through inappropriate use of statistics. *Weed Research* 28:281 289.

Cousens, R. D., P. K. Ades, M. B. Mesgaran, and S. Ohadi. 2013. Reassessment of the invasion history of two species of *Cakile* (Brassicaceae) in Australia. *Cunninghamia* 13:275–290. doi:10.7751/cunninghamia.2013.005

Crameri, F., G. E. Shephard, and P. J. Heron. 2020. The misuse of colour in science communication. *Nature Communications* 11:5444. doi:10.1038/s41467-020-19160-7

Daly, C. 2006. Guidelines for assessing the suitability of spatial climate data sets. *International Journal of Climatology* 26:707–721. doi:10.1002/joc.1322

Davis, A. J., L. S. Jenkinson, J. H. Lawton, et al. 1998. Making mistakes when predicting shifts in species range in response to global warming. *Nature* 391:783–786. doi:10.1038/35842

Dormann, C. F., O. Purschke, J. R. García Márquez, et al. 2008. Components of uncertainty in species distribution analysis: A case study of the great grey shrike. *Ecology* 89:3371–3386. doi:10.1890/07-1772.1

Douglass, N. A. K., and C. S. Fish. 2022. That's a relief: Assessing beauty, realism, and landform clarity in multilayer terrain maps. *Cartographic Perspectives* 100:45–66. doi:10.14714/CP100.1727

Elith, J. 2017. Predicting distributions of invasive species. In *Invasive species: Risk assessment and management*, eds T. R. Walshe, A. Robinson, M. Nunn and M. A. Burgman, 93–129. Cambridge: Cambridge University Press. doi:10.1017/9781139019606

Elith, J., and J. Franklin. 2013. Species distribution modeling. In *Encyclopedia of Biodiversity*, ed S. M. Scheiner, 2nd edition, 692–705. San Diego: Elsevier.

Elith, J., and C. H. Graham. 2009. Do they? How do they? WHY do they differ? On finding reasons for differing performances of species distribution models. *Ecography* 32:66–77. doi:10.1111/j.1600-0587.2008.05505.x

Elith, J., C. H. Graham, R. P. Anderson, et al. 2006. Novel methods improve prediction of species' distributions from occurrence data. *Ecography* 29:129–151. doi:10.1111/j.2006.0906-7590.04596.x

Elith J., M. Kearney, and S. Phillips. 2010. The art of modelling range-shifting species. *Methods in Ecology and Evolution* 1:330–342. doi:10.1111/j.2041-210X.2010.00036.x

Elith, J., S. J. Phillips, T. Hastie, et al. 2011. A statistical explanation of MaxEnt for Ecologists. *Diversity and Distributions* 17:43–57. doi:10.1111/j.1472-4642.2010.00725.x

Ellenberg, H. 1974. Zeigerwerte der Gefässpflanzen Mitteleuropas. *Scripta Geobot Göttingen* 9:1–97.

Fick, S. E., and R. J. Hijmans. 2017. WorldClim 2: New 1-km spatial resolution climate surfaces for global land areas. *International Journal of Climatology* 37:4302–4315. doi:10.1002/joc.5086

Fitzpatrick, M. C., and W. W. Hargrove. 2009. The projection of species distribution models and the problem of non-analog climate. *Biodiversity and Conservation* 18:2255–2261. doi:10.1007/s10531-009-9584-8

Forcella, F. 1985. Final distribution is related to rate of spread in alien weeds. *Weed Research* 25:181–191. doi:10.1111/j.1365-3180.1985.tb00634.x

Fréjaville, T., and M. B. Garzón. 2018. The EuMedClim database: Yearly climate data (1901–2014) of 1 km resolution grids for Europe and the Mediterranean basin. *Frontiers in Ecology and Evolution* 6:31. doi:10.3389/fevo.2018.00031

Grinnell, J. 1917. The niche-relationships of the California thrasher. *The Auk* 34:427–433.

Guisan, A., and N. E. Zimmermann. 2000. Predictive habitat distribution models in ecology. *Ecological Modelling* 135:147–186. doi:10.1016/S0304-3800(00)00354-9

Guisan, A., and W. Thuiller. 2005. Predicting species distribution: Offering more than simple habitat models. *Ecology Letters* 8:993–1009. doi:10.1111/j.1461-0248.2005.00792.x

Guisan, A., B. Petitpierre, O. Broennimann, et al. 2014. Unifying niche shift studies: Insights from biological invasions. *Trends in Ecology and Evolution* 29:260–269. doi:10.1016/j.tree.2014.02.009

Hallgren, W., F. Santana, S. Low-Choy, et al. 2019. Species distribution models can be highly sensitive to algorithm configuration. *Ecological Modelling* 408:1–23. doi:10.1016/j.ecolmodel.2019.108719

Hao, T., J. Elith, G. Guillera-Arroita, and J. J. Lahoz-Monfort. 2019. A review of evidence about use and performance of species distribution modelling ensembles like BIOMOD. *Diversity and Distributions* 25:839–852. doi:10.1111/ddi.12892

Hargreaves, A. L., K. E. Samis, and C. G. Eckert. 2014. Are species' range limits simply niche limits writ large? A review of transplant experiments beyond the range. *The American Naturalist* 183:157–173. doi:10.1086/674525

Holt, R. D. 2009. Bringing the Hutchinsonian niche into the 21st century: Ecological and evolutionary perspectives. *Proceedings of the National Academy of Sciences of the United States of America* 116 (Suppl. 2):19659–19665. doi:10.1073/pnas.0905137106

Hutchinson, G. E. 1978. *An introduction to population ecology.* New Haven: Yale University Press.

Jackson, S. T., and J. T. Overpeck. 2000. Responses of plant populations and communities to environmental changes of the late Quaternary. *Paleobiology* 26:194–220.

Keane, R. M., and M. J. Crawley 2002. Exotic plant invasions and the enemy release hypothesis. *Trends in Ecology and Evolution* 17:164–170. doi:10.1016/S0169-5347(02)02499-0

Kearney, M. R., and W. P. Porter. 2020. NicheMapR: An R package for biophysical modelling: The ectotherm and dynamic energy budget models. *Ecography* 43:85–96. doi:10.1111/ecog.04680

Keyfitz, N. 1972. On future population. *Journal of the American Statistical Association* 67:347–363.

Kriticos, D. J., B. L. Webber, A. Leriche, et al. 2012. CliMond: Global high-resolution historical and future scenario climate surfaces for bioclimatic modelling. *Methods in Ecology and Evolution* 3:53–64. doi:10.1111/j.2041-210X.2011.00134.x

Kriticos, D. J., D. C. Le Maitre, and B. L. Webber. 2013. Essential elements of discourse for advancing the modelling of species' current and potential distributions. *Journal of Biogeography* 40:608–613. doi:10.1111/j.1365-2699.2012.02791.x

Kriticos, D. J., L. Morin, and B. L. Webber. 2014. Taxonomic uncertainty in pest risks or modelling artefacts? Implications for biosecurity policy and practice. *NeoBiota* 23:81–93. doi:10.3897/neobiota.22.7496

Lande, R. 2014. Evolution of phenotypic plasticity and environmental tolerance of a labile quantitative character in a fluctuating environment. *Journal of Evolutionary Biology* 27:866–875. doi:10.1111/jeb.12360

Liu, C., C. Wolter, W. Xian, and J. M. Jeschke. 2020. Most invasive species largely conserve their climatic niche. *Proceedings of the National Academy of Sciences of the United States of America* 117:23643–23651. doi:10.1073/pnas.2004289117

Lowry, E., E. J. Rollinson, A. J. Laybourn, et al. 2013. Biological invasions: A field synopsis, systematic review, and database of the literature. *Ecology and Evolution* 3:182–196. doi:10.1002/ece3.431

Maycock, C. R., E. Khoo, C. J. Kettle, et al. 2012. Using high resolution ecological niche models to assess the conservation status of *Dipterocarpus lamellatus* and *Dipterocarpus ochraceus* in Sabah, Malaysia. *Journal of Forest and Environmental Science* 28:158–169. doi:10.7747/JFS.2012.28.3.158

Merow, C., M. J. Smith, and J. A. Silander. 2013. A practical guide to MaxEnt for modeling species' distributions: What it does, and why inputs and settings matter. *Ecography* 36:1058–1069. doi:10.1111/j.1600-0587.2013.07872.x

Mesgaran, M. B., R. D. Cousens, and B. L. Webber. 2014. Here be dragons: A tool for quantifying novelty due to covariate range and correlation change when projecting species distribution models. *Diversity and Distributions* 20:1147–1159. doi:10.1111/ddi.12209

Meyer, H., and E. Pebesma. 2021. Predicting into unknown space? Estimating the area of applicability of spatial prediction models. *Methods in Ecology and Evolution* 12:1620–1633. doi:10.1111/2041-210X.13650

Meyer, C., P. Wiegelt, and H. Kreft. 2016. Multidimensional biases, gaps and uncertainties in global plant occurrence information. *Ecology Letters* 19:992–1006. doi:10.1111/ele.12624

Morales, N. S., I. C. Fernández, and V. Baca-González. 2017. MaxEnt's parameter configuration and small samples: Are we paying attention to recommendations? A systematic review. *PeerJ* 5:e3093. doi:10.7717/peerj.3093

Newbold, T., T. Reader, A. El-Gabbas, et al. 2010. Testing the accuracy of species distribution models using species records from a new field survey. *Oikos* 119:1326–1334. doi:10.1111/j.1600-0706.2009.18295.x

Noce, S., L. Caporaso, and M. Santini. 2020. A new global dataset of bioclimatic indicators. *Scientific Data* 7:398. doi:10.1038/s41597-020-00726-5

Peterson, A. T., and J. Soberón. 2012. Integrating fundamental concepts of ecology, biogeography, and sampling into effective ecological niche modeling and species distribution modeling. *Plant Biosystems* 146:789–796. doi:10.1080/11263504.2012.740083

Petitpierre, B., C. Kueffer, O. Broennimann, et al. 2012. Climatic niche shifts are rare among terrestrial plant invaders. *Science* 335:1344–1348. doi:10.1126/science.12159

Phillips, S. J., M. Dudík, J. Elith, et al. (2009). Sample selection bias and presence-only distribution models: Implications for background and pseudo-absence data. *Ecological Applications* 19:181–197. doi:10.1890/07-2153.1

Phillips, S. J., R. P. Anderson, M. Dudík, et al. 2017. Opening the black box: An open-source release of Maxent. *Ecography* 40:887–893. doi:10.1111/ecog.03049

Pyron, R. A., G. C. Costa, M. A. Patten, and F. T. Burbrink. 2015. Phylogenetic niche conservatism and the evolutionary basis of ecological speciation. *Biological Reviews* 90:1248–1262. doi:10.1111/brv.12154

Ratcliffe, S. (ed). 2017. *Oxford essential quotations*, 5th edn. Oxford: Oxford University Press.

Roughgarden, J. 1974. Niche width: Biogeographic patterns among *Anolis lizard* populations. *The American Naturalist* 108:429–442. doi:10.1086/282924

Royle, J. A., R. B. Chandler, C. Yackulic, and J. D. Nichols. 2012. Likelihood analysis of species occurrence probability from presence-only data for modelling species distributions. *Methods in Ecology and Evolution* 3:545–554. doi:10.1111/j.2041-210X.2011.00182.x

Schoener, T. W. 1968. Anolis lizards of Bimini: Resource partitioning in a complex fauna. *Ecology* 49:704–726. doi:10.2307/1935534

Schouten, R., P. A. Vesk, and M. R. Kearney. 2020. Integrating dynamic plant growth models and microclimates for species distribution modelling. *Ecological Modelling* 435:109262. doi:10.32942/osf.io/ja4m6

Schröter, M., Crouzat, E., Hölting, L., et al. 2021. Assumptions in ecosystem service assessments: Increasing transparency for conservation. *Ambio* 50:289–300. doi:10.1007/s13280-020-01379-9

Sutherst, R. W. 2003. Prediction of species geographical ranges. *Journal of Biogeography* 30:805–816.

Syfert, M. M., M. J. Smith, and D. A. Coomes. 2013. The effects of sampling bias and model complexity on the predictive performance of MaxEnt species distribution models. *PLoS ONE* 8:e55158. doi:10.1371/journal.pone.0055158

Thuiller, W., B. Lafourcade, R. Engler, and M. B. Araújo, et al. 2009. BIOMOD: A platform for ensemble forecasting of species distributions. *Ecography* 32:369–373. doi:10.1111/j.1600-0587.2008.05742.x

Tyberghein, L., H. Verbruggen, K. Pauly, et al. 2011. Bio-ORACLE: A global environmental dataset for marine species distribution modelling. *Global Ecology and Biogeography* 21:272–281. doi:10.1111/j.1466-8238.2011.00656.x

van Boheemen, L. A., D. Z. Atwater, and K. A. Hodgins. 2019. Rapid and repeated local adaptation to climate in an invasive plant. *New Phytologist* 222:614–627. doi:10.1111/nph.15564

van Proosdij, A. S. J., M. S. M. Sosef, J. J. Wieringa, and N. Raes. 2016. Minimum required number of specimen records to develop accurate species distribution models. *Ecography* 39:542–552. doi:10.1111/ecog.01509

Warren, D. L., N. J. Matzke, and T. L. Iglesias. 2020. Evaluating presence-only species distribution models with discrimination accuracy is uninformative for many applications. *Journal of Biogeography* 47:167–180. doi:10.1111/jbi.13705

Webber, B. L., C. Born, B. J. Conn, et al. 2011a. What is in a name? That which we call *Cecropia peltata* by any other name would be as invasive? *Plant Ecology and Diversity* 4:289–293. doi:10.1080/17550874.2011.610372

Webber, B. L., C. J. Yates, D. C. Le Maitre, et al. 2011b. Modelling horses for novel climate courses: Insights from projecting potential distributions of native and alien *Australian acacias* with correlative and mechanistic models. *Diversity and Distributions* 17:978–1000. doi:10.1111/j.1472-4642.2011.00811.x

Webber, B. L., D. C. Le Maitre, and D. J. Kriticos. 2012. Comment on 'Climatic niche shifts are rare among terrestrial plant invaders'. *Science* 338:193. doi:10.1126/science.12259

Wessels, B., R. Finn, T. Sveinsdottir, and K. Wadhwa. (eds). 2017. *Open data and the knowledge society*. Amsterdam: Amsterdam University Press.

Wiens, J. A., D. Stralberg, D. Jongsomjit, et al. 2009. Niches, models, and climate change: Assessing the assumptions and uncertainties. *Proceedings of the National Academy of Sciences of the United States of America* 106 (Suppl. 2):19729–19736. doi:10.1073/pnas.0901639106

Wisz, M. S., R. J. Hijmans, J. Li, A. T. Peterson, et al. 2008. Effects of sample size on the performance of species distribution models. *Diversity and Distributions* 14:763–773. doi:10.1111/j.1472-4642.2008.00482.x

Xu S., J. Wang, Z. Guo, et al. 2020. Genomic convergence in the adaptation to extreme environments. *Plant Communications* 1:100117. doi:10.1016/j.xplc.2020.100117

Yackulic, C. B., R. Chandler, E. F. Zipkin, et al. 2013. Presence-only modelling using MAXENT: When can we trust the inferences? *Methods in Ecology and Evolution* 4:236–243. doi:10.1111/2041-210x.12004

Zizka, A., D. Silvestro, T. Andermann, et al. 2019. CoordinateCleaner: Standardized cleaning of occurrence records from biological collection databases. *Methods in Ecology and Evolution* 10:744–751. doi:10.1111/2041-210X.13152

Zurell, D., J. Elith, and B. Schröder, B. 2012. Predicting to new environments: Tools for visualizing model behaviour and impacts on mapped distributions. *Diversity and Distributions* 18:628–634. doi:10.1111/j.1472-4642.2012.00887.x

Zurell, D., J. Franklin, C. König, et al. 2020. A standard protocol for reporting species distribution models. *Ecography* 43:1261–1277. doi:10.1111/ecog.04960

8

Theory, prediction and application

MARIA PANIW, ROGER COUSENS, CHRIS BAKER AND THAO LE

A PLACE FOR MODELLING IN ECOLOGY

Prediction has a prominent place in both fundamental and applied ecology. In principle, we learn from using our knowledge to make predictions and then comparing those predictions with what we observe. If our predictions are good, then we can be reassured that our knowledge *may* be reasonable; if predictions are poor, then we may need to reconsider what we think we know. Peters (1991) was of the view that the ability to make predictions is the yardstick by which all scientific theories should be measured, while Houlahan et al. (2017) considered prediction to be the only way to demonstrate scientific understanding.

The need for predictions is also becoming increasingly more important. Anthropogenic environmental change is fundamentally altering natural systems, and we have a responsibility to alleviate the impacts that we cause. Ecological forecasting – near-term predictions that can be validated with independent data — has therefore emerged as a research frontier, with a primary focus on robustly and iteratively testing ecological predictions across different ecological scales (Dietze et al. 2018). If we can demonstrate that our predictions are trustworthy – according to some appropriate assessment – then we should be able to tell managers what the implications of their decisions are likely to be, i.e. what is likely to happen if they conduct some form of intervention.

Ecological prediction is inextricably linked to models. Models are inevitably simplifications of the real world that we *hope* capture the essence of nature, using the abstract tools of mathematics. They are a way of formulating a best guess based on our current ideas and information. But there are always potential errors involved in prediction: our data are limited and subject to uncertainty, we are forced to make assumptions and simplifications, and our ecological understanding will always be imperfect.

Realistically, there will always be limits to how accurate and precise our models and predictions can be. However, the process of modelling is, itself, an educational exercise and we learn a great deal simply from putting the model together, encapsulating our knowledge in a few succinct terms and subsequently seeing what is predicted. We also learn a great deal from our *failures* to predict, perhaps even more than when our predictions turn out to be good. Scientists in general learn a great deal from their mistakes (Bronowski 1979) – a fact of life that the public may not be keen to hear!

There are many different types of models – we will deal with some aspects of their structure in the next section. There are also many different uses of models. One important distinction is between predictions *sensu stricto* and projections: these are commonly confused but are quite different. Predictions are a model's ability to reflect the observed data *while assuming that those conditions will persist*. Projections, on the other hand, refer

DOI: 10.1201/9781003314332-8

to a model's ability to reflect future dynamics of the system *under plausible sets of conditions, i.e.* under various scenarios proposed by the modeller or their stakeholders that deviate from previously observed conditions. Projections typically cannot be validated with independent data in the near term.

An obvious example is the distinction between weather forecasts and climate change projections. The former *predict,* over a short time window, what will happen if current trends persist, whereas the latter *project* what would happen under certain scenarios of greenhouse gas emission such as those considered by the Intergovernmental Panel on Climate Change. More complex models that account for mechanisms may be relatively worse at replicating past observed trends but better at forecasting or projecting when compared with those models that merely assess patterns within data (Hefley et al. 2017).

Merely using a model to make a prediction or a projection is rarely a sufficient outcome, unless the aim is to demonstrate a new technique. The modeller needs to produce predictions that are reliable enough for the task at hand. We often have ethical responsibilities for our work: if we make a prediction that turns out to be inaccurate, we might cause an ecosystem to collapse, a species to go extinct or an enterprise to lose money. Users of the predictions also need to develop a rigorous opinion of what models tell them: just because a model gives a certain answer (perhaps the one that they were expecting) does not necessarily mean that it will be reliable, no matter how sophisticated or biologically realistic the model. It is easy to become over-confident.

So, how good does a decision-maker need a prediction to be for it to be useful to them? Or alternatively, how wrong are they prepared to be? This important design criterion seldom seems to be considered explicitly in ecological research. From a pragmatic perspective, models might not need to be highly accurate: an improvement of the quality of prediction in comparison with the status quo might be regarded as a worthwhile investment.

But, if we are to satisfy both ourselves and our peers, we still need to be able to assess the quality of a prediction, to measure any improvement that we have achieved and to base model selection on objective criteria. Obviously, the better

the prediction is, or the more often it is accurate enough, then the more confident we will be in any recommendations that we make.

It is a worthwhile exercise for a modeller to consider how good they can expect their predictions to be and where improvements will come from: otherwise, they may be chasing a quality of prediction that is almost impossible to achieve. Improvements to prediction might come from several avenues, for example: future technical advances in programming and mathematics; the collection of more data (and with reduced bias that can improve our estimation of parameter values); changes to the model's structure (either greater elaboration in order to make it more realistic or simplification to make it more tractable); or from replacing proxy variables by directly relevant variables (Yates et al. 2018). However, there will always be trade-offs to be made in improving model performance. Better parameter estimates will only come from more activity, at the cost of diverting resources away from other priorities. Even the act of applying for additional research resources – perhaps with low success rates – diverts activity from the research itself. More biological components in a model require knowledge – or guesses – of the values of more parameters. Levins (1966) famously proposed that there is a trade-off between model precision, generality and realism. All three characteristics can be improved, but at a cost, and with limited resources we will have to choose between them – although this claim has been the target of much debate.

In this chapter, we will explore a range of issues faced by those making forecasts for populations. We have chosen population dynamics as a case study of prediction in ecology, since these have the longest history and are perhaps the simplest to discuss, with issues that will apply to prediction in ecology more generally.

We consider three somewhat disparate topics that cover a range of issues that are faced by researchers working on various types of predictions. These are: how we can test the predictions of theoretical models; the many decisions that must be taken when constructing and testing empirical models; and the use of forecasting in the development of policy and management decisions. But first, we will consider a few important points about the ways in which population models are formulated.

TYPES OF POPULATION MODEL

Population models allow us to make predictions about how real populations might behave, based on the assumptions that we choose to make. These predictions may, in many cases, be the prime reasons for modelling: we need models in order to make informed decisions. If we predict a catastrophe for a species, then practical conservation action is warranted. But models also give us a way of working in the opposite direction: to determine the importance of the assumptions that we have made to the model's outcomes and *what* type of actions we might consider. In most cases we use computers to do the calculations, to perform simulations and thus to perform 'experiments' *in silico*. We can readily change our assumptions and incorporate different scenarios to see what effect this has on the model's predictions. Once again, this will guide our management decisions.

A wonderful and topical example of this use of models was provided by the development of COVID-19 simulation models, from which governments could predict the numbers of illnesses, hospital patients and deaths that would result from different policy options, such as travel restrictions, mask use and vaccination strategies (e.g. Doherty Institute 2021).

A model consists of one or more equations that describe the relationships between variables. In general terms, the mathematical form of the equations and its parameters determine the shape, scale and strength of the relationships and interactions. In a population model, the output variable ultimately predicted could be a variety of things: the total number in the entire population; a measure of local abundance (such as number per unit area, population density); frequency of particular genotypes; presence or absence; or the locations of every individual within the population. In practice, the decision on what to predict should be determined collaboratively between the modeller and the end user, predicated on the objectives of the research and the type of population data available. The predictor variables, explanatory variables and 'drivers' of abundance depend on which processes the development team considers to be important and on the information available. This can include anything that determines a demographic or dispersal process, such as resource supply, weather variables, population density or the abundance of organisms whose effect on the target species is positive or negative.

Forecasting necessarily considers time and it may involve space. In reality, both are continuous entities, but as soon as we seek to increase model complexity, we are forced for pragmatic reasons to break both time and space into discrete units. The discrete units of time may often be related to seasonal demographic events. Space may be ignored altogether, assuming that the same temporal dynamics occurs throughout the landscape. Alternatively, space may be divided into discrete cells with or without gaps between them, according to the grain of the environment, the plausible scales of ecological processes or an arbitrary guess.

One of the most important spatial population processes is dispersal: assumptions are made about whether to measure this in radial or Cartesian coordinates, whether dispersal 'kernels' are continuous or discrete, or whether dispersal is reduced to a single migration rate parameter. For populations modelled in a discretely bounded arena, another decision is how to treat population processes at the boundary. We end up with an array of named spatial model forms, such as reaction-diffusion, integro-difference, coupled map lattice, cellular automaton, stepping stone array (in either one or two dimensions), individual-based, agent-based and metapopulation models. See Bolker (2004) for a more comprehensive discussion of model terminology and Cousens et al. (2008) for examples of different model outputs.

Given all the models and variables we have mentioned, how do we choose which model structure in practice?

Say we want to predict the abundance of species A that lives across 20 sites. Imagine that we have information on survival, but not reproduction, at a couple of sites. We have crude data on spatial variation in vegetation and geology. We have climate predictors. We have estimates of the abundances of species B (a competitor) and natural history records on which species are predators. The choice of model is not simple. The final selection will be guided to a considerable degree by attributes of the modeller: art, experience, knowledge, instinct, familiarity and habit. Those with mathematical or computational expertise may prefer to develop a model from first principles. Those who do not have the expertise or resources but nevertheless want to model could pick one of the various user-friendly software packages available – but these force the user into a model that may not be ideally suited to their purpose and mistakes (or suboptimal decisions) can be made by those unfamiliar with the model's assumptions. A user may choose a type of model favoured by their mentor, or that they have been taught in a class. They might use someone else's model for another species, if they consider it to be sufficiently 'transferable' (Yates et al. 2018) – though it is hard to decide in advance how reliable those predictions will be until we have estimated the appropriate parameter values. Given these various limitations and compromises, it is always best to try to assemble a research team that includes experienced modellers, empirical ecologists and end users.

If we have access to a wealth of data, 'black-box'-like machine learning techniques can be used without explicitly choosing a model structure (though inputs and the machine learning algorithm will still need to be chosen) (Olden et al. 2008). Ecologists, however, tend to favour models into which we explicitly incorporate ecological processes.

In principle, we could construct a model that includes every population process and every interaction that we can think of, but we are then immediately faced with compromises. Do we have the data to support it, adequately estimate all of its parameters and test all its components and their interactions? If we want a complicated model, then we must commit to obtaining more and perhaps different types of data. [We will deal with this issue later in the context of 'decision science' (see Box 8.1).] If not, we will be acting under a false sense of scientific rigour: we may have been smart in model design, but we have a model that will be unable to provide sound or testable predictions.

We must, somehow (there are methods to help us to do this: see discussion in Hooten and Hobbs 2015), choose a simpler model (but which one?) that suits the data, but one that also still serves the purposes of the research. We are frequently called upon to make population predictions for conservation or policy purposes in situations where information is distinctly limited, if not completely absent (Burgman et al. 2005). To refuse to make a prediction due to imperfect data is not an option if, for example, a species' survival is at stake. A model is needed to provide a best guess for what remedial or control actions we should take, and to achieve

that we must make guesses about what to include in the model. We may —albeit reluctantly — need to guess at the likely values of the parameters that we put in the model (when experts do this it is legitimised as 'expert opinion': e.g. Lele and Allen 2006). And we may not even be able to test those predictions! But we do so in full awareness of the limitations of what we are doing.

There is vast population modelling literature to which we cannot do justice in this brief chapter. Useful introductions might be Salguero-Gómez and Gamelon (2021) and Gustafsson and Sternad (2016). We will leave the topic of model construction for now, having barely touched the surface, at the point where the modeller decides on the basis of whatever criteria they consider appropriate. It may be an outstanding model or a poor one, and it may be well or poorly suited to the situation. Having chosen the model structure, the modeller must then make it perform as well as possible and they must have a method and criteria for testing it.

TESTING THE PREDICTIONS OF THEORETICAL MODELS

Theoretical models seek to predict what *might* happen to a system and under what sorts of conditions (modellers refer to a system's 'parameter space'), based on assumptions about the processes which we believe might occur. These models have played a significant historical role in the development of ecology, forming a building block on which much of ecological education is based, and remains an active area for ecological research.

Is it possible to validate theoretical models? This is an issue with which many ecologists have struggled (e.g. Dayton 1979). And if we cannot, does that make them useless – as champion of empiricism Simberloff (1981) insisted? Some modellers have argued that ecologists may have an undue expectation of theory: theory only helps us to understand the sorts of things that *could* happen (Caswell 1988), not what *will* happen. But that, in itself, is valuable in the generation of hypotheses.

We face a serious, logical trilemma if we set out to look for supporting evidence for a theoretical model in the real world: (1) We might fail to find any evidence, but does that mean that it will *never* happen? (2) We may search for many decades in the hope that eventually we find one exception that proves the rule. Perhaps we have not yet looked at the particular —perhaps rare – conditions under which it *would* happen. (3) Or we might simply be unable to detect the predicted behaviour even if it *actually* happens, because the real ecological world is far more complicated, and much noisier, than a model. There will always be uncertainty in drawing discrete conclusions (whether the model is satisfactory or not) from continuously varying evidence.

There are a number of things that we can do to test a theoretical model's predictions. Three approaches are common: (1) we can examine data from case studies to see how often the appropriate parameter values occur and hence how likely it is that the dynamics will occur; (2) we can examine time-series data, with its inherent variability, to see whether we can detect evidence – a signal – that the particular form of population dynamics is found in nature; and (3) we can conduct experiments to see whether the predictions can be (readily) replicated under controlled conditions. All of these things together may build a substantial case for or against the theory.

A problem is that there may be other theories, other processes and other models that could lead to the same dynamics. We need to be able to exclude them (though at this point in research we may not know exactly what those alternatives are) and/or to provide evidence through further research that the ecological processes necessary for those dynamics, i.e. the required drivers, do indeed occur in the case study. Otherwise we will be in danger of committing 'confirmation bias' by reaching the conclusion that we would most like to make (Zvereva and Kozlov 2021).

Here, we will discuss two case studies of attempts to test theoretical predictions. One concerns a famous prediction that when a predator and a prey species interact, it is possible that the result will be persistent, displaced cycles of abundance in the two species. The second is the prediction that a spatially expanding population will approach a constant rate dictated by its net reproductive rate and the frequency distribution of distances dispersed by offspring.

Case study 1: predator-prey cycles

Predator-prey cycles feature in just about every ecology textbook, perhaps giving the impression that they are fact, rather than just a prediction of a simple model based on particular mathematical assumptions. The logic behind the model is as follows: When the abundance of predators is low, the organisms on which they rely for food are able to increase rapidly. The predators, with lower rates of population increase, take time to respond but eventually they reach levels at which they consume so much of the prey that the prey species declines. Lack of prey then drives predator populations down and the cycle starts over again.

Laboratory experiments, field surveys and field experiments have all been used to try to test this prediction of predator-driven cycles. Attempts over many decades to replicate the model prediction experimentally met with no success, until Blasius et al. (2020) managed to generate around 50 predator-prey cycles in two freshwater organisms. So, does a single positive result in nine decades really constitute validation of the theoretical model? Why did this study succeed when all others have failed? Hastings (2020) suggested that the reason was the complexity of the life history of the particular predator and urged future researchers to test that additional hypothesis. It is worth noting that in a strictly predator-driven system, there should be a time lag, with peaks in predator populations following *after* peaks in the prey population. Yet, for a considerable period the experiment's cycles – although maintained – were not in the correct order.

The most quoted empirical example of predator-prey cycles is the (roughly) 10-year cycles of lynx (*Lynx canadensis*) and snowshoe hares (*Lepus americanus*) in Canada. The original time-series data were compiled from furs sold to the Hudson Bay Company between 1821 and 1934. The cycles in lynx and snowshoe hares were originally thought to be synchronous across much of the continent, but more recent evidence suggests that there may be a wave of abundance that moves across the landscape, at least in some regions (Krebs et al. 2018). While it is indisputable that these cycles exist, are they actually driven by predation? There are climatic oscillations from both the North Atlantic Oscillation (Hurrell 1995) and the polar vortex (Lu and Zhou 2018) that drive seasonal variation in climate at northern latitudes, which might affect snow depth and persistence in winter and vegetation growth, both of which could affect animal demography (Peers et al. 2020).

While the population data are clearly cyclic and the cycles are mostly in the correct sequence, are they the result of lynx *driving* the abundance of the hares? The predators might be *responding* to the abundance of prey rather than causing it. Hares might cycle in abundance even if the lynx were absent, for an alternative reason such as over-grazing. In some cases, cycles in hares persist where lynx are absent or rare (Krebs 2002). The data in favour of hare over-grazing are weak. Neither application of fertiliser to stimulate plant growth (Turkington et al. 1998) nor the addition of food (Krebs et al. 2001) were able to stop the declines in hare abundance. Even at the peak in hare abundance, the most plentiful foods were still poorly grazed – although a decline in food quality was not discounted.

The idea of predation as the prime driver of hare abundance has thus maintained its appeal. Few hares die of starvation: most are predated upon (Krebs et al. 2018) (though malnourished hares would also be easier for predators to catch). There is some evidence that the decline in reproductive rate in hares at their peak abundance may be a physiological result of stress (Sheriff et al. 2011) caused by higher risk of predation. Thus, there may be an indirect effect through predator abundance as well as a direct effect of predation.

In an unreplicated study, the addition of food and the exclusion of ground predators by a fence maintained female hare body mass and reproductive output but did not completely prevent a hare population decline (Krebs et al. 2018). The fact that cycles in hares persist even where lynx are absent (Krebs 2002) has been used to suggest that the cycle in hares may be driven more by predators in general than specifically by the lynx. Stenseth et al. (1997) concluded that hare numbers were best explained by a three-level trophic model (vegetation-hare-lynx) whereas the lynx numbers were best explained by just a two-level model (hare-lynx). They also pointed out that the trophic webs in these regions are highly complex and although lynx are primarily specialist predators on hares (and the only species for which historical trap data were available), they are by no means the only hare predators. By adding coyote and great horned owl to a hare-lynx population model, Tyson et al. (2010) were able to predict the metrics of the cycles more accurately than with a lynx-hare model; they also found that owls were crucial for the prediction of low hare densities.

The many different lines of enquiry of the hare-lynx system have each added to our ability to make educated guesses about what is driving population dynamics, but absolute certainty will always be lacking – even if there is continued investment in research. Some of the studies would benefit from repetition and there are still unanswered questions about the drivers of demography at low hare population levels (Krebs et al. 2018).

How much further research of this system is warranted? What will it take to satisfy us that we have satisfactorily explained the system and thus validated the theoretical prediction? Some might argue that we already have explanations which are sufficient to allay our curiosity. Even if there is still a possibility that those explanations are partly or completely wrong, do we need to chase the unattainable goal of absolute certainty in every case study?

Case study 2: rate of population spread

Our second example of a test of a theoretical model prediction concerns rates of population spread. The test of a theoretical prediction failed, but this led to the realisation that the appropriate processes had not been built into the model. Various models, beginning with Fisher and Kolmogorov in 1937, showed that a population spreading unimpeded through a homogeneous landscape and with a normal distribution of dispersal distances should travel at a rate of $\sqrt{4\alpha D}$, where D is the root mean square dispersal distance and α is the exponential population growth rate.

Skellam (1951) used this prediction to estimate the rate of spread of oak populations after the last Ice Age. His (rough) calculations were as follows:

- Although the number of acorns produced over the life span of a tree must be prodigious, mortality is very high (1% reach 3 years of age). According to Skellam, '*it seems safe to assume that the average number of mature daughter oaks produced by a single parent oak did not exceed 9 million*'.
- Acorns are usually produced when a tree reaches around 60 years of age and continues for seven hundred years, so the generation time is at least 60 years.

- Oak populations have travelled 600 miles since the last Ice Age, as estimated from pollen cores.
- Assuming a generation time of 60 years and that the retreat of the ice started around 20,000 years ago, approximately 300 generations had passed.

From these values, and using a bivariate normal distribution of *realised* dispersal distances (distances of offspring trees rather than of acorns), the root mean square dispersal distance required to explain the observed rate of spread was calculated to be in the region of $600/[300\sqrt{\log_e(9,000,000)}]$, or about 0.5 mile per generation. However, only a very small proportion of acorns is ever found beyond the edge of a tree canopy. A similar conclusion, that oak populations spread faster than they *should*, was reached by Reid (1899) and 'Reid's paradox' was named after him. The conclusion was that animals, such as corvids, must move some acorns by large distances and leave them uneaten; subsequent studies of seed caching confirmed that this is possible.

Although we might regard these calculations as being the musings of an ecologist from a less rigorous era (though Skellam's mathematics was by no means lacking in rigour!), we would still be hard-pressed to come up with any better estimates for lifetime reproductive output of a forest tree now (Clark 1998). However, the consensus seems to be that the model predictions for rate of spread failed primarily because seed dispersal does not follow a simple normal distribution. Clark et al. (1998) showed that Reid's paradox can be overcome by a model that incorporated a thin-tailed dispersal kernel for most short-distance dispersal agents and a fat-tailed kernel for a few long-distance agents. This 'stratified' model of dispersal was sufficient to predict the rates of spread after the Ice Age while at the same time explicitly recognising that most acorns disperse only short distances.

After Clark's paper, there was a great deal of activity aimed at estimating plant dispersal distributions empirically, fitting frequency distributions to data and modelling dispersal of individual propagules. The dilemma is that we cannot accurately determine the long tails of real dispersal frequency distributions (Cousens et al. 2008, section 6.4.4), even though we know them to be (theoretically) crucial. Fits of frequency distributions to empirical data are likely to be influenced strongly by the more precise estimates of dispersal close to the source. Rare long-distance events are too infrequent to be sampled adequately and so we must resort to mechanistic models to predict long distances (using one theoretical model to justify another).

PREDICTIONS GENERATED FROM EMPIRICAL DATA

The wave front velocity case study was a demonstration of theory being challenged by empirical data. A great many ecologists, however, use population models because they want to predict not what outcomes might be possible, but what is *likely* to happen in a particular case. For example, what is likely to happen to a particular population of an endangered species if we do nothing or if we carry out some form of management intervention? The models used for such purposes are usually based on a determination of the important factors – the 'drivers' of abundance – and their effects on demographic rates. A simple flowchart for a demographic model is given in Figure 8.1, based on a self-fertile annual plant. The number of starting individuals is multiplied by each 'transition probability' in the sequence indicated by the flowchart.

In species with overlapping generations, it is common to elaborate the model so that probabilities are a function of the ages, the sizes or the sexes of the individuals. Since we must then keep track of the numbers in each of these classes, we end up with a matrix of probabilities for each step rather than a single value. Typically, the probabilities are expressed via equations, for example, relating fecundity in some way to abundance (i.e. density dependence) of the focal species or relating survival to some extrinsic variable such as rainfall. Thus, we end up with a set of equations connected by simple rules and a set of parameters to which we need to ascribe values.

In a spatial model, we must also include probabilities for immigration and emigration and we can make demographic parameters spatially explicit, perhaps based on spatial variation in habitat characteristics. In principle, there is no limit to the complexity that we can introduce into one of these models.

At this point, we are faced with three problems: which drivers do we include? How do we include

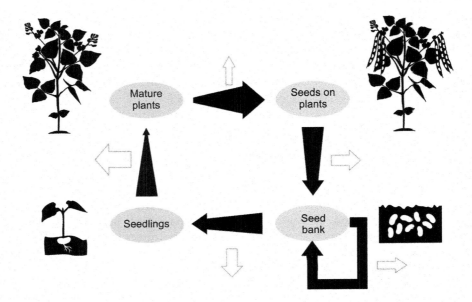

Figure 8.1 Flow chart illustrating the life-cycle of an annual plant (modified from Cousens et al. 1986). Solid arrows indicate the number of individuals at each stage (expanding arrows indicate reproduction; contracting arrows are the result of losses). Open arrows show losses due to various processes, including consumption, disease, germination, dispersal and density-dependent mortality.

them (what equations should we use)? And what are appropriate values for the parameters?

Which drivers are important for prediction?

It is intuitive to think that gaining a mechanistic understanding of a system will allow us to achieve better forecasts and thereby make better management decisions. However appealing that logic is, it is not always true and should be evaluated on a case-by-case basis. In ecological forecasting, data limitation is often a problem; and it is more important to achieve reliable predictions within acceptable tolerances, for which very simplistic methods may be adequate, than to include elaborate mathematics and a multitude of interacting variables for which the relevant data are scarce. And even if the model contains all the important mechanisms, it could be highly sensitive to the data (as in chaos theory).

An important example showing that accurate forecasts can be achieved with a basic knowledge of mechanisms comes from atmospheric science, where the art of prediction is much better developed than in ecology. Edward Lorenz (1963) published a system of three ordinary differential equations, designed to be a simplified model of atmospheric flows. He found that any change, no matter how small, in the initial system state led to vastly different forecasts. The system is now known as the Lorenz attractor and spurred the growth of chaos theory. While Lorenz's conclusion was that long-term weather forecasting is impossible, it also proves that a perfect mechanistic understanding of a system is not enough to make accurate forecasts. While weather forecasts may seem removed from forecasts of organism abundance, the principles of chaos theory have shown that accurate forecasts of fish abundance may be attainable without a deep mechanistic understanding of underlying biotic and abiotic drivers (Perretti et al. 2013; Ye et al. 2015).

In practice, it is the data we have available that decide how mechanistic our models can be. The past decade of ecological research has been driven by the practice of model selection, either hypothesis driven (testing the effects of specific drivers using, for instance, regularisation) or data driven (selecting the most parsimonious model structures among several candidate models by removing parameters) (Hooten and Hobbs 2015). This practice determines the significance of certain drivers, but most frameworks have also been designed to avoid over-parameterisation, that is, fitting and choosing models that are too complex for the data at hand. For instance, if we only have 15 years of abundance data, it is unlikely that we can assess non-linear effects or interactions among climate variables on abundance. Otherwise, we run the risk of inaccurate predictions and especially of extrapolation error.

Beyond being able to predict or forecast, we may want to understand why we see certain patterns within empirical data. For instance, sophisticated methods now exist to use intrinsic properties of abundance time series to forecast future changes in abundances with acceptable accuracy and precision (Pennekamp et al. 2019). Inevitably, when discussing such projected changes, researchers must at least speculate about the mechanisms. Are decreases in survival the culprit? Is lower survival perhaps compensated by reproduction? Are spatial differences in abundance changes due to different responses to a common factor or different underlying factors? Understanding such mechanisms can provide a way to model various scenarios of potential responses of populations to environmental change.

One key source of variation in abundance is the effect of abiotic variables on demographic rates. So, which variables should we include in our models? Sophisticated methods now exist to link variation in survival, reproduction and movement to extrinsic conditions such as weather, soil conditions or disturbances (e.g. Pedersen et al. 2019). However, even if such variables explain much of the past variation in demographic rates, forecasts are only as robust as (1) our predictions of future values of the abiotic variable itself and (2) our ability to extrapolate responses in response to future abiotic conditions. For instance, if fires are projected to double in intensity in the future, our forecasts of effects on abundances will be more precise if we had captured population responses to high-intensity fires in the past instead of 'blindly' extrapolating.

Our ability to accurately specify the relationship between demography and one or more environmental variables will depend on issues such as:

- *Omitted variable bias.* Some important drivers may be missed altogether by the researcher. There may be little a priori information on which to base variable choice and data might be entirely lacking for many variables. So, we make arbitrary choices based on what is available.

- *Relevance of the variable.* Although data on some variables may be readily available, they may be of limited use, such as when they are crude surrogates for the true driver, or where they are combinations of many different processes, such as biomass.

- *Data quality and extent.* Some data may be heavily affected by measurement error, while other data may have limited numbers of observations. Short time series or data collected in remarkably benign periods may fail to have a signal strong enough to be detected.

- *Strength of the causal relationship.* We need to select variables in terms of their impact on abundance. Although statistical significance is often used as an indicator of the importance of variables, this can be misleading: even weak drivers can be significant if enough measurements are made.

- *Correlation with unobserved predictor variables.* Many variables may be involved in driving the dynamics of a population, but we may only have data on one or two of them. El Niño events, for example, are typified by changes in rainfall and fire incidence on land, and changes in ocean currents. Extremely low continent-wide winter temperatures are accompanied by periods of reduced river flow followed by extreme discharge as snow and ice melt, with consequent effects on salinity in estuaries and changes in nearshore currents.

An example of how difficult it is to determine the drivers of demography again comes from fisheries. A huge amount of effort is put into the collection of fisheries data in order to inform management decisions. Although there is little that the fishing industry can do to cope with variation in recruitment – other than taking this into account when later setting quotas – there has been a great deal of interest in explaining sources of this variation.

Shepherd et al. (1984) reviewed 47 studies that reported significant correlations with environmental variables, including temperature, salinity (or a surrogate, the inverse of rainfall), wind speed, pressure gradients, upwelling, river discharge and various other proxies (including tree ring width), as well as nine of their own data sets. When re-tested by Myers (1998), around half the correlations were not supported. Myers noted also that there would have been many non-significant correlations generated by researchers that never would have been reported, so the ability to statistically explain variation in fish stock recruitment is much lower than a meta-analysis of published studies would show. The only consistent signal was that correlations with temperature tended to be significant in cases where the species were towards the northern or southern limit of their ranges. It was also notable that there were no significant correlations with the environment for the most intensively studied fisheries (the North Sea and Georges Bank).

Thus far in this section we have considered only extrinsic variables. An important component of many population models is intrinsic population regulation. Not only is this in recognition that abundance – of the focal species or of other species at the same or different trophic levels – is likely to affect demography, but it stops the model from predicting unrealistically high levels of abundance. The way that density dependence is incorporated into population models is based on a variety of well-established relationships, typically either exponential or hyperbolic functions and usually with asymptotic behaviour.

Different branches of ecological research may, for historical reasons, choose particular equations, such as the Beverton and Holt (1957) and Ricker (1975) 'stock and recruitment' functions in fisheries. The parameters required for more complex forms of density dependence, such as power terms, can unfortunately be difficult to confidently estimate from empirical data.

Although developing robust predictive models that account for both abiotic and biotic mechanisms in parameterising and projecting demographic rates is difficult, examples exist and show the opportunities and challenges of such approaches. Here we describe just one of them.

Case study 3: meerkat abundance

Kalahari meerkats (*Suricata suricatta*), social mongooses, have been studied in South Africa since 1993 as part of the Kalahari Meerkat Project. As a result, weekly phenotypic trait (body mass) and demographic data on over 3,000 individuals are currently available – an ideal basis to develop mechanistic forecasting approaches and projections (Clutton-Brock et al. 2016). The meerkats live in a harsh desert climate and have adapted an effective strategy to deal with unpredictable

fluctuations in rainfall: cooperative breeding. Only the dominant female reproduces and her young are co-reared by nonbreeding helpers, typically related to the dominant female. This interesting social system is the reason that meerkats have been studied for so long. However, over the years, it has become evident that meerkats, as well as other arid environment specialists, are facing an increasing frequency of temperature extremes under climate change (Bourne et al. 2020). Recent work on meerkats has therefore repurposed the detailed individual data to assess the demographic mechanisms of meerkats' population responses to ongoing climate change.

The first step in linking trait and demographic data of meerkats to abiotic (temperature and rainfall) and biotic drivers (density and group size) was to parameterise models that allowed the assessment of non-linear effects of different variables and their interactions on body mass change, survival, reproduction and dispersal. Such state-of-the-art modelling approaches offer flexible tools to describe non-linearities inherent in biological data, and their 'flexibility' of response curves can be adjusted depending on how much data are available for model fitting. GAMs (generalised additive models) provided good fit to observed variation in meerkat demography and abundances (Paniw et al. 2019). Although the effects on outputs of various sources of uncertainty in the underlying data (such as body mass) were assessed, uncertainty in climatic variables when fitting demographic-rate models was not considered (but was accounted for in projections). Uncertainty in derived climate indices is usually ignored, despite the fact that weather stations in remote areas are sparse and interpolation results in considerable uncertainty.

Once demographic rates were parameterised, population models for meerkats could be built and projected. Because climate variables were included into the GAMs, determining demographic rates, the fate of meerkats under IPCC climate change scenarios could be investigated. This showed that climate change could result in elevated local extinction risk. Their models allowed researchers to propagate various sources of uncertainty in projections, including uncertainty in climate change models. A challenge of such projections is typically that local or regional climatic data are used to parameterise the demographic models while global climate change indices are used for projections, thus creating mismatches in scale. There are ways to alleviate this issue – for instance using probabilistic forecasting (Fronzek et al. 2010) – but no solution is completely satisfactory.

The accuracy of predictions and projections can be assessed by using a training data set for model parameterisation and a separate test data set for validation. Although this approach is ideal, such partitioning of data is not always practical in biological time series. The meerkats are a prime example: despite having over 25 years of continuous data collection, the effects of climate change on meerkats are best understood when modelling the entire time series. This is because the most dramatic effects have occurred in the past eight years, where increases in temperature extremes were accompanied by increases in disease outbreaks, decimating meerkat groups and putting the population at serious risk of extinction (Paniw et al. 2022). These indirect effects of climate change are therefore lagged as, in the case of diseased meerkats, individuals take some time to die. Removing some of the critical years (where disease outbreaks increased) for model validation therefore comes at a loss of power for model fitting – whereas hindcasting (using past years for model validation) may not be appropriate as climate-disease interactions were rare. Thus, paradoxically, as the collection of long-term data in meerkats allowed researchers to understand some key mechanisms of climate change effects on an arid environment specialist, validating the likelihood of these mechanisms to bring about a local population collapse will require even more data collection. This is, of course, not a desirable scenario for most management interventions.

Despite the challenges of validating mechanistic models, the meerkat study system is also a fantastic example of the opportunities that understanding these mechanisms bring to ecological research and management. The detailed demographic models in meerkats have been able to demonstrate that the relevant aspects of climate are not just the average annual or seasonal temperatures or precipitation. The timing of climate extremes matters as much as the nature of the extremes, for meerkats and likely most other species (Li et al. 2021).

For the meerkats, under variable rainfall patterns that do not necessarily decrease in the future, higher temperatures may benefit individuals if they occur in the rainy but typically colder season. But if temperatures increase in the hot and dry season, they can bring about dramatic weight loss in individuals which then affects reproductive output further on. Weight loss is stressful and may also exacerbate the risks of deadly infections from endemic diseases (tuberculosis in the case of meerkats). Most social species carry endemic diseases, so that climate change potentially altering disease dynamics is therefore of concern for a wide range of taxa (Plowright et al. 2008; Russell et al. 2020). A better understanding of the mechanisms that affect population dynamics therefore allows us to discuss different 'what-if' scenarios beyond specific case studies.

Model parameterisation and validation

If we have sufficient knowledge, then we can put together a complex model. If we have the resources, then we can obtain good estimates of many parameters. We can expect to achieve good accuracy and precision of our predictions. If we invest further resources, then we might expect further precision and accuracy.

But there is a limit. Every system has what can be referred to as its 'intrinsic predictive ability' (Pennekamp et al. 2019) and no matter how much we try, we will never be able to keep making significant improvements to our predictions. An analogy might be the rate at which the world 100 m running record is improved. The trouble is knowing where the limit for population prediction is. In a practical sense, we also run the risk that increases in model complexity will outstrip our ability to estimate the parameters. Model complexity and 'parameterisation', as the attribution of values to parameters is called, is always a compromise and it always has the potential to affect the quality of predictions. However, complexity is not always necessary.

COVID-19 modelling provides an example of how we can use models to inform policy without modelling the entire system. The objective of one particular study (Baker et al. 2021) was to explore how polymerase chain reaction (PCR) tests can reduce disease spread at a population level. One approach would be to model the full system, by implementing a PCR testing model within a disease transmission model with multiple disease classes (susceptible, exposed, infectious) and parameterisation of human behaviours regarding mixing and testing, and so on. While theoretically feasible, that model would be quite complex and, from experience, data to estimate parameters would not exist, or, at best, be hard to access.

Detailed mechanistic models not only require a lot of data to parameterise them, but they can also give inaccurate predictions. Accuracy on known data does not give guarantee of accuracy under all other possible actions (Boettiger 2022; Geary et al. 2020). Instead, by framing the question as 'what reduction in COVID-19 transmission do we get from a given strategy', a simpler question was posed – one from which we can get important insights without modelling the entire system in detail. Thus, rather than using a large mechanistic model that directly included all the complexities of disease transmission and human testing behaviour, a model of the testing system was developed with relatively simple onward transmission, focusing on important parameters involving laboratory testing capacity and surge testing capacity. Using this model, the COVID-19 researchers produced exemplar scenarios, showing that more testing is not always better if laboratories are overwhelmed.

Model structure and the drivers and the values of the parameters that we include in it will determine the quality of our predictions. In many instances, we use simple models because our ecological knowledge is limited and our estimates of the parameters are weak. But this is one of the important reasons for using models.

We may not want – or expect to achieve – accurate predictions of the abundance of species X at some specified future date. Instead, we want to see what our limited knowledge can tell us about what might plausibly happen: perhaps whether the population is likely to increase, decrease or remain roughly the same or how much impact some environmental perturbation might be expected to have. Many management decisions must be made with incomplete and uncertain information (Burgman et al. 2005). We cannot defer decisions on an endangered species because we do not know enough: we may never know enough and/or we cannot conduct the experiments needed to get better knowledge. So, we make our best attempt. We may guess at some parameters, or 'borrow' them from other species. Simple predictions of this type have been used, for example, to determine the ways

that we can manage crops to minimise pest resistance (Holst et al. 2007).

How do we assess the quality or the reliability of our predictions? This is usually referred to as model 'validation'. If our predictions involve time trends of abundance, then strictly speaking we would need an *independent and appropriate* time series with which to compare our forecasts. The prediction error is then the difference between the observed abundance and the prediction. We must take into account the fact that both the observed and the predicted have error associated with them – in other words, we must partition the contribution of different sources of uncertainty to our metrics of interest (Petchey et al. 2015). We do not know the actual abundance, we just have an estimate of it that may be quite crude. And although it is rarely calculated, our predictions involve errors due to the estimates of the parameters and the structure of the model. One way of addressing the precision of the model's predictions is to use a Monte Carlo simulation: we can do multiple runs of the model, with parameter estimates, initial conditions and drivers taken from a frequency distribution based on the raw data used for parameter estimation. We can even use prior knowledge to help us estimate parameters and their uncertainty, undoubtedly an important reason for the popularity of Bayesian methods in applied ecology. We might even have situations where the precision of the prediction is good, but accuracy of prediction might be very poor because we have failed to identify bias or because the model is structurally unsound.

The lack of appropriate validation data is a common hurdle in population modelling. For a scenario prediction, we often speculate about the amount by which a given parameter might change; this may be informed by evidence or it may be a 'ballpark' guess. For example, we might say '*suppose hunting causes a 50% reduction in male survival*' – something that we put out there for the sake of argument when we actually have no idea. A rigorous test of a model prediction would need data that have been assembled under those specific scenarios. But we do not have such data, because those scenarios have never occurred and have never been included in an experiment.

In cases such as climate change, we cannot validate our predictions of the future until those changes have happened – though we could test it to some degree retrospectively on older time series.

We must, therefore, treat scenario predictions and projections with an appropriate degree of caution. No matter how complex the model, we have made no more than a best guess and we must be honest about this and communicate the uncertainties in the model and in the forecasts.

Model validation is important and is often stressed in introductory materials about modelling. In practice, it has traditionally been overlooked in many modelling papers because the appropriate data are too often lacking. A prediction is made and validation must wait until someone comes along in the future. Many models, however, are never really complete and validation, model development and the collection of new data go hand in hand. The model is never finished, it is constantly under review and its predictions are – we hope – constantly improving. We know the predictions have some error, whether we can measure it or not, but through sustained effort that error will continue to fall. This process has been formalised with the term 'iterative near-term forecasting' (analogous to the ideas of adaptive management and rapid prototyping) (Dietze et al. 2018).

It is self-evident that if we want a high level of precision and accuracy, then we will need to invest adequate resources into assembling the information needed.

We take it for granted that in every modelling project there will be care taken to generate the best estimates of parameters that we can from the data that we have on hand. As we have indicated elsewhere in this chapter, we glean parameter values from a range of sources. These may include long-term demographic studies with intensive monitoring, large sample sizes and extensive data sets: i.e. high-quality data that would make most modellers' mouths water! We spend a great deal of effort in using state-of-the-art methods to obtain the best estimates of our parameters; there is a great deal of literature on these methods. But parameter estimates also include data from short-term studies (perhaps graduate theses), means reported in (or calculated from) published papers, unreplicated observations and expert opinion (best guesses).

We know that parameterisation of models is crucial to model performance, yet we often take what we can get, publish the results and reflect on the predictions made from a job well done. Some studies – particularly well-funded long-term studies of iconic species – do put a great deal of effort

into further research to improve parameter estimates. However, increasing accuracy and precision requires effort and investment that may be better utilised elsewhere.

In predictive modelling, we should more frequently ask *'how much investment is additional parameter improvement worth?'*, and *'which parameters justify the greatest research effort?'*. We can perform sensitivity analyses for any model, altering the values of each parameter systematically and then observing the incremental impact on the quantity predicted (in our case population abundance).

Linear models of simple life histories are often examined using elasticity metrics, while sensitivity analyses have also been developed for 'Bayesian belief networks'. We will say more about this when we discuss 'value of information' analysis later. And however simple or complex the population model is, we still need to conduct optimisation to find the best management strategy (optimisation methods have their own entire field, which we won't talk about here).

FROM FORECASTS TO POLICY

So far, this chapter has explored models of population dynamics and using them to make predictions. But what do we do with a model once we have it? Apart from using models to improve our fundamental understanding of species, we can use them to improve management decisions. There is an entire area of research – 'decision science' – devoted to the study of making decisions (Box 8.1).

The use of decision science in ecology has increased particularly over the last decade: some prominent examples include spatial planning for conservation (Ball et al. 2009) and the Project Prioritisation Protocol for targeting and prioritising investment in threatened species (Joseph et al. 2009).

In management contexts, predictions fall into three broad categories: nowcasting, forecasting and scenario analysis. All play a role in management, but they are used in very different ways. 'Nowcasting' is about estimating the current state of a system from observations. As defined earlier in the chapter, 'forecasting' is predicting the future state of a system, given current knowledge, while 'scenario analysis' is about modelling a range of potential future management options and/or

BOX 8.1: What is decision science?

While we do not provide a detailed guide to decision science here (instead, see Hemming et al. 2021), we provide a brief description to enable discussion of modelling. The process of framing problems by focusing on the objectives and actions – rather than on fundamental science – is key to the decision science approach to solving problems. Beyond specifically helping people to make decisions, another important use of the approach is in helping with questions about model complexity. It is easy to make models more complex to try to capture more realism; however, as we have mentioned elsewhere in this chapter, it is difficult to determine how much complexity is enough. While we cannot resolve this issue in general, decision science allows us to ask the related question: *'how much complexity do I need to make a useful model to inform my current decision?'*

Central to the approach is a structured decision-making workflow. Broadly, the steps are:

1. Set management objectives and performance measures.
2. Decide on potential actions, which includes 'no action'.
3. Estimate consequences of different actions on the objective.
4. Evaluate trade-offs.
5. Make the decision.

In a fully-fledged structured decision-making workshop, researchers can guide stakeholders through the entire structure of the decision-making process. However, addressing every point in the structured decision-making process is not necessary for it to be a useful concept for all scientists trying to make a policy impact with science. The key role of population modelling is at step 3, to estimate how different actions will affect a system and our management objectives. Note that uncertainties are inherent in decision-making (Milner-Gulland and Shea 2017), though it is possible that the decision will remain the same even if uncertainties are resolved (see the discussion on value of information later in the chapter). Quantifying the uncertainties in the subsequent population model (such as providing credible intervals) can reveal actions that are robust to the remaining uncertainties.

In recent years, there has been an increasing number of papers modelling population dynamics with species interaction to predict potential management outcomes (e.g. Baker et al. 2017). However, in terms of direct impact to policy, one of the most recent applications of decision science with wide-ranging impact is the National Plan for COVID-19 Modelling in Australia (Doherty Institute 2021). In this study, modelling was used to advise the Australian Government on potential policies, steps and actions to bring Australia out of lockdown due to the COVID-19 pandemic. This model provides an interesting case study, because it is purely focused on step 3, estimating consequences, and not the entire structured decision-making workflow. Awareness of the other steps was critical to ensure that the correct questions were being answered.

---

across a range of plausible, but uncertain, model parameters.

There are two broad types of decision-making questions we may seek to answer with mathematical models. The first is *'do we need to act?'* And the second is *'what action should we take?'* The types of models required for the former are nowcasts and forecasts, while the latter is typically done with scenario analysis (which may be built on, or incorporate, nowcasts and forecasts). When using these modelling tools in a decision-making framework, we need to think carefully about how models will be used within the decision-making process. Models are often designed to answer specific types of questions and, if those questions do not align with the decisions being made, then the potential for impact of that model in the decision-making process will be limited.

When creating models to inform management, we face different criteria for what makes a *good* model. Often in ecology we are concerned about making accurate and precise predictions of populations into the future. However, in a decision-making setting, our aim is to correctly distinguish between a set of management options and select the truly best option, and *not* to make our models maximally accurate and precise *per se*. The accuracy and precision required depend on the question being asked, who is asking it and how it is being asked.

Aside from the 'standard' structured decision-making process (Box 8.1), there are a range of other techniques that fall under the decision science umbrella. Two particularly important concepts are 'adaptive management' and 'value of information' theory. Adaptive management is in some ways an extension of structured decision-making (Walters and Holling 1990), where decisions are made regularly with updated information (for example, yearly decisions on population control). We can repeat the same decision-making process, refining and updating our models each time and learning from past actions as we proceed. Value of information theory focuses on learning about the uncertainties in models and how they affect the outcomes, to determine whether it is worth the resources to acquire more information before making the decision (Canessa et al. 2015). It is related to optimal experimental design, which seeks to determine how to optimally design an experiment to reduce system uncertainty.

In the face of a constantly changing world, our knowledge about ecological systems and our ability to forecast what would happen under various management actions are imperfect. Adaptive management acknowledges this, allowing us to iteratively make improvements rather than decide and keep to a fixed set of actions. It can be the most optimal and cost-effective management scheme (Walters and Holling 1990). In addition to repeating the decision-making process regularly, adaptive management also involves monitoring and using that information to inform the next decision-making process. Updating information, data and predictions is key to reducing uncertainties and improving outcomes at each cycle.

To make use of adaptive management, after making and implementing a decision, the results should be monitored. It is important to pick indicators or measurements that can detect the changes in the system when management is changed. Did the results play out as expected or not? During the implementation process, can we uncover more information that could now inform a better decision? The decision-monitoring process of adaptive management allows researchers to test the forecasts of their model on real impacts and measure how robust the original predictions were. Repeating this allows us to thus expand, modify and iteratively correct forecast models, leading to a better understanding of the important factors and major interactions in ecological systems, similar to how weather forecasting has improved over recent decades (Bauer 2015).

There are many specific adaptive management models created for different ecological systems and requirements. A number of proposed frameworks include management strategy evaluation (MSE) (Punt et al. 2016) and strategic adaptive management (SAM: Kingsford et al. 2011). Adaptive management requires strong and continuous communication between multiple parties, from stakeholders, to decision-makers and scientists.

Whether we spend the time or resources to gain more information is itself a decision, but it is not guaranteed that knowing more would lead to a better decision, nor whether the cost of doing more research will lead to a better return on the decision. Eventually, one must stop monitoring and start taking direct actions, lest one ends up '*monitoring a species until it becomes extinct*' (Lindenmayer et al. 2013). While more information can be tempting, especially to researchers, more research may not be the best action to take: gathering information takes time and resources, delaying a potential management decision and action and potentially allowing the current state of the system to worsen. However, without sufficient information, we are at risk of making uninformed decisions.

Similar to the problem of '*how complex should the model be*' is the problem '*how much information do we need?*' Value of information theory is a formal framework that allows us to estimate the cost and return on further information gathering. We can use a model to conduct a value of information analysis, which involves a structured analysis of trade-offs between obtaining more information versus acting with the current available information, and to determine what would be *useful* information to obtain.

These are not the only frameworks for making decisions. Different ecological and real-world systems contain complexities, and there are a wide range of decision science tools to address them. For example, rapid prototyping can produce quick initial decisions, which are then iteratively improved over a series of small/frequent milestones. There are decision science frameworks for multiple objectives (i.e. multi-criteria decision analysis: Mendoza and Martins 2006).

To ecological complexity must be added the complexity from other humans: decision-makers, titleholders and stakeholders. Researchers who are tasked with modelling the ecological system must be in constant communication with these groups as the resulting actions are made by them and will affect them directly (Gibbons et al. 2008). When running forecasts for decision-making, it is important to communicate uncertainty (Baker and Bode 2020) and also to understand how risk-averse the decision-maker is. For example, whether they prefer to minimise the probability of the worst outcome, or whether they want to maximise the probability of a good outcome and so forth. One approach for dealing with risk and uncertainty is 'stochastic dominance', which can be used to rank alternative management actions using probability distributions (Canessa et al. 2016). In addition, involving titleholders and stakeholders in the decision-making process can improve the future decision implementation (Bennett et al. 2019). It would not be surprising if decision-makers, titleholders, stakeholders and even the modellers have conflicts. If so, then other methods under decision science might need to be used, such as negotiation theory and conflict resolution.

There are many complexities to consider when it comes to using modelling to make real policy impact. Earlier in the chapter, we mentioned how decision science was used in the context of COVID-19 modelling and PCR testing. To put the above discussion in context, we will now give another example of COVID-19 modelling, as well as a case in which ecological modelling has been used to help inform policy and management decisions for a threatened species.

Case study 4: dynamical population modelling for COVID-19 policy

Writing about modelling and policy in 2023, it is hard not to reflect on the role of modelling for decision-making throughout the COVID-19 pandemic. Rarely – if ever – have mathematical models of biological dynamics featured so prominently in our society. Hence, COVID-19 modelling gives us a range of recent examples of how mathematical modelling has been used to engage with policy. Although this book's focus is on ecology and modelling, we make no apology for using another COVID-19 example. Its topicality will resonate with the reader: both humans and diseases can be studied ecologically (they are both organisms within an environment) and they have populations.

In 2020, COVID-19 spread to Australia, triggering nation-wide lockdowns that successfully prevented the wide destructive spread of the disease. As vaccines were becoming available, in 2021 the Australian Government decided that they wanted to end the lockdowns and reopen borders, which would necessarily mean accepting the spread of COVID-19 through its population. Scientists modelled population and infectious disease dynamics to inform government decisions (Doherty Institute 2021), using a range of models from simple dynamical systems to complex and highly parameterised agent-based formulations. The modelling team's role was to engage with the Australian Government to understand the objectives and the potential decisions and develop models where they could explore various actions for ending lockdowns since vaccines were finally available for use. The objectives, actions, trade-offs and final decisions (i.e. steps 1, 2, 4 and 5 of the decision-making process in Box 8.1) were all determined by the Australian Government, not by the modellers. Using modelling, the team could simulate the given actions, mapping the outputs to the real-world objectives. The team had a close collaboration with the Department of the Treasury to evaluate various trade-offs, considering the broad impacts of disease spread alongside other metrics, including economic impact of both restrictions and public health impacts (Australian Government 2021). The modelling team ultimately delivered a range of scenarios from which government could choose, depicting how border opening at different thresholds of vaccination coverage would likely affect future infections, disease outcomes and the clinical impacts.

This case study exemplifies that a decision science approach is not only relevant when scientists can provide significant input into each step. By engaging with relevant groups and understanding steps 1, 2, 4 and 5 from their perspective, we can use scientific modelling to inform step 3 (i.e. estimating the consequences of different actions on the objective). If scientific modelling is done without understanding the broader scope of potential actions and objectives, the work may not be usable and may be unable to affect decisions – for example if the considered actions will never be considered realistically (e.g. due to cost) or politically, or the objectives are not actually being considered by the policy makers.

The COVID-19 case study had the benefit of a wealth of data from around the world to inform the models, and hence the subsequent actions. Few programs on important, unique and rare ecological species are in that position! In the next case study, we look at the management of one threatened Australian animal with uncertain information about how it interacts with its threats and how this is now being resolved.

Case study 5: adaptive management of malleefowl

The malleefowl (*Leipoa ocellata*) is a ground-dwelling bird that builds large mounds to incubate its eggs. It is found across southern Australia and is formally recognised as being endangered. Threats include historical habitat clearance, predation from introduced and native species, and changing fire regimes. The National Malleefowl Recovery Team have been implementing a recovery plan since 1989, working with many other organisations across southern Australia (The National Malleefowl Recovery Team 2022). Nesting activity has been monitored since the 1990s and, at present, a number of different ongoing management activities aim to increase abundance, including fox baiting, fencing and re-vegetation. However, data analysis over time has drawn conflicting conclusions as to whether fox baiting in particular was effective.

Hauser et al. (2019) worked in collaboration with multiple groups such as land managers, experts and many other stakeholders including government agencies, mining companies, traditional owners, farmers, private landholders and leaseholders to facilitate a decision science process (steps 1–5 listed in Box 8.1). They developed an ensemble ecosystem model to predict malleefowl abundance, involving 80 different interactions between 14 different ecological components, including malleefowl density, vegetation density, rainfall quality, rabbit density and fox density. They simulated the five-year consequences of various potential management actions on abundance. The model predicted that management actions targeting disease and inbreeding had a high probability of producing positive effects. In contrast, management action addressing fox predation could lead to both large positive effects *and* large negative effects in their abundance. In short, there was high uncertainty.

The decision-makers and stakeholders wanted to resolve the uncertainty about the interactions between malleefowl and its predators. Hence, the research team developed a predator control experiment. They also conducted a statistical power analysis to determine how many sites and how long the experiment needed to run in order to resolve the uncertainties. After multiple workshops and the involvement of multiple organisations and groups across Australia, the Adaptive Management Predator Experiment is now in-progress. As part of this experiment, different sites were strategically chosen to either be managed (fox baiting) or purposefully unmanaged (no fox baiting). There are 22 control-treatment paired sites in eight clusters, chosen such that they have similar environmental conditions. The known malleefowl nesting mounds (found in various monitoring efforts) are monitored for activity, as a proxy for abundance (since it is difficult to monitor the malleefowl themselves).

The experiment will run for five years. As part of their experimental plan for learning, the researchers presented statistical methods to evaluate the future results after monitoring, with a model to estimate the effect of fox baiting on malleefowl nesting mounds that can be updated as data come in. It remains to be seen how the malleefowl management will change *after* this experiment concludes. If decision-makers adjust their management actions in the future, then this would become a rare example of successful adaptive management in biodiversity conservation at a landscape scale. Decision-makers could even embark on a new experiment to resolve other uncertainties relating factors that affect malleefowl abundance.

While there are many examples of adaptive management of natural resources in the context of harvesting, there are few successful implementations in biodiversity conservation for various reasons (Westgate et al. 2013). Biodiversity conservation adaptive management publications tend to be light on the follow-up after the first cycle of the decision-making process. If adaptive management is truly to be implemented, then it is not enough for the research team to meet with the decision-makers and stakeholders to help make one decision; they need to continue the conversation, play a role in updating the models and thus aid decision-makers to adaptively make decisions over time. This requires strong relationships and connections – a difficult human problem that needs to be overcome before one can start working on the ecological problem together —and ongoing access to funds (another difficult problem).

SO WHAT?

In this chapter, we have delved into population models and touched on the numerous aspects that affect their accuracy and reliability. Predictive modelling is an extremely important part of empirical ecology, requiring sufficient expertise and resources. The availability of user-friendly software has made predictive modelling much more accessible, but it can be misused in the wrong hands.

We have considered how predictions should be based, where possible, on sound empirical data and should be revised upon new information. Researchers need to consider not just whether more empirical data are needed, but what data and why. Although there has been a tendency among ecologists to believe that more research will serendipitously result in better insights into management options, this is not necessarily the case, and some types of research are more useful than others.

Regardless of how and what model ecologists ultimately choose for their context and purpose, there will always be limitations and uncertainty. A detailed understanding of fundamental ecology often helps us to model, especially when we have limited data. But we also note that in many situations – such as policy impact – high precision and accuracy may not be necessary, and that it is much more important to have good predictions for broad scenarios targeted towards well-defined objectives in a decision science framework. Prediction is both a way to demonstrate scientific understanding about scientific theories, and also what we can use to make scientifically rigorous decisions to positively change the world around us.

Historically, empirical ecology has largely consisted of case studies of numerous species and corresponding population models, representing isolated or small systems as they are right now. However, with increasingly many challenges facing the ecological landscape and species worldwide, we need ecological forecasting to predict what may happen in the future and to explore how we can prevent negative outcomes – and ensure maximum benefits – under alternative scenarios.

In other disciplines, such as economics, engineering or climatology, generalisable outcomes of studies are used as reliable indicators of future trends. Can we achieve this in ecology? Or is ecology simply too complex? Or perhaps, are the assumptions in other disciplines simply not complex enough? Answering these questions will likely determine the future of ecological research because in order to be taken seriously, ecologists need to show confidence in their forecasting ability to mitigate emerging global threats. The first step towards this goal would require us to propose generalisable rules for predictions. But how do we want to achieve this? Is the future to work on even more local case studies and generalise from these – as has been done for life history theory? How many such studies are needed: or is the need unbounded? Every ecosystem, community or population needs case-specific data, to help formulate models and to test them. Or is global large-scale research the way to go (such as DroughtNet: Sevilleta 2022)? There are trade-offs in relation to scale. Local studies are more equitable, but produce a lot of noise. Global approaches may produce too little noise and tend to be exclusionary. In short, there is no one-approach-fits-all method when it comes to ecological forecasting.

We currently have a wide range of techniques that allow us to model just about whatever we want, and many more are under development. Theoretical model complexity itself is now only constrained by computational power. However, this comes at the cost of uncertainty or high data requirements to parameterise and calibrate a model to reflect the current known ecological status. Furthermore, there is *no guarantee* that a complex model will do any better than a simple model at predicting what is unknown. Even if a model can successfully predict the outcome of one ecological action, it may be completely wrong about the outcomes from other ecological actions.

For each situation, researchers must carefully choose which predictive or forecasting models are most suitable for their context. There is no easy way to do this. The end use of the model – what it is that we want to achieve – should dictate much of what we do.

In the case of fundamental ecological research designed to extend our basic understanding, it is a difficult question to answer what the biggest goals are. We delve ever deeper into the details of every issue. Others before us have argued that any further developments in theoretical ecological modelling need to go hand in hand with research that aims to test not just their qualitative predictions (Simberloff 1981; Haller 2014), but also the assumptions they make and the processes that were incorporated. But as we have seen in the case of predator-prey cycles, testing may be difficult and illusory.

For applied ecology, the situation might be quite different. There may be a plethora of contexts and objectives, but the use of structured methods and processes within decision science can help enormously. There are methods to help to better establish what we truly want to achieve, identifying what the constraints to decisions are, guiding us to options and evaluating what the trade-offs are in their implementation. Decision science can help considerably in this way and is better than trying to make decisions purely by instinct.

So, should every ecologist become a decision scientist? No! Although some funding agencies are urging researchers towards more applied outcomes, there is no requirement for every ecologist to do work that has a clear path from research to impact. However, for anyone who wants to impact decision-making and policy, decision science provides a useful perspective to better understand how to contribute.

For some, that engagement may be running structured decision-making workshops and working through each step of the decision-making process with relevant stakeholders. For others, it may focus solely on improving how we model systems, so we can better estimate the consequences of actions. And for some, it could be investigating the fundamental building blocks of ecosystems, enabling better modelling in the future. For this final group, the use of the decision science perspective is not about solving problems directly, but as an aid in understanding what fundamental mechanisms are critical to understand in order to facilitate better decision-making in the future.

There is no universal correct answer for what type of work to do, there is only what is right for each project.

REFERENCES

Australian Government. 2021. Economic impact analysis: National plan to transition to Australia's national COVID-19 response. https://treasury.gov.au/publication/p2021-196731 (accessed 17 August 2022).

Baker, C. M., and M. Bode. 2020. Recent advances of quantitative modeling to support invasive species eradication on islands. *Conservation Science and Practice* 3:e246. doi:10.1111/csp2.246

Baker, C. M., A. Gordon, and M. Bode. 2017. Ensemble ecosystem modeling for predicting ecosystem response to predator reintroduction. *Conservation Biology* 31:376–384. doi:10.1111/cobi.12798

Baker C. M., I. Chades, J. McVernon, A. P. Robinson, and H. Bondell. 2021. Optimal allocation of PCR tests to minimise disease transmission through contact tracing and quarantine. *Epidemics* 37:100503. doi:10.1016/j.epidem.2021.100503

Ball, I. R., H. P. Possingham, and M. E. Watts. 2009. Marxan and relatives: Software for spatial conservation prioritization. In *Spatial conservation prioritization: Quantitative methods and computational tools*, eds A. Moilanen, K. A. Wilson, and H. P. Possingham, 185–195. New York: Oxford University Press.

.Bennett, N. J., A. Di Franco, A. Calò, et al. 2019. Local support for conservation is associated with perceptions of good governance, social impacts, and ecological effectiveness. *Conservation Letters* 12:e12640. doi:10.1111/conl.12640

Beverton, R. J. H.; and S. J. Holt. 1957. On the dynamics of exploited fish populations. *Fishery Investigations Series II Volume XIX, Ministry of Agriculture, Fisheries and Food.*

Blasius, B., L. Rudolf, G. Weithoff, U. Gaedke, and G. F. Fussmann. 2020. Long-term cyclic persistence in an experimental predator–prey system. *Nature* 577:226–230. doi:10.1038/s41586-019-1857-0

Boettiger, C. 2022. The forecast trap. *Ecology Letters* 25:1655–1664. doi:10.1111/ele.14024

Bolker, B. 2004. Continuous-space models for population dynamics. In *Ecology, genetics, and evolution of metapopulations*, eds I. Hanski, and O. E. Gaggioti, 45–69. San Diego: Elsevier Science.

Bourne, A. R., J. J. Cunningham, C. N. Spottiswoode, and A. R. Ridley. 2020. Hot droughts compromise interannual survival across all group sizes in a cooperatively breeding bird. *Ecology Letters* 23:1776–1788. doi:10.1111/ele.13604

Bronowski, J. 1979. *The origins of knowledge and imagination.* New Haven: Yale University Press.

Burgman, M. A., D. B. Lindenmayer, and J. Elith. 2005. Managing landscapes for conservation under uncertainty. *Ecology* 86:2007–2017. doi:10.1890/04-0906

Canessa, S., G. Guillera-Arroita, J. J. Lahoz-Monfort, et al. 2015. When do we need more data? A primer on calculating the value of information for applied ecologists. *Methods in Ecology and Evolution* 6:1219–1228. doi:10.1111/2041-210X.12423

Canessa, S., J. G. Ewen, M. West, M. A. McCarthy, and T. V. Walshe. 2016. Stochastic dominance to account for uncertainty and risk in conservation decisions. *Conservation Letters* 9:260–266. doi:10.1111/conl.12218

Caswell, H. 1988. Theory and models in ecology: A different perspective. *Ecological Modelling* 43:33–44.

Clark, J. S. 1998. Why trees migrate so fast: Confronting theory with dispersal biology and the paleorecord. *American Naturalist* 152:204–224.

Clark, J. S., C. Fastie, G. Hurtt, et al. 1998. Reid's paradox of rapid plant migration: Dispersal theory and interpretation of paleoecological records. *BioScience* 48:13–24.

Clutton-Brock, T. H., and M. Manser. 2016. Meerkats: Cooperative breeding in the Kalahari. In *Cooperative breeding in vertebrates: Studies of ecology, evolution*, eds W. D. Koenig, and J. L. Dickinson, 294–317. Cambridge: Cambridge University Press. doi:10.1017/CBO9781107338357.018

Cousens, R., C. J. Doyle, B. J. Wilson, and G. W. Cussans. 1986. Modelling the economics of controlling *Avena fatua* in winter wheat. *Pesticide Science* 17:1–12.

Cousens, R., C. Dytham, and R. Law. 2008. Dispersal in plants: A population perspective. Oxford: Oxford University Press. doi:10.1111/j.1095-8339.2012.01210.x

Dayton, P. K. 1979. Ecology: A science and a religion. In *Ecological processes in coastal and marine systems*, ed. R. J. Livingstone, 3–18. New York: Plenum Press.

Dietze, M. C., A. Fox, L. M. Beck-Johnson, et al. 2018. Iterative near-term ecological forecasting: Needs, opportunities, and challenges. *Proceedings of the National Academy of Sciences of the United States of America* 115:1424–1432. doi:10.1073/pnas.171023111

Doherty Institute. 2021. Doherty Institute modelling report for national cabinet. https://www.doherty.edu.au/news-events/news/doherty-institute-modelling-report-for-national-cabinet (accessed 16 August 2022).

Fisher, R. A. 1937. The wave of advance of advantageous genes. *Annals of Eugenics* 7:355–369.

Fronzek, S., T. R. Carter, J. Räisänen, L. Ruokolainen, and M. Luoto. 2010. Applying probabilistic projections of climate change with impact models: A case study for sub-Arctic palsa mires in Fennoscandia. *Climatic Change* 99:515–534. doi:10.1007/s10584-009-9679-y

Geary, W. L., M. Bode, T. S. Doherty, et al. 2020. A guide to ecosystem models and their environmental applications. *Nature Ecology and Evolution* 4:1459–1471. doi:10.1038/s41559-020-01298-8

Gibbons, P., C. Zammit, K. Youngentob, et al. 2008. Some practical suggestions for improving engagement between researchers and policy-makers in natural resource management. *Ecological Management and Restoration* 9:182–186. doi:10.1111/j.1442-8903.2008.00416.x

Gustafsson, L., and M. Sternad. 2016. A guide to population modelling for simulation. *Open Journal of Modelling and Simulation* 4:55–92. doi:10.4236/ojmsi.2016.42007

Haller, B. C. 2014. Theoretical and empirical perspectives in ecology and evolution: A survey. *BioScience* 64:907–916. doi:10.1093/biosci/biu131

Hastings, A. 2020. Long-term predator-prey cycles finally achieved in the lab. *Nature* 577:172–173. doi:10.1038/d41586-019-03603-3

Hauser, C. E., D. Southwell, J. J. Lahoz-Monfort, et al. 2019. Adaptive management informs conservation and monitoring of Australia's threatened malleefowl. *Biological Conservation* 233:31–40. doi:10.1016/j.biocon.2019.02.015

Hefley, T. J., M. B. Hooten, R. E. Russell, D. P. Walsh, and J. A, Powell. 2017. When mechanism matters: Bayesian forecasting using models of ecological diffusion. *Ecology Letters* 20:640–650. doi:10.1111/ele.12763

Hemming, V., A. E. Camaclang, M. S. Adams, et al. 2021. An introduction to decision science for conservation. *Conservation Biology* 36:e13868. doi:10.1111/cobi.13868

Holst, N., I. A. Rasmussen, and L. Bastiaans. 2007. Field weed population dynamics: A review of model approaches and applications. *Weed Research* 47:1–14. doi:10.1111/j.1365-3180.2007.00534.x

Houlahan, J. E., S. T. McKinney, T. M. Anderson, and B. J. McGill. 2017. The priority of prediction in ecological understanding. *Oikos* 126:1–7. doi:10.1111/oik.03726

Hooten, M. B., and Hobbs, N. T. 2015. A guide to Bayesian model selection for ecologists. Ecological Monographs 85:3–28. doi:10.1890/14-0661.1

Hurrell, J. W. 1995. Decadal trends in the North Atlantic Oscillation: Regional temperatures and precipitation. *Science* 269:676–679.

Joseph, L. N., R. F. Maloney, and H. P. Possingham. 2009. Optimal allocation of resources among threatened species: A project prioritization protocol. *Conservation Biology* 23:328–338. doi:10.1111/j.1523-1739.2008.01124.x

Kingsford, R. T., H. C. Biggs, and S. R. Pollard. 2011. Strategic adaptive management in freshwater protected areas and their rivers. *Biological Conservation* 144:1194–1203. doi:10.1016/j.biocon.2010.09.022

Kolmogorov, A., I. Petrovskii, and N. Piskunov. 1937. Study of a diffusion equation that is related to the growth of a quality of matter and its application to a biological problem. *Moscow University Mathematics Bulletin* 1:1–26.

Krebs, C. J. 2002. Beyond population regulation and limitation. *Wildlife Research* 29:1–10. doi:10.1071/WR01074

Krebs, C. J., R. Boonstra, S. Boutin, and A. R. E. Sinclair. 2001. What drives the 10-year cycle of snowshoe hares? BioScience 51:25–35. doi:10.1641/0006-3568(2001)051[0025:WDTYCO]2.0.CO;2

Krebs, C. J., R. Boonstra, and S. Boutin. 2018. Using experimentation to understand the 10-year snowshoe hare cycle in the boreal forest of North America. *Journal of Animal Ecology* 87:87–100. doi:10.1111/1365-2656.12720

Lele, S. R., and K. L. Allen. 2006. On using expert opinion in ecological analyses: A frequentist approach. *Environmetrics* 17:683–704. doi:10.1002/env.786

Levins, R. 1966. The strategy of model building in population biology. *American Scientist* 54:421–431.

Li, G., X. Wan, B. Yin, et al. 2021. Timing outweighs magnitude of rainfall in shaping population dynamics of a small mammal species in steppe grassland. *Proceedings of the National Academy of Sciences of the United States of America* 118:e2023691118. doi:10.1073/pnas.2023691118

Lindenmayer, D. B., M. P. Piggott, and B. A. Wintle. 2013. Counting the books while the library burns: Why conservation monitoring programs need a plan for action. *Frontiers in Ecology and the Environment* 11:549–555. doi:10.1890/120220

Lorenz, E. N. 1963. Deterministic nonperiodic flow. *Journal of the Atmospheric Sciences* 20:130–141.

Lu, C., and B. Zhou. 2018. Influences of the 11-yr sunspot cycle and polar vortex oscillation on observed winter temperature variations in China. *Journal of Meteorological Research* 32:367–379. doi:10.1007/s13351-018-7101-2

Mendoza, G. A., and H. Martins. 2006. Multicriteria decision analysis in natural resource management: A critical review of methods and new modelling paradigms. *Forest Ecology and Management* 230:1–22. doi:10.1016/j.foreco.2006.03.023

Milner-Gulland, E. J., and K. Shea. 2017. Embracing uncertainty in applied ecology. *Journal of Applied Ecology* 543:2063–2068. doi:10.1111/1365-2664.12887

Myers, R. A. 1998. When do environment-recruitment correlations work? *Reviews in Fish Biology and Fisheries* 8:285–305

Olden, J. D., J. J. Lawler, and N. L. Poff. 2008. Machine learning methods without tears: A primer for ecologists. *The Quarterly Review of Biology* 83:171–193. doi:10.1086/587826

Paniw, M., C. Duncan, F. Groenewoud et al. 2022. Higher temperature extremes exacerbate negative disease effects in a social mammal. *Nature Climate Change* 12:284–290. doi:10.1038/s41558-022-01284-x

Paniw, M., N. Maag, G. Cozzi, T. Clutton-Brock, and A. Ozgul. 2019. Life history responses of meerkats to seasonal changes in extreme environments. *Science* 363:631–635. doi:10.1126/science.aau5905

Pedersen, E. J., D. L. Miller, G. L. Simpson, and N. Ross. 2019. Hierarchical generalized additive models in ecology: An introduction with mgcv. *PeerJ* 7:e6876. doi:10.7717/peerj.6876

Peers, M. J. L., Y. N. Majchrzak, A. K. Menzies, et al. 2020. Climate change increases predation risk for a keystone species of the boreal forest. *Nature Climate Change* 10:1149–1153. doi:10.1038/s41558-020-00908-4

Pennekamp, F., A. C. Iles, J. Garland, et al. 2019. The intrinsic predictability of ecological time series and its potential to guide forecasting *Ecological Monographs* 89:e01359. doi:10.1002/ecm.1359

Perretti, C. T., S. B. Munch, and G. Sugihara. 2013. Model-free forecasting outperforms the correct mechanistic model for simulated and experimental data. *Proceedings of the National Academy of Sciences of the United States of America* 110:5253–5257. doi:10.1073/pnas.1216076110

Petchey, O. L., M. Pontarp, T. M. Massie, et al. 2015. The ecological forecast horizon, and examples of its uses and determinants. *Ecology Letters* 18:597–611. doi:10.1111/ele.12443

Peters, R. F. 1991. *A critique for ecology.* Cambridge: Cambridge University Press

Plowright, R. K., S. H. Sokolow, M. E. Gorman, P. Daszak, and J. E. Foley. 2008. Causal inference in disease ecology: Investigating ecological drivers of disease emergence. *Frontiers in Ecology and the Environment* 6:420–429. doi:10.1890/070086

Punt, A. E., D. S. Butterworth, C. L. de Moor, J. A. De Oliveira, and M. Haddon. 2016. Management strategy evaluation: Best

practices. *Fish and Fisheries* 17:303–334. doi:10.1111/faf.12104

Reid, C. 1899. *The origin of the British flora.* London: Dulau.

Ricker, W. E. 1975. Computation and interpretation of biological statistics of fish populations. *Bulletin of the Fisheries Research Board of Canada* 191, Ottawa.

Russell, R., G. V. DiRenzo, J. Szymanski, et al. 2020. Principles and mechanisms of wildlife population persistence in the face of disease. *Frontiers in Ecology and Evolution* 8:569016. doi:10.3389/fevo.2020.569016

Salguero-Gómez, R., and M. Gamelon (eds). 2021. *Demographic methods across the tree of life.* Oxford: Oxford University Press.

Sevilleta Long-Term Ecological Research. 2022. https://sevlter.unm.edu/droughtnet-experiment/#:~:text=The%20Drought%20 Network%20is%20aacross%20biomes%20 and%20climate%20gradients (accessed 1 September 2022).

Shepherd, J. G., J. G. Pope, and R. D. Cousens. 1984. Variations in fish stocks and hypotheses concerning their links with climate. *Rapports et Proces-verbaux des Réunions. Conseil International pour l'Éxploration de la Mer* 185:255–267.

Sheriff, M. J., C. J. Krebs, and R. Boonstra. 2011. From process to pattern: How fluctuating predation risk impacts the stress axis of snowshoe hares during the 10-year cycle. *Oecologia* 166:593–605. doi:10.1007/s00442-011-1907-2

Simberloff, D. 1981. The sick science of ecology. *Eidema* 1:49–54.

Skellam, J. G. 1951. Random dispersal in theoretical populations. *Biometrika* 38:196–218.

Stenseth, N. C., W. Falck, O. N. Bjørnstad, and C. J. Krebs. 1997. Ecology Population regulation in snowshoe hare and Canadian lynx: Asymmetric food web configurations between hare and lynx. *Proceedings of the National Academy of Sciences of the United States of America* 94:5147–5152.

The National Malleefowl Recovery Team (2022) Protecting our iconic Malleefowl. https://www.nationalmalleefowl.com.au/ (accessed 9 September 2022)

Turkington, R., E. John, C. J. Krebs, et al. 1998. The effects of fertilization on the vegetation of the boreal forest. *Journal of Vegetation Science* 9:333–346.

Tyson, R., S. Haines, and K. E. Hodges. 2010. Modelling the Canada lynx and snowshoe hare population cycle: The role of specialist predators. *Theoretical Ecology* 3:97–111. doi:10.1007/s12080-009-0057-1

Walters, C. J., and C. S. Holling. 1990. Large-scale management experiments and learning by doing. *Ecology* 71:2060–2068. doi:10.2307/1938620

Westgate, M. J., G. E. Likens, and D. B. Lindenmayer. Adaptive management of biological systems: A review. *Biological Conservation* 158:128–139. doi:10.1016/j.biocon.2012.08.016

Yates, K. L., P. J. Bouchet, M. J. Caley, et al. (2018) Outstanding challenges in the transferability of ecological models. *Trends in Ecology and Evolution* 33:790–802. doi:10.1016/j.tree.2018.08.001

Ye, H., R. J. Beamish, S. M. Glaser, et al. 2015. Equation-free mechanistic ecosystem forecasting using empirical dynamic modeling. *Proceedings of the National Academy of Sciences of the United States of America* 112:e1569–e1576. doi:10.1073/pnas.141706311

Zvereva, E. L., and Kozlov, M. V. 2021. Biases in ecological research: Attitudes of scientists and ways of control. *Scientific Reports* 11:226. doi:10.1038/s41598-020-80677-4

9

From pattern to process in the search for generality

FRANÇOISE CARDOU AND MARC CADOTTE

THE PATTERN-FIRST APPROACH TO ECOLOGY

Science seeks to understand and predict the natural world. While the wondrous complexity and diversity of biological systems has inspired countless generations of romantics and thinkers, to the scientist, it presents potent challenges. If every biological phenomenon is a unique and special event that is dependent in some way on the particular context in which it is observed (in other words, if it is fully 'contingent'), then understanding even something so routine as the effect of herbivory on prairie plants could reasonably entail measuring every blade of grass in every prairie on every continent, every day of the year. While this prospect might still attract a few patient and dedicated souls, for many others, this would be a deflating prospect.

General theories are statements about nature that propose specific relationships between observable phenomena and which are thought to apply to a range of conditions (Peters 1980) – for instance, a statement about the effect of large herbivores on graminoid species, independent of climate. Because they have '*fewer or less restrictive pre-conditions*', general theories contain more information about the world (Peters 1991). Thus, a statement about '*plant leaf response to physical damage*' contains information about many more individuals than a similar statement about '*leaf response to*

physical damage under drought in the rare Western prairie fringed orchid Platanthera praeclara', which addresses only a small subset of cases. For much of the 20th century, the grinding search for such general theories was thought of as the main mechanism for progress in science. Think of the simple caricature of science (Figure 9.1) where arrows take us from question to hypothesis to experiment to conclusion or theory. By eliminating unsuccessful theories using experiments and observation, successive theories might approach the truth (Niiniluoto 2019).

Where do ecologists typically look for such general theories? In a famous quote from MacArthur (1972) '*to do science is to search for repeated patterns, not simply to accumulate facts*'. Readers of ecological textbooks will be familiar with extensive discussions of canonical ecological patterns like latitudinal diversity gradients, multi-annual population cycles and species-area relationships. The idea is that if patterns repeat predictably in a wide array of ecological contexts, they may be amenable to explanation by single, general all-or-nothing processes. Take for instance the very basic processes of distribution and diffusion of chemicals across membranes with which scientists were able to explain ubiquitous scaling laws in biology (Brown et al. 2004). General patterns are therefore often thought to be good contenders to yield general theories (e.g., Lawton 1999).

DOI: 10.1201/9781003314332-9

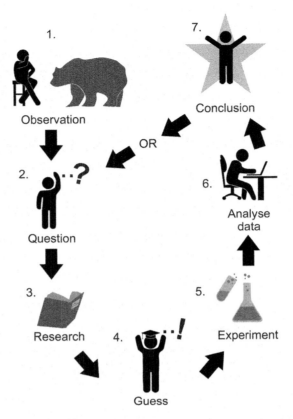

Figure 9.1 According to Popper's 'falsificationism', science progresses by subjecting general theories (statements about how phenomena relate to each other) to testing via experimentation or other means. If the general theory is not supported by testing, it is eliminated from the range of theories that we have about the world. If it is not eliminated, it survives only until it can be tested again.

For the philosopher Kuhn, scientific progress was anything but assured. He argued that scientific disciplines tended to go through phases, but movement from one to the other was not assured. He called disciplines that do not share an underlying framework or conceptual basis 'pre-paradigm' sciences. Here, scientists can work, but this work is neither well-organised nor effective (Godfrey-Smith 2003). If a piece of work emerges that suddenly provides a common model from which further investigation can grow, a field now has a 'paradigm', and can establish a new tradition. Kuhn called this phase 'normal science', where day-to-day scientific activity might look a lot like Figure 9.1. Although new paradigms can initially yield new and unexpected insight, over time, any new observation that does not conform to the paradigm is taken as a sign of researcher error, rather than a challenge to the paradigm. As more and more evidence accumulates that conforms poorly to the reigning paradigm, scientific disciplines can stagnate, until such time as a crisis arises that opens the door for scientific revolution and the emergence of a new paradigm.

Scientific disciplines can stagnate for a range of reasons, and Ecology has always benefited from a range of critiques seeking to catalyse change (e.g. Peters 1991; Shrader-Frechette 2001). However, at least one has had disproportionately larger impact: in 1999, Lawton published an influential assessment of ecology's progress towards generality. His view was a pessimistic one. While ecology had yielded some recurring patterns, few of them were generalisable in any useful sense. In particular, he (famously) singled out one subdiscipline as a laggard: for him, ecology's reputation as 'soft' science was largely due to the overwhelming emphasis on community ecology.

Lawton bemoaned the fact that community ecology had few, if any, general patterns. Because here the focus is on the study of ecological phenomena at a scale that is sandwiched between population-level and macroecological processes, he concluded that communities were too contingent, complex and confounded to yield generalities. It should be jettisoned from the ecological program. He believed that population ecology, with just a handful of parameters describing population growth, and macroecology, with few broad environmental and geographical variables controlling range size and diversity, were the appropriate scales of study for ecology to progress. Lawton was not alone in this view. Many scholars felt that community ecology, and perhaps ecology in general, had hit the end of the road and that sustained scientific progress was unlikely, at least unless new ways of thinking emerged (Simberloff 1980; Peters 1991; Ricklefs 2008).

Twenty-five years later, community ecology is still clearly alive and well: it endures as a core and (we would argue) energised subdiscipline in ecology. How did it overcome the crisis illustrated by Lawton's critique? Although pattern-first approaches have been popular in ecology (MacArthur 1972; Lawton 1999) they are not the only pathway to generality (Cooper 2003; Fox 2019), and are arguably incapable of providing alone the theoretical basis for novel predictions (Cadotte and Tucker 2017; Kraft et al. 2015a).

Community ecology is not the first scientific discipline to tackle complex, confounded and contingent phenomena (Vellend 2016). Rather than be deterred by repeated failures to find general patterns and drawing inspiration from parallel fields like evolutionary biology, community ecology has undergone a rapid shift towards a new source of generality: processes. Beginning with a brief tour of community ecology, we retrace the move from pattern-first to process-first approaches and how it has helped achieve greater generality across three of community ecology's core goals. Despite these advances, we argue that community ecology is still hindered by the search for single all-or-nothing explanations. We conclude that even in 'pluralistic' systems that are contingent, complex and confounded, ecologists have a range of approaches at their disposal to achieve generality. Though process-first approaches likely still have untapped potential to achieve greater generality, ecologists should continue to assess progress critically.

BOX 9.1: Glossary of some terms used in this chapter

Contingent: Synonymous with 'context dependent', referring to situations where relationships vary depending on the conditions – the context – under which they are observed (Catford et al. 2022; Lawton 1999).

Coexistence theory: Posits that species coexistence is regulated by two inequalities: fitness differences (where fitness captures growth and reproduction) and niche differences. According to this theory, two species with similar fitness values need only a small niche difference to coexist, and species with large fitness differences require a much greater niche difference (Chesson 2000).

Ecosystem function: Stocks of energy and materials, fluxes in energy and material processing, and the stability of these fluxes in time (Pacala and Kinzig 2013).

Generality: Property of knowledge (concerning a question, system, species or situation) that is transferable to other questions, systems, species or situations (Fox 2019).

Scientific theories: Predictive and falsifiable statements about nature that propose relationships between observable phenomena (Peters 1980).

Pattern: Regularity in what we observe in nature, or in other words 'widely observable tendencies' (Lawton 1999).

Process: *'A continuous and regular action or succession of actions occurring or performed in a definite manner, and having a particular result or outcome; a sustained operation or series of operations'* (Oxford University Press 2022).

COMMUNITY ECOLOGY: A BRIEF OVERVIEW

Any scientific discipline must define a fundamental unit that provides the origin of explanation, or is the thing being explained, whether we are talking about energy, genetic variation or ecological communities. As early as the 19th and early 20th centuries, ecology witnessed the development of contrasted perspectives: proto-ecologists hailing from scientific traditions of taxonomy and systematics had a tendency to classify and categorise plant 'societies' into complex hierarchies (Schröter and Kirchner 1896; Braun-Blanquet 1932). In comparison, early ecologists hailing from physiology and natural history tended to focus on functionality (Drude 1896; Warming 1925), a view which, if applied at the individual species or whole community level, led to a famous debate between the so-called Clementsian and Gleasonian views and which we will return to in the next section. Fundamentally, what distinguishes these views is the level of predictability that we can expect from the association that exists among species that form communities.

Communities are now commonly defined as a group of interacting populations in a given area, or the area that contains all interacting individuals (Ricklefs and Relyea 2018; Smith and Smith 2014). Such a definition is of course imprecise and difficult to implement: it requires that we know both the precise extent of each constituent population and have information on the extent to which these populations interact. This is simply implausible. Populations themselves defy a simple delineation of boundaries, and interactions among species can take place across broad spatial and temporal scales. Take for instance the case of migrating birds or predators with home ranges many orders of magnitude larger than that of their prey.

In reality, ecologists do not study communities *per se*. What they frequently study is an arbitrary area that they believe captures an adequate representation of the types of interactions and mechanisms structuring species abundances and diversity within it, regardless of the trophic complexity of the study question. With this pragmatic approach to the study of communities in hand, we still need to determine what community ecologists typically aim to achieve.

What do community ecologists try to predict and understand?

Ecology as a whole can be defined in a number of ways, and emphasis provided by different authors can lend community ecology a range of flavours. For instance, definitions emphasising the 'abundance and distribution' of species used in popular textbooks like Krebs (2000) originate from biogeography. Other definitions emphasise the study of pools and fluxes of energy through both biotic and abiotic components in order to understand the physiology of whole ecosystems (Odum 1953).

Up until relatively recently, a majority of community ecologists would have probably identified most closely with the first of these definitions. From early studies of desert plant assemblages and plankton communities, a large proportion of the work that is still done by community ecologists comes down to understanding a handful of 'first-order' community-level attributes (*sensu* Vellend 2016), such as species diversity and composition, and linking these properties with other site-level characteristics, like environmental gradients (Figure 9.2, I and II).

In contrast, inspired by Odum's ecosystem-centric view of ecology, another line of enquiry has emerged which is not simply concerned with how species respond to the environment or one another, but how they themselves drive ecosystem processes via close ecological interactions (Figure 9.2, III). Spurred initially by a factious debate on the importance of diversity for the stability of ecosystems, this line of enquiry has bloomed in recent decades into a rich body of knowledge on the multifarious repercussions of community structure on the functioning of ecosystems.

Crisis

Lawton's critique rightly pointed out that community ecology was an attempt to understand ecological relationships at an awkward scale, sandwiched between population biology and macroecology. As a result, community ecology suffered from the accumulated complexity and contingency of each constituent population, but at a scale too small for this variability to be ignored or abstracted away, or perhaps superseded by larger-scale patterns with regularity. In the 25 years since Lawton's

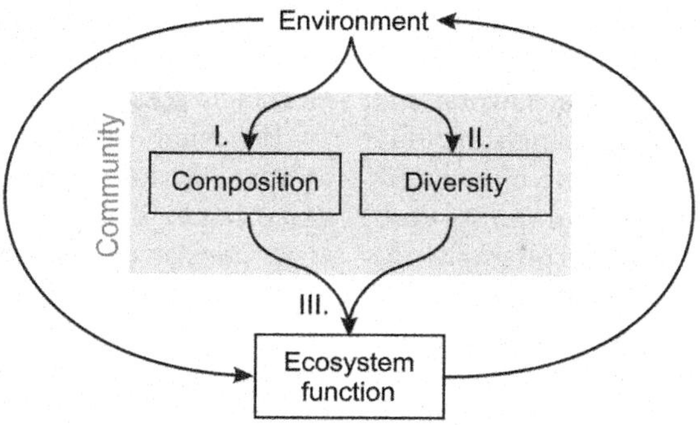

Figure 9.2 An illustration of the main phenomena that community ecologists try to understand and predict. This includes 'first-order' properties of ecological communities, like composition (I) and diversity (II), as well as ecosystem-level properties, such as stocks of energy and materials (III).

indictment, macroecology has certainly exploded as an ecological discipline that addresses the geographic, climatic and other large-scale drivers of ecological patterns (Smith et al. 2008). Community ecology, on the other hand, far from fading from the spotlight, seems to have been rejuvenated by not just Lawton's criticism but other salvos across community ecology's bow.

The ascent of a process-first approach for ecology

In 2002, Lavorel and Garnier proposed the unification of the approaches that had been developing to understand the abundance and distributions of species (Keddy 1992; Westoby 1998; Grime 1977; Figure 9.2, I and II), with those schemes that attempted to measure the impact of communities on ecosystem processes (Grime 1998; Figure 9.2, III). They did this by moving away from species identities and instead defining species by their suite of 'response' and 'effect' traits. Here a response trait is a measurable attribute of a species (usually, physiological, morphological or phenological) that influences its response to abiotic and biotic influences, as captured by its growth and reproduction. Effect traits are those that impact ecosystem processes.

With plant ecologists in the vanguard, the unification of community ecology under the common currency provided by traits has had an impact that can hardly be overstated. Because traits provide a mechanistic basis for generalised predictions that are independent of taxonomy (McGill et al. 2006;

Shipley 2016), they have opened the door to a generality in our understanding of the selective forces that shape communities that did not exist at the time of Lawton's critique.

Selective forces that operate on traits are just one of several processes that have been proposed as the explanation for diversity and composition. Against the backdrop of a booming enthusiasm for the deterministic component of community assembly ('rules of assembly') and species coexistence (Chesson 2000; Weiher and Keddy 1995), the last 25 years have also seen the formalisation of ideas surrounding processes that are blind to species' differences. With Hubbell's neutral theory of biodiversity (2001) and the advent of metacommunity ecology (Leibold et al. 2004), what has emerged are not universal laws that govern community dynamics in predictable ways, but a finite set of general high-level processes that fully specify the range of mechanisms about which community ecologists make predictions (Vellend 2016).

THE HOLY GRAIL: UNDERSTANDING AND PREDICTING COMMUNITY COMPOSITION

Ecologists commonly chide each other for having what they term 'physics envy'. This is usually levelled at those who might aspire to a level of generality and predictability that is considered incompatible with the features of biological systems or who are dissatisfied with the current ability to predict variables of interest. Realistic or not, there is a belief among some community ecologists that our ultimate goal is to predict the exact species composition that one might find in a given environment, under given biotic conditions (Lavorel and Garnier 2002; Laughlin et al. 2012; Laughlin 2014). To achieve this would go to the heart of Lawton's critique and cement the status of community ecology as a predictive science. Not surprisingly, the regularity and predictability of community composition is a topic that has generated both a range of perspectives and fierce debates.

As early as 1909, Spalding was observing that species in desert plant communities seemed to shift when and where they occurred from year to year (Spalding 1909). Around the same time, however, Clements (1916) working in Nebraska was describing the deterministic nature of plant succession and developing the firm belief that there were such things as stable and predictable associations between species. The successional trends that he was witnessing were so regular and predictable that Clements thought plant communities were analogous to organisms, with each constituent species in the community playing a particular and important role, like organs in the body. Much like ambient temperature might affect a person as a whole, Clements thought that external processes acted on the community 'super-organism' collectively, leading to predictable associations among species that resulted in climax communities (Figure 9.3a).

This view was strongly criticised by Gleason. While Gleason agreed that plant communities exist, can be mapped and studied, he also thought that, consistent with observations like those of Spalding, species respond to the environment individually (Figure 9.3b). Because species could not be expected to co-occur predictably in any general sense, species associations were therefore coincidental, rather than fundamental organic entities (Gleason 1926; Nicolson and McIntosh 2002). By the 1980s Gleason had largely won the debate: his individualistic view of species distributions became a *de facto* null model for explaining community composition. Any departure from this expectation involving more complex interactions among species had to be demonstrated with solid evidence.

But the success of Gleason's ideas begs one important question: if species respond individually to environmental gradients, is there any hope of achieving community ecology's 'Holy Grail'? Recurrent patterns of compositional change across environments are some of the most striking features of ecological systems. An individualistic view

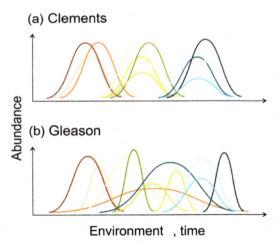

Figure 9.3 The early days of community ecology were concerned in large part with the debate between Clements' view of communities as stable and predictable 'societies' determined by strong inter-species interaction (a). He expected that this should result in stable clusters of species (represented by groups of individual curves in panel a across environmental or temporal gradients). This view was strongly opposed to Gleason's individualistic view of species' relation to the environment (b). While the empirical record now chiefly supports Gleason's view, we also now know that interactions between species can have strong impacts on community composition. Each curve represents a different species.

of species' distribution like Gleason's could lead to the conclusion that assemblage membership is simply context dependent. Since context dependency is generally a placeholder for a current lack of sufficient explanation, this would be a somewhat unsatisfactory conclusion. On the other hand, if all species respond individually but predictably to the environment, then all that one would theoretically need to predict community composition would be sufficient information concerning the preferences of individual species. The (non)-random structure of communities across environmental gradients has provided motivation and fuel for the search for a general explanation (Whittaker 1960; Laughlin et al. 2012).

Challenge (or strawman) from Hubbell's neutral theory: do species differences even matter?

Building on Spalding's initial observations on the transience of desert plant species associations, ecologists have long suspected the importance of stochasticity as a driver of community structure. Yet, the notion that patterns of community composition could be sufficiently explained by processes that are indifferent to the clear differences that exist between species was not formalised until the publication of Hubbell's 'neutral theory' in 2001. Under this theory, species are assumed to have identical niche requirements and to be competitively equivalent: what determines community structure (its diversity and composition) is strictly the outcome of stochastic births and deaths. More specifically, the idea is that a species that sustains some decrease of its population will be statistically more likely to go extinct, regardless of how well it is adapted to its environment. As a result, stochastic deaths (or births) due to, say, the fall of a meteorite can have long-term consequences. Given enough time, neutral theory posits that markedly different community structures can emerge simply by chance.

This was a bold claim and flew in the face of much established wisdom. Ecologists had long been used to devising refined hypotheses to predict species' responses to their environment that were based on their features. One need only think of the timeless proverb contrasting the oak and the reed and their ability to withstand storms based on their stem properties. What was especially remarkable

was that Hubbell's theory proved able to reproduce species abundance distributions in high-diversity communities quite well (Hubbell 2001). Could community structure really be contingent 'all the way down', as Hubbell's theory suggested?

Neutral theory has had two distinct impacts on ecology research. The first has been to serve as a foil against the overwhelming reliance on deterministic niche-based processes to explain differences among communities. Here, the response was swift and largely negative (e.g. McGill 2003), highlighting for instance the fact that species niche differences are easily observable and demonstrable. However, beyond the apparent strawman presented by neutral theory was its second impact – neutrality as an emergent process.

While species have differing adaptations, there are a suite of mechanisms and influences that can equalise fitness such that species with, for example, competitive differences might appear as though their interactions are governed by neutral processes. Any process, either density independent or density dependent, that reduces reproduction or increases mortality can potentially reduce competitive differences, allowing species to persist together (1) if these external influences create the conditions for coexistence (i.e., fitness differences lowered to the point where the positive influence of niche differences can be realised) or (2) if these species exhibit very little niche difference, then this persistence can appear as apparent neutrality (Chesson 2000; MacDougall et al. 2009; Chave 2004).

Predictive community-environment relationships based on processes

If Hubbell's expectation of species' equivalence is so unrealistic, then how should we express species' differences in a way that can capture the deterministic selection forces to which they are responding? A species, name tells us very little about how it interacts with the world. Rather, it is the measurable physical and biochemical aspects of an individual's phenotype (traits) that dictate how it perceives and responds to environmental stimuli and how it interacts with competitors, predators, parasites, pathogens and microbial mutualists (McGill et al. 2006; Cadotte et al. 2011). Traits are functional when their variation has demonstrable influences on species performance or other trophic levels or processes like nutrient cycling. By linking traits to species performance across environmental gradients, we can predict the composition and direction of community change because we can evaluate the relationship between, say, the abundance of species that have different wood densities and a soil moisture gradient (Laughlin et al. 2012).

Take, for instance, the change in forest composition that occurs predictably with increasing elevation: this is a regular pattern in temperate environments. In the Smoky Mountains (Tennessee, USA), this trend can be articulated as a transition between *Tsuga canadensis* at low elevations to *Acer rubrum* at mid-elevations and *Pinus rigida* at high elevations (Whittaker 1956). Because this specific group of species does not occur on mountainsides located in Japan or Austria, the previous sentence provides no information as to what forest composition we might find as we climbed these other mountains. In other words, this is a pattern without process and does not provide a general prediction that can be tested in other biomes. However, it does become predictive when we articulate this pattern in terms of the traits that might respond to selective forces at play along this and other altitudinal gradients, resulting in lower water evapotranspiration and greater shedding of snow at higher elevations.

More specifically, such trait-environment correlations capture two interrelated processes. Firstly, the change in trait values reflects the fit between trait and local environmental conditions. This is the signal of the selective forces that progressively sift out species with ill-adapted traits. Secondly, species fitness, which is influenced by trait values, results in changes in competitive hierarchies, and an inferior competitor could persist in a suboptimal environment in the absence of a species with better-adapted traits (Cadotte and Tucker 2017; Kraft et al. 2015a).

As they have done since the days of Clements and Gleason, community ecologists will no doubt continue to debate the importance of deterministic and stochastic processes in community assembly. The emergence around the same time of both functional community ecology and neutral theory shows that this is not a debate that can be resolved by single decisive tests of each theory. As

in population genetics, 'drift' within communities is more important in small communities. For their part, trait-based approaches have yielded a number of robust trait-environment relationships that successfully generalise across broad sets of environmental conditions, like water availability, shade or altitude (Poorter et al. 2019; O'Brien et al. 2017; Delhey 2019). What neutral theory really highlighted was that we cannot assume the supremacy of deterministic processes and that, thanks to Chesson's (2000) expansion of coexistence theory, species interactions fall along a continuum from approximating neutral to very deterministic processes. In other words, both processes co-occur continuously and predictably.

MORE THAN ONE PATH: UNDERSTANDING AND PREDICTING DIVERSITY

The core of community ecology is focused on testing hypotheses about not just the kinds of organisms that we might find in a given place, but their diversity as well. Specifically, for much of the field's history, community ecologists have developed theory and collected data focused on the number of species in a community.

As early as the 19th century, biogeographers knew that surveys carried out over larger spatial extents would yield a higher number of species (McIntosh 1986). From terrestrial plant communities to freshwater lakes, early quantitative ecologists set about counting how many species might be found if they sampled increasingly large areas (Arrhenius 1921). Formalised into an equation, the resulting relationship yields a characteristic curve (a so-called 'species-area' curve; Figure 9.4a) that allowed scientists to make educated guesses about the quantities of species that might be present in areas they had yet to sample. Because such curves tend to share a basic shape, reflecting the balance of common species relative to rare ones, the species-area relationship became known as one of the canonical patterns in community ecology (Preston 1960). Even today, this relationship is still one of community ecology's very few robust and general patterns (Lawton 1999), holding up across several scales. Its impact on the next several decades of (community) ecology research can hardly be overstated.

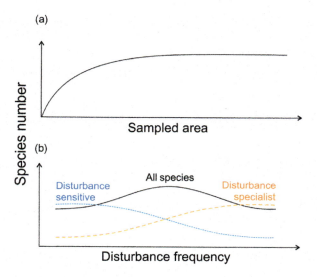

Figure 9.4 Ecologists have tried to find generalisable relationships between diversity and many environmental features. Some have proven robust, like the relationship between species number and sampled area (a), while others like the 'intermediate disturbance hypothesis' (b) have been shown to produce divergent patterns based on the traits of species in the species pool.

MacArthur and Wilson were the first to really put the species-area relationship to work. Building on Wilson's work on ant communities, the pair hypothesised that in an archipelago, the number of species that might be found on a given island would be determined by its total area. Because immigration and extinction are dynamic processes that depend both on the isolation of the island from the mainland (via propagule pressure) and the number of species already present (via competition), the dynamic process of arrivals and extinctions would maintain the number of species in each community around an equilibrium that, despite turnover in species, could be predicted based on just a few parameters (MacArthur and Wilson 1967).

Diversity patterns depend on species pool

Following MacArthur and Wilson's lead, community ecologists set about exploring many other potential predictors for the number of species that might be found in a given area, beyond its extent and its isolation. In 1918, Thienemann had predicted that communities in areas with a greater diversity of environmental conditions would be composed of a greater number of species. The species richness-heterogeneity relationship has turned out to be another example of a robust and predictive relationship in community ecology, holding up to scrutiny across both plant and animal communities (Stein 2014; Allouche et al. 2012). If we were to stop the roundtable here, one might get the impression that the search for predictors of diversity has on the whole provided community ecology with a firm basis from which to derive general theories. As it turns out, Lawton had ground for concern.

The intermediate disturbance hypothesis (IDH), formulated by Connell in 1978, predicts that diversity should peak at disturbance levels that are moderate enough for sensitive species to survive, but frequent enough to allow disturbance specialists to still colonise, yielding a diversity peak at intermediate disturbance intensities (Figure 9.4b). That this prediction tracks well with the experience of many ecologists, particularly those working in temperate plant communities, is probably not independent of the speed at which this prediction has become common ecological wisdom, or of its tenacity in entry-level ecological textbooks (e.g. Krebs 2000). But while this is probably one of the most frequently tested hypotheses in ecology, there is good reason to doubt its generality. Meta-analyses of empirical results have shown that diversity-disturbance relationships are in fact not peaked or general (Mackey and Currie 2001).

There are conceptual reasons why we might expect diversity-disturbance relationships to have different shapes in different ecological situations (Cadotte 2007). In its original formulation, the IDH assumed that species would be drawn from a pool where species are evenly distributed between disturbance-sensitive and disturbance-specialist species. In this scenario, a progressive increase in disturbance might thus very well lead to a progressive shift from one group to the next, as predicted. There is however no *a priori* reason why a regional pool would contain even proportions of either group: after all, adaptation to recurrent disturbances depends on suites of traits that can evolve, and thus it is entirely reasonable to expect greater proportions of disturbance specialists in disturbance-prone environments. In this case, rather than a peaked relationship, one would therefore expect a directional increase in diversity with increasing disturbance intensity (Cadotte 2007).

It would be a mistake to think that the particular failures of the IDH are its alone: other hypotheses that attempt to predict robust trends in species diversity along complex ecological gradients have also yielded mixed or weak evidence. For instance, diversity was also long thought to peak at intermediate levels of productivity, but this effect has failed to generalise robustly outside the plant communities where it was first addressed (Mittelbach et al. 2001). Underlying these weak relationships is the fact that they are based on hypotheses that make assumptions about the composition of the species pool: in other words, they rely on a selection mechanism that will yield different results depending on species identity, and as such, their predictions are contingent on the properties of those species that are available to colonise (Ricklefs 2008).

Matching diversity measures to hypotheses to capture processes

If we looked closely at many of the earliest community ecology theories, we would see that they are ultimately based on predictions about the effect of numbers and relative abundance of species on species' niches and niche differences (Chesson 2000). For example, Lotka-Volterra competition models included a parameter describing the strength of the magnitude of the reduction in population growth of one species on another (Lotka 1925; Volterra 1931), assuming that species are likely to coexist if these impacts are low relative to intraspecific density dependence (Chesson 2000); this is what we expect if species occupy distinct niches. Similarly, one of MacArthur's fundamental insights was that species co-occur and coexist only when they use different resources by partitioning niches, also commonly referred to as Gause's principle (MacArthur 1958; Gause 1934).

Despite this, we still routinely use species richness as a surrogate for niche differences (Box 9.2). In essence, we assume that a greater number of species should result in more niches being represented, or in a greater amount of niche space. This poor match between the mechanisms underpinning our hypotheses and what we measure – the patterns we seek to explain – have existed in ecology for much of its history. The problem with such surrogacy is that studies which failed to support the intermediate disturbance hypothesis (for example) did not disprove the underlying mechanisms, but rather were unknowingly testing for the relative numbers of species that occupy different niches (e.g. disturbance-sensitive versus disturbance-specialist species).

This type of problem was fully exposed by a seminal paper by Webb showing how the phylogenetic distances among species could be used to assess whether communities were comprised of more closely or distantly related species than expected by random draws from a regional species pool (Webb 2000). Because we do not always know which traits are important for a given species and because functional characteristics tend to be retained within phylogenies, phylogenetic differences provide a holistic proxy for niche differences: these distances can be assessed at the community level in a way that is independent of differences in the number of species. For instance, phylogenetic dissimilarity among species were hypothesised to reflect changes in the relative importance of competition (and thus niche differences) versus environmental filtering (e.g. Bässler et al. 2016).

As we saw in the previous section, predictable relationships between traits and environment allow us to make educated guesses about the presence or abundance of individual species, based on their traits, and about the average trait values of entire assemblages (Laughlin et al. 2012; Laughlin 2014). Species traits and phylogenetic distances are complementary approaches (see Box 9.2; Cadotte et al. 2019) that both connect more directly to the

BOX 9.2: Measures of diversity

There are many ways to quantify the diversity of species in a given community. Species richness provides a first-cut measure that simply tallies the number of species present in a community. In cases where we only know which species were present or absent at a site, this is the best we can do. But species' relative abundances are also an important feature of community diversity, and can vary markedly even when species richness remains constant, as illustrated in Figure 9.5.

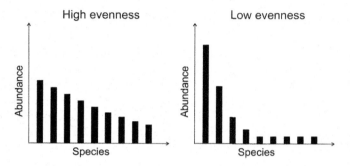

Figure 9.5 Illustration of the principle that either high or low evenness can be found in communities with similar species richness.

A number of indices exist that capture species' abundance-weighted diversity (evenness). Popular examples include the Shannon-Weiner index and Simpson's index. The merits of these different indices were a recurrent topic of debate among ecologists through the 1980s and 1990s. We now generally agree that species richness and measures of evenness capture different facets of species' abundance distribution in a community: they are complementary tools to common questions, and new unified measures based on Hill numbers now allow the computation of diversity measures that incorporate evenness in a variety of ways across a common mathematical formulation (Chao et al. 2014).

Importantly, the critique levelled at indices like species richness in the main text hold equally for all other measures of diversity. When they are based on taxonomic species identity, these indices offer equally poor ways of testing hypotheses that are implicitly based on species' niche differences. Since the advent of functional community ecology, a full suite of both functional and phylogenetic (based on shared evolutionary ancestry) alternatives to these measures have been developed, such that it is now possible to describe trait distributions to the same level of detail. Incorporating functional and phylogenetic information into diversity measures provides a basis to account for species dissimilarities while still calculating richness or evenness type measures (Mason et al. 2005; Chao et al. 2014; Cadotte et al. 2010).

processes underlying coexistence than species richness. For instance, returning to our example of how disturbance shapes communities, a number of studies have shown how variation in disturbance alters both the phylogenetic and functional trait composition of communities in predictable ways (e.g. Helmus et al. 2010). These new approaches to measuring community diversity have opened the floodgates for empirical tests of community assembly mechanisms.

Inferring process from (diversity) pattern: a many-to-one problem

The abiotic environment can influence species fitness directly, by limiting growth and reproduction through constraints that are common to all species in a community. This is termed 'environmental filtering'. The abiotic environment is also ultimately the source of resources that support populations. For plants, for example, local pools of nutrients like nitrogen and phosphorus, along with water and light fuel growth. As these and other resources are consumed or occupied, they begin to limit population growth: this is the stage at which we expect there to be a shift in the processes driving community assembly, away from environmental filtering and towards competition between individuals within and across species.

Of course, because of local environmental heterogeneity and variability, and because different species are unlikely to be limited by the same resources, no single species has the capacity to consume all available resources. This means that species that can access resources unavailable to others, or are limited by different resources, are able to coexist (Tilman et al. 1982; Gause 1934). As a result, species that are similar in their niches, and by extension their traits, are likely to either face competition resulting in competitive exclusion or will persist neutrally if they have relatively equivalent fitness (Chesson 2000; Adler et al. 2007). Either way, these species will not deterministically coexist. Instead, coexistence will be more likely between those species that exhibit trait differences. Evidence from successional studies generally confirms that as ecosystems become more diverse, interactions play out, heterogeneity increases and communities become more diverse in their traits and more distantly related (Meiners et al. 2015; Li et al. 2015).

It is now routine for ecologists to assess whether communities contain species that are similar or dissimilar to one another (Cadotte et al. 2019). These community-level dissimilarity patterns are typically assessed against randomly generated communities that are sampled from a larger regional species pool. Communities that are functionally or phylogenetically underdispersed (i.e. containing species that are more similar to one another than expected by random sampling) are often assumed to have adaptations allowing them to persist under a severe environmental regime (i.e. environmental filtering; e.g. Bässler et al. 2016). Conversely, communities that are overdispersed are presumed to reflect the outcome of competition, specifically limiting similarity, that selects for dissimilar species.

The problem with these inferences is that these mechanisms (environmental filtering, limiting similarity) cannot be directly assessed from changes in dissimilarity. Different mechanisms and processes can lead to convergent community phylogenetic and functional diversity patterns (Mayfield et al. 2010; Cadotte and Tucker 2017). For example, species facilitation, small-scale soil heterogeneity and limiting similarity can all result in overdispersed communities. Further, different processes can act on different elements of species' phenotypes, meaning that some traits might be underdispersed because of convergent evolution while they are dissimilar on other trait axes that promote coexistence (Cadotte et al. 2019).

This is a potent example of community ecology's many-to-one problem. Because different processes can lead to the same patterns (Lawton 1999; Vellend 2016), additional information or experiments are required to rule out or account for potentially co-occurring mechanisms. Without these, reliance on patterns of dissimilarity can lead to erroneous inferences about process, even when measures of dissimilarity are well aligned with niche differences. For instance, to differentiate between different community assembly mechanisms, additional information might be needed on environmental heterogeneity, how individual species abundances covary with environmental gradients and the presence/absence of other species (Cadotte and Tucker 2017). One might even use experiments to determine how species respond to environmental gradients in the absence of competition (Kraft et al. 2015b). Even as community ecology has pivoted towards a process-first approach, the search for all-or-nothing explanations continues to be a stumbling block.

A LITTLE BIT OF EVERYTHING ALL OF THE TIME: ECOSYSTEM FUNCTION

The term 'ecosystem function' classically refers to three types of ecosystem properties: stocks of energy and materials, fluxes in energy and material processing, and the stability of these fluxes in time (Pacala and Kinzig 2013). In contrast with the challenges encountered in preceding sections, it is noteworthy (and perhaps, to be expected) that attempts to understand how communities affect ecosystem functioning have been process-driven from the start. Still the reliance on species richness in experiments has nonetheless created a mismatch between the measure of diversity employed and the hypothesised mechanisms. In addition, this area of research continues to be hindered by a search for all-or-nothing mechanisms, and by a narrow focus on a subset of ecosystems functions.

From an ecosystem view, plants represent a single functional group that converts energy, light and nutrients into organic matter. This means, first, that plants determine the amount of energy available to all other players in the ecosystem, and second, that their contribution to ecosystem functioning can be assumed to depend on a common set of characteristics. As a result, the study of ecosystem function through the lens of community ecology has been overwhelmingly focused on terrestrial and plant communities. Of course, even in the 1950s, ecologists (not to mention farmers and foresters) knew very well that plants could determine ecosystem properties like soil fertility: farmers have for centuries increased yield by alternating between crops and leaving fields fallow. However, 'how' and 'how much' plants affect ecosystem functions are questions that have generated at least two fruitful but (until relatively recently) largely orthogonal perspectives, with each side favouring one causal pathway over the other.

The perspective from mathematical ecology

In the 1970s and 1980s, some community ecologists became embroiled in a series of raucous debates surrounding a set of related questions. Several authors had previously converged on the hypothesis that more diverse communities should also exhibit more stable ecosystem properties. When research turned up mixed evidence and weak patterns, the debate eventually shifted to a narrower question. Setting aside their stability in time, could diversity predict ecosystem properties?

Favouring experimental approaches, ecologists of the 1990s set about assembling grassland communities to see whether those with higher numbers of species would turn out to be more productive (Naeem et al. 1994; Tilman et al. 1996; Hector et al. 1999). In general, they did! Of course, these experiments, carried out in tightly controlled environmental conditions, creating relatively homogeneous conditions that likely limited niche opportunities and once again focused on species richness as a proxy for underlying niche differences. They assumed that richer communities would also contain species with more different niches, allowing them to make more efficient use of resources ('niche complementarity') and increasing the likelihood that they might establish mutually beneficial interactions.

With such a tenuous link with species' actual contribution to ecosystem function and little means of distinguishing the effect of diversity *per se* from the disproportionate contribution of particular species, this line of research soon came under heavy criticism from researchers who had already been chipping away at the problem in natural and agricultural systems (Wardle 1999; Huston 1997; Grime 1997). After all, in natural conditions, the most productive ecosystems are often glaringly species poor. Though community ecologists quickly devised methods to isolate the effects of biodiversity *per se* (Loreau and Hector 2001) and to capture directly species' niche differences (e.g. Cadotte et al. 2013; MacIvor et al. 2018), opposing evidence from experiments and *in situ* studies reinforced disagreements.

The perspective from ecosystem ecology

Meanwhile, ecosystem ecologists and community ecologists had been peeling back layers of abiotic and biotic drivers to reveal complex causal hierarchies that explain local ecosystem properties like productivity and decomposition in natural systems. They were able to show not simply that species composition matters for ecosystem function, but that this impact can be explained by species fundamental properties (effect traits) like growth form and level of investment in various plant structures (Sims and Singh 1978; Lavelle et al. 1993). Because these properties are also involved in how species respond to environmental conditions, they generate biophysical feedbacks that can stabilise ecosystem properties or shift them into entirely new states, with ecological succession being just one of many examples (Vitousek and Reiners 1975; Hobbie 1992).

Biomass is not usually evenly distributed among species within communities. Thus, there was reason to suppose that species would affect ecosystem properties to different degrees, and proportionally to their contribution to the total biomass of the community. This insight was formalised by Grime (1998) under the name 'mass ratio hypothesis', and proved critical for the integration of effect traits into mainstream community ecology. In an influential study of a grassland chronosequence, Garnier et al. (2004) demonstrated that, weighted by the contribution of each species to total community biomass, species' traits could explain (once the effects of environmental heterogeneity are accounted for) upwards of 70%, 80% and even 90% of the variation in ecosystem properties. From this point forward, there was great hope that community ecology might close the loop between the response of community composition to environment change and the repercussions of these changes for ecosystem functioning (Figure 9.2).

All-or-nothing explanations

Global environmental change is associated with pervasive shifts in environmental conditions, accelerating land use change and the increased movement of species from place to place. Even while global losses in biodiversity are incontrovertible, there is also clear evidence that species diversity is just as likely to increase as to decrease at local scales where the close species interactions that matter most for ecosystem function occur (Vellend et al. 2013; Dornelas et al. 2014). But while diversity might appear stable at small scales, communities are undergoing substantial changes in composition (Blowes et al. 2019). Anticipating the effect of global change on ecosystem services, and, therefore, on ecosystem functioning, has become one of the great challenges of community ecology.

Given the extensive work done by scientists in experimental settings and in the field, we might have been forgiven for thinking that this area of research would be more than ready to step up to the plate. However, protracted debates between proponents of community composition versus diversity as the main driver of ecosystem function continue to span theoretical, methodological and even sometimes ethical grounds. Though both sides have agreed that plants affect ecosystem processes through their traits (Hooper et al. 2005), ecologists still routinely focus and emphasise the predominance of single all-or-nothing drivers of ecosystem function (e.g. Hooper et al. 2012). Moving forward requires integrating these various traditions to understand which of the three causal pathways in Figure 9.2 predominates, at which scale and in which situations. This may not be entirely enough, either.

On both sides of this debate, ecologists have overwhelmingly focused on one single ecosystem function: productivity. Though studies on occasion have extended their focus to other functions in which plants are known to be involved, like decomposition and soil respiration (Spehn et al. 2005; Cardou et al. 2020), this remains a woefully small subsample of all ecosystem functions on which we depend for ecosystem services. Global environmental change is driving rapid 'rewiring' of biotic interactions (Bartley et al. 2019), and it is not clear that community ecology (as we have described it thus far) is ready to tackle this challenge.

Pending challenge: when the pattern is the process

From predator-prey systems to complex food webs, communities that span more than one trophic level have always been recognised as falling under the umbrella of community ecology. Yet, despite the fact that vertical plankton communities provided some of the earliest examples of community ecology (Forbes 1887), the study of communities that include trophic interactions ('vertical') versus those that only examine patterns within a trophic level ('horizontal') have since largely gone their separate ways.

One reason for this split is most likely a methodological one: sampling across trophic levels requires broad and diverse skill sets, including different sampling techniques and complementary taxonomic identification abilities (Seibold et al. 2018). More fundamentally, these two fields also typically test different hypotheses and rely on different definitions of what an ecological niche is. For horizontal community ecologists, the niche refers to the various strategies that organisms can adopt to ensure their own survival under various environmental conditions (Hutchinson 1978) while vertical community ecologists understandably think of it as the role that species play within the system: it is defined by species-to-species interactions, such as predator and prey (Elton 1927). Vertical communities therefore challenge theories developed for horizontal community in fundamental ways.

Within-community interactions in horizontal communities are assumed to be primarily defined by competition: while different pairs of species can be involved in different levels of competition, the interaction is assumed to be symmetrical, with both partners incurring similar cost from their shared overlap. Vertical communities are defined by the asymmetrical exchange of energy between species: interactions can be assumed to be diverse, strong and negative as well as positive. Another assumption of modern coexistence theory is that species success is the additive outcome of direct pairwise interactions, but strong indirect effects are widely described in food webs (e.g. Godoy et al. 2018).

If species coexist and persist not through varying responses to shared constraints on their fitness but instead as a direct result of trophic exchanges, then the structure of these interactions provides another entry point into community assembly. So far, however, the study of ecological networks has focused overwhelmingly on describing network structure and identifying linkages with other network-level measures, like 'stability' (Marjakangas et al. 2022). Because the latter case treats interactions (ecosystem processes) as the explanatory variables and stability (coexistence) as the response, the resulting knowledge maps awkwardly onto the insights pursued by horizontal community ecologists, and for whom properties of communities like diversity and composition are the variables among which an explanation of ecosystem process might be found.

Still, several recent studies attempt to bridge the conceptual gap between horizontal and vertical communities to explain not just species composition and diversity, but also interactions themselves (Godoy et al. 2018; Marjakangas et al. 2022; Gravel et al. 2016; Ponisio et al. 2019). The stage therefore appears set for field-wide synthesis on processes that underlie species coexistence.

A final word on communities

With plant ecologists in the vanguard, the unification of functional approaches under the common currency provided by traits has had an impact that can hardly be overstated. In re-centring research on those specific characteristics that affect species fitness, functional community ecology has allowed scientists to identify and measure directly those variables that are thought to determine species coexistence and persistence. Because traits provide a basis for generalised predictions that are independent of taxonomy (McGill et al. 2006; Shipley

2016), they have opened the door to a generality in our understanding of the selective forces that shape communities that did not exist at the time of Lawton's critique.

This is not to say that functional methods have 'solved' community ecology. Functional community ecology, which has grown so rapidly in the last decades, has yet to truly resolve several of its foundational tenets (Shipley 2016); some have even wondered whether the subfield has begun to 'drift' (Mittelbach and McGill 2019) or failed to live up to its promise (van der Plas et al. 2020). More to the point, current enthusiasm for the deterministic component of community assembly ('rules of assembly') denotes the influence of niche theory, but selective forces that operate on traits are just one of several processes that have been proposed as the singular explanation for diversity and composition. With Hubbell's neutral theory of biodiversity (2001) and the advent of metacommunity ecology (Leibold et al. 2004), trait-neutral processes like drift and colonisation have also had their moment. What has emerged from these ideas are not universal laws that govern community dynamics in predictable ways, but a finite set of general high-level processes that fully specify the range of mechanisms about which community ecologists make predictions when they try to explain community structure (Vellend 2016).

SO WHAT?

Virtually all ecologists seek generality in their work. Statistical inference is based on the idea that what is true for a sample of cases is likely to generalise to a certain population of cases that have not been directly measured. This is formalised in scientific publications by statements about the range of conditions that our results extend or apply to.

Though individual ecological subdisciplines vary in scale and scope, they have this in common that they generally do not lend themselves to clean 'yes or no' answers. This is true for population dynamics, where both stochastic and deterministic factors interact to yield an endless variety of patterns. It is also true for macroecology, where even bold and robust trends like latitudinal diversity gradients are likely to be the result of both speciation and selective forces. As we have seen, this is most definitely the case of community ecology. McIntosh called this ecology's 'pluralism' (1987), and it is a feature that ecology shares with several disciplines, including geology, evolutionary biology and all of the social sciences. But generality is not determined solely by system-level properties: it is a product both of the system and how we choose to study it (Fox 2019).

Thankfully, there are a number of ways to achieve generality (Cooper 2003; Fox 2019). The pattern-first approach has undoubtedly had resounding successes, not the least of which being the development of metabolic theory to explain robust scaling laws that had puzzled ecologists for decades. As we have shown, however, such an approach reaches its limits in cases where contingency and complexity are high and mechanisms are confounded.

The key to understanding the post-Lawton era of community ecology, and what will drive its future advance, is the move away from a pattern-based heuristic approach to explaining community patterns to a theoretically informed process-based perspective that relies on predictions and the evaluation of multiple competing or interacting mechanisms. Questions like *'how does disturbance influence community diversity?'* should not rely on a unique and idiosyncratic hypothesis, but rather, on how a finite set of discrete high-level processes – immigration, drift and speciation, and finally selection (Vellend 2016) – combine to explain how communities change in response to disturbance.

This is not the first time that in the search for generality, Ecology has undergone a rapid shift towards more mechanistic approaches. With some fanfare, the rapid development of mathematical ecology through the 1980s came with the hope that mathematical models involving just one or two key processes would provide the firm basis that ecology needed. Throughout this chapter, we have intentionally remained vague on the question of whether the recent shift to trait-based approaches in community ecology constitutes a true Kuhnian paradigm shift. Writing in 2002, Paine argued that, because of its pluralism, ecology is unlikely to undergo changes that are quite so radical. After all, whether it is mathematical ecology, niche theory, neutral theory, metabolic theory or metacommunity theory, none of these advances have achieved quite the level of generality that they initially aspired to. Yet, all of them have been fully integrated into the ecological canon and now contribute to our understanding of ecological systems.

Whether the goal of ecology is to understand and predict the abundance and distribution of species, or how energy flows through the biotic and abiotic components of the ecosystem, it is unhelpful to declare that generality is impossible, or that ecologists should be satisfied with less of it. Achieving generality is, at least partially, under our control. Ecologists should continuously evaluate new methods and approaches critically, based on how much generality they help us achieve. It is our view that process-first approaches have propelled community ecology forward, a subdiscipline notoriously plagued with context dependence and complexity. We also believe that such approaches still have vast untapped potential, though this comes with significant (but bracing) challenges. Like opportunistic tinkerers, however, we will be keeping our eyes open for diminishing returns and on the lookout for the next idea that might take us even further.

REFERENCES

Adler, P. B., J. HilleRis Lambers, and J. M. Levine. 2007. A niche for neutrality. *Ecology Letters* 10:95–104. doi:10.1111/j.1461-0248.2006.00996.x

Allouche, O., M. Kalyuzhny, G. Moreno-Rueda, et al. 2012. Area-heterogeneity tradeoff and the diversity of ecological communities. *Proceedings of the National Academy of Sciences of the United States of America* 109:17495–17500. doi:10.1073/pnas.1208652109

Arrhenius, O. 1921. Species and area. *Journal of Ecology* 9:95–99. doi:10.2307/2255763

Bartley, T. J., K. S. McCann, C. Bieg, et al. 2019. Food web rewiring in a changing world. *Nature Ecology and Evolution* 3:345–354. doi:10.1038/s41559-018-0772-3

Bässler, C., M. W. Cadotte, B. Beudert, et al. 2016. Contrasting patterns of lichen functional diversity and species richness across an elevation gradient. *Ecography* 39:689–698. doi:10.1111/ecog.01789

Blowes, S. A., S. R. Supp, L. H. Antão, A. Bates, et al. 2019. The geography of biodiversity change in marine and terrestrial assemblages. *Science* 366:339–345. doi:10.1126/science.aaw1620.

Braun-Blanquet, J. 1932. Plant sociology. *The study of plant communities*, first edn. New York: McGraw-Hill.

Brown, J. H., J. F. Gillooly, A. P. Allen, et al. 2004. Toward a metabolic theory of ecology. *Ecology* 85:1771–1789.

Cadotte, M. W. 2007. Competition–colonization trade-offs and disturbance effects at multiple scales. *Ecology* 88:823–829. doi:10.1890/06-1117

Cadotte, M. W., C. H. Albert, and S. C. Walker. 2013. The ecology of differences: Assessing community assembly with trait and evolutionary distances'. *Ecology Letters* 16:1234–1244. doi:10.1111/ele.12161

Cadotte, M. W., M. Carboni, X. Si, and S. Tatsumi. 2019. Do traits and phylogeny support congruent community diversity patterns and assembly inferences? *Journal of Ecology* 107:2065–2077. doi:10.1111/1365-2745.13247

Cadotte, M. W., K. Carscadden, and N. Mirotchnick. 2011. Beyond species: Functional diversity and the maintenance of ecological processes and services. *Journal of Applied Ecology* 48:1079–1087. doi:10.1111/j.1365-2664.2011.02048.x

Cadotte, M. W., T. J. Davies, J. Regetz, et al. 2010. Phylogenetic diversity metrics for ecological communities: Integrating species richness, abundance and evolutionary history. *Ecology Letters* 13:96–105. doi:10.1111/j.1461-0248.2009.01405.x

Cadotte, M. W., and C. M. Tucker. 2017. Should environmental filtering be abandoned? *Trends in Ecology and Evolution* 32:429–437. doi:10.1016/j.tree.2017.03.004

Cardou, F., I. Aubin, A. Bergeron, and B. Shipley. 2020. Functional markers to predict forest ecosystem properties along a rural-to-urban gradient. *Journal of Vegetation Science* 31:416–428. doi:10.1111/jvs.12855

Catford, J. A., J. R. U. Wilson, P. Pyšek, et al. 2022. Addressing context dependence in ecology. *Trends in Ecology and Evolution* 37:158–170. doi:10.1016/j.tree.2021.09.007

Chao, A., C.-H. Chiu, and L. Jost. 2014. Unifying species diversity, phylogenetic diversity, functional diversity, and related similarity and differentiation measures through Hill numbers'. *Annual Review of Ecology, Evolution,*

and Systematics 45:297–324. doi:10.1146/annurev-ecolsys-120213-091540

Chave, J. 2004. Neutral theory and community ecology. *Ecology Letters* 7:241–253. doi:10.1111/j.1461-0248.2003.00566.x

Chesson, P. 2000. General theory of competitive coexistence in spatially-varying environments'. *Theoretical Population Biology* 58:211–237. doi:10.1006/tpbi.2000.1486

Clements, F. E. 1916. *Plant succession: An analysis of the development of vegetation*. Washington D.C.: Carnegie Institute of Washington.

Connell, J. H. 1978. Diversity in tropical rain forests and coral reefs. *Science* 199-1302-1310.

Cooper, G. J. 2003. The pursuit of ecological generality. In *The science of the struggle for existence: On the foundations of ecology*, first edn, 96–127. Cambridge: Cambridge University Press. doi:10.1017/CBO9780511720154.

Delhey, K.. 2019. A review of Gloger's rule, an ecogeographical rule of colour: Definitions, interpretations and evidence. *Biological Reviews* 94:1294–1316. doi:10.1111/brv.12503

Dornelas, M., N. J. Gotelli, B. McGill, et al. 2014. Assemblage time series reveal biodiversity change but not systematic loss. *Science* 344:296–299. doi:10.1126/science.1248484

Drude, O. 1896. *Manual de geographie botanique*. Paris: Librairie Des Sciences Naturelles.

Elton, C. S. 1927. *Animal ecology*. New York: Macmillan.

Forbes, S. A. 1887. *The lake as a microcosm*. Peoria: Bulletin of the Peoria Scientific Association. .

Fox, J. W. 2019. The many roads to generality in ecology. *Philosophical Topics* 47:83–104. doi:10.5840/philtopics20194715

Garnier, E., J. Cortez, G. Billès, et al. 2004. Plant functional markers capture ecosystem properties during secondary succession. *Ecology* 85:2630–2637. doi:10.1890/03-0799

Gause, G. F. 1934. Experimental analysis of Vito Volterra's mathematical theory of the struggle for existence. *Science* 79:16–17.

Gleason, H. A. 1926. The individualistic concept of the plant association. *Bulletin of the Torrey Botanical Club* 53:7–26. doi:10.2307/2479933

Godfrey-Smith, P. 2003. *Theory and reality: An introduction to the philosophy of science*. Chicago: University of Chicago Press.

Godoy, O., I. Bartomeus, R. P. Rohr, and S. Saavedra. 2018. Towards the integration of niche and network theories. *Trends in Ecology and Evolution* 33:287–300. doi:10.1016/j.tree.2018.01.007

Gravel, D., C. Albouy, and W. Thuiller. 2016. The meaning of functional trait composition of food webs for ecosystem functioning'. *Philosophical Transactions of the Royal Society B: Biological Sciences* 371:20150268. doi:10.1098/rstb.2015.0268

Grime, J. P. 1977a. Evidence for the existence of three primary strategies in plants and its relevance to ecological and evolutionary theory. *The American Naturalist* 111:1169–1194. doi:10.1086/283244

Grime, J. P. 1997b. Biodiversity and ecosystem function: The debate deepens. *Science* 277:1260–1261. doi:10.1126/science.277.5330.1260

Grime, J. P. 1998. Benefits of plant diversity to ecosystems: Immediate, filter and founder effects. *Journal of Ecology* 86:902–910. doi:10.1046/j.1365-2745.1998.00306.x

Hector, A., B. Schmid, C. Beierkuhnlein, et al. 1999. Plant diversity and productivity experiments in European grasslands. *Science* 286:1123–1127. doi:10.1126/science.286.5442.1123

Helmus, M. R., W. Keller, M. J. Paterson, et al. 2010. Communities contain closely related species during ecosystem disturbance. *Ecology Letters* 13:162–174. doi:10.1111/j.1461-0248.2009.01411.x.

Hobbie, S. E. 1992. Effects of plant species on nutrient cycling. *Trends in Ecology and Evolution* 7:336–339. doi:10.1016/0169-5347(92)90126-V

Hooper, D. U., E. C. Adair, B. J. Cardinale, et al. 2012. A global synthesis reveals biodiversity loss as a major driver of ecosystem change'. *Nature* 486:105–108. doi:10.1038/nature11118

Hooper, D. U., F. S. Chapin, J. J. Ewel, et al. 2005. Effects of biodiversity on ecosystem functioning: A consensus of current knowledge. *Ecological Monographs* 75:3–35. doi:10.1890/04-0922

Hubbell, S. P. 2001. *The unified neutral theory of biodiversity and biogeography.* Princeton: Princeton University Press.

Huston, M. A. 1997. Hidden treatments in ecological experiments: Re-evaluating the ecosystem function of biodiversity. *Oecologia* 110:449–460. doi:10.1007/s004420050180

Hutchinson, G. E. 1978. *An introduction to population ecology.* New Haven: Yale University Press.

Keddy, P. A. 1992. Assembly and response rules: Two goals for predictive community ecology. *Journal of Vegetation Science* 3:157–164. doi:10.2307/3235676

Kraft, N. J. B., P. B. Adler, O. Godoy, et al. 2015a. Community assembly, coexistence and the environmental filtering metaphor. *Functional Ecology* 29:592–599 doi:10.1111/1365-2435.12345

Kraft, N. J. B., O. Godoy, and J. M. Levine. 2015b. Plant functional traits and the multidimensional nature of species coexistence. *Proceedings of the National Academy of Sciences of the United States of America* 112:797–802. doi:10.1073/pnas.1413650112

Krebs, C. J. 2000. *Ecology: The experimental analysis of distribution and abundance,* fifth edn. San Francisco: Benjamin-Cummings Publishing Company.

Laughlin, D. C. 2014. Applying trait-based models to achieve functional targets for theory-driven ecological restoration. *Ecology Letters* 17:771–784. doi:10.1111/ele.12288

Laughlin, D. C., C. Joshi, P. M. van Bodegom, et al. 2012. A predictive model of community assembly that incorporates intraspecific trait variation. *Ecology Letters* 15:1291–1299. doi:10.1111/j.1461-0248.2012.01852.x

Lavelle, P., E. Blanchart, A. Martin, et al. 1993. A hierarchical model for decomposition in terrestrial ecosystems: Application to soils of the humid tropics. *Biotropica* 25:130–150. doi:10.2307/2389178

Lavorel, S., and E. Garnier. 2002. Predicting changes in community composition and ecosystem functioning from plant traits: Revisiting the Holy Grail. *Functional Ecology* 16:545–556. doi:10.1046/j.1365-2435.2002.00664.x

Lawton, J. H. 1999. Are there general laws in ecology? *Oikos* 84:177–192. doi:10.2307/3546712

Leibold, M. A., M. Holyoak, N. Mouquet, et al. 2004. The metacommunity concept: A framework for multi-scale community ecology. *Ecology Letters* 7:601–613. doi:10.1111/j.1461-0248.2004.00608.x

Li, S., M. W. Cadotte, S. J. Meiners, Z. Hua, et al. 2015. Species colonisation, not competitive exclusion, drives community overdispersion over long-term succession. *Ecology Letters* 18:964–973. doi:10.1111/ele.12476

Loreau, M., and A. Hector. 2001. Partitioning selection and complementarity in biodiversity experiments. *Nature* 412:72–76. doi:10.1038/35083573

Lotka, A. J. 1925. *Elements of physical biology*. Baltimore: Williams and Wilkins.

MacArthur, R. H. 1958. Population ecology of some warblers of northeastern coniferous forests. *Ecology* 39:599–619. doi:10.2307/1931600

MacArthur, R. H. 1972. *Geographical ecology: Patterns in the distribution of species*. Princeton: Princeton University Press.

MacArthur, R. H., and E. O. Wilson. 1967. *The theory of island biogeography*. Princeton: Princeton University Press.

MacDougall, A. S., B. Gilbert, and J. M. Levine. 2009. Plant invasions and the niche. *Journal of Ecology* 97:609–615. doi:10.1111/j.1365-2745.2009.01514.x

MacIvor, J. S., N. Sookhan, C. A. Arnillas, et al. 2018. Manipulating plant phylogenetic diversity for green roof ecosystem service delivery. *Evolutionary Applications* 11:2014–2024. doi:10.1111/eva.12703

Mackey, R. L, and D. J Currie. 2001. The diversity-disturbance relationship: Is it generally strong and peaked? Ecology 82:3479–3492.

Marjakangas, E.-L., G. Muñoz, S. Turney, et al. 2022. Trait-based inference of ecological network assembly: A conceptual framework and methodological toolbox. *Ecological Monographs* 92:e1502. doi:10.1002/ecm.1502

Mason, N. W. H., D. Mouillot, W. G. Lee, and J. B. Wilson. 2005. Functional richness, functional evenness and functional divergence: The primary components of functional diversity. *Oikos* 111:112–18. doi:10.1111/j.0030-1299.2005.13886.x

Mayfield, M. M., S. P. Bonser, J. W. Morgan, et al. 2010. What does species richness tell us about functional trait diversity? Predictions and evidence for responses of species and functional trait diversity to land-use change. *Global Ecology and Biogeography* 19:423–31. doi:10.1111/j.1466-8238.2010.00532.x

McGill, B. J. 2003. A test of the unified neutral theory of biodiversity. *Nature* 422:881–885. doi:10.1038/nature01583

McGill, B. J., B. J. Enquist, E. Weiher, and M. Westoby. 2006. Rebuilding community ecology from functional traits. *Trends in Ecology and Evolution* 21:178–185. doi:10.1016/j.tree.2006.02.002

McIntosh, R. P. 1986. *The background of ecology: Concept and theory*. Cambridge: Cambridge University Press.

Meiners, S. J., M. W. Cadotte, J. D. Fridley, et al. 2015. Is successional research nearing its climax? New approaches for understanding dynamic communities. *Functional Ecology* 29:154–164. doi:10.1111/1365-2435.12391

Mittelbach, G. G., C. F. Steiner, S. M. Scheiner, et al. 2001. What is the observed relationship between species richness and productivity? *Ecology* 82:2381–2396. doi:10.1890/0012-9658(2001)082[2381:WITORB]2.0.CO;2

Mittelbach, G. G., and B. J. McGill. 2019. *Community ecology*, second edn. Oxford: Oxford University Press. doi:10.1093/oso/9780198835851.001.0001

Naeem, S., L. J. Thompson, S. P. Lawler, et al. 1994. Declining biodiversity can alter the performance of ecosystems. *Nature* 368:734–737. doi:10.1038/368734a0

Nicolson, M., and R. P. McIntosh. 2002. H. A. Gleason and the individualistic hypothesis revisited. *The Bulletin of the Ecological Society of America* 83:133–142.

Niiniluoto, I. 2019. Scientific progress. In *The Stanford encyclopedia of philosophy*, ed. E. N. Zalta, Winter 2019 edn. Stanford: Metaphysics Research Lab, Stanford University. https://plato.stanford.edu/archives/win2019/entries/scientific-progress/ (accessed 23 December 2022).

O'Brien, M. J., B. M. J. Engelbrecht, J. Joswig, et al. 2017. A synthesis of tree functional traits related to drought-induced mortality in forests across climatic zones. *Journal of Applied Ecology* 54:1669–1686. doi:10.1111/1365-2664.12874

Odum, E. P. 1953. *Fundamentals of ecology.* Philadelphia: W. B. Saunders.

Oxford University Press. 2022. *Oxford English dictionary.* https://www.oed.com/ (accessed 12 December 2022)

Pacala, S., and A. P. Kinzig. 2013. Introduction to theory and the common ecosystem model. In *The functional consequences of biodiversity,* eds. S. Pacala, A. P. Kinzig, and G. D. Tilman, 169–174. Princeton: Princeton University Press. doi:10.1515/9781400847303.169

Peters, R. H. 1980. Useful concepts for predictive ecology. *Synthese* 43:257–269.

Peters, R. H. 1991. *A critique for ecology.* Cambridge: Cambridge University Press.

Plas, F. van der, T. Schröder-Georgi, A. Weigelt, et al. 2020. Plant traits alone are poor predictors of ecosystem properties and long-term ecosystem functioning. *Nature Ecology and Evolution* 4:1602–1611. doi:10.1038/S41559-020-01316-9

Ponisio, L. C., F. S. Valdovinos, K. T. Allhoff, et al. 2019. A network perspective for community assembly. *Frontiers in Ecology and Evolution* 7. doi:10.3389/fevo.2019.00103

Poorter, H., U. Niinemets, N. Ntagkas, et al. 2019. A meta-analysis of plant responses to light intensity for 70 traits ranging from molecules to whole plant performance. *New Phytologist* 223:1073–1105. doi:10.1111/nph.15754

Popper, K. 1959. *The logic of scientific discovery,* second edn. London: Routledge. doi:10.4324/9780203994627

Preston, F. W. 1960. Time and space and the variation of species. *Ecology* 41:612–627. doi:10.2307/1931793

Ricklefs, R. 2008. Disintegration of the ecological community. *The American Naturalist* 172:741–750. doi:10.1086/593002

Ricklefs, R., and R. Relyea. 2018. *Ecology: The economy of nature.* New York: Macmillan.

Schröter, C., and O. Kirchner. 1896. *Die vegetation des bodensees.* Kommissionsverlag der Schriften der Vereins für Geschichte des Bodensees und seiner Umgebung von J. T. Stettner.

Seibold, S., M. W. Cadotte, J. S. MacIvor, et al. 2018. The necessity of multitrophic approaches in community ecology. *Trends in Ecology and Evolution* 33:754–764. doi:10.1016/j.tree.2018.07.001

Shipley, B. 2016. *Cause and correlation in biology: A user's guide to path analysis, structural equations and causal inference with R.* Cambridge: Cambridge University Press.

Shrader-Frechette, K. 2001. Non-indigenous species and ecological explanation. *Biology and Philosophy* 16:507–519. doi:10.1023/A:1011953713083

Simberloff, D. 1980. A succession of paradigms in ecology: Essentialism to materialism and probabilism. *Synthese* 43:3–39. doi:10.1007/BF00413854

Sims, P. L., and J. S. Singh. 1978. The structure and function of ten western North American grasslands: III. Net primary production, turnover and efficiencies of energy capture and water use. *Journal of Ecology* 66:573–597. doi:10.2307/2259152

Smith, F. A., S. K. Lyons, S. K. M. Ernest, and J. H. Brown. 2008. Macroecology: More than the division of food and space among species on continents. *Progress in Physical Geography: Earth and Environment* 32: 115–138. doi:10.1177/0309133308094425

Smith, T. M., and R. L. Smith. 2014. *Elements of ecology,* ninth edn. Boston: Pearson.

Spalding, V. M. 1909. *Distribution and movements of desert plants.* Washington: Carnegie Institution.

Spehn, E. M., A. Hector, J. Joshi, et al. 2005. Ecosystem effects of biodiversity manipulations in European grasslands. *Ecological Monographs* 75:37–63. doi:10.1890/03-4101

Stein, A., K. Gerstner, and H. Kreft. 2014. Environmental heterogeneity as a universal driver of species richness across taxa, biomes and spatial scales. *Ecology Letters* 17:866–880. doi:10.1111/ele.12277

Thienemann, A. 1918. Lebensgemeinschaft und lebensraum. *Naturwissenschaftliche Wochenschrift* 17:282–290.

Tilman, D., S. S. Kilham, and P. Kilham. 1982. Phytoplankton community ecology: The role of limiting nutrients. *Annual Review of Ecology and Systematics* 13:349–372.

Tilman, D., D. Wedin, and J. Knops. 1996. Productivity and sustainability influenced by biodiversity in grassland ecosystems. *Nature* 379:718–720. doi:10.1038/379718a0

Vellend, M. 2016. *The theory of ecological communities.* Princeton: Princeton University Press. doi:10.1515/9781400883790

Vellend, M., L. Baeten, I. H. Myers-Smith, et al. 2013. Global meta-analysis reveals no net change in local-scale plant biodiversity over time. *Proceedings of the National Academy of Sciences of the United States of America* 110:19456–19459. doi:10.1073/pnas.1312779110

Vitousek, P. M., and W. A. Reiners. 1975. Ecosystem succession and nutrient retention: A hypothesis. *BioScience* 25:376–381. doi:10.2307/1297148

Volterra, V. 1931. *Leçons sur la théorie mathématique de la lutte pour la vie.* Paris: Gauthier-Villars et cie.

Wardle, D. A. 1999. Is 'sampling effect' a problem for experiments investigating biodiversity-ecosystem function relationships? *Oikos* 87:403–407. doi:10.2307/3546757

Warming, E. 1925. *Oecology of plants: An introduction to the study of plant-communities.* Oxford: Oxford University Press.

Webb, C. O. 2000. Exploring the phylogenetic structure of ecological communities: An example for rain forest trees. *The American Naturalist* 156:145–55. doi:10.1086/303378

Weiher, E., and A. Keddy. 1995. Assembly rules, null models, and trait dispersion: New questions from old patterns. *Oikos* 74:159–164. doi:10.2307/3545686

Westoby, M. 1998. A leaf-height-seed (LHS) plant ecology strategy scheme. *Plant and Soil* 199:213–227. doi:10.1023/A:1004327224729

Whittaker, R. H. 1956. Vegetation of the Great Smoky Mountains. *Ecological Monographs* 26:2–80. doi:10.2307/1943577

Whittaker, R. H. 1960. Vegetation of the Siskiyou Mountains, Oregon and California. *Ecological Monographs* 30:279–338. doi:10.2307/1943563

10

Effective ecology

ROGER COUSENS

HOW TO INCREASE THE EFFECTIVENESS OF ECOLOGICAL RESEARCH

It would be great to finish with a chapter that gives instructions, a recipe or a 'road map' to success: follow these steps and everyone will be the ultimate, effective ecologist... But no! The many factors that make ecology difficult will persist and progress will always be hard. There are no magic recipes for success in ecology, despite the prevalence of popular research techniques in our publications! The approach required depends on each researcher's aim in any particular instance, but it is possible to identify generally good and bad research practices, and to provide some guidance.

Problem-solving requires a knowledge of what the problems are and it requires vigilance; critique needs to become a habit. That is why the book's authors have identified the *sorts of problems* that face us, and the hurdles that we must attempt to overcome, rather than providing specific *solutions* to the problems. Some of the hurdles may be overcome by a combination of skill, ingenuity, critical evaluation and good research design. Different researchers may identify different solutions, but many will be only partially effective. There is no perfect solution and good judgement is required to achieve even partial insight. Some barriers may be insurmountable (at least for now): we must identify these and not waste time on misguided research and misleading inferences.

A more critical approach to ecology should achieve more effective research. Stronger criticism of ourselves and of others may be the best recipe for effective ecology. By questioning everything, perhaps against our instincts to trust and respect our peers, we are more likely to identify what is holding us back. Although a piece of research may appear good and interesting, issues may become apparent upon closer scrutiny. It is not a case of trying to find faults, but of finding a better way, a way of answering a question more effectively. For example, a particular study may lack certain approaches that were beyond the skills of the researchers; this could be resolved by finding collaborators who have those skills.

As we discussed in Chapter 2, Ecology evolves as the outcome of the behaviours of the individual researchers. Therefore, we need to examine how individuals make project design decisions. For simplicity, consider design as three phases: goals (the outcomes sought); actions (our *modi operandi*); and application (how we proceed with actions). As discussed in Chapter 2, however, the evolution of Ecology into its current form is embedded in and constrained by the multilayer network that is Ecology and all the interactions it includes (Figure 2.2). We must therefore consider all the various layers and nodes in the network and determine how they can be modified to make the whole system more effective.

Although the authors of the book are all proud of what Ecology has achieved, and confident in its

DOI: 10.1201/9781003314332-10

ability to deliver excellence, we are also certain that ecology can be more effective; it is not ineffective currently, but it could be better. The question is: how?

WHAT WE SEEK TO ACHIEVE

In *The Role of Critique in Science* in Chapter 1, we argued that the effectiveness of a project should be evaluated based on its goals. We did not suggest that merely having a goal *will* result in better research outcomes, but goal orientation in planning research makes sense. It seems logical to say *'this is what I want to achieve, and this set of actions appears the most likely to succeed'*. The alternative is to believe that following a program of habitual actions based on experience will, somehow, lead to benefits. Many ecologists have built successful careers on this latter model. Goal-orientated research does not necessarily produce outcomes that are narrower; and both approaches can lead to unexpected spin-offs. An explicit goal provides greater likelihood that the outcomes include those intended.

There are practical reasons why good intentions to be goal-driven may not reach fruition. One is funding. Resources are limited and usually competitive. Do we determine our scientific goal, work out the budget required and then try to find that funding? The resource requirement may be beyond the limits of granting agencies or the project may not fit their criteria. Unconventional (for scientists) entrepreneurial, lobbying and collaboration skills may be required to find atypical funding. The effort required may be great, but a rare success may be worth the time invested. This is how the CERN and Deep Space networks came about. It is also how we need to proceed if ecological research is to be internationally coordinated and funded to tackle the most important goals. The alternative is to start with the budget (e.g. an agency's project funding limit) and design a project with an objective that fits the budget. The purse limits the proposal scope, but success rates can still be low. This is the way many of us play the funding game. It can provide scientifically valuable research, but probably not be what we really need.

Most ecologists have some idea of an end-point for their research, perhaps in their subconscious, but it may not be explicit, perhaps because it is rarely given the opportunity to develop. Early on in our careers our approaches to research are determined for us. Initially, we inherit (or accept) a research style from our supervisors and bosses, but over time, we gain more flexibility and respond to other influences. We are influenced most by those whose research impresses us, those who judge our work and those who pay for our research (usually the same bodies that set the criteria on which we are judged). It seems quite likely that these people will not be goal-orientated in the same way and we act accordingly and conservatively. The *status quo* is maintained. Under a system of passive diffusion of ideas, even the most influential goal-driven research will take a long time to change researcher behaviour.

So... How could the Ecology network and its components become more goal-orientated?

If funding agencies were to ask researchers for explicit long-term goals for their programs and not just the expectations for current projects, then the applicants and reviewers would react accordingly. Researchers would set explicit goals for peers to adjudicate (see *Ecological goals* in Chapter 1). Moreover, if the agency's priorities specified types of *outcome*, not just fields of activity, very different projects would be submitted. For example, rather than broad 'research on ecological aspects of climate change', the agency could specify mitigation options for known climate impacts. Such a shift in policy would require a clear and radical decision by a leader with authority who understood the benefits of goal-setting.

Another layer in the ecological network is our professional societies. Could these play a part in encouraging more goal-focused research? While societies fill many valuable roles, including knowledge dissemination, they have generally not played a role in setting the scientific agenda. One exception was a survey, with repeated rounds of voting and discussion, conducted by the British Ecological Society (Sutherland et al. 2013) which produced a list of 100 'questions of fundamental importance', divided into seven subject areas. We can imagine a similar exercise focusing on the goals to be achieved. More recently, that same society has been undertaking a process *'to develop a unified community vision of the grand challenges for ecology and how best these can be met'* (British Ecological Society 2022). Societies could also have influence on behaviours through themed symposia in their conferences or through plenary sessions addressed by leading exponents of goal-focused research.

Finally, and most importantly, we are influenced by active discourse with others in our field. Workshops have a long tradition in ecology, often including formal presentations and posters, but with time allocated to the exploration and synthesis of ideas. Typically, workshops produce lists of future research opportunities (i.e. things to *do*). Sets of goals (to *achieve*) and challenges to peers are less common outputs. Conventional workshops can be transformed into effective debates about goals and challenges; it just needs a different philosophy from the organisers. The Andina workshops (Cousens 2017), which were mentioned in the Preface, were set up to provide an environment for open debate, with an emphasis on bringing together early-career and more experienced researchers. They are always over-subscribed. Up to five discussion papers have been published from each of the six biennial workshops thus far and feedback from attendees has been outstanding. Another example of goal-orientated workshops is the 'sandpits' scheme run over five days by the Engineering and Physical Sciences Research Council in the UK (UK Research and Innovation 2021). That program uses lateral thinking and radical approaches to address research challenges, and the outcomes can include funding for projects.

A perennial problem for all debate-style workshops is funding. They lack economy of scale and have limits on attendance; to be effective, they need more than just one or two days. Each Andina meeting faces a funding challenge that must be solved. Some ecological societies provide limited funds for short meetings of members' working groups, but their scope is often very restricted. Other workshops are *ad hoc*, organised by informal networks of colleagues, perhaps with funding included in a research grant (and, sadly, often by invitation only). NCEAS, one of the most successful long-term centres for ecological synthesis (and discourse: Halpern et al. 2020), received core funding from the National Science Foundation in the US from 1995 to 2010. This, and similar centres, have been forced to close or to develop alternative and often less secure funding (Baron et al. 2017). If ecologists are to take goal-setting workshops seriously, we need organisations, whether societies or government agencies, to recognise them as priorities and to allocate sufficient funds. This may divert some of the limited resources from actual research, but it may prove more effective in the long term.

HOW WE GO ABOUT ECOLOGY

Ecology is a multidimensional science: there are many things that we do and many ways we do them. There has never been a comprehensive analysis of everything that we do, only restricted discussions on particular methods or broad issues. In a survey of almost 111,000 articles in 136 journals, Carmel et al. (2013) classified research as observational (59%), experimental (28%), modelling (12%), analysis of existing data (9%) or problem-solving (17%) [note that some articles were scored in multiple categories]. Other studies have focused on the topics we research and the vocabulary we use (Andersen et al. 2021), rather than how we do the research. This section will focus on just three overlapping and common approaches to ecological research: our acceptance of weak inference from descriptive observations; research that focuses on system outputs rather than ecological processes; and the collation of evidence that supports a particular proposition.

Descriptive ecology

Ecology's history began with description. This is how we generate our ideas and hypotheses: we collect data, summarise and analyse them as best we can and then speculate on explanations. Only then can we start to test our ideas.

Carmel et al. (2013) found that descriptive studies using data exploration methods still represent over half of published papers. Indeed, the 'new era' of data-driven ecology (McCallen et al. 2019), big data and deep learning (Guo et al. 2020) is still a form of description although the wealth of detail makes more perceptive analysis possible. Remember, however, that big ecological data sets are usually full of autocorrelation, in both space and time, and autocorrelation can strongly influence both analysis and interpretation (Dale and Fortin 2014). All that really differs from past efforts are the tools now at our disposal. Ecology has maintained an approach in which the analysis of pattern still dominates as an attempt to understand process (McCallen et al. 2019).

As Ecology matures in seeking insights more definite than speculation, efforts may swing to more investigative approaches, using experiments and modelling, but descriptive work still dominates, in part because the natural world is so diverse that there are many things not yet described. Plausible explanations are developed based on intuition or expert opinion, on comparisons with other systems (perhaps including experimental results) or from detecting relationships between variables (such as correlations). Although correlation is limited in determining causal relationships for several reasons, many ecologists are happy to leave their research at that point (see Chapter 7 for prime examples of this). The correlation gives them a *plausible* explanation for their observations and that is sufficient; or perhaps any further progress is beyond their technical or resource capabilities.

Predictive capacity is a valid goal and does not *ipso facto* require a knowledge of mechanisms (see Chapter 3) and so we cannot fault those who seek to establish it through correlation. Indeed, it can be argued that our insistence on explanations has been somewhat counter-productive (Currie 2018). Many years of research can lead to only a partial understanding of mechanisms, with a long list of caveats and little ability to predict. The search for mechanistic understanding will never be complete and will always require further work. Correlations, however, offer an ability to predict statistically even in the absence of understanding. Provided that the limitations of the approach are fully appreciated and nothing changes, we should be able to develop some robust rules and generalisations through descriptive data alone. One major concern is that correlative prediction requires stationarity (i.e. that statistical properties of data do not change over space or time). If the processes are not stationary, we need to know more than correlation, otherwise our conclusions can be spurious and unreliable.

If we want to progress from speculation about mechanisms towards better justified, confident statements about ecological processes, then we need to proceed through a sequence of steps of questions and answers (as discussed in Chapter 6 and depicted in Figures 1.1b and c). Correlations generate hypotheses, which may be followed up experimentally to put together a stronger body of evidence (regardless of whether a hypothesis can be categorically proven or falsified; see Chapter 3). Models can put together the available information in ways that reflect a belief about how the system works and they, too, can produce hypotheses that can be followed up. However, in a set of five major ecological journals Grace (2019) reported that only 25% of articles used the word 'hypothesis', but that the proportion had increased from 15% over a 30-year period (Grace was responding to a criticism made of ecology by Peters (1991)). Betts et al. (2021) concluded that the frequency of hypotheses in eco-evolutionary publications over the same period was low and static. Based on this scant data, the testing of hypotheses does not seem to feature highly in ecological research, at least not explicitly stated.

The problem is that we tend to leave our search for explanations merely started: we collect descriptive data, we analyse them and we make an inference. Period. We are content to stop where we have an idea that is plausible, based on the limited available data; it may be correct but has not been rigorously investigated with all the methods available.

Alternative explanations for observations may not have been considered, or not yet, and papers describing these incomplete searches are published in many journals: not the best journals, perhaps, but the sheer number bias Ecology's literature. Compare this with the standard of evidence in a legal system. If we gave expert evidence in a court case and we could only say that our *'data suggest'* or that *'there is a correlation'*, does this fulfil the criterion of *'beyond reasonable doubt'*? No... and any student of logic would point out the weakness of such statements; as scientists, we need to raise our standards for the strength of evidence in ecological research.

Black box ecology

Much of ecology takes what we might call a 'black box' approach to science. It is indirect. We focus on the *outputs* of a system and then try to work backwards, attempting to postulate the processes inside the system which might explain our observations, but those processes are essentially unknown to us (Figure 10.1). We can't see inside the box! We can change the inputs to the system and observe the way that the outputs change; this also might help us to understand how the system works. The alternative to a black box approach is a mechanistic approach, in which we observe the processes directly and try to build a picture (perhaps also a model) of the system itself: the 'nuts and bolts'

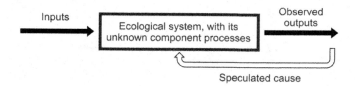

Figure 10.1 The black box approach to ecological understanding.

of the system's internal structure and how it is expected to function. Peters (1991) criticises this treating of ecological systems as if they are human-engineered machines, which they are not. They are more complex. Thus, our attempts to envisage the workings of ecological systems are doomed to be incomplete or naïve; again, a lack of stationarity in the processes we cannot see may threaten any understanding we have developed.

The problem with a black box approach is that we never know how far from reality our explanations are because we cannot examine the processes in the system. Our speculations provide explanations for the outcomes that may be sufficient but are not necessary. Other explanations are possible. Consider the example of the evolution of increased competitive ability (EICA) in invasive species. With this hypothesis, Blossey and Notzold (1995) suggested that the removal of a selection pressure on the invader that is present in the region of origin, such as specialist herbivores, should allow the evolution of traits to deal with new selection pressures in a new region. The removal of one selection pressure frees resources to address others. Specifically, *'In the absence of herbivores, selection will favour genotypes with improved competitive abilities and reduced resource allocation to herbivore defence.'* Several researchers then looked for examples in which invasive plants were larger (size considered a surrogate for competitive ability) in introduced regions than in their putative source regions. The examples that were found were taken as evidence for the plausibility of the EICA hypothesis.

There are, however, other reasons for plants to grow bigger in their new locations, as Colautti et al. (2009) showed, such as adaptation to different growing season length. Even random processes, founder effects and genetic drift could produce some introductions that are larger than in the native region (and some that are smaller). Meta-analyses of similar data sets for native and introduced locations, whether they are biomass or competitive ability (by valid measurement, see Zhang et al. 2018), may show that individuals in introduced populations are often larger and from that point of view *could* support EICA, but they do not eliminate other possible mechanisms.

Meta-analyses may also be subject to a kind of sampling bias. It may have been easier to publish apparent support for EICA than studies that are non-significant or seem to contradict the hypothesis. For each suspected EICA case, we need to see evidence for the other conditions stipulated in the hypothesis: that the selection for herbivore defence is reduced, and defensive structures or secondary compounds are reduced in the introduced populations. These conditions must be all tested at the same time and in the same systems. We are trying to infer adaptation from a long-past event, and we require the assumption that the current post-adaptation introduced genotype's mean phenotypes were originally identical to the current native-range genotypes that are being compared. This assumption might be false. Here is another case where non-stationarity in the form of unseen changes over time can undo our conclusions.

Black box approaches have also dominated ecological research on competition. Competition is defined as the differential access to resources in limited supply. Ecologists rarely investigate the processes that occur between individuals at a physiological level (i.e. their use of the resources in different aspects of development). Typically, we vary the intensity of competition by either altering the density and frequencies of individuals of coexisting species (resource demand) or the availability of particular resources in their shared supplies (resource supply). We then measure reproductive output and the rate of population growth. In mixtures of plant species, it was common to measure biomass and to calculate indices based on relative performances in mixture and in monoculture as surrogate measures of competition. Jolliffe (2001) listed more than 25 such indices. There was an intense argument about which indices to use and how such experiments should be conducted (see also Box 1.2), and attempts to interpret indices in quasi-scientific terms such as 'aggressivity'.

There are some examples of competition research where the physiological processes themselves were studied, measured and modelled, particularly in the eco-physiological modelling of competing weed-crop systems (Kropff and van Laar 1993; Louarn and Song 2020), but these never became popular beyond agricultural systems. The tradition of focusing on outputs and trying to infer processes continues in studies of species introductions into complex assemblages of plants and functional types.

Seed dispersal is one area in which there has been a swing from black box ecology to more mechanistic approaches. Models of dispersal derived from basic fluid mechanics have been developed over several decades, culminating in the work of Nathan and Katul (2005). These studies focus on movement of individuals from point sources under specified conditions (projections as defined in Chapters 7 and 8, not predictions). A realisation from this work is that to predict dispersal distances requires an understanding of 'movement ecology' (Nathan et al. 2008), such as the rules governing the locomotion of an animal and meteorological vectors affecting dispersal. This has much in common with another process-based modelling approach, agent-based modelling (McLane et al. 2011), and is highly relevant to wildlife conservation (Fraser et al. 2018).

This discussion of the limitations of black box ecology may sound like a plea to re-establish physiological ecology into mainstream ecology. Perhaps and perhaps not! The black box approach may well be holding the discipline back in many areas. In cases like EICA, we will only make progress by the direct study of the evolutionary and ecological processes, rather than system outputs such as phenology, moving from speculation to evidence-informed predictions. Many ecological systems, however, might be too complex to allow anything other than a black box approach as Peters (1991) argued and which we hinted in Chapter 2 in discussing complex multilayer networks. Many concepts that have dominated community ecology relate to attempts to predict system output or overall behaviour from its structure. In community ecology (see Chapter 9) progress has been made by moving the focus from the description of community structure towards understanding processes.

Peters (1991) suggested that we might 'operationalise' ecological concepts by placing them within testable theories, thus connecting them to hypotheses about the underlying processes. Ecosystems have long been studied at a process level, using simplifications that permit a focus on the physical-chemical processes rather than communities' complexities.

Collection of supporting evidence

Ecologists have been engaged in a long struggle to find rules that are sufficiently general to apply throughout ecology (see discussions in Chapters 3, 5 and 9): whether or not these rules are laws of nature (we'll postpone that discussion). If our ideas, derived from many studies in different systems and locations, are truly sound, then they should apply across the variation found in the natural world. General rules would allow us to predict function in systems not yet studied. In recent decades, meta-analyses (with their own, formal methodology) have tried to establish whether or not there is evidence for such generalisations. Studies announce (or deny!) generalisations in their titles: *'Climate niche shifts are common in invasive species'* (Atwater at al. 2017); *'Climate niche shifts are rare among terrestrial plant invaders'* (Petitpierre et al. 2012). Generalisations have even been boldly announced on the results of a single study, encouraged by the modern trend towards 'banner headlines' for article titles.

It is no surprise that some ecologists hunt the literature for studies that support their favoured idea, based on the thought that if most studies support the generalisation, it has greater credence, even if the support is not universal. The term *context dependency* refers to the fact that different systems or different regions can give different results (Chapter 5), but this overall vote-counting procedure risks misleading the ecology community. Logical problems emerge if it seems that not all studies have equal weighting.

A well-known source of error is 'confirmation bias', where studies in favour of the expectation are collected, but contrary studies are ignored or discredited. The proportion of studies that support the expectation will be overestimated. This bias may be inadvertent: even if a meta-analysis does its best to access all published studies, there may well be an under-representation of contrary studies in the literature. It has always been easier to get a positive (statistically significant) result published in a journal ('publication bias'), rather than an unclear (non-significant) or contrary (significant) result. Confirmation bias can also enter into individual studies when researchers expect to see a particular outcome and their observations become biased. Examples have been suspected and reported particularly in animal behaviour research (Marsh and Hanlon 2007).

Something similar to confirmation bias occurs when the attention of the observer is caught by exceptions and these become overemphasised. The statement that '*hybridisation is an important factor influencing adaptation in invasive species*', for example, is based on an observation that several significant invasions have involved hybridisation. If 'important' is treated as synonymous with 'often', depending on the definitions of 'often' or 'common', it may overstate the situation.

How can we improve what we do?

As in other walks of life, some of us are more adept at difficult things than others, and so there are a range of standards of ecological research. A systematic appraisal of our research outputs, if that were possible, would be unlikely to reveal the greatest frequency in the 'most outstanding' category. There would probably be a broad spread, perhaps with a significant proportion being far from the best possible (as has been shown in surveys of our applications of particular techniques). Even the best products of the most lauded ecologists will not be perfect; like the rest of us, they are trying to find their way in an inexact, complicated discipline. Some will choose one approach, some another; and each approach will have limitations and may produce different interpretations of the results. While the best studies are praised, many lesser studies also provide worthwhile information and are published, and our emerging scientists may be tempted to see the norm, rather than the very best, as the benchmark.

We can warn our colleagues of potential problems in ecological methods. Those practices that are regarded as strong or weak can be highlighted through education and communication, but for these efforts to be effective, receptivity is crucial. There must be a general appreciation by ecologists that suboptimal research is common and that we – not someone else – need to take action. Will the

community of proud practitioners, whose research is published and widely read, accept this admission of weakness and embrace the need for concerted action? Both denial and ignorance are likely to stifle uptake of even the best advice.

Even when evidence of poor standards has been widely communicated (such as the poor standards of species distribution modelling or of statistical analysis and interpretation), remedial action has not followed. The publication of awareness papers in journals that highlight and explain the problems, and even the adoption of best practice guides by journals, seems to be ineffective in inspiring action by editorial boards (see Chapter 7).

The inability of the peer review system to filter out poor research practices and to discriminate between good and bad use of research techniques has been widely and frequently described.

Despite the huge investment of time in the peer review process, its statistical power is poor because of high variances among reviewers and small sample sizes (Cousens 2019). It is difficult to see how to improve the peer review system without greatly increasing our investment in it. It may always be an ineffective sieve for weak research because those assessing the work have the same level of expertise as those whose work is being judged. In the case of journal articles, the research has been completed, and so there is no opportunity for formative evaluation and iterative improvement. What will be published in the future reflects the standards of what is already published and not what the standards ought to be.

Rather than try to solve the problem too late in the process, can we be proactive? Perhaps we need a new approach to how the discipline of Ecology is taught. In the limited curriculum time available, we tend to focus on the state of ecological knowledge, but founded on textbooks that had their first drafts decades ago, often with methods and case studies that have historical rather than current relevance. It is important for students to have an appreciation for the historical development of ecology, so that they can learn from how our predecessors made progress and so that they can appreciate how that history constrains current thinking. Practical classes give students limited experience with a few classical and experiments and procedures. It may be that we need a new curriculum that focuses on how to conduct effective ecological research.

Many scientists have argued that we learn best from our mistakes, not just from our successes. We need to open students' eyes early, to appreciate how easy it is to do ecology *poorly*. It would be useful to have resource material that illustrates poor practices and how methods can be misused and results misinterpreted, and examples of critiques of published research. Resource material could also explore what we might do, and the various choices and compromises we have to make when the real world departs from the ideal.

AND, FINALLY, SO WHAT?

If you were expecting this book to tell you how the entire discipline of Ecology can be made more effective, we will have disappointed you.

No matter how passionately some people call for new approaches to sweep through our discipline, that will not happen readily or swiftly. If it happens at all, it will take an extremely long time. The entrenched nature of our approaches and the complexity of Ecology's disciplinary network ensure lasting inertia. Our journals will continue to publish descriptive studies that barely touch the surface of a problem, with weak inferences and inconsistent quality control. On the other hand, Ecology will continue to be populated also by outstanding projects and syntheses of great depth and novel insight.

Rather than trying to set the entire ecological research world to rights, it is perhaps more a matter of altering the balance. We can do this by anticipating, recognising and addressing the discipline's weaknesses and broadening the appreciation of its strengths: by strengthening critique, discourse, communication and education. This still requires a groundswell of opinion that we need to do it. How will *that* be achieved?

Those who are interested in more altruistic actions, who are in privileged positions and with influence, need to pursue ways to make better education and training available, and to ensure that more of the appropriate opportunities are in place for all ecologists to synthesise, to challenge and to debate.

Collecting data is easy. Making speculations based on that data is easy. It will always be hard, however, to make significant intellectual progress in ecology, and it will always be harder for some of us than for others and in some fields of research than in others. It is the improvements in the individual actions of its practitioners, acting within and enabled by their multilayered network, that will result in more effective ecology. We need

more explicit goals, the right questions, the most effective actions, the right data, the right analyses and the right interpretations. This requires careful deliberation, common sense and something that we might consider art.

Significant change to standards in ecology requires appropriate attitudes:

- acceptance that we are not experts in everything, even in simple things that we do routinely (there is an ever-present danger that we will make mistakes)
- perception that we need help (and cultivate effective collaborations) and that we need to educate ourselves from the literature that indicates the best use and the misuse of our techniques
- recognition of the powers of critique applied to everything that we do and everything that we read and hear (Gide 1952: '*Believe those who are seeking the truth. Doubt those who find it.*')
- deliberately search for weaknesses in what we do or have done, rather than hoping that they will not be found
- preparedness to go against the trend of what our respected colleagues are doing
- realisation that we make assumptions (and use surrogates or other indirect approaches) in almost everything and that those assumptions need to be checked and shown to be appropriate
- recognition that black box approaches lead to weak inference and that we need to focus on biological, ecological or evolutionary processes and system function

Perhaps above all, we need to grasp the challenge *to raise our expectations, from the search for the merely plausible to the demonstration of the most probable* ('beyond reasonable doubt').

Plausible explanations may often turn out to be correct, but the most effective, highest quality science does not stop at initial investigations and first-pass conclusions. It applies the most appropriate subsequent methods to assemble the most comprehensive evidence that we can.

In following this path, we may cover less of nature's diversity, but the strength of our arguments and our progress on those things that we do study will be so much more powerful. We are more likely, in this way, to push the boundaries of our knowledge more effectively.

REFERENCES

Anderson, S. C., P. R. Elsen, B. B. Hughes, et al. 2021. Trends in ecology and conservation over eight decades. *Frontiers in Ecology and the Environment* 19:274–282. doi:10.1002/fee.2320

Atwater, D. Z., C. Ervine, and J. N. Barney. 2018. Climatic niche shifts are common in introduced plants. *Nature Ecology and Evolution* 2:34–43. doi:10.1038/s41559-017-0396-z

Baron, J. S., A. Specht, E. Garnier, et al. 2017. Synthesis centers as critical research infrastructure. *BioScience* 67:750–759. doi:10.1093/biosci/bix053

Betts, M. G., A. S. Hadley, D. W. Frey, et al. 2021. When are hypotheses useful in ecology and evolution? *Ecology and Evolution* 11:5762–5776. doi:10.1002/ece3.7365

Blossey, B., and R. Nötzold. 1995. Evolution of increased competitive ability in invasive non-indigenous plants: A hypothesis. *Journal of Ecology* 83:887–889.

British Ecological Society. 2022. Future of ecological research in the UK. https://www.britishecologicalsociety.org/policy/future-of-ecological-research-in-the-uk/ (accessed 27 October 2022).

Carmel, Y., R. Kent, A. Bar-Massada, et al. 2013. Trends in ecological research during the last three decades: A systematic review. *PLoS ONE* 8:e59813. doi:10.1371/journal.pone.0059813

Colautti, R. I., J. L. Maron, and S. C. H. Barrett. 2009. Common garden comparisons of native and introduced plant populations: Latitudinal clines can obscure evolutionary inferences. *Evolutionary Applications* 2:187–199. doi:10.1111/j.1752-4571.2008.00053.x

Cousens, R. 2017. Do we argue enough in ecology? *Bulletin of the British Ecological Society* 48:58–61.

Cousens, R. 2019. Why can't we make research grant allocation systems more consistent? A personal opinion. *Ecology and Evolution* 9:1536–1544. doi:10.1002/ece3.4855

Currie, D. J. 2019. Where Newton might have taken ecology. *Global Ecology and Biogeography* 28:18–27. doi:10.1111/geb.12842

Dale, M. R. T, and M.-J. Fortin. 2014. *Spatial analysis: A guide for ecologists*, 2nd edition. Cambridge: Cambridge University Press. doi:10.1017/CBO9780511978913

Felker-Quinn, E., J. A. Schweitzer, and J. K. Bailey. 2013. Meta-analysis reveals evolution in invasive plant species but little support for evolution of increased competitive ability (EICA). *Ecology and Evolution* 3:739–751. doi:10.1002/ece3.488

Fraser, K. C., K. T. A. Davies, C. M. Davy, et al. 2018. Tracking the conservation promise of movement ecology. *Frontiers in Ecology and Evolution* 6:150. doi:10.3389/fevo.2018.00150

Gide, A. 1952. *Ainsi-soit-il, ou: Les jeux sont faits.* Paris: Gallimard.

Grace, J. 2019. Has ecology grown up? *Plant Ecology and Diversity* 12:387–405. doi:10.1080/17550874.2019.1638464

Guo, Q., S. Jin, M. Li, et al. 2020. Application of deep learning in ecological resource research: Theories, methods, and challenges. *Science China Earth Sciences* 63:1457–1474. doi:10.1007/s11430-019-9584-9

Halpern, B. S., E. Berlow, R. Williams, et al. 2020. Ecological synthesis and its role in advancing knowledge. *BioScience* 70:1005–1014. doi:10.1093/biosci/biaa105

Jolliffe, P. A. 2001. The replacement series. *Journal of Ecology* 88:371–385. doi:10.1046/j.1365-2745.2000.00470.x

Kropff, M. J., and H. W. van Laar. 1993. *Modelling crop-weed interactions.* Wallingford: CAB International.

Louarn, G., and Y. Song. 2020. Two decades of functional–structural plant modelling: Now addressing fundamental questions in systems biology and predictive ecology. *Annals of Botany* 126:501–509. doi:10.1093/aob/mcaa143

Marsh, D. M., and T. J. Hanlon. 2007. Seeing what we want to see: Confirmation bias in animal behaviour research. *Ethology* 113:1089–1098. doi:10.1111/j.1439-0310.2007.01406.x

McCallen, E., J. Knott, G. Nunez-Mir, et al. 2019. Trends in ecology: Shifts in ecological research themes over the past four decades. *Frontiers in Ecology and the Environment* 17:109–116. doi:10.1002/fee.1993

McLane, A. J., C. Semeniuk, G. J. McDermid, et al. 2011. The role of agent-based models in wildlife ecology and management. *Ecological Modelling* 222:1544–1556. doi:10.1016/j.ecolmodel.2011.01.020

Nathan, R., and G. G. Katul. 2005. Foliage shedding in deciduous forests lifts up long-distance seed dispersal by wind. *Proceedings of the National Academy of Science of the United States of America* 102:8251–8256. doi:10.1073/pnas.050304810

Nathan, R., W. M. Getz, E. Revilla, et al. 2008. A movement ecology paradigm for unifying organismal movement research. *Proceedings of the National Academy of Science of the United States of America* 105:19052–19059. doi:10.1073/pnas.0800375105

Peters, R. F. 1991. *A critique for ecology.* Cambridge: Cambridge University Press

Petitpierre, B., C. Kueffer, O. Broennimann, et al. 2012. Climatic niche shifts are rare among terrestrial plant invaders. *Science* 335:1344–1348. doi:10.1126/science.121593

Sutherland, W. J., R. P. Freckleton, H. C. J. Godfray, et al. 2013. Identification of 100 fundamental ecological questions. *Journal of Ecology* 101:58–67. doi:10.1111/1365-2745.12025

UK Research and Innovation. 2021. Sandpits. https://beta.ukri.org/councls/epsrc/guidance-for-applicants/types-of-funding-we-offer/transformative-research/sardpits/ accessed 19 September 2022.

Zhang, Z., F. Zhou, X. Pan, et al. 2018. Evolution of increased intraspecific competitive ability following introduction: The importance of relatedness among genotypes. *Journal of Ecology* 107:387–395. doi:10.1111/1365-2745.13016

Index

abandonment 103, 110–111
abiotic niche 71
absence
    of data or information 119
    of evidence 109
accuracy 104, 127, 135–144
achievement 5–8, 145, 154, 174–175
adaptation 82–87, 112
adaptive
    loci 86
    management 139–143
    trait 87
adaptive behaviour 24–26
adaptive explanations 82–88
agent-based models 20, 129, 142, 178
aggressivity 178
Agouti gene 89
allele
    effect size 87
    frequency 86
alternative explanations 4, 14, 57, 131, 144, 176
altitudinal gradients 158
analysis of variance 51, 121
applied ecology 18
art in science 129
assembly/assemblages of communities 71, 155–165
assumptions 3, 42, 57, 60, 82, 97–122, 129–130, 160, 177, 180
    cost 122
    validity 121–122
autocorrelation 175

balancing selection 87
Bayesian
    belief networks 139

statistics 50–51, 55, 138
best practice 98
bias 75, 104–109, 115, 119, 128, 138, 177
    confirmation 4, 14, 131, 178
    from omitted variables 135
    publication 179
    sampling 105, 108, 111, 116
big data 175
Bioclim variables 105–107
bioclimatic models 112
biodiversity 37, 70
biogeography 154, 158
bioinformatics 87, 90
biological invasions 37, 67
bionomic variable 99, 100, 103
biophysical feedbacks 163
biosecurity 116
biotic interactions 103
black box ecology 176–178
bullying 5
busy work 4, 14

calibration of models 114
camouflage 89
candidate models 134
case studies 41, 131, 140, 144
causal
    factors 35, 86, 135
    hierarchies 163
    process 81
    relationships 36, 49, 82, 88, 163, 176
casual users of methods 98, 109
causality 14
centroid 104, 107–110
change of ecological practices 10, 15, 27, 28
chaos theory 134

citizen scientists 16, 104
climate 106
    availability 110–111
    average 104
    change 9, 36, 71, 105–106, 113–117, 128, 136–138, 174
    change impacts 174
    gradient 87
    layers 105
    matching 112
    niche 105, 110
    niche shifts 111, 178
    non-analogue 115
climax communities 156
Climond 106, 117
coat colour 89
coexistence
    of species 74, 99, 155–165
    theory 153, 158, 165
cognitive ability 1
collaboration 9, 28, 92, 129, 173–174, 180
colour phenotypes 90
common garden experiments 85–90
communication 15–28, 119, 142–143, 180
community
    assembly 63, 71, 76, 155, 158, 161–165
    biomass 164
    composition 155
    definition 154
    drift 158, 166
    ecology 152–153, 178
    horizontal 164
    structure 99, 157, 178
    vertical 164

183

184 Index

competition
    among organisms 177
    among researchers 9, 19, 174
competitive
    exclusion 99, 102, 162
    hierarchies 158, 162
complex systems 27, 33–35
complexity 1, 3, 22–26, 33, 42, 92, 137, 142, 151–154, 166
components of fitness 82–83, 86
composite variables 106–107
computational power 144
concept 3, 7, 14, 17–18, 20, 33, 100
    maps 23
    operationalisation of 178
confidence levels 4
confirmation bias 4, 14, 131, 178
conflict resolution 142
confounding factors 64, 67
confronting models with data 57
connectance 27, 34
connectivity 27
conservation 17, 37, 129
constructive criticism 5
context dependence 56, 63–76, 153–158, 166
    apparent 66–67, 74–75
    mechanistic 66–67, 74
    methodological 66, 75
context specificity 6
contingency 151–166
contingent generalisations 40
convergent evolution 162
copper toxicity/tolerance 90–91
correction for spatial scale 70–91
correlated walk 14, 55, 82–84, 176
correlations 14, 55, 82–84, 176
correlative species distribution models 112
covariance 83
COVID-19 137–138, 142–143
criticism 4–6, 14, 173
    constructive 5
    of ecology 13
critique 4–5, 10, 152–154, 161, 165, 173, 180
culturomic analysis 18
curriculum 179

Darwin 72–74
data
    absence 130

cleaning 104, 109, 114–115
distributions 60
exploration 18
for model validation 138
remedial actions 109
smoothing 108
training 137
databases 102, 105, 119
debate 4, 6, 175, 180
decision-making 140–141
decision science 130–145
decisions 9, 129, 138, 145
deduction 38–39
deductive-nomological model 39
deer mouse 89–90
default values 109, 117, 122
definition of ecology 2, 15
degrees of freedom 60
deleterious variation 87
demography 17
density-dependence 133, 157
descriptive studies 14, 175–176, 180
detection capacity 51
discourse 5–6, 175
disease transmission model 137
disorder 24–25
dispassionate scientists 8
dispersal
    ability 76, 129, 133, 178
    barriers 115
    limitation 101, 111
    realised 133
dissimilarity methods 113
disturbance-sensitivity 160
diversity 1, 24, 68, 99, 154–163
    gradients 151, 165
DNA sequence 87
drivers of ecological processes 69, 129–138, 155–157, 164
Duhem-Quine problem 42

eco-physiological modelling 178
ecological
    assembly 69
    effects 57
    niche model 112
    scale 63–76
    scientists 2
    societies 175
ecology
    network 23, 165

applied 7
definition 2
fundamental 7
economic impact 142
economics 17
ecosystem
    function 68, 153, 162–164
    processes 154–155
    services 17, 164
    stability 163
edge effects 68
editorial boards 120, 179
education 28, 179–180
effectiveness 5–6
effects
    detection of 55
    ecological 57
    fixed 50–59
    random 50–59
    size 55, 69
    strength 51
    trait 155, 163
elasticity 139
emergent processes 67
emigration 133
employers 20
El Niño 135
enemy
    pressure 72
    release 72, 111
    richness 72
energy flows 166
ensemble ecosystem model 143
envelope models 105, 112
environmental
    coordinates 106
    drivers 73
    filtering 73–74, 160–162
    gradients 154, 162
    layers 113
    space 100, 105
epistasis 83
errors 5, 104, 108, 114, 119–120, 138, 152
    extrapolation 135
    independence of 51
    in inference 97, 162
    in measurement 135
    statistical 13, 57
ethics 164
evapotranspiration 158
evenness 161

Index 185

evidence 1, 4–5, 17, 131, 176–180
evolution 17, 153
   of ecology 13–28
   of ideas 21
   of increased competitive
      ability 177
evolutionary ecology 17, 81–82, 91
expectations 43–44
experience 129
expert judgement/opinion 8, 130,
    139, 176
explanations 35–37, 57, 81, 176
extent 63–76
extinction 137, 159
extrapolation 117, 135
extremophile 102
extrinsic variables 136

fads 14
failures 127, 153, 160
false
   inference 98
   negatives 109
falsification 38–41, 152
fat-tailed dispersal kernels 133
feedback loops 24–25
feminist perspective 37
fitness 82–89, 157–158, 165
   components of 83, 86
   lifetime 83–84
   relative 82
   total lifetime 83, 86
fixed effects 50–59
flaws in research 13, 28, 57
food webs 68, 164
forecasting 127–144
fragmentation 68, 71
fraud 56
frequentist statistics 50–51
function 81
functional traits 157
functionality 154
fundamental
   ecology 7
   niche 99–111
funding agencies 20, 175

Gasterosteus 88–89
Gause's principle 160
gene flow 86–87
general
   laws 41, 178

theories 151
generalisable rules 128, 144
generalisations 17, 33–44, 75,
    151–166,
    176, 178
   accidental 39–40
generalised additive mixed
    models 54
generalised additive models 51,
    54, 136
genes
   candidate 86
   causal 86
genetic
   architecture 83, 87
   drift 87, 91
   mapping 83
   variation 17, 86, 89
genome wide association studies 87
genomics 86–87
geographic space 100
global change 17, 122, 141, 164
goal-orientated research 174–175
goals of research 5–10, 15, 41, 81,
    112, 132, 142, 145, 153,
    156, 173–176, 180
government 15, 142
grain 63–76
grand challenges 174
guesses 8, 130

habitat
   distribution model 112
   suitability 105, 114
hares 131–132
herbivore defence 177
heritability 84
hierarchies 154
hindcasting 137
historical
   contingency 86
   development 26
homogeneity of variance 51, 97
host-parasite interactions 67–69
human constructs 67, 97
humans as observers 1
hybrid lethality 90–91
hybridisation 179
hypotheses
   alternative 131, 164
   enemy release 72
   frequency of 176

generation of 81, 176
   mass-ratio 163
   paucity of 14
   revision 157
   testing 4, 39, 41, 55, 59, 158–164
hypothetico-deductivism 38

immigration 133, 159, 166
impact
   economic 142
   of research outputs 9, 50, 145
implied criticisms 14
improvement of quality 13
inbreeding 87
individualistic view of communities
    156–157
induction 38–39
inductive skeptics 39
inference 82, 97
   false 98
   weak 111
inferential robustness 45
instability 25
interacting factors 67
interactions 34, 55, 60, 73–74, 82,
    103, 154, 165
   competitive 74
   indirect 25
interdisciplinarity 18–19, 28
intermediate disturbance
    hypothesis 159–160
intervention 33–37, 127, 133, 137
intrinsic predictive ability 137
introduced species 98, 106
introgression 91
invasion
   success 75
   biological 37, 112
invasion paradox 64, 74–75
iterative near-term forecasting 139

key performance indicators 9
keystone species 36
knowledge 21, 41, 129
   graphs 23, 27

lag phases in invasions 106, 110
landscape heterogeneity 68
law of diminishing returns 4
laws 14–17, 33, 35, 39–40, 155, 178
least squares method 56
life histories 17, 68, 144

life history traits 6
lifetime
    fitness 83, 86
    reproductive success 83
limiting similarity 73, 162
linear regression 51
linkage 87, 91
    disequilibrium 83
    map 88
local adaptation 91, 111
logic 4, 15–16, 60, 109, 112, 131,
    134, 176
Lorenz attractor 134
Lynx 131–132

machine-learning methods 113
macroecology 153–155
male reproductive success 83
malleefowl 143–144
management
    advice 8
    decisions 128, 133–144
    options 139–141
    outcomes 8, 140
    of pests 17
    strategy evaluation 141
    wildlife 18
mass-ratio hypothesis 163
MaxEnt 113–118
maximum likelihood estimation
    54, 56
measurement error 135
mechanistic understanding
    135–136, 176–178
meerkats 136–137
memory 26
Mendelian crossing 90
Mendel's laws 40
meta-analysis 36, 41, 51, 60, 75, 109,
    121, 136, 159, 177–178
metabolic
    rates 105, 166
    relationships 40, 166
meta-community ecology 155,
    165–166
methodological pluralism 44–45
methods
    choice of 112–114
microclimate 104

microsatellite markers 88
Mimulus 90–91
minimum convex hull 108
misclassification of effects 51
mistakes 1, 3, 52, 97, 112, 127, 130,
    179–180
misuse of research methods 114,
    120–121, 180
mitigation 7, 129, 144, 174
model 49, 97, 112, 127
    agent-based 20, 129, 142, 178
    calibration 114–115
    complexity 137, 140, 144
    disease transmission 137
    fitting 57, 137
    goodness of fit 118
    mechanistic 134–135
    mixed effects 50–51, 54
    parameterisation 113, 136
    precision 128, 141
    predictions 127–145
    projections 113, 127, 136, 139, 178
    selection 50, 129
    simulations 129
    species distribution 36, 51, 71,
        106, 112–120, 179
    structure 130
    validation 130, 138–139
modifiable areal unit problem 70
modularity 24
molecular ecology 17, 92
monitoring 141
monkeyflower 90–91
Monte-Carlo simulation 138
mouse 89–90
movement ecology 178
multi-criteria decision analysis 142
multi-layered networks 22–27,
    173, 178
multiple regression 83
mutation 86–87
mutualism 100

n-dimensional hypervolume
    99–100, 106
native enemies 72
native range 102
natural experiments 102
natural history 16, 82, 84, 92

natural selection 17, 83, 87–89
naturalisation conundrum 64
NCEAS 175
negotiation theory 142
nestedness 24–25
net reproductive rate 100
network
    analysis 76
    complexity 24
    evolution of 27
    multi-layered 22–27, 173, 178,
        180
    stability 24
    structural properties 22
neutral
    processes 86
    theory 6, 155–157, 165–166
neutral-based dynamics 63
niche 99–101, 157, 162–164
    abiotic 71
    apparent shifts 109–116
    climatic 110, 178
    complementarity 102, 163
    conservatism 102
    differences 160–163
    Eltonian 99, 102, 164
    fundamental 99–103, 111
    Hutchinsonian 99, 164
    overlap 102
    potential 101
    realised 100–103, 107, 111–112
    shifts 98, 102–116, 178
    theory 102, 165–166
niche-based processes 63, 157
noise 35, 49–51, 57–59, 131, 144
non-analogue climates 103, 107, 115
non-expert/inexperienced users
    117–119
non-linear responses 24–25, 34
non-native species 68, 73
non-significant 51, 109
normal science 152
norms of ecological research 42, 179
nowcasting 139
null prediction 120
numerosity 25
nutrient
    cycling 158
    pools 161

oak 132–133
objectivity 5, 9, 37, 42–43
occurrence thinning 104, 116
occurrences 102, 105, 108, 112–114, 118
omitted variable bias 135
open data 121
operationalisation of concepts 178
opinions 3
optimal
    experimental design 141
    model complexity 44
outcomes of research 174
outliers 60, 104, 115
outputs 114
over-fitting 117
over-parameterisation 134
overlap 108

p-hacking 50
paradigm 43, 99, 152
    shift 10, 13, 166
parameter
    estimates 130, 136, 139
    values 133, 139
parameterisation 113, 137
parasite
    communities 68–69
    prevalence 73
paternity 83
path dependence 34
pattern 35, 40, 72, 151–166, 175
peer review 5, 8, 98, 119–121, 174, 179
periodicity 73
permutation test 108
Peromyscus 89–90
persistence 17, 157
pest resistance 138
phenotypes 82–83, 90
phenotypic
    convergence 87
    differences 88
    plasticity 111–112
    selection 84
phylogenetic
    constraint 102
    dissimilarity/distance/
        relatedness 73–74, 160
physics envy 14, 155

physiological variation 90
pigmentation 89–90
pioneering in invasions 103
pixel size 119
plausibility 138, 177
plausible explanations 176
pleiotropy 83, 87, 91
pluralistic strategy 45, 165–166
point sources 178
policies 15, 37, 128, 140–143
politics 9
polymerase chain reaction 137
pooling of data sets 115
population 98
    cycles 151
    dynamics 17
    genetics 87, 91, 100
    growth rates 17, 100
    models 17, 127–145
    regulation 136
    structure 87
potential distribution 114
power analysis 55, 143
pre-adaptation hypothesis 73–74
precision 105, 127–128, 135–144
predation 89
predator-prey cycles 131, 164
prediction 8, 10, 33–37, 113, 127–145, 156
    intrinsic ability 137
    quality 128
predictors 60, 135
preregistration of research 50, 54, 60
presence data 104
principle components analysis 106–107, 117
PRISMA 60
probable explanations 81
problem of induction 39
problem-solving 18, 173–175
process 131, 151–166
productivity 164
professional societies 174
progress in science 3, 7–8
project prioritisation protocol 139
projection 113, 127, 136, 139
propagule pressure 159
proxy variables 128, 135

pseudo-absence 116
pseudoreplication 57–59
pseudoscience 41
publication
    bias 179
    metrics 120
    pressure 120
purpose of research 5
Python 122

quality
    assurance 28
    control 3, 10, 14, 98, 104, 119, 122, 180
    of science 5
quantitative trait loci (QTL) 87–88, 90
questions
    in science 1, 3–4, 6, 9, 151, 176, 180
    unresolvable 18

R 55, 122
random
    effects 50–59
    walk 20, 24, 27
rapid prototyping 139, 142
raster data 105
rate of spread 132–133
rationality 43
realised
    niche 100–112
    dispersal distance 133
realism of models 105, 119, 128
reality 177
reasonable doubt 4, 176, 180
recessive alleles 88
reciprocal transplant experiments 86–91
recombination 86
Reid's paradox 131
relative fitness 82
repeated measures design 54
repetition of studies 50
replacement series 6
replication 51–59, 75
research
    design 98, 173
    waste 50
resolution 64, 105, 119

188 Index

resources
    biological 99–100
    for research 20
response trait 155
restricted maximum likelihood
        estimation 56
risk aversion 142
robustness of conclusions 45, 50
rules of assembly 155, 165

sample size 49
sampling
    bias 105, 108, 111, 116
    effort 108
    structure 60
sandpits 175
scale 154
    correction for 69
    dependence 63
    ecological 63–76
    mismatches 137
scaling
    differences 70
    laws 151, 166
scenario analysis 139–144
scenopoetic variable 99, 101, 103
science social space 19–20
scientific
    knowledge 41
    landscape 15
    method 38
    natural history 16
selection
    balancing 87
    bias 119
    directional 85
    phenotypic 84
    pressures 21
    stabilising 85
selective
    agents 91
    forces 158
    sweep 86
self-organisation 24, 26
semantics 99
seminars 92
sensitivity analysis 17, 139
sequencing 86
serendipity 8

signals 49–51
simulation 129
    Monte-Carlo 138
site-specificity 63
social
    components of systems 18
    contribution 7
    implications 9, 18
    relationships 20
society 3, 8, 156
sociopolitical constraints 115
software 117
    developers 122
    user-friendly 98, 112, 114, 122,
        129–130
soil colour 89
space
    geographic 102
space-for-time substitution 73
spatial
    attractors 20
    coordinates 106
    scale 63–76, 154
    turnover 76
species
    accumulation curves 70–71
    co-occurrence 6, 99, 155
    distribution models 36, 51, 71,
        106, 112–120, 179
    equivalence 157
    pool 159–162
    richness 69–75, 159–163
species-area relationships 40, 151,
        158–159
speculation 8, 180
stability of communities 103,
        154–156, 165
stakeholders 140–145
standards of rigour 1
standing genetic variation 89
stationarity 67, 176–177
statistical
    analysis 49, 179
    errors 13
    model 50, 59–60
    significance 50–59, 97, 108–109,
        179
stickleback 88–89
stochastic dominance 142

stochasticity 73, 157
stock and recruitment models 136
strategic adaptive management 141
structural hierarchies 26
structure of data 57–59
structured decision-making 141
sub-disciplines 15
subsamples 59–60
succession in communities 156, 162
super-organism view of
        communities 156
surrogates 3, 27, 100, 105–106,
        112–116, 135, 160, 177, 180
synthesis 4, 28, 63, 76, 175, 180

taxonomic resilience 41
technical ability 1
temporal variances 52
testable theories 14
theoretical
    ecology 7
    modelling 81, 84, 102, 128,
        130, 145
    population genetics 87
theories 7, 36, 131, 151–153, 178
theory 22, 127–133
theory-laden concepts 43
time series 131
tolerance limits 100
trade-offs 128, 140
trait
    correlations 83
    effect 155, 163
trait-neutral processes 165
trajectories of research 20
transdisciplinarity 28
transferability 130
transition probability 133
trophic levels 35, 133, 158
truth 39, 97, 151

uncertainty 3–4, 140–144
unfilling 103, 110–112
unresolvable questions 18

vaccines 142
validation data 138
validity of assumptions 121–122

value of information analysis
139–141
values
epistemic 37, 43
ethical 37, 42
non-epistemic 37, 43
role of 33
scientific 20, 37, 42
variables
among scientists 3
bionomic 99
climatic 105
ecoclimatic/bioclimatic 105
extrinsic 136
scenopoetic 99, 101
variation
physiological 90
viability 1, 35
water uptake 69
weather forecasting 134
whole genome sequencing 87
wildlife management 18
working groups 175
workshops 92, 175
WorldClim 105–106

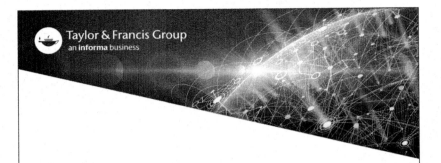